# CENTURIES OF TUTORING

## A History of Alternative Education in America and Western Europe

By
**Edward E. Gordon**
DePaul University
Chicago, Illinois

With
**Elaine H. Gordon**
DePaul University
Chicago, Illinois

UNIVERSITY
PRESS OF
AMERICA

Lanham • New York • London

Copyright © 1990 by
**University Press of America®, Inc.**
4720 Boston Way
Lanham, Maryland 20706

3 Henrietta Street
London WC2E 8LU England

**Library of Congress Cataloging-in-Publication Data**

Gordon, Edward E.
Centuries of tutoring : A history of alternative education in
America and Western Europe / by Edward E. Gordon
with Elaine H. Gordon.
p.      cm.
Includes bibliographical references.
1. Tutors and tutoring—Europe—History.   2. Tutors and
tutoring—United States—History.   3. Domestic
education—History.   I. Gordon, Elaine H.   II. Title.
LC41.G58      1990      371.3'94—dc20      89–27430 CIP

ISBN 0–8191–7641–9 (alk. paper)
ISBN 0–8191–7642–7 (pbk. : alk. paper)

 The paper used in this publication meets the minimum requirements of
American National Standard for Information Sciences—Permanence
of Paper for Printed Library Materials, ANSI Z39.48–1984.

# ACKNOWLEDGMENTS

The scope of this book made my heavy reliance upon many scholars very essential. I wish to thank the Reverend F. Michael Perko, S.J., Ph.D. for his many helpful suggestions and patient support, and also Joan Smith, Gerald Gutek and Hans Schieser who gave me invaluable research assistance and counseling.

The staff members at many research libraries were invaluable in finding the diaries and letters of tutors including: Albert C. King at Rutgers University, Sara S. Hodson at the Huntington Library, the University of North Carolina Library, Virginia State Library, University of Texas Library, the Newberry Library and the University of Chicago Library. I wish to make special mention of my appreciation to David C. Duniway for the use of his father's records as a tutor and C. Jamie Johnston for his research assistance in organizing these papers.

Margaret Schieser's translation assistance was invaluable to me. It goes without saying that my school's staff has shown great patience during this long writing process particularly, Judy Slee who prepared the final manuscript from its first draft with the assistance of Sandra Gula Gleason. The support of my family has never wavered in their son's effort to become Cleo's disciple.

Above all I wish to thank my wife, Elaine Gordon the Instruction Librarian of DePaul University. Elaine worked with me to gather the research for this entire book. In many instances her research insights provided important material that otherwise would have been overlooked. Her critical editing added clarity and may insights. However, for all the many shortcomings found by the reader in this work I take sole responsibility.

# TABLE OF CONTENTS

# PREFACE

## DOES TUTORING HAVE A HISTORY?

Consider the education of an aristocratic boy, to which one man's whole time
is devoted. However excellent might be the
results of such a system, no man with a
modern outlook would give it serious
consideration, because it is arithmetically
impossible for every child to absorb the
whole time of an adult tutor. The system
is therefore one which can only be employed
by a privileged caste; in a just world, its
existence would be impossible.[1]

The very word "tutor" reflects for a modern
audience images of the aristocracy. Educational
history concluded long ago that the common school
rose in spite of tutorial education; that tutoring
was the outmoded prerogative of a few affluent
children.

The purpose of this book is to investigate
tutoring's widespread applications throughout the
history of childhood in the Western world. Both
women and men as philosopher-tutors, some well-
known, others obscure, made a significant contribution to modern educational philosophy that remains a
cornerstone in contemporary schooling.

Horace Mann, the great American advocate of
universal schooling, argued that education in groups,
not by tutors, was both more practical and necessary
in a democracy. He believed that only mass schooling
could establish the vital foundation of a representative form of government. Rousseau, Pestalozzi and

1

others laid the groundwork for Mann's ideal. He reconciled their view of a free society of individuals with mass education which had as its goal the improvement of character of children by modifying behavior in the classroom.

Twentieth century learning theory formalized this study of behavior in its research. However, the recognition of Jean Piaget and other cognitive psychologists has brought back our attention to the study of individual learners. The history of children and their tutors reveals a great deal on this subject. The focus of this book will be confined mainly from the Renaissance to the end of the Victorian age.

The word "tutor" has a long and confusing history. Its meaning as an educational concept has shifted over time, country and culture. Many other terms were brought into use that have related meanings. Any search for the "history of tutoring" must first come to grips with all these related concepts and word variations. A principal cause for the lack of a unified history of tutoring may be that the concept of tutoring has been called so many different names and that it exists only as a jumble of related terms dispersed over 2,500 years of social history.

The Oxford English Dictionary lists eight main definitions of the word "tutor." Only two of these meanings are in modern use, the other six are now obsolete. During the course of this book we will review over thirty different words used for "tutor," but in other words.

### Ancient Greece

paidagogós — A Greek slave who tutored the young.

Sophists — Greek tutors that worked for a fee.

### Ancient Rome

tutela — A Roman tutor.

2

| rhetores | - Roman tutors. |
|---|---|
| domi | - A residential tutor. |
| fori | - A visiting tutor. |
| pedagogue | - A Greek slave brought to Rome as a tutor of the young. |
| pedisequis | - Roman attendants who tutored. |
| comes | - A companion tutor. |
| custos | - A guardian tutor. |
| rector | - A tutor. |
| governor | - A male tutor. |
| governess | - A female tutor. |

## Medieval Europe

| escalastre | - Latin term used by the Third Lateran Council (1179) for a tutor of non-theological subjects. |
|---|---|
| theologal | - Lateran Council term for a tutor of theology. |

## Ireland

| fosterage | - Medieval term used for tutoring in the monasteries. |
|---|---|

## Italy

| courtesy education | - The Renaissance tutoring of a gentleman. |
|---|---|

## England

| maistresse | - Medieval female tutor known to Chaucer's England (14th Century). |
|---|---|

3

| | |
|---|---|
| master of the henchmen | – Royal Court tutor of the king's servants (15th century). |
| scrivener | – A tutor of writing (15th century). |
| governor | – A male tutor (15th century). |
| governess | – A female tutor usually for women (14th century). |
| domestic education | – In the 18th and 19th centuries often used to describe one-to-one education at home. |
| bear leader | – A tutor accompanying a boy on the "Grand Tour" of Europe in the 18th century. |
| monitor | – A student peer-tutor common in the 19th century. |
| nanny | – A combination nurse and early childhood tutor common in the 19th century. |
| fireside education | – A term directly related to domestic education from the 19th century. |
| private tuition | – A paid tutor at home first commonly used in the 15th century, but still in widespread use today. |
| tutorial college | – Institutions found in Oxford or Cambridge that tutor students for national secondary examinations and for the "Oxbridge" university entrance examinations. |

écolâtre   - A medieval French tutor.

candidatus  - An 18th century term referring to "a private tutor."

## Germany

Wohnstubenerziehung
- A 19th century term based on Pestalozzi's educational philosophy meaning a "living room education."

Erziehungskuenstler
- Herbart's 19th century description of "a genius in education," i.e. a model tutor.

## United States

peer-tutors - Student tutors found in many schools from the 18th century and still in use today.

Old Field
School
- 17th century term used in the Southern American colonies to describe private tutoring on a plantation.

private
tutor
- A 20th century term used to describe a teacher's after-school remedial work with a student at home or in a "tutoring center."

home
schools
- The 20th century equivalent of "domestic education" describing parents teaching their children at home as a substitute for regular school attendance.

What is the definition of "tutoring" that will guide us through this present study? How is tutoring different from small group instruction and "schooling" in larger groups? Tutoring, as we will use it, encompasses the academic, moral and philosophical growth of the individual child. Tutors identified themselves closely with their pupils. When a family allowed a tutor to enter their home, he worked not only to help a child mature intellectually, but also intimately shared in the family's day-to-day life experiences. Unlike his counterpart in the classroom, many tutors lost their distinction as outsiders and became quasi-family members. Tutoring made education a family affair. It often involved the parents with the tutor in combining education and the family as a unified life-long experience. This is what distinguished a "tutor" from a "classroom teacher." The tutor's highly individualistic approach transcended education's academic lessons. At its best tutoring attempted to reach out and touch a child's intellectual, moral and spiritual fiber in a dynamic personal process. The tutor remained a counselor into adulthood, long after the lessons had ceased. These concepts were found originally in the "tutorial ideal" of the ancient world. We will follow their development in the educational history of the West.

For the purpose of this present study tutoring is defined as one-to-one or small group instruction. Only the tutoring of academic subjects will be considered, not apprenticeship education or "coaching." We will investigate how tutoring was accomplished at home as a substitute for "schooling." In some instances the contributions of these tutorial programs influenced classroom instruction.

Who were these tutors? Our focus will concentrate on individual adults who tutored often, not just on an occasional basis. Many tutors were university professors, others primary or secondary teachers, clergymen, college students, governesses, parents, family relations and even neighbors. A review will be made of tutor attitudes toward children and their education. Childhood here is defined as beginning with infancy and continuing into the teenage years. We will also trace the history of the education of women at home by their tutors. We will only concentrate on tutoring in the Western

6

world.

This book will examine both the development of tutoring as a form of education, and its influence on "schooling." We will undertake a review of what these educators wrote on their work, the lives of their students, and the wider socio-cultural ramifications during centuries of tutoring.

The introductory chapter will examine the origins of antiquity's "tutoring ideal." We will then consider how this concept was adapted in southern and northern Europe during the Renaissance and Reformation. England's Tudors will then create a backdrop of scholarly literature that formalized educational thought on tutoring for subsequent centuries. The Age of Reason and the Enlightenment will chronicle the rise of the famous continental tutors: Rousseau, Fénelon, Locke, Herbart among others, and the popular support they built for "domestic education." The role of the tutor and the tutor-governess will then be reviewed as education at home, and the corollary use of tutors in the school. The nineteenth century in Europe and America witnessed the widespread use of tutors, and the gradual adoption of mandatory tax-supported public schooling. The study concludes with a brief review of the contemporary uses of tutoring and an analysis of its historical contributions to Western education.


Endnotes


1.  7th Modern Meaning of "Tutor" - "To act the part of a tutor towards; to give special or individual instruction to; to teach, instruct (in a subject)." This is the central concept of the word tutor used for the present study. 8th Modern Meaning of "Tutor" - "To instruct under discipline; to subject to discipline, control or correction, to school; also to admonish or reprove. Oxford English Dictionary, 1st ed., s.v. "tutor."


7

CHAPTER 1

THE CLASSIC IDEAL AND THE MEDIEVAL TRANSITION
(1500 B.C. - 1400 A.D.)

To gain a perspective on the historical origins of tutoring, this study will deal with many published sources in the history of education. A review will be made of selected Western teachers, Socrates, Plato, Aristotle, Cicero, Quintilian among others, and their thoughts on this instructional method. These individuals played a multi-dimensional role in the history of education. In one sense they were general theorists; additionally many established schools. Their careers as tutors, however, have generally been ignored. Without diminishing the general importance of schooling, we will now reconsider the foundational concepts of tutoring and its development.


1. EARLY BEGINNINGS (7000 B.C.)

The story of tutoring began in early civilization with the transmission of knowledge through oral tradition. The family was the school. Parents tutored their children by practice in life skills and the recitation of folklore.[1] Only much later (5000 B.C.?) did writing begin, probably as a record of these oral traditions of families.[2] Sumerian priests (2800 B.C.) used one-to-one instruction to teach mythology and train scribes. Early Jewish history (800 B.C.) is devoid of schools. Fathers taught their children religious traditions, the law and some writing. The royal children of Israel had their own special tutors.[3] The ancient Druid (500 B.C.),

9

Brahmin (600 B.C.), Aztec, Inca and Mayan (100 B.C.-
1400 A.D.) civilizations taught their religious
beliefs and culture through one-to-one instruction.
During the later Chinese empire students were
frequently tutored at home in preparation for the
civil service examination system.[4]

Schools appeared in these first civilizations
only when the family no longer provided a child's
basic education. As the great oriental cultures
became empires, schools were established to meet the
needs of a society of specialists. In Egypt by 200
B.C., even though many fathers still taught their
sons, other children attended the temple schools.
These students, upon graduation, would attend the
school of government to learn public administration.
Later they were sent to public officials to be
individually instructed in their new occupations.[5]

Many of the first tutors were certainly unpaid.
An important bond approximating the closeness between
family members existed between them and their
students. It was in Greece that the "classic ideal"
of man's individual relationship to the universe
became intertwined with an "educational ideal." The
Greek Homeric hero, "was the pattern held up by the
tutor for emulation by the pupil. . . ."[6] Here
existed a model of "absolute beauty" and a "perfect
valor" that transcended any real heroic deed. This
Greek concept of the ideal man dominated their
education. Here was the guide and criterion that
shaped all human character. This unique Greek
conception became the source of later Western notions
of "culture." Each subsequent generation of tutors
in some way drew upon it.[7]


2. THE IDEAL TUTOR OF GREECE


During the formative years of Greece (750-650
B.C.) education was limited mainly to individual
tutoring of members of the upper classes. Since most
of the written records that have survived were kept
by the aristocracy, what we know of education in
these early societies centered mostly on education of

the aristocrats.[8] Homer, in the ninth book of the
Iliad, implies that boys were educated by their
fathers or an appointed tutor.[9] The "classic ideal"
of education between master and pupil resulted in the
tutoring of the young through the counsel and example
of an older man. An atmosphere of virile camaraderie
shaped and molded the young boy's character. The
relationship between the two became personal,
intimate and lasted for life. It extended beyond the
home to the marketplace, battlefield and all aspects
of daily life.[10] In the Greek tutorial method of
education the pupil associated constantly with his
tutor. He observed his speech, manner, social and
moral attitudes.[11] Isocrates (436 B.C.-338 B.C.)
tells us,

> In this process, master and pupil each
> has his place; no one but the pupil can
> furnish the necessary capacity; no one but
> the master, the ability to impart know-
> ledge; while both have a part in the
> exercises of practical application; for the
> master must painstakingly direct his pupil,
> and the pupil must rigidly follow the
> master's instruction.[12]

Lessons were given in oratory, etiquette, music and
poetry. The whole process of tutoring became one
long informal examination whereby the tutor determined how much the child had learned. He advanced
the pupil according to his achievement. The tutor
strove to always act as a role model in the eyes of
the young. Public opinion, and in some instances the
law, held the tutor morally responsible for the
development of his student. The tutor was himself
usually an aristocrat. He was not required to tutor
but recognized this activity as a fulfillment of his
obligation to society. However, the tutor had the
right to reject a new student. The personal relationship became so close that the tutor was regarded
in many instances as a second father.[13]

Oral instruction dominated tutoring in Greece.
Great stress was placed on memorization. Literature
in early Greece seems to have been taught solely by
oral tradition. The "tutor-disciple" method dominated early and to some extent, later Greek educa-

11

tion. The student had to prove himself worthy to be chosen and retained as a "disciple." This followed the Platonic belief in the superiority of oral lteaching and direct communication. The written word was too impersonal. Memorization was considered a cultural safeguard.

It is impossible for what is written not to be disclosed. That is the reason why I have never written anything about these things, and why there is not and will not be any written work of Plato's own.[14]

The Greek educational ideal was intended only for men. Women had limited educational opportunities. But their social position in early Greece seems to have been higher and their education more complete than at the later stages of Greek civilization. Yet no Greek city state established girls' schools. Girls belonging to the better classes were taught some reading and writing at home by their mothers or nurses. Hypatia (c370 B.C.-415 B.C.) was the daughter of the mathematician Theon, who was Director of the University of Alexandria. He tutored her in the style of the dialogue. Hypatia later established her reputation as a mathematician while studying under the instruction of Plutarch the younger. She became a popular teacher in her own right and became known simply as "The Philosopher." It was historically significant that tutoring became the primary source of education for women in ancient Greece. This social practice continued well into modern European history.[15]

One notable exception of educational opportunity among Greek women was the intellectual attainment of the hetaerae. They were the prostitutes of Greece. Some became high-priced courtesans who spent a great deal of money on their own tutorial education. A few reached a level of higher intellectual development. Some, such as Aspasia, a common law wife of Pericles, educated herself so well that her wit and grace attracted the leading men of society to her home.[16]

By 500 B.C. it became a common practice in Greece to entrust a boy at age six to a paidagogos. In some cases the Greek paidagogos was a most worthy

12

and valuable servant. But sometimes he was a slave, too old to work, with a vile accent and character to match. Until the boy reached age eighteen, the paidagogos was his constant companion.[17]

Considerable disagreement exists over the paidagogois' exact role. Lodge confined his duties to that of a slave escorting his master daily to and from the palestra or gymnasium. For Freeman the paidagogos was "a mixture of nurse, footman, chaperon and tutor." There is no English word which covers all these activities, and nothing in the English educational system which corresponds closely to the concept. The word "tutor" is commonly used in translation, even if it is inadequate.[18] Beck and Ely gave the paidagogos a far more significant educational role. He taught the child propriety in all situations, to walk with dignity and grace. He awakened in the youngster a sense of modesty and shame. He acted as the role model for the child's sense of courtesy, modesty, good manners and inspired in his charge an ambition to live his life as a credit to his family. All other learning was subordinated and played a contributing role.

Jaeger and Yannicopoulos take a middle view that the paidagogos role did not remain static throughout antiquity. In earlier times he probably functioned as both a teacher and guardian. At some point these roles diverged and teaching passed into the hands of a master or tutor, while governance over conduct remained with the paidagogos. Plato referred to the well-known tutor "Phoenix" as a paidagogos. In Laws he wrote that, "just as sheep, or any other creatures, cannot be allowed to live unshepherded, so neither must boys be left without the care of tutors." Plato described in Lysis the scene of Socrates trying to teach a student the necessity of discipline, training and control. "Do they let you rule yourself. . . . I should think not," said he. "You have someone to rule you then? Yes, my tutor here."

In the early aristocratic days of Greece, technical and literacy instruction were combined and taught by a paidagogos. Only later with the advent of schools did this function change. But the

13

paidagogos never lost his connection with technical and moral instruction. He became the descendent of the Roman pedagogus and the later European aristocratic private tutor.[19] The modern concept of a well-educated teacher is still designated by the Latin term, pedagogue.


## 3. GREECE'S ILLUSTRIOUS TUTORS

History's most honored Western teachers were tutors--Socrates, Plato, Aristotle. They each engaged their students one at a time in a profitable dialogue.[20] This allowed their students to learn gradually through the principle of imitation. Isocrates (436 B.C.-338 B.C.) based his entire system of instruction on the imitation of models. This form of instruction was the hub around which turned the Greek tutoring method. The small enrollment in Isocrates' school allowed him to tutor one or two students. He taught them carefully in the basic principles of a subject. This technique required a well-educated, versatile master, a quality not found then in every domestic tutor. Out of his school came Speusippus, the successor of Plato, and possibly Aristotle (384 B.C.-322 B.C.) himself.[21]

Many tutors were foreign slaves who learned their trade by association with family members. The tutor learned to imitate what he thought was relevant in each society from his master by association, imitation and practice. These tutors were often semi-independent artisans who taught the arts as a sideline.[22] They tutored their pupils in what they knew themselves and the household's cultural values and lived on the small fees a pupil's parents were able to pay. Smith has found that Protagoras was the first (505 B.C.) known person who "publicly declared himself to be a professional teacher."[23]

Socrates (469 B.C.-399 B.C.) is remembered as being the foremost of these tutors in Ancient Greece. He is famous for developing the dialogue as a teaching method.

14

If I think that any person is not wise, I try to help the cause of God by proving that he is not. . . . A number of young men with wealthy fathers and plenty of leisure have deliberately attached themselves to me because they enjoy hearing other people cross-questioned. These often take me as their model, and go on to try to question other persons. Whereupon, I suppose, they find an unlimited number of people who think that they know something, but they really know little or nothing.[24]

Plato (427 B.C.-347 B.C.) continued this practice later at his Academy in Athens. He combined this method with lectures and posing problems to the students. Plato's Academy was not a research seminar. Instead, Plato's Dialogues sought to offer advice and methodical criticism to other individual thinkers. He tells us how Socrates argued with his disciple, Crito, against bribing the prison guards and escaping after his condemnation to death by an Athenian court. Socrates asked Crito if it can ever be right to defend oneself against evil by doing evil. Crito answered, "If you leave the city, Socrates, you shall return wrong for wrong . . . and injure . . . your friends. . . ." Socrates explained that a man must always do what his country orders him unless he can change its view of what the law should be.[25] This conversational form of tutoring between a student and a mythical master stimulated thinking and sharpened reason in the search of ideal truth. Later, Aristotle's Lyceum bore a resemblance to Plato's Academy.[26]

Aristotle (384 B.C.-322 B.C.) was born at Stagira, a colony on Thrace. His father was a physician. Losing his parents at an early age, Aristotle was given to a "foster parent," Proxenios, who tutored him. Traveling to Athens, Aristotle hired tutors familiar to Plato. For the next twenty years he attended first the school of Isocrates, then Plato's Academy, and became so well educated that Plato remarked, "Aristotle is the mind of my school."[27]

According to one legend Philip the Warrior, King

15

of Macedonia (382 B.C.-336 B.C.), upon the birth of his son Alexander (356 B.C.-323 B.C.), looked about for the age's greatest teacher to tutor the future master of the world.[28] Aristotle in the _Politics_ had acknowledged the importance of a good tutor even for the very young child.

> When the children have been born, the particular mode of rearing adopted must be deemed an important determining influence . . . the question of the kind of tales and stories that should be told to children of this age must be attended to by the officials called Children's Tutors. For all such amusements should be imitations of the serious occupations of later life . . . . The Tutors must supervise the children's pastimes.[29]

Phillip supposedly wrote to Aristotle, "like a peer putting his son down for Eton," the following letter:

> I give you notice that I have a son born to me, but I am not so much obliged to the gods for his birth, as for the happiness that he has come into the world while there is an Aristotle living. For I hope that being brought up under your direction and by your care, he may deserve the glory of his father and the empire which I shall leave him.[30]

To further induce Aristotle to become Alexander's tutor, Philip rebuilt Stagira, the philosopher's home town, which Philip had leveled in a war. He also brought back its citizens whom he had either exiled or enslaved. The persuasion worked. A school was built on the foothills of Mount Bermion, twenty miles west of Pella, Philip's capital, with outdoor gardens, a gymnasium and stone lecture seats. Here Aristotle tutored Alexander and his friends, (343 B.C.-336 B.C.) in morals and politics, the art of medicine, Homer's _Iliad_, poetry, and rhetoric. Aristotle made an immediate appeal to his pupil's practical and inquisitive intellect, as well as to his thirst for exploration and discovery. Alexander became so fascinated with biology and zoology that the subjects became life-long interests.

They had just four years together. Philip, committed to a long foreign war, appointed the young sixteen-year-old Alexander, Regent of Macedon. After Philip's death, Alexander set out to conquer Persia. Aristotle sent an associate scholar, Callisthenes, to continue tutoring Alexander. His reward was the collection of natural specimens selected from conquered lands, which in turn formed the material for Aristotle's History of Animals. Plutarch observed that Alexander loved Aristotle no less than his own father because "he was indebted to the one for living, and the other for living well."[31]

By 300 B.C. the palestra served as the preferred method for primary education though private tutoring persisted in many homes. Enrollment followed in the gymnasium. Both schools gave a form of physical training in the open air. Instruction was also individualized in both these schools. At the higher stages of Greek education individual or small group instruction were always the preferred modes. The Sophists (500 B.C.-300 B.C.) (philosopher-teachers) did not usually organize a formal school or regular course. Among them were Protagoras (481 B.C.-411 B.C.), Gorgias (485 B.C.-380 B.C.), Prodicus (5th Century B.C.), Hippias (5th Century B.C.), Antiphon (480 B.C.-411 B.C.), Thrasymachus (5th Century B.C.), and Callisthenes (360 B.C.-327 B.C.). Instead, they traveled from place to place gathering local students. They made a contractual arrangement to teach a precise subject for a specified fee and length of time. In the opinion of Socrates this was an evil thing to do. If someone had something good to teach, he should do it without pay.

> There is another expert, too, from Paros, who I discovered was here on a visit; I happened to meet a man who has paid more in Sophist's fee than all the rest put together. So I asked him . . . if your sons had been colts or calves, we should have no difficulty in finding and engaging a trainer to perfect their

17

qualities. . . . But seeing that they are human beings, whom do you intend to get as their instructor? Who is the expert in perfecting the human and social qualities? . . . Is there such a person or not? Certainly, said he. Who is he? . . . said I. And what does he charge? Evenus of Paros, Socrates, said he, and his fee is five minas. I feel that he was to be congratulated if he really was master of this art and taught it at such a moderate fee. I should certainly plume myself and give myself airs if I understood these things, but in fact, gentlemen, I do not.[32]

The Sophists taught a variety of subjects on how to improve oneself and succeed in life (techne). This they substituted for the Socratic dialogue. Techne referred to professional knowledge of doing things. Plato divided this instruction into three categories, the musical arts, the visual arts and the literary arts. The practical useful education of the Sophists seemed to contrast the deeper thought provoking process of the dialogue. Marrow has characterized the Sophist teaching method as nothing less than "collective tutoring."[33]

The philosopher-scholars of early Greece established tutoring as a definitive educational form. Their Socratic tutoring methods modelled on the dialogue, embodied the classical education tradition that encouraged educated persons to become "free thinkers." Each succeeding generation of tutors embellished upon these methods and broadened the scope of tutorial education.


4.   TUTORS IN ANCIENT ROME (200 B.C. - 500 A.D.)


From the Republican third century B.C. until the empire, private home education by a tutor was regarded by the Roman aristocracy as the normal mode of instruction. This was equally true in the Hellenistic states after their conquest by Rome (146 B.C.). The writings of both Quintilian and Pliny the

Younger indicate what tremendous prestige private tutoring retained until the beginning of the second century A.D.[34]

The Roman word "tutela" (tutors) had much broader connotations than those related only to a teacher and his pupil. In Latin tutela also means guardian and ward. Under Roman law the person and property of an orphan were entrusted to a tutela, usually a discrete friend of the family. Later, Emperor Marcus Aurelius made this function a public office "praetor tutelaris." Until the orphaned infant could speak and think, he was represented by his tutor. From the age of fourteen to twenty-five a curator was imposed on the youth to protect him from immorality and subterfuge. Roman women in general were reduced to permanent "tutelage" by parents, husbands or guardians. Here Romans used tutoring in a much broader sense. All freedmen were under the "tutela" of their patron. But a woman "created to please and to obey was never supposed to have attained the age of reason and experience."[35] Thus the Roman concept of tutoring helped to partially support a general inequality between the sexes.

Since tutoring for the Roman family had such broad cultural implications it is understandable why the family long remained the chief educational agency in early Rome. During the republic many parents tutored their children at home.

Like the Greeks, this familial tutoring relied heavily upon direct observation and imitation. Education concentrated on the formation of moral character, the right conduct of the individual, and the social obligation to the state. The father was the role model for Roman virtue, but it was the Roman mother who gave her children their first education. As the child matured he was tutored by the father in reading, writing and simple mathematics. Boys and girls shared the same tutoring experience, except that boys learned physical exercises and girls domestic art. Roman domestic education was very narrow with an emphasis on the practical and moral.[36]

At age sixteen or seventeen boys were given the "toga virilis," the garb of manhood. Their families then placed them under the charge of a tutor, who was usually a family friend. "My school," Crassus says in _De Oratore_, "was the forum, my master's experience, the laws and institutions of Rome and the customs of our ancestors."[37] Under the supervision of his tutor the boy memorized the Law of the Twelve Tables in the forum at Rome. He also learned a great number of legal precedents and the complex system of prescriptions that characterize Roman law. Other less well-born young men received instruction in practical skills such as fighting or farming. The final phase of a young man's education was the so-called "tirocinium fori." This was a form of advanced tutoring under a leading orator in the law for those who planned to become barristers, enter politics, or who came from the patrician aristocracy of Rome. Tacitus described this old Republican tradition.

> In the days of our ancestors a young man who was being prepared for the law and oratory, after having been trained at home and thoroughly instructed in the liberal arts, was brought by his father or relations to the leading orator at Rome. By following him and frequenting his company, he had the opportunity of listening to all his speeches in the law courts or at public meetings; he could hear him in argument and debate and, so to speak, learn to fight by taking part in the battle.[38]

Here was the essential difference between Roman and Greek tutors. In Rome the rhetorical argument supplanted the Socratic dialogue. Cicero, Quintilian and other rhetoricians provided an education model that advocated an ordered, legalistic style in education. Rome needed a more practical tutorial education that provided the skills and ideas to rule an empire.

After Rome had conquered Greece, there followed the Greek conquest of Rome in education, the arts, religion and philosophy. A swelling tide of _Graeculi_, ("Greeklings") came from the East and dominated Roman education. Many were slaves who became tutors in Roman families, others were rhetores. They gave private instruction in oratory, philosophy and literary composition. Livius Andronicus (3rd Century B.C.) was taken as a slave from the Greek-speaking city of Tarentum. In Rome (272 B.C.) he became the tutor to the children of the Roman Consul, Livinus Salinator, who later emancipated Andronicus. He was given his freedom in recognition of his intellectual ability.[39] He taught his students the philosophy of Plato and Aristotle and rhetorical culture. In 250 B.C. to supplement his income from tutoring, Andronicus translated Homer's Odyssey into Latin. This was the starting point of Latin literature with a tutor as its founder. This work remained a standard textbook in Roman education down to Horace's day (65 B.C.). Andronicus chose the Odyssey since he felt its adventures would appeal more to his Roman audience. Thereafter, he produced the first Latin play (240 B.C.) and even composed a "State Hymn."[40]

Another Greek tutor in the tutor-scholar tradition was Ennius of Rudiae (2nd Century B.C.). He wrote Greek tragedies based upon Euripides while he tutored leading Roman families, including Scipio Africanius (234 B.C.-183 B.C.), the conqueror of Hannibal. Both Andronicus and Ennius began at Rome what had existed previously at Alexandria, scholar-poets acting as tutors. This tradition later included Cato at the close of the Roman Republic, the historian Polybius and Ausonius of Bordeaux towards the end of the Empire.

Julius Caesar's (100 B.C.-44 B.C.) tutor, Antonius Gnipho (1st Century B.C.), was part of this tutor tradition. Left on a hillside to die of exposure at birth, he was rescued and later given his freedom by his foster parents. Gnipho became skilled in Latin and Greek, acquiring a reputation as a tutor. He was the first person to apply the principles of analogy to Latin in order to determine the correct word form. This practice of rational deduction from existing forms in other similar words was continued by Caesar himself in a work On Analogy (54 B.C.) Gnipho also taught rhetoric. Even Cicero, at the height of his oratorical renown, attended this tutor's declamations. (66 B.C.)

21

Other Greek tutors arrived in Rome searching for lucrative fees and a wider reputation. Philo of Larissa (1st Century B.C.), who founded the New Academy, arrived in 88 B.C. He was followed by Antiochus of Ascadon (1st Century B.C.), who later headed the Academy in Athens. Even the greatest thinker of that age, Posidonius (135 B.C.-51 B.C.), came to Rome where he tutored both Cicero (106 B.C.-43 B.C.) and Pompey (106 B.C.-48 B.C.). Later Virgil (70 B.C.-19 B.C.) was tutored by the Greek poet, Caecilius Epirota (1st Century B.C.), whose excellent teaching helped Virgil become a dominant force in literature.[41]

With the dawn of the imperial system and the Augustan peace (30 B.C.-14 A.D.), the available supply of tutors increased, as did the demand for their services. Even during the empire, elementary tutoring was still done at home. How widespread was this practice? Wilkins maintains the traditional belief that "for middle and poorer classes going to school was the rule from the first."[42] Yet Bonner has found evidence that there continued to be widespread use of tutors throughout the history of Rome and the Empire and at many levels of society, not just the rich. As late as the fifth century A.D. in Constantinople, when teachers had been publicly appointed by the municipality or the state, "special mention is made of those who were accustomed to conduct their classes in numerous private homes and this practice would also have been common at Rome."[43] Gradual deterioration of discipline in Roman schools caused anxious parents to look for reputable tutors. Even Emperor Marcus Aurelius, at the height of imperial Rome (121-180 A.D.), complained that Roman schools had such a corrupting influence "that the employment of good tutors at home was far better, and that no expense should be spared in acquiring them."[44]

Many Greeks acted as residential tutors (domi) for a period with a particular family. Some, from time to time, became visiting tutors (fori). Their curriculum included Greek, Latin, literature, rhetoric, philosophy, painting, modeling and field sports. Initial contact with a perspective tutor was made by a parent at the morning lucem (early morning reception in a Roman household). During this job interview parents sought to discover the tutor's knowledge and qualifications. Later, the father took time to make discreet inquiries of any person who knew the tutor's character and previous teaching record. If a second interview occurred, an arrangement was negotiated covering the terms of the tutor's services and his fee. The traditional Roman tutor earned his keep, regular compensation and if the tutoring was well received, an occasional gift as a token of appreciation. The treatment of tutors depended upon the integrity and generosity of the tutor's client. Some Roman families treated their tutors as mere hirelings, (or as slaves, which many were), subjecting them to humiliating indignities beneath the teacher's rank. Others were mean and stingy in payments. However, this seems to be the exception, since most private Roman tutors found their occupation satisfying and rewarding.[45]

Marcus Fabius Quintilian (40-118 A.D.), a famous Roman rhetorician, recorded three types of tutors who contributed to a Roman child's earliest education at home. First, the nurse in charge for the first three years of life. Then, a Greek slave or pedagogue became a moral and intellectual force for the child. He was a teacher in basic writing and reading and an intimate exemplar of all those important Roman virtues. Finally, in some instances, at age seven the Roman boy or girl entered a ludus (primary school) accompanied each way by a pedagogue to guard his safety and his morals (unless the child was tutored at home). He also had the important task of monitoring the pupil's progress and the schoolmaster's teaching skills. The pedagogue was sometimes called a "pedisequis" (attendant), or "comes" (companion) or "custos" (guardian) or even "rector" (governor--boys, governess--girls). Some of these Roman titles for tutor reappeared in later eras. According to Wilkins, the pedagogue starting at age seven also taught the child Greek. The Latin author Varro describes his duties as that of a tutor, not just an attendant. Sometimes an old female slave became the pedagogue of a girl. The use of pedagogues for tutoring, a paid residential tutor (domi), or a visiting tutor (fori), was widespread in Rome and throughout the Empire. They made a signifi-

23

cant contribution to the educational experience of Roman children.[46]

Because of the extensive use of tutors during the Roman epoch, Quintilian warned parents that if a _pedagogue_ was not well educated, he might pass along his ignorance to his pupil. Some _pedagogues_,

> delude themselves into the belief that they are the possessors of real knowledge . . . they disdain to stoop to the drudgery of teaching and conceiving that they have acquired a certain title to authority . . . become imperious or even brutal. . . in teaching their own narrowness and prejudices to their pupil. . . . Their conduct is no less prejudicial to morals.[47]

Quintilian, like Emerson, warned against the practice of using tutors because it deprived the child of formative friendships and stimulating rivalries. These were important virtues in Republican Rome. The use of "public instruction," said Quintilian, has won "the approval of most eminent authorities" and those men "who formed the national character of the most famous states."[48]

According to Quintilian, the two principal reasons some parents preferred tutors were that they wished to protect youth from teachers of low morality, and they believed in the ideal that a tutor of one student could offer more than a teacher of many. He dismissed the first concept with the belief that only in the presence of these others can one become a great orator. Though he did admit that if a school became injurious to a child's morality, "I should give my vote for virtuous living in preference to even supreme excellence of speaking."[49] Quintilian's strongest argument against tutoring was that good teachers wanted a large audience and poor teachers one pupil. Even if a great teacher were employed, the majority of "the learner's time ought to be devoted to private study."[50] Only a small time is needed each day "to give purpose and direction . . . thereafter, the teacher can give individual instruction to more than one pupil."[51] Some subjects (rhetoric) are only properly taught in a large group where the student will learn from the progress and faults of others in the schoolroom.

Quintilian's argument for preferring schools over tutors was to be repeated innumerable times during the following centuries. It was the Roman rejection of the classic Greek model for the education of the individual. The oratory of the Roman forum replaced the endless philosophical dialogue at the Greek academy. But even Quintilian did not deny completely the ancient heritage of the tutor.

Would Philip of Macedon have wished that his son Alexander should be taught the rudiments of letters by Aristotle, the greatest philosopher of that age. . . if he had not thought that even the earliest instruction is best given by the most perfect teacher and has real reference to the whole of education?[52]

Other notable Romans did not accept Quintilian's concept of tutoring. Marcus Tullius Cicero (106 B.C.-43 B.C.), orator and man of letters, was tutored in rhetoric by the greatest jurist of the time, Quintis Mucius Scaevola (1st Century B.C.). The Greek poet, Archias (ca. 120? B.C.), taught Cicero his own language and literature. For his own son Marcus and his nephew Quintus, Cicero engaged (56 B.C.) Tyrannio (1st Century B.C.), a tutor from Amisus on the Black Sea. Captured in 70 B.C., he became a tutor to a Roman family. He was freed as an expression of gratitude, then journeyed to Rome and became a wealthy man. Along the way he acquired a large library and published a variety of scholarly books. Tyrannio became an authority on geography, Homeric meter and Greek accentuation. As a tutor for Cicero's children he taught them grammar, literature and rhetoric.[53] He also worked with Cicero in the classification and organization of Cicero's library. Cicero supplemented this tutoring by writing Partitiones Oratoriae, a rhetorical textbook in question and answer format.[54]

By 70 B.C. the use of tutors to educate girls to a higher intellectual level was no longer uncommon. Pompey the Great, for instance, had his two sons

Gnaeus (1st Century B.C.) and Sextus (?-35 B.C.) and his daughter Pompeia (1st Century B.C.) tutored (65 B.C.) by a Greek teacher at his home. From the later republican era onward, the compliment "docta puella" came into use to designate those women who were well educated in Greek and Latin poetry.[55]

No portrait of Roman tutoring can be complete without the experiences of the imperial family. From Augustus (30 B.C.-14 A.D.) onward, tutors were employed to guide the emperor's children with widely varying degrees of success.[56]

Claudius (10 B.C.-54 A.D.), being out of the emperor's favor as a child, had an ex-transportation officer assigned as his tutor. A quiet bookish child, he later wrote that, "The man was a barbarian . . . who had been assigned the task of punishing me savagely whatever I might do."[57] As Emperor, Claudius adopted his ten-year-old nephew Nero (37 A.D.-68 A.D.), and appointed Lucius Seneca (4 B.C.-65 A.D.), at that time a Roman Senator, as his tutor (47 A.D.). A Spanish rather than Greek philosopher, Seneca was a leading writer, orator, essayist, playwright and poet. It was unusual that this outstanding foreign intellectual also became a consul of Rome. As Nero's tutor, he worked to alter the young man's worst excesses. After becoming emperor, Nero demonstrated the limits of Seneca's influence by murdering his mother, aunt, wife and daughter. Even Seneca was not subtle enough to keep up with Nero's rages. He committed suicide (65 A.D.) to avoid being brutally murdered.[58]

Titus (40-81), as a youth was taught by many different tutors in a wide array of subjects. Domitian (51-96) had Quintilian tutor his two great nephews.[59] But it was in the remarkably diverse education of Marcus Aurelius (121-180), that the age of imperial tutors reached its zenith. Young Marcus never went to school. Instead he studied with tutors at home. His adoption by the Emperor Antonius Pius (86-161), and their close intimacy were crucial factors in his education. His adoptive father's devotion to honest government became a lasting influence in his development. Taught by tutors mostly of the Stoic school, he learned Stoic morality; to have few wants, to welcome hard work and to tolerate plain speech. Marcus also learned rhetoric, mathematics, grammar, Greek and Latin. His most distinguished tutors included Marcus Cornelius Fronto (2nd Century A.D.), Herodes Atticus (104-180), and Sextus (2nd Century A.D.), (grandson of Plutarch). His Meditations credit his various tutors and family members with what they had taught him. To his great-grandfather he gives high recognition for teaching him, "not to have frequented public schools, and to have had good teachers at home, and to know that on such things a man should spend liberally." From his other tutors he learned,

> to write with simplicity, to read care-
> fully, not superficially, the power of free
> will, to reason, a benevolent disposition,
> to speak well of teachers, to love my
> children truly, to love truth, to love
> justice, a love of labour and perseve-
> rance.[60]

In the life of Marcus Aurelius the classic model of tutor and student made their perfect match. To Rome's great misfortune, his contribution to the empire was negated by a questionable wife and a worthless son, Commodus, who started Rome's gradual decline.[61]

As the political power of the Roman world weakened, the church continued its educational traditions. One of the first to mention tutors in the early Christian era was St. Jerome (342-420). In a letter to a Roman lady, the lady Laeta, regarding the education of her daughter Paula, he recommended a female tutor--a governess to teach the child. An "honest woman of sad age." He describes the governess as "gravis, pallens, sordidata, subtristis." She was a melancholy tutor first drawn in somber tones by a saintly man of God.[62] Tutoring continued to thrive during the waning years of the empire. In large university centers throughout the Mediterranean world, many scholars outside the university derived their entire income solely from tutoring fees (400 A.D.). Tutor-philosophers again began traveling from city to city in the empire. This movement flourished throughout the Roman world for the first three centuries A.D.[63]


### 5. THE MEDIEVAL TRANSITION (500-1440)

At the termination of the Roman Empire in the West only fragmented records on tutorial education survived during the next several hundred years. The preservation of the tutorial model of Rome dominated the activities of medieval educators. In this context the Christian church controlled education. The tutors of the Middle Ages developed a new focus on theological ideals (scholasticism) rather than secular training.

In early medieval Britain (550) the first mention of a tutor-governess was Hildelith, Abbess of Barking (5th Century). Her schoolroom was the nunnery. Her pupils were either young nuns in training or an early Saxon princess. Holy women taught them to spell, write and to compose Latin verse.[64]

Irish monasteries began the instruction of boys at an early age or at adolescence. A monk became the child's tutor. They lived together. Here the child learned to become a copyist based on the ancient Irish tradition of fosterage. The child was entrusted to his tutor for all his care as if he were the tutor's son. The monk taught the alphabet, reading psalms, copying and memorization. More advanced students were taught basic arithmetic and astronomy. The "system of fosterage" seems to have been the rule among well-to-do families for their younger sons who did not inherit the family's land. This custom placed young children in monasteries between babyhood and age seventeen for boys, age fourteen for girls. According to Ryan "there is nothing peculiarly Irish about the custom which is found in many countries in the East and West since the beginning of monasticism."[65]

Gradually private tutoring revived as a home centered activity. Instruction was usually limited to children of royal or noble birth. The first palace school was established (782) by Charlemagne (768-814). Alcuin of York (735-800), a Saxon educator, tutored Charlemagne, his queen, three sons, two daughters, and Charlemagne's sister, son-in-law and three cousins. Alcuin used the discursive tutoring method since Charlemagne had an infectious eagerness and curiosity for learning. His task was to tutor them thoroughly in Latin so that they could read and write correctly both from scripture or the classics. Alcuin's De grammatica, De orthographia, Disputatio and De rhetorica employed the Platonic dialogue as a teaching method, but at a fundamental level. Alcuin had to teach elementary knowledge to students who were mature in body, but whose minds lacked formal educational experience. Charlemagne kept him at his side to the end of his life. Alcuin even traveled with him on the various circuits of his empire.[66]

England's first court tutor-governess had to wait until the reign of Alfred the Great (849-901). The king had a great love of learning from his childhood.

> Now on a certain day his mother was showing him and his brothers a book of Saxon poetry, which she held in your hand, and finally said: "Whichever of you can soonest learn this volume, to him will I give it." Stimulated by these words, or rather by divine inspiration, and allured by the beautifully illuminated letter at the beginning of the volume, Alfred spoke before all his brothers, who, though his seniors in age, were not so in grace, and answered his mother: "Will you really give that book to that one of us who can first understand and repeat it to you?" At this his mother smiled with satisfaction, and confirmed what she had before said: "Yes," said she, "that I will." Upon this the boy took the book out of her hand, and went to his master (tutor) and learned it by heart, whereupon he brought it back to his mother and recited it.[67]

At Reading, Alfred established a palace school for his sons and daughters. Elfgifn (9th Century) was the first royal governess. Little else is known about her other than her existence. Alfred did import scholars from abroad to instruct him and his people.[68]

On the European continent the church's educational influence grew steadily during the Middle Ages. The practice of prominent churchmen serving as the tutors of emperors continued with the instruction of Otto III of Germany (983-1002), Holy Roman Emperor, by Gerbert of Aurillac (940-1003), a scholar and scientist (990). Gerbert became known for his construction of astronomical instruments and the reintroduction of the abacus to the West. He also was elected Pope Sylvester II in 999. The tutor inspired his former student with the church's vision of the empire and Rome harmoniously ruling Christian Europe for the glory of God and the welfare of the faithful. It was not to be; Otto died in 1002, and Sylvester died the following year.[69]

The church was also notably active in preserving an abundance of classical literature that otherwise would have been lost to posterity. Monastic copyists who were tutored in their art by other monks left us most of our present knowledge of Greece and Rome. Their occupation was tedious. Haskins relates a fable from Ordericus Vitalis who tells us that tired monks were told that God forgave them one sin for each line they copied. One monk escaped hell by the margin of a single letter.[70]

Tutors also were active in clerical learning. The Third Lateran Council promulgated a decree (1179) that called for the appointment of a tutor at every cathedral.

> The Church of God, being obliged like a good and tender mother to provide for the bodily and spiritual wants of the poor, desirous to procure for poor children the opportunity for learning to read, and for making advancement in study, orders that each cathedral shall have a teacher charged

with the gratuitous instruction of the clergy of that church, and also of the indigent scholars, and that he be assigned a benefice, which, sufficient for his subsistence, may thus open the door of the school to the studious youth. A tutor shall be installed in the other churches and in the monasteries where formerly there were funds set apart for this purpose.[71]

One tutor taught ordinary subjects (esolastre), another theology (theologal). This practice continued for some time as bishops took a strong stand against an illiterate clergy. The register of Walter Stapledon, Bishop of Exeter from 1308-1326, records the use of tutors for insufficiently literate candidates for the priesthood. English bishops continued this practice into the fifteenth century.[72]

Beginning in the twelfth century, the modern history of English and European education can be delineated with some degree of accuracy. Significant quantities of educational source material began to survive from the twelfth century onward making it a reasonable point to resume a detailed chronicle in the story of tutoring. The concept of tutoring became more sharply defined as educators began to write entire books on their experience as an instructor of one child at a time. To an ever increasing extent the "ideal form" of individual education will be defined in these terms, separate from the history of schools, but still of great importance in shaping the Western tradition of education.

Popular medieval writers lead us to believe that every household of substance maintained its own domestic or family school. A boy of a noble family was left for his first seven years in the charge of women who tutored him in names and letters. From age seven to fourteen, a student from the university, the castle's private chaplain, or a priest from a local abbey tutored him in religious education, reading, writing and Latin.

Girls also had private tutors. Wright believes that domestic scholarship in the Middle Ages seems to have been chiefly preserved and employed for the education of women. Their tutoring centered on Latin, reading, and committing lessons to memory. A famous tutorial relationship was carefully recorded by the noted scholastic philosopher, Peter Abelard (1079-1142), in the Historia Calamitatum (The Story of My Misfortunes, 1135). Abelard tells the story of his instruction with the beloved Heloise (1101-1164).[73]

Children of nobility were often sent to another household for their education. Many boys were trained in the code of chivalry. Squires were taught by knights until they had learned the duties and responsibilities of the knightly class.[74] Some families maintained outstanding home tutors. The church again played a prominent role in this practice. Archbishop Thomas á Becket (1118-1170) had many sons of great Anglo-Norman families taught in his household. Both the bishops of Ely and Lincoln did the same. This practice produced a scholarship described by learned men in the Middle Ages as "urbanitas," a polite education belonging to the city. The French named this tutoring "curtoisie" or courtly manners. A Latin metrical piece, the Boke of Curtasye (Liber Urbanitatis) (circa 1100), became a very popular description of medieval tutoring. Thus was born the tradition of "courtesy education" as a distinctive tutorial form. For the next five hundred years this concept was enhanced by subsequent philosophers of education.[75]

We know that medieval tutors were serious scholars. John of Salisbury (1117-1180) represented the finest traditions of twelfth century learning. He wrote about his becoming the tutor of some noble's children (1140). "I was stimulated by the requirements of my position and the urging of the boys to recall more frequently to mind what I had heard."[76] Another tutor, Peter of Blois (12th century), thought his compensation inadequate for teaching a child and his adolescent brother (1160).

> For I hope better things of the education of him who comes to me rude and unformed, than from another whose character has already begun to harden and has as it

32

were impressed on itself the stamp of another teacher. . . . Indeed Quintilian says in the book <u>On the Training of the Orator</u> that Timotheus, a famous artist with the flute, was wont to ask double pay from those who had had a previous teacher.[77]

How many future tutors would bemoan their master's failure to follow the advice of Emperor Marcus Aurelius regarding ample compensation?[78]

Educational arrangements during the Middle Ages did not favor women. Outside of the nunnery school for girls, home tutoring was the only educational path opened to the medieval woman. It appears that more studied at home with private tutors than attended outside schools. The instruction was for many only in the fundamentals. By the fifteenth century some women spoke French, but writing was a much rarer accomplishment. Study ended at age twelve. In medieval towns the daughters of the higher class, artisan members of guilds or daughters of petty merchants, might go to the nunnery schools. Many stayed at home to study under a tutor. In many respects there appears to have been little difference between what was taught to the sexes until about the thirteenth century. With the rise of the medieval university more rigorous education for males began in order to prepare them for admission. This opportunity was usually closed to women during the Middle Ages. Only later during the Renaissance did limited numbers of women attend the university.[79]

By sharp contrast, the Middle Ages provided a solid educational foundation for the institutionalized university. In the history of tutoring the rise of the university is of no small importance. University students and their professors acted as tutors outside their school. They ultimately dominated instruction at the university. This was a natural expansion of the tutor's role. In the first student hospices, (circa 1100) older students began to tutor younger ones. With the establishment by William of Wykeham of New College, Oxford (1379), the Bishop of Winchester began a tutor system at Oxford. However, only gradually did instruction at Oxford and later Cambridge pass into the hands of a single

33

tutor.    This  tutorial  system  allowed  tutors  to
respond  to  each  student's  educational  interests  by
extensive reading and individual discussion.

By   the   fifteenth   and   sixteenth   centuries
tutorial  instruction  became  so  general  that  it  led  to
the   decline   of   the   professional   studies   of   law,
medicine  and  theology  and  opened  the  studies  of  the
humanities.   The  ideal  of  the  generalist  helped  pass
instruction  into  the  hands  of  the  tutor.[80]    There
began  a  close  relationship  between  tutor  and  student.
It  is  not  a  simple  coincidence  that  the  subsequent
"new  learning"  of  the  Renaissance  spread  so  rapidly
across  European  society.    The  growing  number  of
university-educated  tutors  propelled  this  revival  in
learning  into  the  leading  families  of  Europe.    Only
the   "black   death"   at   the   end   of   the   fourteenth
century   temporarily   slowed   an   improvement   in
literacy.    So  many  university-trained  tutors  and
clergy  died  of  the  plague  that  four  of  Europe's
thirty  universities  vanished  and  a  shortage  of  tutors
developed  to  privately  teach  grammar.    This  was  only
a  temporary  setback,  for  soon  the  tutor  would  come  to
center   stage   in   the   development   of   Western
education.[81]

The  growing  domination  in  education  by  tutors
extended  into  the  education  of  kings.    From  1200  all
the  English  kings  had  private  tutors.    It  was  about
that  time  that  the  reigning  house  in  England  came  to
have  a  "state  governess."    As  a  position  it  carried
great  responsibility  and  influence,  for  this  person
in  turn  controlled  the  royal  children's  other  tutors.
A boy would be supervised by a "state governor."

The  education  of  princes  was  a  theme  of  a  number
of  treatises  circulated  in  Western  Europe  during  the
Middle  Ages.    This  included  a  book  allegedly  compiled
by  Aristotle  for  his  pupil  Alexander  the  Great,
another  by  Thomas  Aquinas  (1225-1274)  and  Giles  of
Rome  (4th  Century).    They  all  sought  to  offer  a
princely  model  of  virtue,  statecraft  and  justice.    By
the  late  medieval  period  Sir  Simon  Burley,  the  tutor
of  Richard  II  (1367-1399),  was  influenced  by  a  French
work  on  "the  govern-ment  of  kings  and  princes."
Henry  V  (1387-1422)  read  the  poet  Thomas  Hoceleve's
(15th  Century)  treatise  The  Regiment  of  Princes

(1411-1412), intended for his education as Prince of Wales.[82]  By 1501 John Skelton (1460-1529) made a gift of his _Speculum Principis_, his brief Latin tract, to his pupil, the future Henry VIII (1491-1547).[83]  The beginning of the Renaissance saw the older concept of "courtesy education" being combined with these works in princely education to produce a new and influential tutorial literature.

From our review of published sources in the history of education, and the writings of the great Western teachers, we have seen tutoring emerge as a definitive educational form.  Though never able to compete with the schools of any era in terms of enrollment, tutoring had deep roots throughout Europe's past supported by both the upper classes and the church.

The Greek "educational ideal" of pedagogue and student developing free speculative thinking was modeled on the Socratic dialogue.  Rome adapted this practice to perfect a rhetorical form of one-to-one instruction that subordinated individual thought to the mastery of Roman law and oratorical form.  This rhetorical form of tutorial education spread throughout the empire and was adopted by the Christian church as Rome declined.  The one-to-one instruction provided by the monasteries helped to facilitate the preservation of our knowledge of antiquity.  However, the Church subordinated her role as record keeper to the greater need of upholding Church law and tradition. From these medieval origins would rise in the Renaissance much of the modern educational philosophy of the West as tutors attempted to restore the "lost" knowledge of antiquity.[84]

Endnotes

1.  Edward Myers, _Education In The Perspective Of History_ (New York:  Harper and Brothers, 1960), 256-259.

2.  W.A. Mason, _History Of The Art Of Writing_ (New York:  Macmillan, 1920), 39.

3.  William Barclay, <u>Educational Ideals In The Ancient World</u> (London:  Collins, 1959), 14-15; Christopher Lucas, <u>Our Western Educational Heritage</u> (New York:  Macmillan, 1972), 149.

4.  Confucius, <u>The Sacred Books of China</u>, <u>The Texts of Confucianism</u>, trans. Legge in <u>The Sacred Books of The East</u>, ed. Muller, vol. 28 (Oxford: at the Clarendon Press, 1885), 82-92; _____ <u>Bhagavad-Gita</u>, <u>(The Song Celestral)</u> trans. Arnold (Boston:  Robert Brothers, 1885), 37-45; _____ , <u>Book of The Dead</u>, trans. Hillyer in <u>Anthology of World Poetry</u> ed. Doren (New York:  Harper, 1928); Elizabeth Godfrey, <u>English Children In The Olden Time</u> (Williamstown: Corner House Publisher, 1980), 30; R. Freeman Butts, <u>The Education Of The West</u> (New York: McGraw-Hill, 1973), 68; <u>Encyclopedia Britannica</u>, 1985 ed., s.v. "History of Education."

5.  Lucas, <u>Educational Heritage</u>, 37-38; Butts, <u>Education</u>, 58.

6.  Homer, <u>The Iliad</u>, trans. Rieu (New York:  Viking Penguin, 1986), 172-177; Homer, <u>The Odyssey</u>, trans. Bryant (Boston:  Estes and Company, 1898); Myers, <u>Education Perspective</u>, 256.

7.  Myers, <u>Education Perspective</u>, 256-257.

8.  Butts, <u>Education</u>, 84; Myers, <u>Education Perspective</u>, 256.

9.  Homer, <u>Iliad</u>, 172-177.

10. Josef Pieper, <u>Scholasticism</u>, trans. Winston (New York:  McGraw-Hill, 1960), 39-40, 155-156.

11. Werner Jaeger, <u>Paideia:  The Ideals of Greek Culture</u>, trans. Highet (New York:  Oxford University Press, 1945), 3-14.

12. Isocrates, <u>Panegyricus, Antidosis, Against the Sophists, Panathenaicus, Areopagiticus</u>, and <u>To Philip</u>, trans. Norlin (London:  Loeb Classical Library, 1928), 188.

13. Pieper, Scholasticism, 39-40, 155-156; Lucas, Educational Heritage, 51-52; Encyclopedia Britannica, 1985 ed.,s.v. "History of Education;" Myers, Education Perspective, 73-75, 256-259.

14. Plato, The Collected Dialogues of Plato, ed. Hamilton and Cairns (Princeton, New Jersey: Princeton University Press, 1961), 1567; Myers, Educational Perspective, 256-259.

15. Myers, Education Perspective, 259; Alice Zimmern, The Home Life Of The Ancient Greeks, trans. Blumner (New York: Cooper Square Publishers, 1966), 129; Jennifer S. Uglow and Frances Hinton, The International Dictionary of Women's Biography (New York: Continuum, 1985), 234.

16. Zimmern, Ancient Greeks, 129, 171-174.

17. Kenneth J. Freeman, Schools of Hellas (New York: Teachers College Press, 1969), 66-69, 279.

18. R.C. Lodge, Plato's Theory of Education (New York: Russell and Russell, 1970), 66; Ibid., 70; Barclay, Educational Ideals, 97.

19. Plato, The Collected Dialogues of Plato, 150, 635-636, 1379, 1481-1482; H.I. Marrou, A History of Education In Antiquity (New York: Sheed & Ward, 1956), 221-267; Jaeger, Paideia, 309; Frederick Beck, Greek Education (London: Methuen, 1964), 106-107; Frederick Ely, This History And Philosophy of Education Ancient And Medieval (New York: Prentice-Hall, 1940), 273-274; A.V. Yannicopoulos, "The Pedagogue In Antiquity," British Journal of Educational Studies 33 (June, 1985), 175. The modern concept of a well-educated teacher is still designated by the Latin term, pedagogue. William Barclay, Educational Ideals in the Ancient World (London: Collins, 1959), 103.

20. Plato, Dialogues, trans., Hamilton, XIII-XXV.

42. Wilkins, <u>Roman Education</u>, 42.

43. Bonner, <u>Education In Rome</u>, 31-33.

44. Bonner, <u>Education In Rome</u>, 21-22.

45. Wilkins, <u>Roman Education</u>, 42; Bonner, <u>Education In Rome</u>, 31-33, 21-11, 105.

46. George Kennedy, <u>Quintilian</u> (New York: Tweyne Publishers, 1969), 42-43; E.B. Castle, <u>Ancient Education and Today</u> (Baltimore: Penguin Books, 1961), 63-64; Butts, <u>Education</u>, 116, 118; Wilkins, <u>Roman Education</u>, 40-42.

47. Marcus Fabius Quintilian, <u>Quintilian</u>, trans. Butler, (New York: Putnam, 1921), 23-25.

48. Ibid.

49. Ibid., 31-49.

50. Ibid.

51. Ibid.

52. Ibid.

53. Quintilian obviously chose to later ignore Cicero's tutoring experiences, thereby trying to refute the education of Rome's greatest rhetorician.

54. Clarke, <u>Rhetoric</u>, 20; Bonner, <u>Education In Rome</u>, 16, 28-30.

55. Bonner, <u>Education In Rome</u>, 27.

56. Ibid., 33, 161.

57. Gaius Suetonius, <u>The Twelve Caesars</u>, trans. Robert Graves (New York: Penguin Books, 1957), 187.

58. Cornelius Tacitus, <u>The Reign of Nero</u>, trans. Ramsey (London: The Folio Society, 1962), 115-122; Michael Grant, <u>Nero</u> (New York: American

Heritage Press, 1970), 27-28, 57, 214.

59. Bonner, Education in Ancient Rome, 33, 161.

60. Marcus Aurelius, The Meditations of Marcus Aurelius Antonius, book 1, in The Social Philosophers, ed. Saxe Commins and Robert Linscott (New York: Random House, 1947), 277-284.

61. Henry Dwight Sedquick, Marcus Aurelius (New Haven: Yale University Press, 1927), 40-41.

62. Bea Howe, A Galaxy of Governesses (London: Derek Verschoyle, 1954), 15.

63. John W. H. Walden, The Universities of Ancient Greece (Freeport: Books For Libraries Press, 1970), 146.

64. Howe, Governesses, 16.

65. Cain Irraith, Law of Fosterage Fees, vol. 1, 147; John Ryan, Irish Monasticism (Ithaca, New York: Cornell University Press, 1972), 209, 213, 216; H. Graham, The Early Irish Monastic Schools (Dublin: Talbot Press, 1923), 79; The Oxford English Dictionary, 1st ed., s.v. "Foster."

66. Alcuin, The Letter of Alcuin, trans. Page (New York: The Forest Press, 1909), 79-80; Alcuin, Disputatio in Thought and Letters in Western Europe A.D. 500 to 900 ed. Laistner (Ithaca, New York: Cornell University Press, 1957), 199; Alcuin, De rhetorica in Thoughts and Letters, 200-201; Eginhard, Early Lives of Charlemagne, trans. A.J. Grant (London: Chatto and Windus, 1926), 61-62; Frank Graves, A History of Education (Westport: Greenwood Press, 1970), 28-29; Duggan, History of Education, 85.

67. James Sutherland, ed., The Oxford Book of Literary Anecdotes (Oxford: Clarendon Press, 1975), 4-5.

68. Howe, Governesses, 16-17.

41

69. Morris Bishop, The Horizon Book of the Middle Ages (New York: American Heritage, 1968), 38, 263-264.

70. C.H. Haskins, The Renaissance of the Twelfth Century (Boston: Harvard University Press, 1928), 72.

71. Teachers taught classes in the cathedral school, while tutors taught individuals in local churches and monasteries. Gabriel Compayre, trans. Payne, The History of Pedagogy (Boston: D.C. Heath, 1886), 69.

72. Nicholas Orme, English Schools In The Middle Ages (London: Methuen and Company, 1973), 18-19.

73. Nicholas Orme, English Schools, 167-168; Butts, Education, 164; Barbara W. Tuchman, A Distant Mirror (New York: Alfred A. Knopf, 1979), 52; Thomas Wright, The Homes of Other Days (New York: D. Appleton and Company, 1871), 133-134, 138-139; Peter Abelard, The Story of My Misfortunes, trans. Bellows, (Glencoe, Illinois: The Free Press, 1958), 16-22.

74. Raymond Lull, The Book of the Order of Chivalry, ed. Byles (London: Kegan Paul, 1926), 77-89; Frances Gies, The Knight in History (New York: Harper & Row, 1984), 101-105.

75. Joan Simon, Education and Society In Tudor England (Cambridge: University Press, 1966), 10-11; Nicholas Orme, From Childhood to Chivalry (London: Methuen, 1984), 17-29, 56; An interesting collection of documents include the Boke of Curtasye related to home tutoring; F.J. Furnivall, The Babee's Book (London: 1868).

76. John of Salisbury, "The Education of John of Salisbury," in University Records and Life In The Middle Ages, ed. Lynn Thorndike (New York: Octagon Books, 1971), 13.

77. Peter of Blois, "Literature versus Logic," Ibid., 15; Christopher Brooke, _From Alfred to Henry III_ (London: Sphere Books, 1969), 159-160.

78. "that on such things (tutoring) a man should spend liberally." (See footnote number 60).

79. James Mulhern, _A History of Education_ (New York: Ronald Press, 1959), 272; Orme, _English Schools_, 55; Shulamith Shahar, _The Fourth Estate_ (London: Methuen, 1983), 157-159, 186, 214-216; Orme, _Childhood_, 58-59, 106-107.

80. Hastings Rashdall, _The Universities of Europe In The Middle Ages_, eds. Powrche, Eneden (Oxford: Clarendon Press, 1936), vol. 1, 528, 532, vol. 3, 216, 231-232.

81. Mulhern, _History of Education_, 286; Rashdall, _Universities of Europe_, vol.3, 2, 16, 231-232; Butts, _Education_, 269-270; Rashdall, _Universities_, vol. 1, 528, 531; Tuchman, _Mirror_, 118-119; Philip Ziegler, _The Black Death_ (New York: Harper and Row, 1969), 252.

82. Thomas Hoceleve, _Works_, ed. Furnivall, vol.3, (EETS, 1897), 1-197.

83. John Skelton, _Works_, ed. Dyce (London, 1843).

84. Orme, _English Schools_, 19-21; Howe, _Governesses_, 19.

CHAPTER 2


THE "NEW LEARNING" OF SOUTHERN AND NORTHERN EUROPE
(1416-1526)


A significant transition occurred during
Europe's fifteenth and sixteenth centuries. The
shift from medieval scholasticism to Renaissance
humanism coincided with the disappearance of the
voluminous Latin chronicles written by monks or
scribes, who admirably had preserved most of
recorded history. This vacuum would gradually be
filled by private correspondence and chronicles
written in the modern languages of Europe. These two
largely new sources of historical information became
very valuable since they existed in considerable
quantity, were contemporary and the majority had been
dated precisely.

Ross states that the greatest value of private
chronicles and correspondence is that they are not
deliberate works of history and thus are unselfcon-
scious. These "informal" historic records include
what medieval history passed by, the use of family
tutors in Western Europe. The historical materials
of the Renaissance and afterwards offer an insight
into educational development by illuminating the day-
to-day events of community life. While chronicling
the rise of tutoring, these same writers also give us
an appreciation of parallel developments of childhood
and women's education in Europe. Woodward argues
that viewing these broader historical issues will
safeguard against exaggeration, which is always a
risk when isolating a social phenomenon, (in this
case the importance of tutors in the history of
education).[1]

# 1. ITALY POINTS THE WAY

Italy's many city-states promoted a commercial rivalry that completed the work of the medieval Crusades in developing Italian wealth. Local independence led to a bountiful rivalry among princes with respect to their cultural patronage. This zeal to excel in sculpture, architecture, painting, poetry, scholarship and education became the theme of the southern Italian humanists. A literary base had been prepared for them in the development of the vernacular, and in the fervor for recovering and studying the classics of Greece and Rome (led by Petrarch and Boccaccio).

The discovery of the complete text of Quintilian's _De Institutione Oratoria_ (1416) and Cicero's _De Oratore_ (1422), as well as other lost works from antiquity, strengthened humanist ties to the classical ideal of education. The humanists also attached great importance to diet, clothing and exercise. The social end was always present in their minds. As the humanists became tutors to Italian noble families, their purpose was to develop an easy graceful learning, suppleness and dignity of figure in the old Greek tradition. This relationship of culture to social gifts was also developed in their educational writing. Between 1465 and 1476 the first printing presses appeared in Italy and Spain. This facilitated the wide and rapid spread of the "new learning" across all of Europe that eventually included an international group of philosopher-tutors. The literature of the Renaissance revealed a new age of individualism.[2]

Vittorino da Feltre (1378-1446) was a classic representative of this Renaissance "new learning," matching a fine intellectual humanism to a standard of physical excellence and personal courtesy.[3] He was born in the Venetian Alps and worked at the University of Padua under Gasparino Barzizza, the pioneer scholar of the Renaissance.[4] Before 1420 he acted as a tutor in Latin and mathematics at a boarding-house he set up for students at Padua. Vittorino's scholarship was so well known that by 1422 he was appointed to the chair of rhetoric at the university.[5] Soon after (1423) the Marquis of Mantua, Gianfrancesco Gonzaga, hired him as a tutor for his children to equip them in the struggle of wits that meant life or death to the noble families of Italy in that day.[6] His "school" was set up in a casino, a sumptuous garden-house that Vittorino named "La casa Giocosa," (the joyful house). He ordered it decorated with frescoes of children at play, in keeping with his philosophy of education. Here he directed the education of the sons and daughters of the princely house of Mantua. Families came from all over Italy and Germany seeking him as a tutor.

Vittorino was no mere "grammar master" teaching a group of children. Instead, he was a true Renaissance humanist who respected student individuality and made a sincere effort to increase it. As soon as a child manifested any special gift, he adjusted subject and method. This approach gained for him the reputation as a great tutor. Without doubt some group instruction occurred at Vittorino's "school" in Mantua, but his emphasis remained on the cultivation of each child's personal intellectual temper through one-to-one instruction and mutual study. The individuality which characterized this teaching rested upon Vittorino's intimate knowledge of the temper and ability of each pupil. Vittorino tutored not only the nobility, but also "the gifted poor" whom he tutored at his home for nothing. There were forty to seventy such pupils at any given time.[7]

Vittorino proposed to train as one the mind, body and spirit of each of his students. His was a thorough, practical discipline. It prepared youth for a life of action by training both mind and character for the exercise of judgment in public affairs. The subjects for tutoring were drawn exclusively from classical and early Christian sources. (This applied equally to mathematics, natural science, ethics, history and geography).[8] Quintilian's Institutio Oratoria expressed the ideal of the educated man accepted by Vittorino. Humanists from Petrarch onwards recognized Quintilian's importance as the prime authority of the Roman educational ideal. As we will see later many philosophers of the "new learning," whether Italian or Teutonic, including Guarino, Agricola, or Erasmus, followed the guidance of this treatise.[9] (They also obviously chose to ignore Quintilian's denunciation of one-to-one instruction, since they were tutors at some point in their lives).

The study of history meant for Vittorino the story of ancient Rome and Greece told by Livy, Thucydides, Xenophon or Plutarch. Geography was learned from ancient sources such as Strabo, Ptolemy, Mela and Dionysius. Aristotle, Pliny and Theophrastus became indispensable manuals of science. Since archaeological, geographical, historical or scientific works coordinating the contents of the classic authors were not yet available, Vittorino believed that the only path to true knowledge lay in studying these ancient books in their original languages. The instruction of Greek and Latin in humanist schools was more literary in context rather than linguistic, for its chief end remained "erudito" or knowledge. There would be some notable future exceptions to this principle in the giftedness of individual Renaissance student linguists.

Vittorino also attached great importance to diet, clothing and exercise. The social end was always present in his mind. As the "new learning" developed in the Italian high Renaissance, the conceptual relationship of culture to social gifts spread through all of Italy.[10]

A contemporary and intimate friend of Vittorino, Guarino da Verona (1374-1460), also established his reputation as a humanist-tutor. In 1429 Guarino was invited by the Marquis Niccolo d'Este to Ferrara to tutor his son, Leonello. He was paid 350 ducats. This was perhaps the highest-paid post held by any of the humanist tutors. He also tutored other children in Ferrara and later all parts of Italy.[11]

Guarino devoted most mornings to his public teaching as a professor of rhetoric at the University of Ferrara. Tutoring generally occupied the rest of his day. His method of instruction fell into three stages: the elementary, the grammatical and the rhetorical. Like Vittorino he searched the entire range of antiquity for the elements best suited to preparing youth for the Italy of their day. Guarino was among the first scholars to conceive and explain a complete scheme of literary education adapted to the modern age. He presented these ideas in <u>Upon the Method of Teaching and of Reading the Classical Authors</u> (1459).

The humanist philosophy of individual education was in sharp contrast to the schools in the Middle Ages that had no established enrollment nor logical progression of studies. As a group the humanists would bemoan the schools as autocratic, brutal, intellectually barren places. Corporal punishment, institutionalized informing and constant surveillance made the schools notorious for punitive discipline rather than scholarship. It is not unusual that most humanists recommended tutoring at home rather than the doubtful education acquired at most schools of this age.[12]

This theme was continued by the Florentine, Leo Battista Alberti (1404-1472), whose <u>Trattato della Cura della Famiglia</u> (1431) was one of the first works written on the requisite tutorial education for an appreciation of classical literature. His early contribution to Renaissance educational literature struck the themes of public duty, respect for family and a simple life.[13]

Matteo Palmieri (1406-1475), a contemporary of Alberti, wrote <u>Della Vita Civile</u>, a work that amplifies his friend's educational themes.[14] From northern Italy, near Venice, Pietro Bembo (1470-1547) composed <u>Gli Asolani</u> (1505) as a series of three dialogues concerning the nature of love and wisdom. He leaves the impression that women, as well as men, had a right to participate in intellectual activities that included tutoring. <u>Gli Asolani</u> became so widely read that by the end of the sixteenth century it had gone through at least twenty-two Italian editions. A Spanish version appeared in 1551, a French translation in 1545. There is no doubt that <u>Gli Asolani</u> was a major influence on an even more important work, Castiglione's the <u>Courtier</u>.[15]

49

Baldassare Castiglione (1478-1529) continued Bembo's theme when he authored what Woodward considers one of the most famous books of the Italian Renaissance, _Il Cortigiano_ (1528), (_The Book of the Courtier_). Castiglione viewed an exemplary gentleman, (named Bembo), as a mixture of Christian virtues and ancient Greco-Roman ideals. "He therefore will be a good scholar, besides the practising of good things must evermore set all his diligence to be like his master, and change himself into him."[16] The courtier represented chivalry at its best. Here was the truly "educated man"--a combination of personal friend, advisor and tutor.

> But in case a philosopher should come before any of our Princes . . . and teach them good manners, and what the life of a good Prince ought to be. . . . Besides this, by little and little distil into this mind goodness, and teach him continence, stoutness of courage, justice, temperance . . . he shall teach the Courtier not only to speak, but also to write well.[17]

The study of music, art, Greek, Latin and history were also among the topics of tutorial study. By 1539 _The Courtier_ was translated into French. In 1561 Sir Thomas Hoby's translation made it an English classic, which every educated sixteenth century Elizabethan read.[18]

Women took a significant part in this general revival of classical learning in Italy. Christine De Pisan (1364-1430) of Venice was a highly respected and widely disseminated intellectual voice on the status of women. She sought to demonstrate that women possessed natural affinities for all areas of cultural and social activity. Her father, Tommaso da Pizzano, was the court astrologer and physician of France's Charles V. Living at this court, Christine was tutored by her father in courtly ways. She obtained a good education in spite of her mother's opposition. Between 1390 and 1429, Christine produced a vast array of works in verse and prose. Her _Cité des Dames_ (_The Book of the City of Ladies_) in 1405 denounced the lack of access women had to education. Warner sees Christine de Pizan assuming the role of a "moral tutor" writing to incline us toward right-thinking and right-doing. Her plea for women's education gave as her reason education's close correlation with good conduct. This argument for learning anticipated The Courtier by over one hundred years. The City of Ladies was the first widely read universal history of women regarding the actual social position of women in fourteenth century Italy and France.[19]

As early as the thirteenth century women attended the University of Bologna. Some became professors. According to Christine De Pisan, Novella D'Andrea (c.1333) at age 21 became a professor at Bologna. Her father, Giovanni d' Andrea, was a professor of cannon law at the university and acted as her tutor. Supposedly, since she was very attractive, Maria delivered her lectures from behind a screen so as not to distract her students by her beauty. Her sister, Bettina, was tutored to become a philosopher, and taught at the University of Padua.[20]

The history of Italian literature mentions other women proficient in Latin and Greek. As early as 1405 Battista di Montefeltro was writing sonnets. She publicly addressed the Emperor Sigismund in 1433 as he passed through Urbino, and she wrote a letter to Pope Martin V. By the middle of the fifteenth century many other women became known for their knowledge of Greek and Latin at an early age. Olympia Fulvia Morata (1526-55) was the daughter of the scholar, Pellegrino Morata. At age thirteen she became tutor to the Princess Anna of Ferrara. She later taught other princesses the classics, geometry, geography and literature. After fleeing to Germany to avoid religious persecution, she tutored students at Heidelberg. The custom of employing tutors for the children of great households was a long established one in Italy. Men dominated this system. Many had been initially trained to teach at the university (Vittorino da Feltre, Guarine da Verona, among others) secured these tutoring positions in families of wealth and distinction. The daughters of merchants, statesmen, and scholars saw for the first time their education treated seriously.

The content and methods of Renaissance education for both girls and boys were much the same. The individuality of women was developed in the same way as a man. The only notable difference in educational content was the humanist's concern for the girl's personal vocation. Most frequently, the girl's future was determined early by her parents. To this end the humanists added the universal principle that true education is preparation for life. Their "new learning" first introduced girls, as well as boys, to a basic learning in the classics. After that goal was reached, additional instruction was determined by each girl's particular needs. A humanistic curriculum was developed gradually and universally adopted before the close of the first quarter of the fifteenth century. It included: Latin, Greek, "humanities," science, mathematics, Christian doctrine, ethics, music, art, dancing, riding, morality and religious practice.

The "rediscovery" in the Italian Renaissance of the "lost" works of antiquity so long repressed by the Church, once again disseminated the "classic ideal" of the educated man. The court tutors of prominent Italian city states taught this "new learning" that helped reawaken the Italian Universities with a distinctive Renaissance flavor. Foreign students that returned to their native lands brought home a new outlook that was concerned with the development of individuals and their role in society. Outside of Italy this type of education was not available for women. One notable exception was Isabella of Castile (1451-1504), mother of Catherine of Aragon (1485-1536). As the wife of Henry VIII (1491-1547), Catherine's influence would be seen in the introduction of a Renaissance education for women in England.[21]


2.  ISABELLA OF SPAIN AND THE EDUCATION OF WOMEN


The Quattrocento in Spain occurred almost exactly one hundred years before the Elizabethan Age and coincided with the reign of Isabella of Castile (1474-1504). Classical learning had survived in the

Middle Ages to a larger extent in the physical isolation of Spain than elsewhere in Europe. Further buttressed by the scholarship of the Moors, a new educational era dawned following the political triumphs of Ferdinand and Isabella. For a brief time this influence of Renaissance learning made their court the most glorious in Europe.[22]

That the Golden Age of Italian humanism coincided with the Age of Isabella was no accident. The best scholarship from Italy, Germany and France was heartily welcomed by her in Spain. In turn, many of the ideals expressed by Spanish humanistic theorists showed evidence of the inspiration which Italy gave to Spain. Throughout the Middle Ages Iberian students sent to Italian universities later influenced their home universities at Salamanca, Valencia, Valladolid and Lisbon. Native Italian scholars came to tutor at the courts of Spain and teach in her universities. Spanish scholars returning from their own College of St. Clement in Bologna or from Aragonese in Naples combined with them to promote the "new learning."[23]

Isabella as Queen of Spain extended her patronage to many individual humanists at Spanish colleges and universities, which became the cultural centers of early humanistic endeavor. Her own education had followed a simple medieval model but had been superior to that of her husband Ferdinand. Tutors under the supervision of her mother taught her both literate habits and Spanish piety. As queen, she dictated her own letters, and, as Prescott tells us, finding herself deficient in Latin set out to learn it. Isabella attained "critical accuracy" in it and became "acquainted with several modern languages." She enjoyed collecting books. In 1477, Isabella founded a library of manuscripts at a Toledo convent. She also donated books to the library at the Escorial. To supplement this knowledge, she brought to the Spanish Court the famous Italian humanist Peter Martyr as her tutor.

Isabella's scholarly fervor became an important impetus to women's education. Her own use of tutors encouraged Spanish families to teach their own daughters at home. Foreshadowing the future "school" that Sir Thomas More used for his own daughters, Prescott gives an account of two sisters, the Marchioness of Monteagudo and the Donna Maria Pacheco, who may well serve as a Spanish parallel of domestic education. The queen herself had a Latin tutor, called for her knowledge, "La Latina." Beatriz Galindo, born in 1475, in Salamanca, rose to influence based on her own scholarship and the fact her brother was the secretary of Ferdinand and Isabella. Whether "La Latina" learned her classical Latin at the University of Salamanca is unclear, though she later became a professor of philosophy, rhetoric, and medicine at that university. Like the Italian universities, those of Spain were open to both men and women. Queen Isabella attended lectures at Salamanca. So many other learned Spanish women claim Salamanca for their birthplace that the presence of women at the university was not an anomaly. "La Latina" was so successful as tutor to the queen that Isabella later arranged her marriage to Francisco Ramirez, a soldier and secretary to King Ferando V. Prescott tells us that two of her contemporaries were also chosen as university professors. One was given a chair in Latin Classics at the University of Salamanca, the other occupied the chair of history at the University of Alcala.[24]

In the same year of the discovery of America and the birth of the famous Spanish humanist, Juan de Vives (1492-1540), Isabella directed Peter Martyr (1500-1562) to establish a court school at Saragossa. From 1492 to 1501 he taught in the Palace School and was at the same time the queen's tutor. The young nobles attended his lectures during the day with their tutors, who in the evening helped revise the lectures. Other Italian scholars came to Spain as teachers or tutors until learning became a cult of the nobility. The schools these humanists founded for boys or girls supplemented the expanding domestic education by tutors.[25]

Nor did this intellectual queen, who was described as "the most vigorous and most learned Princess in Europe," leave the education of her children to the whim of her courtiers. Isabella gave personal tutoring to her four daughters. She had the learned Italian brothers Antonio and Alessandro

Geraldino brought to Spain to teach in the palace school. Under Antonio, Isabella's eldest daughter, the Infanta Isabella (1470-1498), attained Latin scholarship of the highest Renaissance Italian order. Her Latin poetry was published at Salamanca in 1505. Catherine (1485-1536), another daughter, could also read and write Latin in her childhood. Vives wrote that the four Infantas, "were well learned all, . . . there were no queens . . . that ever did more perfectly fulfill all the points of a good woman."

The royal families of Europe profited from the fruits of their advanced education. Isabella and Maria each in turn became the Queen of Portugal, Juana, Queen of the Netherlands (1479-1555), and Catherine in 1501 married Arthur, Prince of Wales (1486-1502). After his death in 1509 she married his brother, Henry VIII. As Queen of England, Catherine would spread the influence of the Southern Renaissance tutors to Northern Europe. She became a significant factor in the general rise of English humanism, and the inception of a "golden age" for learned women in England.[26]

### 3. THE HUMANIST TUTORS OF NORTHERN EUROPE

The roots of humanism north of the Alps was the "new learning" that was spread by the Italian noble houses to the trade centers of the Netherlands and Germany. Here the dispersion of Renaissance culture went even further geographically than in the south and its scope was changed by the social interests and varied life of northern Europe.

The tutors of southern Europe limited the spread of their talents largely to the ruling families of Italy or the Spanish court. Almost without exception they tended to glorify the established political order. Southern humanists remained more sophisticated and secular than their other European counterparts. The northern humanist and Reformation tutors extended their thinking beyond courtly "courtesy education," to include families of the gentry, mercantile and professional groups. These tutors and schoolmen fostered a more practical education than found in southern Europe. They envisioned education as a nationalistic instrument that complemented the age of exploration and its fierce competition for markets overseas. This fueled the rediscovery of science, that had been born in the Renaissance south, but made even greater strides in northern Europe and England. Most of all, they remained deeply colored by the piety and mysticism of the late Middle Ages. Erasmus may have been its most illustrious exponent, but it was left to Luther and Melanchthon to mold the faith and intellectual outlook of a generation of young scholars.

With the general support of the aristocracy many of the northern humanists such as Erasmus, Comenius and Vives, supported tutorial instruction at home as a better educational plan than the group instruction of a school. This preference came in part because the universities of northern Europe resisted abandoning medieval scholasticism. Since the northern gentry were largely rural, home tutoring was a more practical solution. However, there still remained for most families a general reluctance to entrust a child to a single tutor. For the great majority of children of the sixteenth century the question remained mute. Most received little, if any, formal education at home or school.[27]

These northern humanists did not look to the university to advance their scholarship toward classical inquiry. Instead, as in Italy, the courts of ruling families gave the first and strongest impulse to the northern Renaissance. In Germany and the Netherlands the hopes of the humanist scholar centered on the local duke, king, or sovereign. In 1450 the German, Aeneas Sylvius (15th century), wrote De Liberorum Educatione as a detailed guide for the tutoring of two young German Habsburg princes. Through courtly education, the Renaissance concern for the individual grew in these societies.[28]

Ties between the north and south of Europe were made stronger by intermarriage among the nobility. Barbara von Brandenburg's marriage to Ludovico Gonzaga of Mantua brought the employment of the humanist Ariginus as court tutor (1512). He tutored

Barbara Gonzaga (16th Century), their daughter, who became a poet and a collector of German poetry. Some of his other students became proficient in the classics. Even earlier Emperor Charles IV (1347-1378), swayed by Petrarch (1304-1374), commanded that all princes of the empire be tutored in its four spoken languages. The same education was mandated even for princesses.[29]

The influence of Isabella of Spain on the Habsburg court is one of the best examples of the effect of humanism on education. Margaret of Austria (1480-1530), daughter of Emperor Maximilian I (1459-1519), became the affianced bride of the Infante Juan, only son of King Ferdinand and Queen Isabella. Margaret remained in Spain less than two years because of the prince's untimely death. During that short time she still benefited from the excellent tutors employed by Isabella for her own daughter. Catherine of Aragon exchanged with Margaret conversation lessons in Castilian for those in French.

Many years later, after the death of her second husband, Margaret became Regent of the Netherlands (1506). When her sister-in-law, Juana of Aragon, had lost both her husband, (Philip the Handsome of the Netherlands), and her sanity, she became the guardian of Juana's three daughters and eldest son, Charles, later Emperor Charles V (1500-1556). At her castle of Malines the library combined the rich treasures of both Greek and Latin manuscripts, and the best literary works of the Renaissance. Here tutors including Adrian Dedel, head of the University of Utrecht, (later Pope Adrian VI) (1522-1523), tutored Charles using the original manuscripts of Christine de Pisan (1364-1430). As an amplification to her writing there hung in the castle library a beautiful tapestry illustrating scenes from her <u>Cité des Dames</u>. Juan de Vives also tutored at this court. While Margaret was regent, Erasmus encouraged her to pursue her own literary projects. At Malines was a new blending of humanist learning from the south with the cultural heritage of northern Europe. Charles V, as an emperor educated in these liberal arts, bequeathed to the Habsburg dynasty its greatest social and economic development.[30]

## 4. <u>THE REFORMATION TUTORS</u>

Humanist principles in education were not dropped by the German Reformation, only modified by Martin Luther (1483-1546) and his supporters. As the German leader of church reform, Luther wielded an important influence in the general education of children. With Melanchthon and Sturm, Luther proposed a new method for the education of boys as either clergymen or civil servants. Women's education was mentioned only as an afterthought. Luther complained (1524) that some boys were in school twenty or thirty years.[31]

> yet have learned nothing. The world has changed, and things go differently. My idea is that boys should spend an hour or two a day in school, and the rest of the time work at home, learn some trade and do whatever is desired, so that study and work may go on together. . . . The same should be done for the education of girls.[32]

This thoroughly practical education was more vocational than humanistic, but revealed a disdain for the worst abuses present in the classical Latin schools of the period. In the preface to his shorter catechism (1529), Luther urged fathers of families to tutor their children and servants in basic religion. This led to early instruction in reading at home.

> For this reason children must be taught the doctrine of God . . . which you must teach your children,--namely to know our Lord Jesus Christ. . . .[33]

In many Protestant farmhouses in Germany the parents taught their children to read many years before sending them to school.

Luther intermingled the religious and educational obligations of parents toward their children. He contributed to the widespread acceptance of domestic education in Protestant Europe and later in Puritan North America. The moral concept of education in the north supplanted the southern humanists' courtly code of good manners. Luther left to his schoolmaster associate, Philip Melanchthon, the translation of these ideals into realistic educational doctrines.

Philip Schwarzerd, known by the Graecised form of his name as Philip Melanchthon (1497-1560), was born at Bretten in the Palatinate. His father was a prosperous armorer of notable intellect. Melanchthon was taught at home by a private tutor, John Unger, a young theological scholar. Unger, later a court chaplain in Baden, remembered Philip as an "excellent linguist." He gave the boy a thorough grounding in Latin and an appreciative taste for languages. From his tutor Philip learned modesty, honesty and the love of truth. Melanchthon later cherished these memories of his early tutoring.

> He drove me to grammar and made me do twenty or thirty verses from Mantua each day. . . . Thus he made me a linguist. He was a good man; he loved me as a son, and I him as a father. . . .[34]

Both teacher and student must have been exceptional, for in 1511 at age fourteen, Melanchthon received his bachelor's degree at Heidelburg. While at that university, he tutored the two sons of Count Ludwig von Lowenstein. This was probably his first teaching experience. Melanchthon's own teachers commented on the young man's extraordinary insight into Greek literature. By his twenty-second year he became beyond question the best humanistic scholar in Germany.[35]

Melanchthon's humanism, moral, national and ethical, came closest to an ideal representation of the Teutonic Renaissance. He believed in the efficacy of letters for training German-speaking children in a nationalistic Christian faith. Under Luther's influence, Melanchthon completed the reconciliation of southern humanism with Protestant and northern European nationalism. By 1534 he had become the supreme educational authority in Germany.

Melanchthon began the reorganization of the universities and secondary schools along German Protestant-humanistic lines. Melanchthon gave to the German Renaissance his genius for systematization by establishing many schools. His countrymen named him the "Creator of the Protestant Educational System of Germany" with good reason, since nearly all the Latin schools and gymnasiums of sixteenth century Germany were founded according to Melanchthon's direction.[36]

Melanchthon still found time to set up a "schola privata" (a small private academy) in his own house at Wittenberg. There he carried out experiments using different methods of organizing an educational course with a small number of pupils. Melanchthon gave each one "direct personal instruction" in Latin and Greek as a preparation for higher education reminiscent of his own childhood tutoring. Even in the more fully developed "trivial school," Melanchthon exhibited a humanistic concern for the individual. He also taught his students mathematics, physics, rhetoric and logic. Boys were grouped by ability and aptitudes. Work with the teacher was largely individual, with only two lessons each week given to the entire class. The continued use of one-to-one tutorials as a supplement to classroom instruction was almost an invariable practice in classical schools of sixteenth century Germany and England.[37]

Melanchthon's educational influence rested upon his German nationalism and his Reformation theology. Many humanists looked upon the Reformation as a step backward, but not Melanchthon. His commitment to this religious movement, combined with the educational attainments of the Renaissance, and inaugurated a new era in German education. For forty-two years he championed humanistic studies throughout German education. Outside of Germany, Erasmus, a contemporary humanist reformer, did not break with the church. He achieved even wider fame as an educational reformer and a contributor to Renaissance tutoring.

## 5.  ERASMUS, THE EDUCATION CATALYST

Born at Rotterdam, Desiderius Erasmus (1466?-1536), whose name meant the beloved one, was the son of humble parents.  Orphaned at eighteen, he was ordained in 1492.  After some years of good service as the secretary of the Bishop of Cambrai, Erasmus convinced the bishop to enroll him at the University of Paris.  While there, he tutored many younger students.  One rich young pupil, Lord Mountjoy, took Erasmus to his country home in Greenwich, England (1499).  There he met the young Thomas More (1478-1535) and briefly attended Oxford.  He made the acquaintance of John Colet (1467-1519), John Fisher (1459-1535), William Grocyn (1446-1519) and other young Englishmen freshly returned from Italy, filled with zeal for the "new learning."  Their association was destined to stimulate a definite humanist movement in England.  Fisher's formation of Christ College at Cambridge, the first humanist college, was probably due to Erasmus' influence.

On a second visit to England (1505-06), Erasmus was engaged as a tutor for the sons of Henry VII's physician.  He accompanied them to Italy on the "Grand Tour" as a "general guide and supervisor."  By this time he was perhaps the best-read Latinist in France or England.  Returning to England yet again (1509), he lived in or near London, where More's house at Chelsea was always open to him.  Erasmus was very impressed by the intellectual atmosphere of More's "school" for his daughters and other family members.  He became More's closest friend.  In turn, More converted Erasmus to a belief in higher education for women.  Erasmus even advised More's eldest daughter, Margaret, on her education in Latin and Greek.

From his educational writings we learn that Erasmus preferred a tutor at home, under the father's direction, once the child reached age seven.  He had a low opinion of schoolmasters of the time and an even lower opinion of schools run by religious orders.

Plato's primary concern in his Republic had been
the education of future rulers, a theme Erasmus now
took up in his Institutio Principis Christiani,
(Education of a Christian Prince, 1516). This work
was read widely in England and took a very concrete
and practical form. Erasmus argued that if the
gentry did not shake off their medieval disdain for
learning, then other men's sons would take their
place as England's future leaders.[38] This argument
of Erasmus generated such consternation among the
upper class that a law was even proposed in Parliament, possibly by Elizabeth's close advisor, William
Cecil, which forbade anybody below the rank of baron
from keeping a tutor at his house. If this law
passed, no evidence exists that it was ever enforced.

Some have criticized Erasmus and other humanist
educators for not recognizing a distinct childhood
education. This was largely true, since few teachers
today prescribe a Latin and Greek curriculum for
five-year-old children. (See Chapter Four on the
royal tutors). Yet Erasmus did understand that this
problem existed and offered a solution. In De Pueris
Instituendis (1529) he recognized the influences of
heredity and the environment on the young child.[39]

Erasmus allowed the mother oversight of the
young in health, habits and religion until the age of
seven. But Erasmus had little enthusiasm for the
Greek interest in physical perfection supported by
Vittorino as an essential factor in forming the
"complete personality" of the Italian Renaissance.

The foundation of instruction belonged to the
home. Here, like Luther, Erasmus saw a parental
obligation to teach the elements of the Christian
faith. Religious instruction assumed teaching in
reading, writing and drawing.

Only at the seventh year did a child reach the
age for systematic instruction. Under ideal circumstances a private tutor at home was the first
preference of Erasmus. The next alternative was to
engage a highly qualified teacher to teach a small
group of children in one of their homes. Erasmus had

a low opinion of most schoolmasters of his day (1520-1530). The tutor's qualifications were to be reviewed carefully by the parents. He should have a thorough mastery of Greek and Latin; be widely read; and possess fluency in Latin. The tutor must be first of all, a man of high character, worthy of fullest confidence. He must be active, vigorous and of healthy habit. His great aim will be to kindle spontaneous interest. Manner is of importance; he must not be gloomy in appearance, nor passionate; he must be serious, indeed, but patient, remembering that he too was once a boy.

Erasmus believed that a tutor's effectiveness depended upon his ability to discern the "natura" of his pupil, the taste, interests and special talents that made each child an individual. In his Cambridge days, Erasmus had earned derision from his professors for urging a tutor's career upon men of standing in the university. Erasmus foreshadowed the profession of tutorial master that originated during the next three hundred years.[40]

In the <u>De Ratione Studii</u> (1511) Erasmus outlined the readings that belonged to a humanist-rhetorical education. He acknowledged Quintilian as the authority on this subject, but added Plutarch, Seneca and Aesop. The goal of education was to uncover the moral ideals of the ancient authors and to draw lessons for politics and society. Unlike other humanists in Italy, Germany and England, Erasmus scorned the development of the vernacular for political writing and in preaching. He regarded Latin oratory as an end in itself.[41]

By age fourteen, a child's education was to be completed. The systematic instruction of morals from ethical writers, historians and poets, including Cicero, Seneca, Terence and Vergil, helped to mold the child's character. This was intertwined with family life and contact with cultured adults. Erasmus sought to encourage individuality. In particular, he encouraged travel to widen mental horizons and induce tolerance. The final end of this humanist education was the development of the personality to serve the community and God. These were the roots of the tradition of liberal education for northern Europe.

In later years Erasmus turned to the subject of the education of girls. In <u>De Matrimonio Christiano</u> (1526), written at the request of Catherine of Aragon, surfaced his impressions acquired at the home of Sir Thomas More. Erasmus had been impressed by the scholarly atmosphere at Chelsea. He desired for women a wholesome and cheerful home life marked by sober decorum, for the worst enemies of character were triviality and indolence. These were the consequences of denying women an uplifting education. Erasmus urged women's education along classical lines found in the more refined society of Italy.[42] Much of what Erasmus wrote followed the earlier work of Vives' <u>De Institutione Christianae Feminae</u>, (<u>On the Education of Christian Women</u>, 1523). This book long dominated the education of women in England and became a guide in the rise of humanist tutors.[43]

Erasmus became the essential catalyst of the earlier northern and southern humanists. He accelerated the transformation of European education from medieval scholasticism to the humanist's "new learning." An international community of fellow scholars recognized his early insights in education for the young child and intellectual pursuits for women. Nowhere was his influence felt more clearly than in England. There the royal court accepted his concepts of education for both prince and princess. Catherine of Aragon blended Erasmus' humanism with ideals learned from her own Spanish courtly education.

It can be argued that for the most part the roots of the "new learning" in England did not spring from its native shores, but from European humanists, (Thomas More being a notable exception). The transformation of English education was delayed longer than its continental counterparts. But once underway, the educational philosophy of England's tutors during the next hundred years, dominated the stage for the development of modern European educational thought.[44]

# Endnotes

1.  Charles Ross, <u>Richard III</u> (Berkeley: University of California Press, 1981), XXXIV-XXXV; William Harrison Woodward, <u>Studies In Education During The Age of the Renaissance. 1400-1600</u> (New York: Teachers College Press, 1967), 48.

2.  Jacob Burckhardt, <u>The Civilization of the Renaissance In Italy</u>, trans. Middlemore (London: Phaidon Press, Ltd., 1940), 128; William Harrison Woodward, <u>Studies In Education During the Age of the Renaissance 1400-1600</u> (New York: Teachers College Press, 1967), 323-326.

3.  Stefano Ticozzi, <u>Storia dei Letterati e\degli Artisti del Dipartimento Della Piave</u> (Belluno: 1813), 18, 182.

4.  Remigio Sabbadini, <u>Epistolario di Guarino Veronese</u> (Salerno: 1885).

5.  Giovanni Maria Mazzuchelli, <u>Gli Scrittori d'Italia</u>, 2 vols. (Brescia: 1753-56), vol. 1, 499.

6.  Sabbadini, <u>Guarino</u>, 65.

7.  Enrico Paglia, <u>La Casa Giocosa di Vittorino da Feltre in Mantova</u> (Milano: 1884), 150.

8.  Francesco Prendilacqua, <u>Intorno alla vita di Vittorino de Feltre</u> (Cosmo: 1871), 86.

9.  A. Benoist, <u>Quid de puerorum institutione senserit Erasmus</u> (Paris: 1876), 44.

10. Woodward, <u>Studies In Education</u>, 8-23; William Harrison Woodward, <u>Vittorino Da Feltre</u> (New York: Teachers College, Columbia University, 1963), 1-92; Burckhardt, <u>Renaissance</u>, 127; J.H. Plumb, <u>The Horizon Book of the Renaissance</u> (New York: Doubleday, 1961), 51-52.

11. Woodward, _Vittorino_, 159-160.

12. Battista Guarino, _Upon the Method of Teaching and of Reading the Classical Authors_, trans. Woodward in _Vittorino da Feltre and other Humanist Educators_ (New York: Teacher College, Columbia University, 1963), 161-178; Burckhardt, _Renaissance_, 128; Woodward, _Studies In Education_, 26-29, 35-38, 45; David Hunt, _Parents and Children In History_ (London: Basic Books, 1970), 34-35, 134.

13. Leon Battista Alberti, _Il Trattato della cura della Famiglia_ (Firenze, 1843); Hunt, _Parents_, 49-51, 59-63.

14. Matteo Palmieri, _Libro della Vita Civile_ (Firenze, 1529); Woodward, _Studies in Education_, 65, 71, 76.

15. Pietro Bembo, _Gli Asolani_, trans. Gottfried (Bloomington, Indiana: Indiana University Press, 1954), 122-150; Louise Buenger Robbert, "Caterina Corner, Queen of Cyprus" in _Female Scholars_ ed. Brick (Montreal: Eden Press, 1980), 24-35.

16. Baldassare Castiglione, _The Book of the Courtier_, trans. Henderson (London: J.M. Dent and Sons, Ltd., 1928), 45.

17. Castiglione, _The Courtier_, 56, 264, 265.

18. Castiglione, _The Courtier_, 58-65, 80-81, 100-103, 285-293; Niccoló Machiavelli's book, _The Prince_, was written in the same tradition as _The Courtier_, but along politic's "darker lines;" Niccoló Machiavelli, _The Prince_, trans. Marriott (London: J.M. Dent and Sons Ltd., 1958); Frederick Ely, _The History and Philosophy of Education Ancient and Medieval_ (New York: Prentice-Hall, 1940), 894.

19. Christine De Pisan, _The Book of the City of Ladies_ trans. Richards, ed. Warner (New York: Persea Books, 1982), XIII-XXX; Leslie Altman, "Christine De Pisan: First Professional Woman

of Letters" in <u>Female Scholars</u>, ed. Brink (Montreal: Eden Press, 1980), 7-23; <u>The International Dictionary of Women's Biography</u>, 1st ed., c.v. De Pisan, Christine.

20. Burchhardt, <u>Renaissance</u>, 85; De Pisan, <u>The City of Ladies</u>, 154; Uglow, <u>Women's Biography</u>, 127.

21. Burckhardt, <u>Renaissance</u>, 85; Mary Agnes Cannon "The Education of Women During the Renaissance" (Ph.D. diss., Catholic University of America, 1916), 7-9, 28-50; Burckhardt, <u>Renaissance</u>, 240-241; Uglow, <u>Women's Biography</u>, 332.

22. Quattrocento is an Italian term taken from the Latin quattnor (four) and centum (hundred). It was used as an abbreviation of mille quattrocento, 1400 or the fifteenth century. The word denoted the period of high Renaissance art and literature in Italy and elsewhere in Europe. Ebenezer Brewer, <u>Brewer's Dictionary of Phrase and Fable</u> (New York: Harper and Row, 1970), 882; Juan de Vives, <u>Vives and the Renascence Education of Women</u>, ed. Wotson (New York: Longmans, Green and Company, 1912), 4-6.

23. Vives, <u>Renascence Education</u>, 6; Cannon, <u>Education of Women</u>, 78-79; Ibid., 51-52.

24. Vives, <u>Renascence Education</u>, 7; Cannon, <u>Education of Women</u>, 53, 88; Prescott also implies that many other women rose to the rank of Professor, but he supplies no additional examples; Myra Reynolds, <u>The Learned Lady In England 1650-1760</u> (Boston: Houghton Mifflin, 1920), 6; Garrett Mattingly, <u>Catherine of Aragon</u> (New York: Vintage Books, 1941), 5, 8-10; Uglow, <u>Women's Biography</u>, 187; Phyllis Stock, <u>Better Than Rubies, A History of Women's Education</u> (New York: G.P. Putnam's Sons, 1978), 51.

25. William Prescott, <u>Prescott's Histories</u>, ed. Blacker (New York: Viking Press, 1963), 29; Vives, <u>Renascence Education</u>, 6-7; Cannon, <u>Education of Women</u>, 91-92; J.H. Elliott, <u>Imperial Spain</u> (New York: New American Library,

1963) 17, 125-126.

26. Vives, <u>Renascence Education</u>, 8, 9; Cannon, <u>Education of Women</u>, 90-92.

27. Mulhern, <u>Education</u>, 355; Butts, <u>Education of the West</u>, 205; Philippe Aries, <u>Centuries of Childhood</u> (New York: Alfred A. Knopf, 1962), 115; Michael Rogness, <u>Philip Melanchthon</u> (Minneapolis: Augusburg Publishing House, 1969), 2-5.

28. Cannon, <u>Education of Women</u>, 154; Woodward, <u>Studies In Education</u>, 129; Burckhardt, <u>Renaissance</u>, 128.

29. Cannon, <u>Education of Women</u>, 155-156.

30. Ibid., 156-159; J.J. Scarisbrick, <u>Henry VIII</u> (Los Angeles: University of California Press, 1968), 107-108. Adrian Dedel was the last non-Italian Pope before John Paul II.

31. Cannon, <u>Education of Women</u>, 169-173.

32. Martin Luther, "Letter To The Mayors and Aldermen of All the Cities of Germany In Behalf of Christian Schools," trans. Painter, in <u>Early Protestant Educators</u>, ed. Ely (New York: McGraw-Hill, 1931), 71.

33. Martin Luther, "Duties of Parents in Training Children," trans. Barnard, in <u>Early Protestant Educators</u>, ed. Ely (New York: McGraw-Hill, 1931), 25; John Knox the Scottish Presbyterian reformer copied Luther's dictate that parents teach their children. "Everie Maister of household must be commandit eather to instruct or ellis caus {to} be instructed, his children, servandis, and familie, in the principallis of the Christiane religioun . . . ", John Knox, "Bible Reading, Family Instruction, Singing," trans. Laing; Ibid., 294; Friedrich Paulsen, <u>German Education</u>, trans. Lorenz (New York: Scribner's, 1908), 78-79.

34. Philip Melanchthon, Corpus Reformatorum Melanchthon Opera, editors, Bretschneider and Bindseil, vol. 25 (Brunswick: C.A. Schwetschke and Son, 1857), 448; Clyde Leonard Manschreck, Melanchthon (New York: Abingdon Press, 1953), 30-31; James William Richard, Philip Melanchthon (New York: G.P. Putnam, 1898), 6-7.

35. Melanchthon, Corpus Reformatorum, vol. 20, 765; Richard, Melanchthon, 28.

36. Richard, Melanchthon, 134.

37. Melanchthon, Corpus Reformatorum, vol. 26, 90; Richard, Melanchthon, 111-112, 133-137; Manschreck, Melanchthon, 35-36; Joan Simon, Education and Society In Tudor England (Cambridge: University Press, 1966), 129.

38. Desiderius Erasmus, The Education of a Christian Prince, trans. Born (New York: Columbia University Press, 1936), 3-241.

39. Desiderius Erasmus, De Pueris Instituendis (Paris: Ex Officina Christiani Wechelf, 1536).

40. Ibid.

41. Desiderius Erasmus, De Ratione Studii (Paris: Ex Officina Simonis Colinaei, 1526).

42. Desiderius Erasmus, De Matrimonia Christiano (Lugdun Batanorum: J. Maire, 1650).

43. Juan de Vives, Vives and the Renaissance Education of Women, ed. Watson (New York: Longmans, Green and Company, 1912), 16-18.

44. William Harrison Woodward, Desiderius Erasmus: Concerning the Aims and Methods of Education (Cambridge: Cambridge University Press, 1904), 104-126; Margareta More, The Household of Sir Thomas More (New York: Charles Scribner, 1852), 57-59; Fritz Caspari, Humanism and the Social Order in Tudor England (New York: Teachers College Press, 1968), 17-20, 258-259, 289.

CHAPTER 3


THE TUDORS' TUTORS
(ENGLAND 1400 - 1600)


The Renaissance revival of classical learning
had come first to Italy and Spain, then penetrated
north of the Alps. England was among the last
nations to be touched by the "new learning."
Tutoring became the idealized form of Renaissance
learning for the English royal family's princes and
princesses. The Tudor dynasty and their private
tutors exerted a considerable educational influence
over all of England's society. The instructional
activities and the writings of Skelton, Vives, More,
Ascham, Elyot, Cheke and other tutor-theorists,
provided a norm for many sixteenth century educators.[1]


1. THE KING'S "HENCHMEN"


The English humanist Richard Pace described a
conversation at a fifteenth century English dinner
table on the education of children. The host had
announced his intention of finding a good tutor for
his children. His guest burst out furiously with
these words,

> Why do you talk nonsense, friend? A
> curse on these stupid letters; all learned
> men are beggars. I swear by God's body I'd
> rather that my son should hang than study
> letters. For it becomes the sons of
> gentlemen to blow the horn nicely, to hunt
> skillfully, and elegantly carry and train a

71

hawk. But the study of letters should be
left to the sons of rustics.[2]

Fortunately for the history of England, this
anti-educational attitude was not shared by many of
the upper class of the day. The desire of the upper
class for education was due to the humanism of the
Renaissance. As we will see, great scholars such as
Erasmus, Vives, Thomas More and others influenced
Henry VIII and particularly his first wife, Catherine
of Aragon, and a fashion for learning spread from the
royal family to simpler homes. In the sixteenth
century children began attending elementary schools
in larger numbers. Many others were taught at home
by tutors. Girls seldom went to school, but were
educated at home. However, the prospects of women's
education became more hopeful. Slowly an intellectual freedom developed that released women from the
"age-old routine" of learning only the domestic arts.
With their brothers, girls were taught a love of the
classics and studied Latin, Greek, Italian and
French. Quite often boys traveled abroad with tutors
to learn the language and government of foreign
countries. This cult of tutoring reached its highest
level with men like Sir Thomas More, whose Chelsea
manor "school" educated his daughters in the new
Renaissance spirit. By contrast the education of the
common people was badly neglected. The majority of
children were left to their ignorance despite the
cultural revival of the fifteenth and sixteenth
centuries.[3]

Catherine Swynford, born in 1350, was one of the
earliest governesses known to history. She taught
the motherless daughters of John of Gaunt, Duke of
Lancaster, first as his mistress, then as his third
wife. Catherine bore him four illegitimate children,
the Beauforts, from one of whom Henry VII was
descended. Henry VII's consort, Elizabeth Woodville,
and her sister, were both carefully tutored. She
boasted of their superior education in Humphrey
Brereton's rhyming history The Most Pleasant Song of
the Lady Bessy.

Good Father Stanley, hearken to me.
What my father, King Edward, that king
royal,

72

Did for my sister, my Lady Wells, and me.
He sent for a scrivener (tutor) to lusty
London,
He was the best in that city;
He taught us both to read and write full
soon;
If it please you, full soon you shall
see;
Lauded be God, I had such speed,
That I can write as well as he,
And also indite and full well read,
And that, lord, soon shall you see,
Both English and also French,
And also Spanish, if you had need.[4]

By 1449 a fully developed system of education
was discernable in the royal household. The king's
"henchmen," or pages of honor, appointed by the king,
were tutored by the "master of the henchmen," a
squire of the household who taught them deportment.
They were also taught by the grammar master in poetry
and grammatical rules. His services were also
extended to the king's clerks and other children of
the court. The earliest known "schoolmaster of the
henchmen" was a certain Francis Philip, who probably
held this post by 1521. He studied at Oxford, but
due to lack of funds, never attained his M.A. In
1523 he was implicated, along with other members of
the king's household, in a curious plot to steal a
shipment of tax money. The plot failed and Philip
suffered a traitor's death. A strange conclusion for
an early royal tutor, but not the last instance of
tutors briefly claiming the center stage of history.[5]

After the accession of Henry VII (1485) both
ecclesiastical schooling and lay tutoring became
increasingly common in England. "Private tuition"
(tutoring) had been mentioned in a Coventry household
as early as 1318. The royal interest in education
stimulated tutoring in many other great households.
Archbishop Morton had the sons of nobles, living with
him at Lambeth Palace, taught by John Holt. Later,
Holt was appointed tutor to the Prince of Wales.
Other English bishops also maintained tutors in their
households. Among the nobility schoolmasters were
employed by the earl of Northumberland (1511), the
duke of Buckingham (1521) and the second marques of

Dorset (1530).   But not all the children of the
nobility were tutored at their own homes.   Some went
to a local school or traveled to an early "public
school."[6]

Henry and Elizabeth Tudor had seven children,
Arthur and Henry being the two oldest boys.
Beginning with these children, almost every English
prince and princess for the next five hundred years
were to be educated by tutors.   Arthur and Henry were
the first English princes to receive an education
influenced largely by the Renaissance.   This was in
response to the influence of the continental Renaissance and partially to protect them from politically
motivated assassination or abduction.   The practical
aim of their education was to engender the concept of
the perfect man--the many-sided man ("l'uomo
universale"),--a person who could do everything and
do it well; a man of culture, but also of action.
This many-sided individual combined all these
qualities with the philosophic outlook of Plato's
philosopher-king (as a model of princely education).
The Renaissance ideal was based on knowledge of the
classical languages (Latin and Greek) and their
accompanying literatures.   For this princely education English and continental scholars became court
tutors.   The subject content of their individual
instruction for these children broadened over the
next century.   Many of the Tudor's tutors chronicled
their work and developed a broader philosophy of
education concerning all children.   Their books
created a framework for a version of modern educational philosophy that rested on classical humanism.[7]

## 2.   JOHN SKELTON AND THE TUTORING OF
## ARTHUR AND HENRY TUDOR

Henry VII gave both of his sons the best
education that the times afforded, particularly for
Arthur (1486-1502), the heir apparent.   The king
apparently did not hire special tutors for Arthur nor
send him to school.   Learned men, already attached to
the court, were pressed into service.   His first
schoolmaster was John Rede, a Master of Arts from New

College, Oxford. He had been a headmaster of Winchester before his appointment as chaplain and tutor to Arthur. Rede taught the prince English grammar and Latin (1491-1496). The royal historiographer, Bernard André, a blind French poet, continued these lessons until 1500. Arthur's tutors also included the royal librarian, Giles d' Ewes, a Fleming, who taught him French, and the court poet, John Skelton.

Arthur was given a complete classical education. He studied grammar, poetry, oratory and history, but not Greek. At least twenty-four Latin grammarians and fashionable new Italian scholars, Guarino, Perotto and Valla, with a wide diversity of classical historians, orators and poets, Ceasar, Cicero, Livy, Ovid, Pliny and Virgil. Before his premature death at age sixteen, Arthur was fluent enough in Latin to correspond with his future bride, Catherine of Aragon. His brother, Henry (1491-1547), was destined to occupy his throne and drastically alter England's course in world affairs.[8]

Henry's education remains largely unknown, since details are lacking of the tutors' precise curriculum. Ridley believes that as a child, Henry was given "an excellent education" by his tutors. Since he was not yet heir to the throne, Henry possibly received the beginnings of an education for an ecclesiastical career as a potential Archbishop of Canterbury. Many historians agree that even if this were not true, with the education he received, Henry was aptly suited for a position in the church. Henry knew Latin, French and some Italian and Spanish. We do not know how he obtained these linguistic skills, only that Richard Croke taught Henry Greek in 1519, when he was an adult. His grasp of theology proved not as strong as he sometimes believed. Henry loved mathematics. Late into the night he discussed astronomy and geometry with the scholarly Thomas More.[9]

Henry had at least four tutors as a child, including John Fisher (1459-1535). The teacher most closely associated with his education was John Skelton (1460-1529), who taught Henry (1495-1502) to spell and read Latin.

> The honor of England I learned to spell
> I gave him drink of the sugared well
> Of Helicon's waters crystalline,
> Acquainting him with the Muses nine.[10]

Skelton had taught Latin at Oxford. He was a good
scholar and the leading poet of his generation.
Henry learned no Greek from Skelton who despised the
language as one of a decadent people. It is probable
that young Henry also absorbed from Skelton a love of
poetry. But when compared to Skelton's, his verse
shows more of a Renaissance influence. Skelton
undoubtedly was learned, but he usually was an ill-
bred, boisterous, rowdy, vulgar person. He used a
sharp satire to attack both church and court.
Skelton was secretly married after taking holy
orders. It was not surprising that Skelton had many
enemies, including Henry's Chancellor, Cardinal
Wolsey.[11]

In 1501, while still acting as court tutor,
Skelton wrote the moral treatise Speculum Principis
(A Prince's Mirror). He was the first English royal
tutor to imitate the European custom of preparing
guidelines for a prince's education. Henry was
instructed to avoid gluttony and adultery, to
cultivate self-restraint and choose a wife carefully
that he would prize forever. Henry's numerous
marriages represent one of history's best examples of
a tutor's counsel gone awry. Skelton's influence
came to an end in 1502, after he was jailed for
speaking "too freely of palace and court matters."
Henry, as king, brought Skelton back to court as
orator regis, a post he held until his death in
1529.[12]

Henry emerged from his studies perhaps more
learned than any of his predecessors on the English
throne. Though not a scholar by nature, he had had
the ability since childhood to become one. In 1499,
at age nine, Henry was introduced by Sir Thomas More
to his friend, Erasmus. The scholar became highly
impressed with Henry's Latin in the correspondence
they exchanged afterward. At first he did not
believe these letters to be the work of a mere child,
but changed his mind when shown the rough drafts

corrected in Henry's own hand. For the rest of his life Henry VIII used Latin with ease in his intercourse with foreigners. As a grown man he also knew French well and retained a keen interest in mathematics. Henry's book The Defence of the Seven Sacraments (1521), while not theology of the highest order, it was one of the most successful pieces of Catholic polemic produced against Martin Luther.[13]

Despite his exposure to many learned men and women, Scarisbrick characterizes Henry as showing little interest in scholarship. The king gave no more than limited patronage to scholars. In many ways Scarisbrick views the court of Henry VIII, as his reign continued, becoming "less open, less cosmopolitan and interesting than his father's."[14]

England's tutors did influence Henry VIII on one issue vital to his realm. According to Richard Foxe's celebrated story, it was Thomas Cranmer, a tutor of two boys at Waltham, who first made the suggestion of collecting opinions from the universities on the legality of Henry's divorce from Catherine (1529). The king was staying at an abbey near Waltham. Two members of his court, Stephen Gardiner (Henry's secretary), and Richard Foxe (Henry's Almoner), were billeted in the house where Cranmer was tutoring. They both knew Cranmer from their school days at Cambridge. When Henry heard Cranmer's suggestion, he exclaimed that the author had "the sow by the right ear."[15] He summoned the tutor to court, and thus began Cranmer's public career. By 1533 he would be Archbishop of Canterbury.[16]

In imitation of the tutor's role in the royal household, Tudor social policy emphasized and enlarged the role of the family as a systematic domestic educator. Henry VIII's Royal Injunctions of 1536 charged churchmen to admonish parents and their tutors to teach their children to read and thereby learn the basic articles of the Church of England. This new formalized social role for domestic education began with Henry, but was respected in the later Injunctions of Edward VI (1547) and Elizabeth I (1559) thus making household education an instrument of social stability. The royal tutors became increasingly the national models for homes across England where parents and masters followed their published curriculum and methods.[17]

### 3. THOMAS MORE, JUAN LUIS VIVES AND THE EDUCATION OF MARY TUDOR

It was the first of Henry's wives, Catherine of Aragon, who had an explicit influence on the future of English education. In 1501 Catherine, at age sixteen, had married Arthur, Prince of Wales, who then died a few months later. She married Henry VIII in 1509, only to be divorced by 1531 due to her failure to produce a male heir.

Catherine had come to England thoroughly tutored in the classics by the leading available Italian humanists. As has already been recounted, Isabella, Catherine's mother, vigorously supported the classical Renaissance in Spain. During her reign she saw to it that women made a greater contribution to the "new learning" in Spain than elsewhere in Europe. Even in Italy fewer women were professors at the universities than in Spain. Henry's marriage to Catherine, rather than another European princess, assured a fundamental improvement in educational opportunity for women in England and influenced the mode of instruction. Catherine's reign marked a remarkable time of expression of views on the education of women. She collected books and helped libraries to grow. She came to England with a critically accurate knowledge of Latin. Thomas More's Latin verses, in honor of her first marriage to Prince Arthur, won Catherine's lasting appreciation and friendship.[18]

Thomas More (1478-1535) established his own household in 1505. A "cult of learning" for women spread from Catherine's court throughout England. More was among the first Englishmen to carefully educate his daughters at home.[19] More frequently wrote to his children and their tutors. Many of these early letters are almost completely concerned with education. More's household earned a contemporary reputation of being a school and was referred to as such by others writing to him. More educated not only his own children, Margaret, Cecilia, Elizabeth and John, but also their stepmother, Margaret Giggs, his wards and eleven grandchildren. Their tutorial education served English humanists as a powerful example for the education of women.

More employed many tutors in his "school." Richard Hyrde (or Hart) became closely associated with More as a tutor and later translated into English, Vives' Instruction of a Christian Woman.[20] Other tutors included Doctor Clement of Oxford, William Gunwell from Cambridge and Nicholas Kratzer, a famous German-born astronomer who made England his home while teaching at Oxford. They taught their students Latin, Greek, logic, philosophy, theology, astronomy and mathematics. Drawing upon details from his book Utopia (1516), More's household tutoring gave a practical demonstration of the application of its educational principles and methods.[21] In his letters More reaffirmed repeatedly the equality of men and women. "Therefore I do not see why learning in like manner may not equally agree with both sexes."[22] More taught his children to esteem a knowledge of human affairs, contemplation and active virtue. These were the aims of a liberal education. He praised this "school" as the ideal Renaissance academy and was converted to the idea of advanced studies for women. The public renown acquired by More's "school" for his daughters, buttressed the later effort by Catherine to educate her daughter Mary.[23]

More's eldest daughter, Margaret, became a notable Latin scholar. Classical scholars have praised her as one of the few women who wrote an excellent translation of a corrupt Latin text. Later Margaret had her three sons and two daughters tutored in Greek and Latin. Their own academic accomplishments and the widespread social acceptance of education for women were eulogized in Latin poetry.

The mystic Art of Reasoning
well they drew.
Then blush you Men if
you neglect to trace

79

These Heights of Learning
which the Female grace.[24]

Catherine's patronage extended beyond humanists
of English birth. Erasmus, as Europe's chief
humanist, maintained a high mutual respect for her.
Undoubtedly influenced by More, Erasmus thought
Catherine to be a better scholar than Henry VIII.
After Erasmus perhaps no other contemporary humanist
became more famous through his close association with
Catherine than Juan Luis Vives.[25]

After the birth of Princess Mary, (1516-1558)
both a state governess and working governess were
appointed to teach Mary manners, deportment and
social accomplishments. Mary's first childhood
tutor, Dr. Lynacre, wrote for the Princess a
Rudiments of Grammar.[26]

In her attempt to overcome the medieval prejudice, especially in England, against learned women,
Catherine asked one of the three greatest Renaissance
scholars, Juan Luis Vives (1492-1540) (the others
being Erasmus and Budé) to come to England and tutor
Mary. Born in Valencia, Spain, Vives was tutored and
attended school there. His education was to prepare
him for a career in the church. In 1509 he went to
the University of Paris. Vives studied in France and
Flanders and became a personal friend of Erasmus. He
met Guillaume Budé (1468-1540) while tutoring a
youthful Cardinal William de Croy, and studied with
these humanists. Vives altered his career by
accepting Catherine's invitation to tutor Princess
Mary in the "new learning" (1522). For five years he
taught the child, though he disliked England
intensely. The origin of these negative feelings
possibly came from the divorce controversy that was
raging and Vives support of the Spanish Queen of
England. Oxford University made him a Doctor of
Classical Letters, and Corpus Christi College, a
fellow. He brought with him the finished manuscript
of De institutione Christianae feminae (The Instruction of a Christian Woman) (1523).[27] Catherine had
commissioned him to write this book that marked a
departure from the medieval cloistering of women that
had limited them to a domestic education. Expanding
on the ideas of More and Erasmus, Vives championed

the ideal of the educated woman instructed by her tutor.

Home instruction was favored by Vives as much as Erasmus or Thomas Elyot. He saw many typical schoolmasters of the sixteenth century as worthless young men, or elderly failures in life. Even men released from prison were in charge of the common schools. Vives warned that a well-raised child would degenerate under these influences. "He goes home rough, heavy, uninterested, a shock to his parents."[28]

Vives' ideas on education seem hardly revolutionary today, but at the time no one wrote about the education of a princess to become queen. In that age all intelligent women were regarded with suspicion. Some men foresaw dangerous consequences in educating a woman. They equated it to giving a madman a sword. Vives dismissed these objections, advising that functional differences between the sexes dictated different subjects, but there was no difference in intellectual ability. Vives recognized that each tutor must teach to the individual aptitude of his student. He emphasized the value of play but also was very harsh and strict recommending to the tutor a Puritan austerity for his student of no jewelry, ostentatious dress, makeup, elaborate food, dice, cards or wine.

In his _Instruction_ and a complementary book a _Plan of Studies_ (1523) Vives outlined the method of education for the seven-year-old princess.[29] His plan was a mixture of classical and humanist works. Cicero, Seneca, Plutarch, the _Dialogues of Plato,_ and the works of the Christian Fathers were supplemented by a twice-daily reading of the Bible, More's _Utopia_ and selections from the writings of Erasmus.[30] Mary's lessons were copious and exacting, and given only by her tutors. She never attended school. By age nine Mary wrote superior letters in Latin and responded in Latin to a court envoy from Flanders. She also learned French from Giles d' Ewes, the same scholar who tutored Henry VIII. Vives taught Mary to write for speed rather than elegance. Her handwriting was not as beautiful as her half-sister's (Elizabeth), who was taught to do the exact opposite. Mary probably studied astronomy, geography, the natural sciences and mathematics. It was also reported that she was able to read both Spanish and Italian. If true, she completed the liberal education outlined by Vives. This advanced education for an English woman of her time not only helped Mary as queen, but established an educational tradition for England's future queens.

Through the royal court's example society came to accept advanced tutoring for girls and many boys as a reasonable alternative to more traditional schooling. Erasmus wrote in 1548 of the great number of women in England well-tutored in science, languages and Holy Scripture. As home tutoring gained acceptance for women, more girls went to a "petty school" to complete their education. Reynolds views this expansion of domestic education for women as a prime determinant for the unprecedented prevalence of women poets in sixteenth century England.[31]

Catherine of Aragon's influence, however, extended far beyond planning the education of her daughter, Mary. Through her royal patronage the education of women in England experienced its strongest advocate. Catherine's own humanistic education, her length of time on the throne, and Catherine's struggle to guarantee Mary's succession to the crown, produced a historic momentum that elevated the place of learned women in English society. Her daughter Mary's greatest rival, Elizabeth, profited from this new liberal attitude favoring the education of a princess. Elizabeth's own powerful influence extended this new English social phenomenon well beyond the death of Catherine, who founded a new English tradition in the education of women.[32]

## 4. COX, ELYOT, CHEKE: THE EDUCATION OF EDWARD TUDOR

Jane Seymour, Henry VIII's third wife, labored three days and two nights to deliver Edward (1537-1553). Her death a few days later left him in the hands of Lady Bryan, a governess to Princess Mary.

Henry VIII took a great interest in Edward's education. It began prematurely, even for that time, at age three. The king brought to court recognized university scholars rather than using persons already part of the royal household. The only exception was Richard Cox, Edward's first tutor. Dr. Cox was chaplain to Henry VIII. A scholar of Eton and a fellow of King's College, Cambridge (1524), he also attended Christ Church, Oxford (1525-1526), and was headmaster at Eton before receiving a Doctor of Divinity at Cambridge in 1537. In the same year Cox became royal chaplain and then tutor to Edward. He was a strident Lutheran, helping pronounce Henry's fourth marriage to Anne of Cleves null and void. He was in the first rank of English Protestantism. In 1540 he helped write <u>The Necessary Doctrine and Erudition of a Christian Man</u> and between 1548 and 1550, and other later English Protestant works.[33]

As Edward's tutor, Cox taught the three-year-old prince Latin and Greek. Confronted with this difficult task he drew upon Ascham's idea that "no learning ought to be learnt with bondage. Whatsoever the mind learns unwillingly with fear, the same it will quickly forget."[34] He made a military game out of the grammar and syntax. The parts of speech were the enemy. Edward became the king, leading the attack to overthrow them, as Henry VIII had defeated the French at Boulogne. This teaching method succeeded at first, but Cox had to resort to corporal punishment when Edward ultimately responded with boredom and then open revolt.

Cox's style of tutoring was influenced by both Ascham and Thomas Elyot. In 1531 Elyot wrote <u>The Boke Named the Governor</u>, (Governor being another term for a male tutor).[35] It was the first humanist book on the "new learning" published in English. <u>The Governor</u> remains one of the finest expressions of the ideal education of a gentleman, and follows in the tradition of earlier Italian Renaissance courtesy education treatises.

Thomas Elyot was born about 1490. His father, a Wiltshire gentleman, had him tutored at home until age twelve. He continued on his own to study the liberal arts and philosophy, teaching himself Greek,

as Erasmus and More had. Elyot never attended a
university, though he studied law at the Inns of
Court and the Inns of Chancery. While attending
school, he was tutored by Thomas Linacre, the best
Greek scholar in London. Since Elyot's father was a
friend of Thomas More, he undoubtedly observed More's
household school, which seems likely to have
influenced his later ideas on the education of women.

In 1511, with his father's influence, Thomas
obtained the post of clerk of Assize. Wolsey later
appointed him Clerk to the Privy Council (1525). The
new royal chancellor, Thomas Cromwell, knighted Elyot
in 1530. The publication of The Governor (1531)
illustrated how the new education was viewed not by a
tutor-philosopher, but by an influential public
official of this new age. Elyot's book became so
popular that it ran into eight editions before 1600.
It became the first "parent primer" on "how to"
educate your child.

The Governor is clearly a product of Elyot's
reading of the politico-social writing of the
Quattrocento and Erasmian humanism. Baldassare
Castiglione's Courtier; Matteo Palmieri's Vita Civile
and Francesco Patrizi's De Regno et Regis
Institutione, and other earlier Renaissance treatises, influenced Elyot's thinking on education for a
modern community's citizens or princes.[36] These
writers had one common viewpoint; that public service
was the end of all education, either of a simple
country gentleman or a member of the royal court.

Elyot begins The Governor by criticizing the
cultural crudity of the English nobility. Diogenes
the Cynic is quoted regarding this class, who seeing
one without learning seated on a stone, remarked,
"Behold where one stone sitteth on another."[37] At
seven a boy should be placed under a carefully
selected tutor. The office of tutor is to first know
the "nature of his pupil," his inclinations and
disposition.[38] A wise tutor commends the virtues of
courtesy, piety, a free and liberal heart and "a
token of grace." This tutor,

> should be an ancient and worshipful man
> [of] much gentleness mixed with gratitude

84

. . . one as the child may follow by imitation [and] . . . grow to be excellent . . . if he be also learned, he is the more commendable.[39]

The tutor must be temperate and not fatigue a child with constant study and learning. He should mix pleasant learning with exercise and music. Elyot joined other sixteenth-century writers who scorned the wages given to tutors in the household of the great. In 1531 he complained, "they chiefly inquire with how small a salary he will be contented . . . using less diligence than in taking servants."[40]

The tutor should teach the child logic, history and cosmology. The boy should also be trained in hunting, shooting, swimming and tennis, but not football which contains only beastly fire and external violence. The student should read the classics throughout his education, first the poets, then the orators, historians, generals and the philosophers.

Elyot borrowed liberally from Erasmus' Education of A Christian Prince (1516) and repeats most of the ideas of Plutarch's Discourse Touching On The Training of Children (1533). Both Plato's Republic and Quintilian's Instituto Oratoria added details to his ideas on education.[41] The three most important areas in the training of young children are: (a) the necessity of careful attention to the habit of clear and refined speech in childhood, (b) the principle of instruction by methods of play in the first stages of tutoring, (c) the value of conversation in learning Latin and Greek. The learning of languages is "but an introduction to the understanding of [the ancient] authors" so that the student can fully understand "the most sweet pleasant readings of the ancient authors." The classics offer "excellent wisdom with divine eloquence, absolute virtue with pleasure incredible." These books by themselves are "almost sufficient to make a perfect and excellent governor (tutor)."[42]

By age twenty-one the young gentleman who has followed Elyot's curriculum should be universally educated. This will not be achieved if a child learns only Latin and the hollow rules of medieval rhetoric. A person can become a humanist only if he learns to recognize the model of humanity in antiquity and makes it an active force by re-creating it in his own life.

Though The Governor was a Renaissance work and not equally applicable for all time, it was the first book written in English recommending a classical, liberal education: physical development, training for government service, painting, drawing and music. It set the tone for aristocratic courtly behavior that ultimately reached into the education of most Englishmen. Elyot wrote The Governor in his mother tongue, English, to enrich his native tongue, a fact appreciated by Henry VIII. His clarity and precision was an achievement of considerable importance in the development of English prose. [More had written Utopia only fifteen years before but entirely in Latin.] Its influence was far reaching. It is virtually certain that Shakespeare borrowed Elyot's ideas on degree and order in Henry V. As the first modern English courtesy education book, it had an impact on Cox, Cheke, Grindal and Ascham. By the end of the sixteenth century the liberal arts curriculum of the newer academies outlined by Sir Humphrey Gilbert was based upon these concepts. John Milton's Tractate on Education framed a similar definition of a liberal education. Other works such as the Institution of a Gentlemen (Unknown Author) (1555), Queen Elizabeth's Academy (Sir Humphrey Gilbert) (1572) and Institution of a Nobleman (James Cleland) (1607) represent the continued force of Elyot's ideas in English education.[43]

Elyot's book had an immediate impact on the education of Edward VI. The Governor was very influential in shaping John Cheke's tutoring of the prince. In 1544 he took over from Cox the duties as primary royal tutor, though Cox was not in disgrace and continued to play a minor role in Edward's education.

Cheke was born on 16 June 1514 at Cambridge. His father, Peter, was a beadle of the university. John Morgan, M.A. gave Cheke his grammatical education before he went to St. John's College, Cambridge.

There he became one of the outstanding scholars of the university. This was due in large part to his tutor, George Day, who encouraged Cheke to study Greek, an area that later made him famous. Cheke was made a fellow in 1592, received a B.A. in 1530, M.A. in 1533 and later earned an additional M.A. from Oxford. As a young scholar he first became a university tutor. At age twenty-six he was made first Regius Professor of Greek at Cambridge. Among Cheke's pupils were William Cecil, Roger Ascham and William Grindal. Ascham and Grindal, as Elizabeth's tutors, showed the influence of Cheke's Protestant Cambridge scholarship. Cheke attempted to introduce an improved, standardized phonetic spelling into English. Though he failed in this attempt, Cheke insisted on a high standard of spelling from his pupils. Rather curiously, like many other learned people of his age, Cheke was a firm believer in astrology. (Elizabeth also shared this penchant in her later years).

Cheke was a friend of Henry VIII's physician, Dr. William Butts. With his recommendation and the support of Catherine Parr, Cheke, age thirty, left Cambridge in 1544 to tutor the seven-year-old Edward. The scholar and master became very close during the next intervening years. With Edward, Cheke was watchful, critical and demanding, but never harsh. He did not talk down to Edward. Following humanistic theory, Cheke arranged that Edward be tutored part of the time with several cousins, including Henry Sidney and Barnaby Fitzpatrick. This arrangement helped the prince "gain experience in humanity . . . " as part of his formal tutoring.[44]

Besides extensive Latin and Greek studies, Cheke tutored Edward in mathematics and geography. As a devoted Renaissance scholar, his educational program stressed the church, the importance of vernacular language and the training of princes for their leadership responsibilities. As he had taught Ascham, Cheke now used the double translation method to tutor Edward in classical languages. This procedure built considerable skills in vocabulary, phrases and idioms of speech. Cheke did sight translations and made this a goal in Edward's education. The prince read the Bible, Plato,

Aristotle, Xenophon, Isocrates, Demosthenes, Melanchthon, all of Cicero, a great part of Livy, the tragedies of Sophocles and the Greek Testament. This is almost identical to Ascham's reading list with Princess Elizabeth. Because of Henry VIII's failing health, Edward's education was pushed forward, perhaps too rapidly. Florian characterizes Cheke's tutoring as "a stern as exacting and an inexorable intellectual discipline."[45] His curriculum neglected the romantic or imaginative aspects of literature.

Humanists, such as Cheke and Ascham, believed that myths, such as King Arthur, were not good for young boys. In 1551 Sir William Thomas, clerk to the council, criticized Edward's education as being too literal, very dry and narrow for a young developing prince. He wrote secretly to the prince, enclosing a list of eighty-five topics on policy and statecraft. Edward asked for several essays on foreign relations, the reform of the coinage, and on whether it was better for England that the power rest with the nobility or the common people. Thomas in turn found Edward already surprisingly proficient in the laws, history and the constitution of England. Edward was undoubtedly a precocious child and rapid learner. Cheke was a shrewd teacher who made the most of Edward's intellectual abilities.

At age nine, Edward VI became king (1547) and thereafter was considered an adult. Cheke remained his tutor, for Edward still reserved several hours each day for private study. The boy king became noted by his council for an intellect and maturity well beyond his years. Cheke and Edward's tutorial relationship was described as "a happy concurrence of sweetness and ingenuity. . . ."[46] Sir John Hayward said that Edward "had great judgement in measuring his words, that his speech was both fluent and weighty."[47] A visiting Italian philosopher was astonished at Edward's abilities in philosophy, logic and the other liberal arts.

One of Cheke's responsibilities was the supervision of the other royal tutors, including Sir Anthony Cooke. His success at tutoring his own four sons and five daughters led to Cooke's appointment as a tutor to Edward.

Edward's other tutors included Roger Ascham, who allegedly worked with him on handwriting. His French tutor was John Belmaise, whom he shared with Elizabeth. Edward's Spanish and Italian tutors are unknown, though he spoke fluently in the two languages by age fourteen.

Archbishop Crammer contributed to Edward's education by encouraging him to keep a journal that included the progress of his studies. This diary or _Chronicle_ recounted daily events. It remains a unique document. Edward's _Chronicle_ is an objective source of information on many aspects of English life during the sixteenth century. It is a symbolic representation of the king's early maturity and Cheke's success in helping a prince become a king.[48]

In time the king's tutor became the king's friend. As a child and young man, when the court and kingship overwhelmed him, Edward repeatedly turned to Cheke for consolation. He was always present by the young boy's side in his times of stress, so much so that Edward's nickname for Cheke was "Diligence." The king rewarded his tutor by heaping honors upon him. Cheke was made the provost of King's College, Cambridge (1553). He became a member of Parliament in 1547, 1552, and 1553. Edward knighted Cheke in 1551 and later appointed him chamberlain of the exchequer (1552), clerk of the council (1552) and secretary of state (1553). The most unusual honor conferred by the king was the privilege of the shooting rights of noblemen. Edward's highest recognition of Cheke's personal worth came in 1549, when his tutor was ill to the point of death. Edward demanded with all his Tudor forcefulness that God should spare Cheke.

Edward's untimely death (1553) has in many ways limited Cheke's prominence as a royal tutor. Ascham acknowledged his old teacher's accomplishments with the king. In his _Schoolmaster_ Ascham was thinking of Cheke when he described the ideal teacher. Some believed that Edward's early death was at least in part due to too much education. However, a great deal of evidence exists that the prince was given adequate time for relaxation.

Edward proved that languages can be learned by young children. He showed well above-average intelligence, though he suffers from comparison with Elizabeth. Most of all, Edward's tutors must have been exceptionally competent. Cheke's success was almost unbelievable in helping Edward master two ancient and at least three modern languages beside his own by age sixteen.

There remains a strong tendency to characterize all the royal children as infant prodigies. The truth falls short of these idealized versions of the queens and kings of England. Elizabeth, for all her brilliance, in her later years believed in an elixir for perpetual youth. As for her half-brother, Edward, we do not know what flaws would have been revealed during his adolescence and maturity, nor the quality of his kingship.[49]

## 5. ROGER ASCHAM AND ELIZABETH TUDOR

Elizabeth I (1533-1603) was educated in the spirit of both the Renaissance and Reformation. At about the age of three she began to learn her letters from a delicate little horn book of silver filigree. Katherine Ashley was appointed (1536) as her first governess and tutored Elizabeth in the essentials of reading and writing. Elizabeth was known to have a beautiful script long before the work of her later tutors. Katherine Ashley was the first tutor-governess of importance to be clearly identified as a woman tutor.

Mrs. Ashley was the daughter of an ancient Norman noble family. Her brother, John, was a confidant of Henry VIII. In addition to her support of the "new learning," Katherine was a devout Protestant. Throughout her entire life this learned woman remained devoted to Elizabeth. She was even lodged in the Tower with the princess on a charge of high treason. As Elizabeth's confidante, Mrs. Ashley was the only woman toward whom the queen is known to have shown real warmth of feeling. After twenty-nine years she died still in Elizabeth's service. She is the person about whom the queen said,

> St. Gregory sayeth that we are more bound to them that bringeth us up well than to our parents, for our parents do that which is natural for them that bringeth us into the world, but our bringers up are a cause to make us live well in it.[50]

J.E. Neale has observed that well-born children of his age "seemed to be born wise, and have gray hairs in their youth."[51] As a child, Princess Elizabeth was dressed as a woman and was taught as an adult. Like other little girls she wore uncomfortable corsets, layers of petticoats and toddled about in voluminous long robes, stiff with embroidery, and puffed sleeves that made little arms too heavy to lift. Education of children at court corroborated the fact that there was no separate world of childhood. Their daily schedule began at 6:00 a.m. with divine service and no breakfast. From 7:00 to 11:00 they were tutored in Latin. At 11:00 the children received their first meal of the day that was eaten until noon. The music tutor occupied them from 12:00 to 2:00, followed by the French tutor from 2:00 to 3:00, and the Latin and Greek tutors from 3:00 to 5:00. Evening prayers were then conducted and the children given supper. In whatever time was left over, the boys and girls played until the music tutor arrived at 8:00. After one last hour of instruction the children retired at 9:00. These rules were followed for children until age sixteen. Very young children had shorter lessons and an earlier bedtime, but a similar demanding academic program. Many children were not up to these intellectual demands. Hole in English Home-Life found in the diary of Sir Henry Slingsby a record of his dissatisfaction of the Latin abilities of Thomas, his four-year-old son.

> I find him duller this year than last which would discourage one but that I think the cause to be his too much minding play which takes his mind from his book.[52]

Only after 1600 did a new conception of childhood emerge that gradually acknowledged different subject material in the education of children, adolescents and adults.[53]

For Elizabeth and all other sixteenth century children tutored throughout Europe, it was not uncommon to see four, five and six-year-old boys and girls conversing with adults in both ancient and modern languages. They were educated as "little adults" with a somber mood to match. Thomas Cromwell, Henry VIII's chancellor in 1539, described a six-year-old Elizabeth's Christmas greeting to her father. After the king delivered his message, Elizabeth thanked him and inquired about his health with the grave demeanor of a forty-year-old.[54]

Until the age of eleven Elizabeth worked with Mrs. Ashley and her brother Edward's three tutors, Richard Cox, John Cheke, and Anthony Cooke. Because of her bright, quick intelligence and a good memory, languages came easily to Elizabeth. She probably had learned to read by age five or six. By then Elizabeth had begun her second language, Latin. In 1544 she was given her first university-trained tutor, William Grindal. Marples described Grindal as charming, with high scholastic standards. He was one of the best Greek professors at Cambridge. Grindal found Elizabeth anxious to learn; Elizabeth found him stimulating. During the next four years, in which Grindal instructed Elizabeth in the classics, he is said to have taught her more than any other tutor.

These men who taught Elizabeth were young, Grindal in his twenties, Cheke barely thirty, Cox, their dean, at forty-four. All Cambridge scholars, they formed an intellectual Renaissance bridge between the international Catholic southern humanism of Vives, Erasmus and More, with the less tolerant radical northern Protestant learning of later Puritanism.[55]

In 1548 Grindal died of the plague. Her new tutor had been Grindal's friend and advisor, Roger Ascham. Elizabeth knew he was a congenial person and lobbied successfully for his appointment. Ascham started tutoring Elizabeth in 1548 when she was fifteen.

Roger Ascham (1515-1568) was a Yorkshireman who first was tutored by his father and then by Anthony Wingfield. At age fifteen he attended St. John's College, Cambridge. He had at least four different university tutors, including John Cheke. While at Cambridge, Ascham taught Greek to younger children. His studies made him an erudite classicist reading extant Latin literature, Greek, mathematics and music. Ascham received a B.A. in 1534, M.A. in 1537, was appointed a Greek reader at St. John's (1538) and was also given a mathematics lectureship (1539). His penmanship was so beautiful that he developed a brisk business writing official letters for many clients.

It remains unverified that Henry VIII hired Ascham (1544) to teach Edward and Elizabeth penmanship. However, by 1548 he became Elizabeth's official tutor until he left in 1550 returning to Cambridge. At Cambridge he tutored two young half-brothers until they died of the plague in 1551. After serving as the secretary to the English ambassador to the Court of Charles V (1551-1552), Ascham was appointed Queen Mary's Latin secretary (1553). Upon Elizabeth's accession (1558) he kept that office and was also made tutor to the queen, reading Greek and playing chess with her until his death (1568). Elizabeth became very fond of Ascham, who was by nature an affable, mellow man, accepting of others and generous with his praise. In 1566 Elizabeth rewarded him with another renumerative post. Yet Ascham, as have many tutors in other times and places, felt underpaid. In 1567 he boldly demanded more money from the queen evidently to no avail since Elizabeth I was notoriously frugal. Ascham was always in dire financial straits, for he enjoyed dicing and cock-fighting. Only after his death did Elizabeth raise her estimate of Ascham's monetary value, saying that she would "rather have lost 10,000 pounds than her old tutor Ascham."[56]

As a princess, Elizabeth spent her mornings with Ascham at Greek (Isocrates, Demosthenes, or Sophocles). In the afternoon she studied Latin, ultimately reading almost all of Cicero and most of Livy. Elizabeth read some theology in Latin and the testament in Greek. This study was later followed by Italian, French, Spanish and German. Beside Ascham's instruction we know only of William Grindal's efforts at introducing Elizabeth to Greek, and of her Italian tutor, Battista Castiglione, a religious exile, who was made a gentleman of her bedchamber.

As Elizabeth grew older she became very adept at the difficult art of double translation that turned Greek and Latin into English and back again. This exacting exercise was an effort to arrive at the original wording. Ascham's emphasis on double translation made Elizabeth's English sound like a literal translation. This caused an awkwardness and obscurity in all that she wrote.[57]

Later as queen she founded Westminster Grammar School and was responsible for the inauguration of the Westminster Latin play. For over 400 years the annual performance still preserves the barbaric Latin pronunciation of Elizabethan England, which foreigners in the sixteenth century found so deplorable.

Ascham was surprised by Elizabeth's rigor of mind, "exempt from female weakness." She possessed the "masculine power of application." Her comprehension of languages was quick and retentiveness superb. Elizabeth's Italian and French became as fluent as her English; her Latin excellent and considered, her Greek moderately good.[58] At age thirty-three Elizabeth spoke at Oxford, saying in perfect Latin:

> My parents took good care that I should be well educated, and I had great practice in many languages, of which I take to myself some knowledge; but though I say this with truth I say it with modesty. I had many learned teachers, but they labored in a barren and unproductive field, which brought forth fruit unworthy of their toil and your expectations.[59]

Elizabeth's handwriting was considered outstanding. Ascham taught her perfect command of the Italian, or italic script (though some credit Castigliano's instruction). She wrote a firm, bold hand. It was not until middle age that the queen's handwriting gradually changed to a scrawl. Elizabeth was a mistress of calligraphy. Many of her letters, even if she had not been the queen, would have been cherished as works of art.

Ascham, as royal tutor, became an influential member of Elizabeth's court. An after-dinner argument arose one night (1563) between him and Sir William Cecil, secretary of state. Some boys had run away from school at Eton for fear of flogging. Cecil and others of the queen's ministers believed in the value of corporal punishment. Ascham argued strongly against it. His friends urged him to put his ideas in a book. The Schoolmaster was published in 1570, two years after his death.[60] As we have seen Ascham was tutored in a nobleman's household and probably never went to school. He never even taught in a school. His experience had been as a university or private tutor. Consequently, Marples concludes that The Schoolmaster "looks at education mainly through the eyes of the tutor rather than the class teacher."[61] This was the typical background for the majority of influential books written "on education" during Europe's sixteenth and seventeenth centuries. There is a warm humanity about this book. Ascham insists on the delights of learning and true scholarship. The Schoolmaster became much more than a mere treatise on tutoring, or a diatribe against flogging. Ascham's acute understanding of child psychology makes this book commendable reading that is still valued by contemporary educators.

The Schoolmaster is divided into two parts. Ascham first described "the chief points . . . for the good bringing up of children and young men."[62] He then described in great detail why Latin is important to learn as the foundation of all knowledge and the best way to learn it. The first section of his work demands the most attention. Ascham states his goals as follows: "In writing this book, I have had earnest respect to three special points; truth of religion, honesty in living, right order in learning."[63] Ascham told the teacher not to rebuke hastily and to always correct gently. He saw love as a better motivator than humiliation.

> For I assure you, there is no such
> whetstone to sharpen a good wit, and

encourage a will to learning, as is praise
. . . teach then more plainly, sensibly and
orderly, than they be commonly taught in
common schools . . . . I would not have
the master either frown or hit the child
. . . . Chide not hastily for that shall
both dull his wit and discourage his
diligence; but nourish him gently; which
shall make him both willing to amend and
glad to go forward in love and hope of
learning.[64]

Ascham differed from Erasmus and Vives who
thought discipline shaped both learning and moral
behavior. He recognized the need for discipline in
the latter area, but unlike most of his contemporaries believed that the tutor had little influence
in this sphere.

Ascham was distressed that parents took greater
care in hiring a man to care for their horses than a
tutor to teach their children. As a result, families
got tame horses and wild children. It was important
that parents not hire a cunning, quick-witted man to
tutor their children. Quick wits have poor manners
and are seldom troubled with right or wrong. Ascham
complained bitterly, as did most humanists, that
schoolmasters who beat their students were found
everywhere throughout England.

With the common use of teaching and
beating in common schools of England, I
will not greatly contend; which, if I did
. . . in the end, the good or ill bringing
up of children, does as much serve to the
good or ill services of . . . our whole
country, as any one thing does beside.[65]

The tutorial education for young children was a
difficult intellectual activity punctuated with
physical punishments. Little allowance was made by
the tutor for a slower child. Girls and boys were
frequently beaten since tutors were not only
permitted, but expected by parents to reinforce their
teaching with a liberal use of the rod.[66]

As an alternative Ascham advocated individualizing the learning of each child. Teaching should be paced only at the student's rate of learning. Ascham agreed with Erasmus, "That experience is the common schoolhouse of fools and ill men."[67] A good education was far better than experiential learning since, "Learning teacheth more in one year than experience in twenty; and learning teacheth safely, when experience makes more miserable than wise."[68]

Unlike Erasmus, Ascham advocated a thorough grounding in the vernacular before beginning Latin. His double translation method was adopted from John Cheke.

Ascham is considered by many as a pioneer in modern educational methods. His theories marked a progressive development from the earliest works of Erasmus and Vives. "I wish to have love of learning bred up in children . . . to have young men brought up in good order of living."[69] Though many of his ideas were not new, Ascham's thoughtful review of educational concepts made The Schoolmaster a significant expression of the English Renaissance.[70]

Ascham's educational efforts with Elizabeth yielded the most capable monarch of the Tudor dynasty. Her ability at statecraft was deft if not profound. Elizabeth's proficiency as a linguist and her knowledge and sense of history gave her at once a modern practical political outlook, and the means to express it. Elizabeth's position was strengthened as a monarch, since she never needed to rely on intermediaries. She was always able to converse directly with foreign envoys who did not speak English. In 1597 a Polish envoy read to the queen a somewhat arrogant letter in Latin from the King of Poland. To the delight of her English court, Elizabeth suddenly leapt to her feet and rebuked the ambassador for his insolence with the utmost fluency in the same language. With a degree of pride Ascham tells us how the queen, at another session of court, made successive extempore speeches in Latin, French and Italian in reply to the addresses of three foreign ambassadors delivered to her in those languages.

Elizabeth's favorite subject was history. Even

in later life she tried to devote three hours each day to reading historical works in many different foreign languages. This was a new departure in the education of women. Even her sister Mary had not been tutored in history.

Elizabeth also studied geography, architecture, mathematics, astronomy, logic and philosophy. Though she continued to move England closer to Protestantism, the queen was a thoroughly secular person. Elizabeth adopted a humanist outlook from her study of the classics and as a response to the religious fanaticism that surrounded her as a child. Standing apart from her success as queen, Elizabeth's tutors helped make her the best prepared of all Tudor monarchs for the crown.

In view of Elizabeth's scholarship, it is surprising that her educational patronage was limited solely to the founding of Westminster School for boys. Indirectly, however, Elizabeth's long successful reign led to a widespread increase in the tutorial education of women. English society accepted intelligent women as a norm, not an anomaly.

Elizabeth might have been a great monarch even without the help of her tutors. Her Renaissance education helped Elizabeth establish England's national identity abroad, and supported her image as "Gloriana" in the hearts of all Englishmen. In 1603 she died after forty-five years as queen. Elizabeth as England's second monarch to be given a humanist education, also improved the educational climate for many other women throughout England.[71]

The period between the accession of Henry VIII (1509) and the death of Elizabeth I (1603) often has been characterized as a "Golden Age" for the education of women in England. This representation can be somewhat deceptive. Reynolds believes that Catherine of Aragon's sponsorship was crucial to the royal tutors and their many treatises of the period concerning learned women. This royal support encouraged part of English society to embrace the education of women. It cannot be disputed that numerous learned women of note lived during the Elizabethan Age. Kamm asserts that during this period "girls could read to an extent incomparably greater than any previous century."[72] However, their learning had few useful outlets, nor did it usually reach beyond the nobility into the general population.

Richard Hyrde, the translator of Vives' Instruction of A Christian Woman (1524), was the tutor to Margaret, the daughter of Sir Thomas More. He wrote the first Renaissance document in English, On the Education of Women (1524). It was used as an introduction to Margaret's translation of an Erasmus treatise Precatio Dominica in Septem Portiones Distributa written a year earlier. Hyrde wrote this essay as a vindication for women students of the humanities. It was soon followed by The Defence of Good Women (1535?) by the influential Sir Thomas Elyot. He wrote more in praise of women than strictly concerning their education.

By the middle of the sixteenth century educational reformers began to agitate for still better feminine education. Thomas Becon called for grammar schools for girls. Edward Mulcaster supported Becon's plea and voiced a request in 1562 for women's education, based on a humanistic ideal of civil and domestic duty.

Private tutors again met a social need that most "public" educational institutions were not yet ready or inclined to acknowledge. Because of published records and diaries we know of many homes where the family tutors were shared by the ladies of the household. Mistress Hamblyn, Mrs. Bland, Anna Hume (daughter of David Hume), the daughters of Sir Thomas More and Sir Anthony Cook, were but a few who were tutored in the "new learning." Several women even began tutoring others themselves, beginning one of the few socially acceptable outlets for a woman's education during the English Renaissance. Cook's daughter, Anne, became so highly skilled in Greek, Latin and Italian that she helped her father tutor Edward VI. Later, she became the mother of Sir Francis Bacon. This educational trend of women tutor-governesses grew with each passing century in England for the next three hundred years. A flourishing Renaissance scholarship for women was confined

99

to those families that could afford to pay for the best tutors. For the vast majority of women learning was as remote as ever.

After the death of Elizabeth the high intellectual temperature soon fell. Erudition went out of fashion. Learned women once again became an object of ridicule instead of an ideal to be pursued.[73]

## 6. THE OTHER TUTORS

During the Elizabethan era many books other than those discussing princely education were written. Thomas Elyot had led this trend publishing his The Governor in 1531, but he also translated Plutarch's Discourse Touching On The Training of Children (1533) while preparing his own work. Other examples of this literature include Francis Clement's (1550-1617) The Pelie Schole (1587), Dominique Bonhours' (1558-1587) The Artes of Logick and Rhetorick (1584), and The Education of Children in Learning (1588) by William Kempe (1563-1601). Ascham's Schoolmaster (1570) remains part of same tradition.[74]

At the twilight of Elizabeth's reign Edmund Coate wrote The English Schoolmaster (1596) as a hybrid of these earlier works. The book contained a seventy-nine page instruction manual in English, not Latin. Schoolmaster had extensive separate topical sections on the alphabet and spelling; catechism, prayers and psalms; chronology; writing examples; arithmetic; and vocabulary. "It was destined for self-teachers (tutors) of all ages." The book was addressed to "such men and women of trade . . . as have undertaken the charge of teaching others (commercial tutors)."[75] Schoolmaster also helped prepare the non-university educated tutor. "This impromptu schoolmaster could earn a little extra money in this way (as a tutor), and at the same time satisfy a need for rudimentary instruction."[76] Tutoring as a profession had developed so much in England during the past one hundred years, that university scholars were now supplemented by a new professional group of tutors.

Woodward's writings on the leading Renaissance educational theorists indicated that these radical thinkers were far from united in their interpretation of how to implement their educational ideals. Some like Vives, Erasmus, Elyot, Ascham and More were thinking about the gentry and the activities of private tutors. Others like Melanchthon favored boarding school. But all these humanists were seeking to educate not just an enlightened prince, but more significantly a cultivated amateur with a taste for public service and a background of classical literature. They were very successful in beginning a trend that increasingly demanded more information on the education process.

Pollock's study of works published during the sixteenth century found twenty-two treatises, (or thirty-five per cent of all English literature) were written on education. These numbers continued to grow with each passing century. (See footnotes). Of these twenty-two educational works at least sixteen discussed tutoring.[77]

The humanistic educational influence on English society spread from the court outward. Parents taught their own children, hired a tutor if they could afford one, or sent their children to the local school to learn their letters. Public clamor for tutors soon outstripped the supply of available scholars. Promising young teachers were in such demand as tutors for households, that the universities became seriously deprived of them as teachers.

In Elizabethan England the sons of the nobility were for the most part taught by private tutors in their own homes. Many of these tutors also worked as the personal secretary of the master and as both family chaplain and physician. Noblemen even vied with each other to engage tutors for themselves. They hired architects, scientists, mathematicians and others who in turn were looking for a patron to advance their own careers.

This great demand for tutors resulted in a decline in their ability as educators. Even young tutors recently graduated from Oxford or Cambridge often lacked the qualities of a qualified tutor. The popularity of English tutorial literature in the sixteenth century was undoubtedly an attempt by many to complete their own education. Though some contemporary educators criticized the use of family tutors, their position in English society remained secure until the close of the nineteenth century.

In addition to their normal tutoring duties, these scholars often accompanied the eldest son of a noble family on what became known as "the Grand Tour." This combined sixteenth century humanist theory concerning the nature of wisdom through practical experience of people, foreign countries and different political systems, with the life of the medieval clerical student who was an inveterate wanderer. Later in the eighteenth century certain routes on the Grand Tour became so fashionable that entire local economies were reorganized around these tutors and their students.

The "Grand Tour" became a recognizable finishing school for the nobility of England. It became the most popular form of tutoring for several centuries. But in its early years the trip was strictly for "useful" and "practical" information, not only on culture, but also on military fortifications, topography and economic resources of foreign countries. All these might prove useful in a future political or military career. This approach took a lesson from Machiavelli who in the Prince had also recommended a young nobleman's travels as a form of well-hidden military reconnaissance. Many books were written on this theme after the second half of the sixteenth century. (An example was Jerome Turler's De Peregrinatione (The Traveler) (1574).

In traveling abroad a prime aim for a student was to acquire foreign language skills. This ability would serve the young gentlemen as both a social accomplishment and a vocational necessity. To help accomplish this end, there arose during the second half of the sixteenth century a new class of modern language tutors. Their texts, (i.e. Alexander Barclay's Here Begynneth the Introductory to Write and Pronounce French (1521) or L' Esclaircissement de la Langue Francoyse by John Palsgrave (1530), played an important part in the cultural life of the English Renaissance. French and Italian became the most popular modern languages taught in England by these tutors.[78]

The use of tutors was not confined to men at the top of the English social hierarchy. The sixteenth century witnessed an ever widening field of world commerce that created a powerful merchant class. They became not only very rich, but also politically and socially ambitious. England's discovery of this wider world and development of industrial production gave rise to a demand for a sound technical education. The universities offered little in the way of systematic instruction in these areas. By default private tutors once again met a new instructional need and wrote most of their own texts. These books on geography, maps, navigation and newly-discovered lands became a crucial part of the educational scene in England not only for the young sons of merchants, but also throughout educated society.[79]


## 7.  THE TUDORS' INFLUENCE ON TUTORING


Renaissance England produced a passionate regard for education. The philosopher-tutors attempt to "methodize" knowledge and communicate it to society was a startling success. The role of the printing press was critical in supporting this new "cult of education" as was the establishment of new schools and the increasing demand for qualified tutors.

English society considered for the first time education to fit individual needs. These same philosophers began the development of a "child-centered" education, that other tutors (Jean-Jacque Rousseau, John Locke, Maria Edgeworth) eventually triumphed during the next two hundred years.

These English tutors also said a great deal favoring women's education and their intellectual equality. Here we see the clear influence of the southern Renaissance humanists, but the English tutors went a step further. The dearth of males in the Tudor dynasty resulted in a far greater emphasis on the education of women than found anywhere else in Europe. Catherine of Aragon's struggle to guarantee Mary's place on the throne of England resulted in her daughter receiving an education for a future head of state. With the help of her humanist friends, Catherine established for this dynasty an equality of education between either a prince or princess. Elizabeth and Edward both received a "liberal education" far in advance of the times. Formal education for women of the upper-classes reached a very high standard during the Elizabethan era. These women proved only too anxious to take advantage of the learning opportunities opened by their learned sovereign.

For all their notable academic accomplishments these royal students regarded their tutors only as a means to an end. They did not pay them well, though Elizabeth seemed fond of her governess and Ascham, while her brother, Edward, was genuinely moved at the thought of losing Cheke. However, none of them showed the slightest evidence of adopting the humanist view of life as their own. Elizabeth was certainly a more effective monarch with her knowledge of languages, history and geography. But the personality of the Tudor family overrode the philosophy of Erasmus, Vives, Elyot, More and their own tutors. They all remained absolute autocrats with a quick disposition to use the block.

These idealistic "Tudor tutors" may have found that scholar princes were not always virtuous, but they engendered in English society a quest for inner knowledge that matched Britain's new exploration of the outer world. That humanists such as Vives, More, Ascham and Elyot successfully popularized education for this society's leading elements was a notable educational achievement. This combination of royal and non-royal tutor philosopher-educators created a new favorable environment for broader-based schooling in England.

These tutors acted as a definitive watershed for England between medieval scholasticism and the "new learning" of the Renaissance. In their writings a cohesive educational philosophy was formed that catered to individual differences. Their concept of tutoring became central to the later seventeenth century educational philosopher, John Locke.[80]

## Endnotes

1. Craig Willis, "The Tudors and Their Tutors: A Study of Sixteenth Century Royal Education In Britain" (Ph.D. diss., Ohio State University, 1969), 34-35; Morris Marples, Princes In The Making (London: Faber and Faber, 1965), 13-14, 17-18.

2. Richard Pace, "De Fructu" in F.J. Furnivall, The Babee's Book, vol. 32 (London: Early English Text Society, 1868), viii.

3. Ibid., 299-301; Linda A. Pollock, Forgotten Children, Parent-Child Relations From 1500 to 1900 (Cambridge: Cambridge University Press, 1983), 240; Howe, Governesses, 24; Cresacre More, The Life of Sir Thomas More, ed. Kennedy (Athen's Pennsylvania, 1941); Margareta More, The Household of Sir Thomas More (New York: Charles Scribner, 1852).

4. Her poetry was reprinted in Humphrey Brereton, The Most Pleasant Song of the Lady Bessy (London: Percy Society, R. Taylor, 1829); Josephine Kamm, Hope Deferred, Girl's Education In English History (London: Methuen and Co., 1965), 30.

5. Ibid., 17; Orme, English Schools, 218.

6. Orme, English Schools, 219-220. The English term "public school" was first used in the fourteenth century and was undoubtedly known earlier. It designated an endowed free grammar-school/boarding school usually open to wealthy titled people. But it was the opposite of the private home or domestic school of tutoring. Therefore, it was called "a public school" (though it did not receive tax support by the

state). Private schools also existed but were operated for profit by their owners. <u>Oxford English Dictionary</u>, 1st ed., s.v. "public school;" Ibid., "private;" <u>The Concise Oxford Dictionary</u>, s.v. "public school."

7.  Willis, <u>The Tudors</u>, 35; Marples, <u>Princes</u>, 13-18. Prince Charles and Princess Anne ended the tradition of royal tutors-governesses. Elizabeth II sent them to boarding school.

8.  Orme, <u>English Schools</u>, 27-28; Willis, <u>The Tudors</u>, 35-41.

9.  Jasper Ridley, <u>Henry VIII</u> (New York: Viking, 1985), 21; J.J. Scarisbrick, <u>Henry VIII</u> (Los Angeles: University of California Press, 1968), 5-6.

10. John Skelton, <u>Works</u>, ed. Dyce (London, 1843), 129.

11. Willis, <u>The Tudors</u>, 41-48; Orme, <u>English Schools</u>, 28-29; Marples, <u>Princes</u>, 19-21; Henry VIII, <u>Miscellaneous Writings of Henry The Eighth</u>, ed. Mac Namara (London: Golden Cockerel Press, 1924), 173.

12. Skelton, <u>Works</u>, ed. Dyce (London, 1843).

13. Great Britain, Public Records Office, <u>Calendar of State Letters and Papers, Foreign and Domestic of the Reign of Henry VIII</u>, vol.4 (London: Longman and Company, 1875), 217; Henry VIII, <u>The Letters of King Henry VIII</u>, ed. Byrne (London: Cassell and Company, Ltd., 1936), 3; Henry VIII, <u>Assertio Septem Sacramentorum</u>, ed. O'Donovan (New York: Harper and Row, 1908); Scarisbrick, <u>Henry VIII</u>, 110-111.

14. Orme, <u>English Schools</u>, 29; Marples, <u>Princes</u>, 19-25; Scarisbrick, <u>Henry VIII</u>, 516-517.

15. Richard Foxe, <u>The Letters of Richard Foxe</u>, ed. Allen, vol. 7 (Oxford: Oxford University Press, 1929), 6-8; (This story seems true and was confirmed by Morice, Cranmer's contemporary

biographer. Criticisms of its authenticity remain unconvincing); Scarisbrick, Henry VIII, 255.

16. Ibid; Francis Hackett, Henry the Eighth (London: Jonathan Cape, 1929), 260-261.

17. Walter Howard Frere, William McClure Kennedy, eds., Visitation Articles and Injunctions of the Period of the Reformation, vol. 2 (London: Longmans, Green and Co., 1910), 6-8, 116-117.

18. Juan de Vives, Vives and the Renaissance Education of Women, ed. Watson (New York: Longmans, Green and Co., 1912), 9; Garrett Mattingly, Catherine of Aragon (New York: Vintage Books, 1941), 9-10; Cannon, Education of Women, 98-99.

19. Kamm, Hope Deferred, 24; Cannon, Education of Women, 98-99.

20. Juan Luis Vives, The Instruction of A Christian Woman (London, 1540).

21. Sir Thomas More, Utopia (London: Walter Scott, 1890).

22. Cresacre More, The Life of Sir Thomas More, ed. Kennedy (Athens, Pennsylvania, 1941), 83.

23. Ibid.; Richard Marius, Thomas More (New York: Vintage Books, 1985), 221-226; R.W. Chambers, Thomas More (London: Jonathan Cape, 1935), 181-182; Vives, Education of Women, 15; Fritz Caspari, Humanism and The Social Order In Tudor England (New York: Teachers College Press, 1968), 118-127; More, Thomas More, 80-95; Sir Thomas More, The Correspondence of Sir Thomas More, ed. Rogers (Princeton: Princeton University Press, 1947).

24. Reynolds, The Learned Lady, 9-12.

25. Mattingly, Catherine of Aragon, 174-175.

26. Dr. Thomas Lynacre, Rudiments of Grammar (Paris: Ex Officina R. Stephani, 1533). The state governess was Margaret Plantagenet, a second cousin to Henry VIII. She was a dear friend of Catherine, and known as an "Amazon of a woman" for she was the tallest and largest woman at court; Willis, The Tudors, 94.

27. Juan Luis Vives, The Instruction of a Christian Woman, (London, 1540).

28. Vives, Renaissance Education; Woodward, Studies In Education, 190.

29. Vives, Renaissance Education.

30. Plato, Dialogues (Princeton: University Press, 1961); Thomas More, Utopia (London: Walter Scott, 1890).

31. Vives, Renaissance Education; C.H. Williams, ed., English Historical Documents, vol. 5 (London: Eyre and Spottiswoode, 1967), 398; Cannon, Education of Women, 108-114, 163-169; Willis, The Tudors, 91; Reynolds, Learned Lady, 6-9; Reynolds believes that between 1523-1538 all the works published in England on the education of women were under the influence of Catherine; Woodward, Studies In Education, 180-210; Willis, The Tudors, 91, 96-112; Kamm, Hope Deferred, 36; Mattingly, Catherine, 175-180; Reynolds, Learned Lady, 17-18.

32. Willis, The Tudors, 72-79; Huw Wheldon and J.H. Plumb, Royal Heritage (New York: Crescent Books, 1985), 71; Scarisbrick, Henry VIII, 456-457, 148; Reynolds, Learned Lady, 13; The International Dictionary of Women's Biography, 1st ed., s.v. Parr, Catherine.

33. Edward Cox, The Necessary Doctrine and Erudition of a Christian Man (London: Thomas Berthelet, 1543).

34. Willis, The Tudors, 181-182.

35. Thomas Elyot, The Boke Named the Governor, ed. Watson (London: 1907).

36. Baldassare Castiglione, The Courtier; Matteo Palmieri, Libro della Vita Civile (Firenze, 1529); Francesco Patrizi, De Regno et Regis Institutione (Paris, 1567).

37. Elyot, Governor, 12.

38. Ibid., 18-49.

39. Ibid.

40. Ibid., 113; Pearl Hogrefe, The Life and Times of Sir Thomas Elyot, Englishman, (Ames Iowa: University of Iowa Press, 1967). Tutors were generally underpaid servants. Edward VI's grammar tutor received a salary of less than four pounds per year and his room, board and clothing.

41. Desiderius Erasmus, The Education of a Christian Prince, trans. Born (New York: Columbia University Press, 1936); Plutarch, Discourse Touching On The Training of Children, trans. Elyot (London: Thomas Barthelet, 1535); Plato, The Republic, trans. Jowett (New York: Bigelow, Brown and Co., n.d.); Marcus Fabius Quintilian, The Institutio Oratoria, 4 vols. (New York: G.P. Putnam, 1921-22).

42. Ibid., 18-49.

43. Willis, The Tudors, 182-189; Woodward, Studies In Education, 268-296; Elyot, Governor, 18-49; Lehmberg, Elyot, 72-74, 82, 85, 91-94; Orme, English Schools, 158-159; Caspari, Humanism, 161-193; John Milton, Tractate on Education (London: Macmillan and Co., 1918);_____, Institution of A Gentleman (1555), ed. C. Whittingham (London, 1839); Sir Humphrey Gilbert, Queen Elizabeth's Academy, ed. Furnivall (London: Published by the Early English Text Society by N. Trubner and Company, 1869); James Cleland, Institution of A Young Noble Man (1607) (New York: Scholars Facsimiles

and Reprints, 1948); William Shakespeare, <u>The Life of Henry the Fifth</u> (New Haven: Yale University Press, 1961).

44. Robert Bruce Florian, "Sir John Cheke, Tudor, Tutor" (Ph.D. diss., West Virginia University, 1973), 86.

45. Ibid., 90.

46. Ibid.

47. Sir John Hayward, <u>The Life and Reign of King Edward the Sixth</u> (London: John Partridge, 1636), 7.

48. Edward VI, <u>The Chronicle and Political Papers of King Edward VI</u>, ed. Jordan (Cambridge, Mass.: The Belknap Press of Harvard University Press, 1968), xix-xxiv, 3, 86, 110.

49. John Strype, <u>The Life Of The Learned Sir John Cheke</u> (Oxford: Clarendon Press, 1821), 73; Florian, <u>John Cheke</u>, 1, 3, 8-11, 80-136, 303-318; Willis, <u>The Tudors</u>, 177,187-202; Marples, <u>Princes</u>, 27-40; Reynolds, <u>Learned Lady</u>, 12-13. A probable apocryphal anecdote concerns Edward at the age of nine, when he was already king and his schoolmate and cousin, Barnaby. Edward started using bad language. Cheke did not believe in chastising the Lord's anointed so he beat Barnaby while Edward watched, warning him that his "whipping boy" would not escape so lightly if the offense was repeated again.

50. Willis, <u>The Tudors</u>, 133-178; The risk that Mrs. Ashley took in publicly advocating the young Princess Elizabeth's cause was underscored by the fact that of the seventeen noble persons attending her christening, ten were beheaded, died in disgrace or saw their family members executed or imprisoned.

51. J.E. Neale, <u>Queen Elizabeth</u> (New York: Harcourt, Brace and Company, 1934), 42.

52. Christinia Hole, English Home-Life 1500-1800 (London: B.T. Batsford, 1947), 45.

53. Ibid; Elizabeth Godfrey, English Children in the Olden Time, (Williamstown: Corner House Pub., 1980), 88.

54. Neale, Elizabeth, 42.

55. Lucy Aiken, Memoirs of the Court of Elizabeth, Queen of England (London: Alex Murray and Son, 1869), 11-13; Howe, Governesses, 25-35; J.E. Neale, Queen Elizabeth (New York: Harcourt, Brace and Company, 1934), 42, 47-48, 55-58, 69, 16-17, 74-78, 147, 153, 214; J.H. Plumle, "The Great Change In Children," Horizon 13 (Winter 1971), 4-12; Elizabeth Godfrey, English Children In The Olden Time (Williamstown: Corner House Publishers, 1980), 88, 95, 147.

56. Willis, The Tudors, 159.

57. Roger Ascham, The Schoolmaster (London: Cassell, 1900), 11-12, 14, 137, 138.

58. Willis, The Tudors, 153-162; Neale, Elizabeth, 69-76; Marples, Princes, 52-57; Agnes Strickland, The Life of Queen Elizabeth (London: Hutchinson and Company, 1904), 42.

59. Neale, Elizabeth, 76; Willis, The Tudors, 170; Wheldon, Royal, 74-76.

60. Roger Ascham, The Whole Works of Roger Ascham, ed. Giles (New York: AMS Press, 1965).

61. Marples, Princes, 55.

62. Ascham, Works of Roger Ascham, 82.

63. Ibid., 86.

64. Ibid., 90-91, 96.

65. Ibid., 96-97.

66. Hole, English Home Life, 42-43.

67. Ibid., 137.

68. Ibid., 136.

69. Ibid., 120.

70. Willis, The Tudors, 156-158; Kamm, Hope Deferred, 37-38; Ascham, The Whole Works, 83, 86, 96-104, 168-276.

71. Marples, Princes, 53-54; Willis, The Tudors, 171, 174, 176, 178.

72. Kamm, Hope Deferred, 52.

73. Juan Luis Vives, Instruction of Christian Women, trans. Hyrde (London: 1540); Reynolds, Learned Lady, 19-23, 35, 44, 160, 426-427, 450-451; Richard Hyrde, "On the Education of Women" in Vives and the Renascence Education of Women, ed. Foster Watson, (New York: Longmans, Green and Company, 1912), 159-163; Thomas Elyot, "The Defence of Good Women" in Vives and the Renascence Education of Women, ed. Foster Watson (New York: Longmans, Green and Company, 1912), 211-214; Kamm, Hope Deferred, 46-47, 52-53; Howe, Galaxy, 31-35; Cannon, Education of Women, 121-123; Desiderius Erasmus, Precatio Dominica in Septem Portiones Distributa, trans. More (Basel: J. Frobenius, 1523).

74. Francis Clement, The Pelie Schole (London: Imprinted by T. Vantroilier, 1587); Dominique Bonhours, The Artes of Logick and Rhetorick (London: Printed for J. Clark, 1728); William Kempe, The Education of Children In Learning (London: T. Orivin for I. Porter and T. Gubbin, 1588); Plutarch, Discourse Touching On the Training of Children, trans. Elyot, (London: Thomas Barthelet, 1535).

75. Edmund Coate, The English Schoolmaster (London: 1596) 4-15; Aries, Childhood, 298-299.

76. Ibid.

77. Robert D. Peppa, Four Tudor Books On Education (Gainsville, Florida: Scholars Facsimiles and Reprints, 1966), VII-XXX; Douglas Bush, The Renaissance and English Humanism (Toronto: University of Toronto Press, 1939), 78-79; Aries, Childhood, 298-299; Woodward, Studies In Education, XIII; Pollock, Forgotten Children, 240.

Percentage of texts providing information on education:

| Century | All texts | American | British |
|---------|-----------|----------|---------|
| 16th | 33 % | 0 % | 35 % |
| n= | 24 | 2 | 22 |
| 17th | 46 % | 40 % | 48 % |
| n= | 80 | 15 | 65 |
| 18th | 46 % | 44 % | 47 % |
| n= | 245 | 98 | 147 |
| 19th | 51 % | 45 % | 55 % |
| n= | 188 | 65 | 123 |

Books written in the sixteenth century that discussed tutoring mentioned elsewhere in this chapter: John Skelton, A Prince's Mirror, 1501; Desiderius Erasmus, The Education of a Christian Prince, 1516; Alexander Barclay, Here Begynneth the Introductory to Write and Pronounce French, 1521; Juan de Vives, On the Education of Christian Women, 1523; Richard Hyrde, "On the Education of Women," 1524; Desiderius Erasmus, De Matrimonio Christiane, 1526; Baldassare Castiglione, The Courtier, 1528; John Palsgrave, L'Esclaircissement de La Langue Francoyse, 1530; Thomas Elyot, The Boke Named the Governor, 1531; Thomas Elyot, The Defense of Good Women, 1535?; Roger Ascham, The Schoolmaster, 1552; Unknown Author, Institution of a Gentleman, 1555; Sir Humphrey Gilbert, Queen Elizabeth's Academy, 1572; Jerome Turler, De Perigrinatione, 1574; Edmund Coate, The English Schoolmaster, 1596.

78. Jerome Turler, The Traveler (London: William How, Abraham Veale, 1575); Alexander Barclay, Here Begynneth the Introductory to Write and Pronounce French (London: Robert Coplande,

1521); John Palsgrave, <u>L'Esclaircissement de la Langue Francoyse</u> (London: John Hawkings, 1530; Niccoló Machiavelli, <u>The Prince</u>, trans. Marriott (London: J.M. Dent and Sons, Ltd., 1958), 79-85.

79. Joan Simon, <u>Education and Society In Tudor England</u> (Cambridge: University Press, 1966) 101, 348-349, 367-368; Butts, <u>Education</u>, 260; Lawson, <u>Social History</u>, 133; Kenneth Charlton, <u>Education In Renaissance England</u> (London: Routledge and Kegan Paul, 1965), 96-97, 213-295.

80. Charlton, <u>Education</u>, 297, 298; Willis, <u>The Tudors</u>, 236-241; G.E. and K.R. Fussell, <u>The English Countrywoman 1500-1900</u> (London: Andrew Melrose, 1953), 51.

CHAPTER 4

TUTORS IN THE AGE OF REASON
(ENGLAND AND FRANCE 1600 - 1700)


1.  THE PRIVATE ENGLISH TUTOR


By the death of Elizabeth I in 1603 the English
public schools were flourishing, training many boys
in manners and the classics. Winchester, Eton,
Westminster, St. Paul's and Merchant Taylors helped
prepare many boys at a young age for the university.
Almost every town of consequence had a grammar
school. Many were established in the seventeenth
century to take the place of monastic or cathedral
schools destroyed by Henry VIII's reformation. But
the private tutor was still preferred by many
parents.

Many families wished to bring up their own
children at home. A resident tutor instructed both
girls and boys. Some also served as both family
chaplain and physician. In seventeenth century
England the patriarchal family was the chief cultural
transmitter across generations. The socialization of
the child remained the family's prime function, a
role not shared as yet by schools, newspapers or even
books. It becomes quite understandable why the
private tutor of the seventeenth century became an
important social agent, since he served as the
educational extension of the family.

In the nursery, mothers or nurses were the first
tutors. One illustration in Andrew Tuer's History of
the Horn-Book (an early teaching device) showed a
child age two years, two months at these early
lessons. For most children normal tutoring started
at age four. Since life expectancy was short,
childhood was brief. Many girls married by age
thirteen, and boys started the university at age

115

twelve.  The typical curriculum time-table began with
the "horn-book" at age four, the psalter at age five,
and by age seven, the Bible.  By age eight many boys
went to the local Latin schools, though many remained
home with their sisters to continue their education.[1]

Pollock's study of seventeenth century educational literature shows a widespread use of tutors as
an alternative to schooling.  She found in surviving
seventeenth century English diaries that forty-two
per cent of the diarists mentioned that their
children either had a tutor or went to school.  Some
of these diaries give a detailed account of how that
society educated its children at home.

One such diary was kept by the countess and
fifth earl, duke of Bedford, who had nine children.
After they had survived the perils of their babyhood,
the earl engaged the Reverend John Thornton, B.A.,
Trinity College, Cambridge, to tutor them (1655).
Thornton lived with the family at Bedford House,
receiving a salary of thirty pounds per year.  Their
tutor was very influential in molding the character
of his pupils, in some ways more than the countess or
earl.  Thornton stressed both the classics and stern
religious principles in his educational program.  At
age three or four each child received two Bibles, one
in Latin, the other English.  They also were given a
catechism and a Book of Common Prayer.  About the age
of seven they received a book of Calvinist doctrines.
Other texts soon followed:  Nicholas Byfield's
Principles or the Pattern of Wholesome Words, Latin
grammar texts, and Corderius or The Dialogues of
Mathurin Cordier.  Latin authors were introduced in
their order of difficulty.  The curriculum included
both The Gates of Languages Unlocked by Johann Amos
and his revolutionary book that used pictures and
illustrations to help educate children, Orbis Pictus
(1658).  As the children grew, other tutors supplemented Thornton.  French, dancing and music tutors
came from London to teach the girls.  While this
occurred, the boys took the "Grand Tour" with yet
another tutor.  In addition to acting as family
tutor, Thornton also assumed the duties of secretary
to the earl, librarian and family physician.

Diana, the eldest of the two daughters, showed

the lasting impression of her private tutor. After her marriage, Diana constantly wrote letters to Mr. Thornton addressed as her "best friend." Thornton received all of Diana's confidence and freely gave her advice on moral, educational and physical problems. How the other eight children later felt about Thornton is unknown. Yet similar instances of this strong, continuing loyalty between a past student and his or her old tutor are recorded with some degree of frequency throughout the history of tutoring.[2]

Henry Peacham was another seventeenth century tutor, but with a different mission. In 1613 he was commissioned to travel abroad as private tutor to Hannibal Baskerville and the sons of Thomas Earl of Arundel and Surrey. By 1622 he was still employed by the earl as the tutor to his youngest son. Peacham published The Complete Gentlemen (1622) with a dedication to his little pupil, William Howard. Most of the book is addressed to his parents and future tutors "to recover (young William) from the tyranny of these ignorant times and from the common education, which is to wear the best clothes, eat, sleep, drink much, and to know nothing."[3] He exhorted against "cockering and apish indulgence" and against a false economy in the matter of tutors.

> Many are satisfied if they can procure some poor Bachelor of Art from the University to teach their children . . . who will be content with ten pounds a year. . . . It is not commonly seen, that the most gentlemen will give better wages, and deal more bountifully with a fellow who can but teach a dog, or reclaim a hawk, than upon an honest, learned and well-qualified man to bring up their children.[4]

Peacham complained that "public school" hours are long, from six in the morning till twelve noon or past. The "folly" of some schoolmasters is their addiction to the rod. In winter it became a habit with one teacher on a "cold morning [to] whip his boys over for no other purpose but to heat himself. . . . Correction without instruction is plain tyranny."[5] A teacher must not belittle his student with such epithets as "blockheads, asses, dolts, which deeply pierce the free and generous spirit."[6] Peacham recognized the need for a teacher to individualize their instruction for each student, "the self-same method agree not with all alike; the duller want helping most."[7] Most tutors are naturally inclined to give their attention to the quick. He advised tutors to emphasize the sober virtues of thrift, frugality, moderation in living. These qualities are to be mixed with abundant common sense, discretion and social judgment in the formation of an upright character.

The Complete Gentlemen offered the good counsel of "the genteel tradition" as well as instruction in grammar and technical education. Peacham's ideas were so well adapted to his period that they became the stock in trade of courtesy writers for the next two centuries.[8]

A great mass of courtesy literature, similar to The Complete Gentlemen, flooded seventeenth century England. Noyes in Bibliography of Courtesy and Conduct Books in Seventeenth Century England provides the most comprehensive index on the topic of education in Europe.[9] Hundreds of these works frequently were reissued from the previous two centuries.[10]

Primarily reflecting an educator's viewpoint, courtesy literature dealt with concrete ways to teach a young man to become a leader in the society of the day. They reflect seventeenth century preoccupation with "right conduct" and religion. It was sometimes extremely difficult to determine whether a book's topical focus was primarily education or morality. However, courtesy literature always thought of education "under a governor" (tutor) at home, followed by university attendance and completed by the "grand tour." These books had broad appeal throughout English society.[11]

This was especially true of the royal household. During the first half of the seventeenth century James VI of Scotland, later James I of England, received a model tutorial education. At age four the Scottish Privy Council appointed a large educational staff: two general education tutors, a French tutor, an Italian tutor, two athletic instructors, two music instructors and a dancing master. They cooperated successfully in planning a curriculum with one overriding purpose--to make the future king a real scholar. George Buchanan, greatest of Scotland's scholars, and Peter Young, a much younger Calvinist tutor, were the principal instructors. James became so fond of Young that he later as king employed him to tutor his son, Charles. Their teaching of the classics predominated, both in the original and in English, Italian and French translations.

There were many serious distractions for the young prince. James was the center of strife between rival factions, and their plots and intrigues. Once he was kidnapped and before age twelve saw four different regents appointed to protect him. The fact that by age eight James was recorded as conversing fluently in foreign tongues with privileged court visitors is a testimony to his tutor's abilities.

James grew up an enthusiastic scholar, but he had little understanding of how to rule his kingdom. Buchanan had given him a classical education without practical political substance. As a child James feared Buchanan, who thrashed and boxed his ears for motivation. James suffered nightmares all his life due to his tutor's treatment.

Like other future kings, James longed to escape the throne for other pursuits. During a visit to the Bodleian Library at Oxford he wistfully remarked, "If I were not a king, I would be a University man."[12] Later that day James was listening to a disputation in the schools. The king suddenly took the floor and amazed the dons with a long and eloquent speech in perfect Latin. Afterward the professors marvelled that James might be the scholar-king of Plato's ideal republic. Obviously this did not occur. Time and again in the education of princes, the best education was compromised by a distracting environment or lack a contemporary informational base. The education of Charles II and the future James II had the same flaws and was more dislocated.

Even more distressing was the education of James II's two daughters, Mary and Anne. It was a dramatic contrast to that of their Tudor ancestors. The princesses' tutors were of an inferior grade. Little attention was given to what they were taught. Aside from an erratic fluency in French, most of their education was spent in acquiring the elegant arts of the drawing room, in dance and music. Their education represented the final abandonment in England of Renaissance ideals for the education of women.[13]

Throughout the rest of English society a growing use of tutors was made after college for the "Grand Tour." Such was the case of Francis and William Russell, who toured the Continent after three years at Cambridge. Their father (the Earl of Bedford) hired Charles Rich, a "traveling tutor," for 100 pounds and his traveling expenses. The regular governor (the tutor in residence) provided their reading materials for the trip: a pocket Latin dictionary, Comenius' Vestibulum and Letters of the Sieur de Balzac. For five years (1660-66) they toured the capitals of Europe at the stupendous cost of 5,000 pounds. The tutor may have been the least expensive part of the trip.

Some Puritans also sent their sons abroad under the charge of a tutor. Even more common was their practice of boarding the young men in the houses of French or Swiss Protestant divines to imbibe the Calvinistic teaching that also was espoused by ultra-Protestant "roundheads."

In the seventeenth century most young men of position took the "Grand Tour" to see the world. In 1670 Richard Lassel's Voyage of Italy first brought the term in common use. The traveling tutor (given the name "bear-leader") taught them in route and kept them out of mischief. Early in this century, before the civil war (1642-1646), many young Englishmen attached themselves to the household of a relative or friend of the family who held a foreign diplomatic appointment. Thus they had access to the best society abroad and a valuable insight into foreign affairs and diplomatic relations. As the sixteenth century drew to a close the numbers of Englishmen who made the "Grand Tour" increased each year. This was partially induced by the establishment of permanent diplomats at many foreign courts. The popularity of this educational practice in 1592 and again in 1595 led the Pope to complain that too many English heretics had found their way to Venice.[14]

## 2. THE DECLINE OF EDUCATION FOR WOMEN

A backlash of male prejudice against learning for women appeared after the Elizabethan age. The seventeenth century educator, Thomas Becon, was in a minority in support of properly trained and paid governesses. Most young women who wished to teach girls professionally met with strong opposition. Seventeenth century male society believed a woman's place was at home. If she must teach, let it be the so-called "feminine accomplishments" (home economics) at a meager salary, but not French or Latin. The first half of the century witnessed a decline in the literacy rate among women in England. Except for upper class families, girls received little private education. Jonathan Swift estimated that hardly one woman in a thousand could read or spell.

The outbreak of the English civil war worsened educational conditions. The disruption of family life ended most educational activities. Still, pious "round-head" mothers somberly tutored their daughters through home study of the Bible. Cromwell's protectorate was grim, making children solemn little creatures. The rod was often used to reinforce the tutor's lesson.

In many cases, the education of young women was curbed by parents. Elizabeth Tanfield, daughter of Sir Lawrence Tanfield, had her scholarly traits discouraged by a jealous mother. Lady Tanfield could scarcely read or write. She resented Elizabeth's scholarly traits, and attempted to whip them out of her. Candles were forbidden in her room to prevent reading, but Elizabeth bribed the servants for them so often, that by the time of her marriage at age fifteen, she had run up a one-hundred-pound debt.

Large families were the rule during the period, with both parents superintending the education of

121

their children. As we have observed, nobles and upwardly-mobile merchant-class families frequently employed a chaplain to tutor their children. Some abused this appointment. Anne Murray visited her friend, Lady Howard, at Naworth Castle. The family chaplain was an "excellent preacher . . . a man of good life, good conversation . . . he [was] their tutor angel." Living in the household were two young "papist" cousins being instructed by this chaplain in the Protestant religion. Much to Anne's consternation, she discovered that he was taking advantage of his position by making love to the elder of the two.[15]

There were, however, some notable exceptions in this general decline of education for women. Hannah Woolley wrote a remarkable book based on her thirty years of teaching experience that responded to this anti-intellectual atmosphere. The Gentlewoman's Companion (1675) drew a portrait of the ideal governess:

> They who undertake the difficult employ of being an Instructress or Governess of children should be persons of no mean birth or breeding, civil in deportment, of an extraordinary winning and pleasing conversation.[16]

Mistress Woolley was interested in the "science of teaching." She expressed some very sound views on the education of women far in advance of her time. The harsh treatment of children shocked her. She told the grim tale of an English governess who, "called up her maid with whose help she so cruelly chastised a young Gentlewoman for some fault that she died."[17] Woolley begged parents to let their children be tutored lovingly and quietly, "blows are fitter for beasts than for rational creatures." Howe believes that Woolley was the first woman tutor to stress the importance of individual difference in methods of teaching. In her own way Hannah Woolley, like Roger Ascham a century before, was a pioneer in the field of child psychology.[18]

Hannah Woolley was not the only well-known seventeenth century English governess. Bathsua Makin

(1608-1675) was the daughter of the Rector of Southwick, Sussex. The famous John Pell, linguist and mathematician, was her brother. At age thirty Mrs. Makin was appointed governess to the six-year-old Princess Elizabeth (1641), daughter of Charles I. Three years later, Elizabeth could read, write, understand and in some measure, speak French, Italian, Latin, Greek and Hebrew. Though Bathsua's brother held a post under Cromwell, the roundhead parliament repudiated her forty-pound-a-year pension as royal governess after the premature death of the princess (1650). Mrs. Makin turned to private tutoring to earn her living. An indication of her success was that she tutored Lucy Davies, daughter of Sir John Davies, Attorney-General for Ireland. After the Restoration she opened a school for gentlewomen at Tottenham, High Cross, built on her reputation as a royal governess. At about this time she published a treatise widely read in that time period, "An Essay to Revive the Ancient Education of a Gentlewoman" (1673).

> Merely to teach gentlewomen to frisk [walk] and dance, to paint their faces, to curl their hair, to put on a Whisk [wig], to wear gay clothes, is not truly to adorn but adulterate their bodies . . . . The Tongues ought to be studied, especially the Greek and Hebrew.[19]

What education a young well-bred woman received was determined ultimately by her mother with the tutor's assistance. The account by Lucy Assley of her education gives an insight into this age.

> As soon as I was weaned a Frenchwoman was taken to be my dry-nurse, and I was taught to speak French and English together. . . . When I was about seven years of age, I remember I had at one time eight tutors in several qualities, languages, music, dancing, writing, and needlework; but my genius was quite averse to all but my book, and that I was so eager of, that my mother thinking it prejudiced my health, would moderate me in it; yet this rather animated me than kept me back,

and every moment I could steal from my play
I would employ in any book I could find,
when my own were locked up from me.  After
dinner or supper I still had an hour
allowed me to play, and then I would steal
into some corner to read.  My father would
have me learn Latin, and I was so apt that
I outstripped my brothers that were at
school, although my father's chaplain, that
was my tutor, was a pitiful dull fellow.
My brothers, who had a great deal of wit,
had some emulation of the progress I made
in my learning which very well pleased my
father; though my mother would have been
contented if I had not so wholly addicted
myself to that as to neglect my other
qualities.[20]

While there were exceptions, education for women
in England was in a state of decline during the
seventeenth century.  Scholarship was not a socially
accepted attainment for women, and therefore, their
education was confined largely to handicrafts and the
social arts.[21]  While educational opportunities
generally declined for women in England, the French
humanists of the period made contributions to
tutorial education that parallelled their English and
Continental counterparts.  They too strove to improve
the status of education for women.


## 3.  FRENCH TUTORS AT HOME


Guillaume Budé (1468-1540) was the great
humanist of France.  He corresponded with Erasmus and
More.  His early education is unknown but like his
foreign colleagues he taught himself Greek and read
widely in Latin.

In 1516 he wrote in French De l' Institution du
Prince addressed to a young Francis I, urging a
humanist education for his prince, achieved through
the classical languages.  History was also to be
studied by princes to judge the present more securely
and forecast the future with greater accuracy.

Though Budé was never a royal tutor, his philosophy spread throughout French society and letters. He held several important offices including Royal Librarian and provost of Paris. Under Budé's influence Francis I established the Corporation of the Royal Readers, a forerunner of the Collège de France. He also suggested that the king begin the famed library at Fontainebleau, which became the basis of the Bibliothèque Nationale.[22]

De Liberis Recte Instituendis (1530) by Jacopo Sadoleto was written for a larger segment of French society than Budé's work. Sadoleto was the bishop of Carpentras in southern France. He was concerned that the state showed little interest in education. Since organized schools of a satisfactory type did not exist, he prepared a guide for home tutoring. Family life was at the center of education. Tutors were to be attentive to the minor details of their work, which was similar to the educational plans of other Renaissance humanists. The aim of Sadoleto was to fashion a man into a cultured citizen in a civilized and secure society. De Liberis became the French contribution to the international "courtesy education" tradition.[23]

A further step in the development of the practical education sought by the humanists was the rise of the realistic movement in education as characterized by Michel de Montaigne (1533-1592). This realistic movement in turn was the touchstone of the scientific movement in education. The writings of Francis Bacon (1561-1626), Advancement of Learning (1605), Novum Organum (1620) and René Descartes' (1596-1650) Discourse on Method (1637), were an outgrowth of the scientific discourses of the sixteenth and seventeenth centuries. Montaigne's focus on tutoring as an educational form, encouraged basic principles of discrimination, independent thinking, and application on the part of the student. Renaissance educational ideals began assuming their modern form.[24]

Montaigne's grandfather was a fishmonger. He made the family fortune and established the family estate outside Bordeaux. While Michel was only a young child, his father provided him a tutor from

Germany who spoke to him only in Latin and other foreign languages. "I was six years old before I understood more of French than of Arabic."[25] Montaigne acquired mastery of Latin without books, rules or grammar, whipping or whining. Later at the Collége de Guienne his teachers were loath to speak Latin to him, he spoke it so well.

In 1580 he published his Essays. Their popularity was attested by the nine editions between 1580 and 1598. Long before Locke, Montaigne believed that all knowledge is addressed to us by the senses, and since reason depends upon them, reason can be unreliable. By applying the philosophy of scientific inquiry to education, he introduced into French thinking the psychological analysis of the mind and character. Voltaire's and Rousseau's philosophy, at least in part, stemmed from Montaigne's Essays.

Montaigne became the mentor of the Age of Reason in France. He rejected the schools or colleges of his day as agencies of education. A student coming back from these institutions was "so awkward and maladroit, so unfit for company and employment . . . all that . . . he has got is that his Latin and Greek have only made him a greater and more conceited coxcomb than when he went from home."[26]

The educational alternative that Montaigne preferred was a tutor. A broadly-based humanistic education would replace the narrow classical formalism of the Latin grammar schools. Montaigne felt the choice of this tutor was the most important and difficult responsibility of any parent. They must find a tutor having a well-composed and temperate brain.[27]

Montaigne's private tutorial system was closely supervised by the tutor at home or abroad. As in England, tutoring became the accepted form of education for boys in France among the upper classes. The "Grand Tour" was also appreciated as an indispensable part of a young man's complete education.[28]

The school career of Henri de Mesmes seems typical of many sixteenth and seventeenth century French children. Henri was born in 1532, the son of

126

a lawyer.

> My father gave me a tutor, J. Maludan,
> a disciple of Dorat's, and a learned man,
> chosen for the innocence of his life and an
> age suitable for the guidance of my youth
> . . . he relinquished his post only when I
> started my career.[29]

His tutoring continued until age eighteen, but it was
not a substitute for regular school attendance.
Between the ages of five to nine the child was taught
reading and grammar at home. When Henri started
school, Maludan accompanied him and acted as a
private coach. This was similar to educational
practices for many boys in England.[30]

Maréchal de Bassonpierre, born in 1579, was
taught reading and writing at home until twelve years
of age. An advanced tutor started working with him
at nine. This scribe taught him writing to perfection. Another tutor was assigned his more "courtly
education" in dancing, lute playing and music. Aries
believes that this method of domestic education was
common, but seldom extended past age twelve or
thirteen when boys were sent to school. The education of Cardinal Armand Jean du Plessis de Richelieu
seems to support this view. Until the age of twelve
Richelieu was tutored on a remote country estate by
the head priest (prior) of a monastery from Saumus.
In 1597 he went to the University of Paris, accompanied by a private tutor, to attend the College of
Navarre.[31] However, the royal court of France
continued private tutoring until the age of adulthood. Extensive use of court tutors followed an
earlier pattern from the House of Tudor with the
publication of philisophical works on education that
were read throughout Europe.


4.  THE "SUN KING" AND HIS TUTORS


In the monarchial state of absolutist France the
Renaissance concept that the happiness of the nation
was tied to the education of its prince found

enthusiastic support. The spirit of Castiglione's The Courtier was emulated ardently by the French. A great deal of attention was given to the duties of the royal tutor by some of the most eminent thinkers of the seventeenth century. The scientist, Blaise Pascal (1623-62), declared that he would dedicate his life willingly to the education of his prince. Pierre Nicole (1625-1695), a philosopher-theologian, wrote a series of treatises on the education of a prince including Essais de Morale (1661).[32]

Two years after the birth of Louis XIV, the Grand Dauphin (1638-1715), the skeptic philosopher, La Mothe Le Vayer (1588-1672), wrote De l'instruction de Monseigneur le Dauphin (1640). By dedicating the work to Cardinal Richelieu he had hoped to secure the office of royal tutor. The political instability of France led to a surprising neglect of the Grand Dauphin's early education. It was not until 1644 that Hardouin De Perefixe, the Abbé of Sablonceau was appointed as the young prince's tutor. In his third year as royal tutor Hardouin composed Institutio Principis (1647) as a code of essential royal virtues that he hoped to instill in the young Louis.[33]

Later Le Vayer was finally appointed royal tutor (1652) due to his success with Louis' younger brother, the Duke of Orleans. He presided over Louis' desultory studies until 1660, when the Grand Dauphin was married to Marie Therese of Spain. Le Vayer's Morale du Prince (1655?), the Logique du Prince (1656?) and other works, gave more precise detail to the teaching methods used with Louis XIV. Le Vayer prepared seven different treatises that revealed his instruction of the prince was largely superficial. His pupil was too distracted by life at court. Even though the seven liberal arts were presented to Louis, the content of each was compromised seriously. Exact knowledge of Latin was a thing for the rabble, wrote Le Vayer. Arithmetic was the science of merchants. Rhetoric was only important to develop oratorical skills. These hollow justifications meant that the young Louis was poorly instructed and received few if any of the benefits that French humanists had been so eager to bestow upon their prince.[34]

Louis XIV's first son was known as Monseigneur (1661-1711). It is obvious that the king carefully planned his son's education. Perhaps he hoped to avoid the pitfalls of his own inadequate tutorials. During his young childhood, Monseigneur remained in the charge of a governess. At the age of seven two tutors, Duc de Montausier and M. de Périgny, were appointed for his upbringing. A governor acted as the first tutor in charge of the prince's person. The précepteur was the second tutor responsible for his education. He took an oath of office.

I swear to employ all my power to bring him up in the love and fear of God, to train his morals, and develop his mind by the knowledge of letters and sciences such as are suitable to an illustrious prince.[35]

In 1670 Jacques Bénigne Bossuet (1627-1704), bishop of Condom and a very distinguished theologian, was appointed the tutor to the eleven-year-old prince. Pope Innocent XI asked Bossuet for an account of his tutoring, and the resulting series of letters left a precise record of their work together. Bossuet taught the prince Latin and French simultaneously. The royal pupil read Sallust, Ceasar, Cicero, Virgil and Terence. Greek was rejected. History was reviewed carefully. Moral lessons were continually drawn for a future ruler. Monseigneur became so interested in history that A History of France was published in his name (probably most of the work was done by Bossuet). When the prince was thirteen, another work, Helvetian War, appeared under the same circumstances. Bossuet later published Discours sur l' Histoire Universelle à Monseigneur le Dauphin (1679) that were undoubtedly the content of his history lessons with the prince. Other treatises followed that give us an overview of the royal tutors curriculum, De la connaissants de Dieu et de Soi-même (pub. 1722) on the function of the human body and psychology; Politique tirée des propres paroles de l' Ecriture Sainte à Monseigneur le Dauphin as public worship and the support of religion. The later also contained a discussion on the theory of divine right, royal authority, war, taxation and the temptations of kings.[36]

Bossuet's tutoring methods went well beyond writing scholarly tomes to instruct his prince. To learn astronomy, they visited an observatory. To learn mathematics Francis Blondel, a famous architect, was hired as a tutor. The greatest contemporary authorities in every branch of knowledge tutored Monseigneur. Bossuet's methods received unstinted praise in France and across Europe. At times it seemed that these extraordinary efforts would bear fruit. The truth was that any interest in learning was stifled by Bossuet's highly intellectual methods for a young boy's general education. Bossuet, in his frustration to motivate Monseigneur, began beating the child. It was alleged that he broke the prince's arm during one "tutoring session." This type of extraordinary corporal punishment was acceptable in seventeenth century society, even as part of a high-born child's education. Bossuet ultimately admitted his failure, though the tutoring continued to 1680 and the prince's marriage to Marie of Bavaria. No ill-feeling existed between the bored, inattentive pupil and his scholarly tutor. The prince had a friendly relationship with Bossuet all his life. This elaborate tutorial program failed not in its ideals, but in the use of methods suitable for advanced scholarship, not a child's basic education, even for a prince.[37]

The education of Louis XIV's grandson, the Duke of Burgundy, was the third phase of seventeenth century princely tutoring to receive widespread attention throughout French society. After the king's son, he was the heir apparent. For this task Louis XIV changed his tactics and chose not a scholar-theologian, but a known successful tutor, Francois de Salignac de la Mothe Fénelon (1651-1715). This young priest had successfully directed a sisterhood of "new Catholics" composed of Huguenot girl converts. Because of his success, a powerful member of the Court, the Duchess of Beauvillies, asked Fénelon for advice on the education of her eight daughters. At age thirty, Fénelon wrote for her guidance On the Education of Girls (1687). The book impressed her and the king. Upon the recommendation of the duchess and her husband, then the prince's tutor, Louis XIV appointed Fénelon to teach his grandson (1689). Fénelon also tutored the duke's brother and sister with the assistance of two other priests that served as under-tutors.[38]

The seven-year-old prince was very intelligent, but highly distractable like many other young boys. Unlike Bossuet, Fénelon used indirect methods to teach his lessons. A collection of fables was written by Fénelon, <u>Recueil des Fables Composées pour l' education du duc de Bourgone</u> that contained morality tales suited to his age and future role. Unlike the scholarly Bossuet, this fatherly priest established an affectionate relationship with his pupil.[39]

Fénelon's method of instruction for children was new for its time. He believed childhood education must combine concern for health, hygiene, a balanced diet, play, and giving children a love of reading through well-illustrated books filled with stories of adventure. Only through this balanced regimen would the mind of a child grow to love learning. The prince lived simply like a child, shielded from the excesses of the French court. He spent only four hours a day at his lessons. Fénelon believed that a child learned more in conversation and example than behind a desk.

Latin was the basis of the Duke of Burgundy's education, but he was not required to memorize Cicero's orations. Instead, Fénelon wrote amusing sentences for him to paraphrase. The child wrote interesting essays, translated anecdotes and fables. Fénelon successfully made the distinction between foreign language instruction for a child, and instruction for an adult. Indeed, much of his success as a tutor rested upon Fénelon's development of an actual early childhood curriculum that embraced the prince's entire education. This included instruction in geography, history and religion. These teaching methods were probably his greatest contribution to education and far overshadows his instruction of the Duke of Burgundy.

Mann in <u>Princes In France</u> tells us that Fénelon made a personal appeal to his pupil's loyalty and made him sign pledges of honor to be well behaved.

I promise to M. l'abbé de Fénelon, on the faith of a prince, to obey him, and if I fail to do so, I submit to any sort of punishment and disgrace. Made at Versailles, 20th of November, 1689.

Signed Louis[40]

One of Fénelon's more important lessons was teaching the prince humility and respect for moral authority. This represents a strong contrast to most royal education programs. Mann in _Princes In France_ relates that one day the princely pupil rebelled against his tutor. "No, sir, No! I will not be ordered about. I know your place, and who I am!" Fénelon left the room without a word. The next day he told the prince sadly,

Do you remember saying yesterday that you know my place, and yours? It is my duty to inform you that you know neither. You imagine yourself above me; perhaps the servants have told you so; I have no hesitation in saying that I stand far above you in learning and experience. . . . You think me happy to be your tutor. You deceive yourself. I accepted the post in obedience to the King and Monseigneur; not at all for the doubtful pleasure of instructing you. So that you may be undeceived, I am taking you to His Majesty to beg him to find you another tutor, whom I pray may be more successful.[41]

The child was thunderstruck. He spent two whole days pleading amidst a flood of tears for forgiveness. Only when Fenelon felt convinced of the child's repentance did he yield.

Of all the princes who were privately educated, the Duke of Burgundy undoubtedly received the least fawning flattery from his royal tutor. Instead, Fénelon substituted the required moral lessons of childhood and adolescence. From being a bad-tempered royal pupil, the prince became pleasant, affable, humble, austere and had no interest in the court life at Versailles.  (Louis XIV began to complain that Fénelon had turned his grandson into a monk!)  A deep friendship persisted between them for life.

Unfortunately for France, after only eight years at the turbulent royal court, Fénelon was banished from the side of his pupil over a theological dispute (1697).  We will never know the quality of kingship that this young prince would have provided France after his successful relationship with Fénelon. Louis XIV's grandson died (1712) one year after the burial of his son, Monseigneur (1711).  The Duke of Burgundy's own son became Louis XV in 1715 at age five.  The friendship between Fénelon and the Duke in some ways was strikingly similar to Cheke and Edward VI.  We can only speculate to what extent their kingships would have been enhanced by their tutorial education.[42]

At the French Court humanist tradition did not neglect the education of women.  The influential courts of Renaissance Italy brought Francis I to first recognize the possibility of applying the classic ideal for the education of women.  Francis I's sister, Marguerite, later Queen of Navarre (1492-1549), received a brilliant if not profound education.  She studied Latin and was tutored in Greek and Hebrew by the Venetian, Paul Paradis (Canossa).[43]

Mary Stuart, later Queen of Scots (1642-1687), was largely educated at this same court under her guardian, Cardinal Lorraine.  As one of the great humanists of his time, this cardinal favored Spanish-Italian Renaissance humanism at the royal court. Mary Stuart's theme book from her tutoring has been preserved and also provides evidence of this same humanistic education at the French court.  Both the form and content of this book have a striking similarity to the tutoring at the English court under Vives and Ascham.  Mary was proficient in Latin, French and even her native Scots.[44]

By the seventeenth century in France the royal court's support of the education of women influenced the nobility to instruct their daughters at home using a governess or private tutor.  Fénelon's On the Education of Girls (1687) received royal support and

133

was widely read throughout French society.  While not a great philosophical work, it marked a turning point in educational development, both for the education of girls and in general educational thought.  The very fact a book was written on the education of women this long after the Renaissance was of great significance for the time.  Society had supported a general belief that even better-class girls should be left uneducated or narrowly trained in convents.

Fénelon did not advocate scholarship for women, but believed that ignorance in women leads to vanity and frivolity that is harmful to both mind and body. The cure for these conditions was "solid learning" in subjects appropriate to their sex.  In addition to religious instruction he would tutor women in reading, writing, arithmetic, music, art and practical household matters.  While this curriculum was not very enlightened, it responded to the Renaissance humanistic tradition of preparing people for their station in life.  This was a new idea that initiated a movement for better feminine education among the French upper classes.  To achieve his ends, Fénelon recommended home tutoring rather than convent education.

Fénelon's general educational philosophy is of equal if not greater importance than his views on women.  A concept of early childhood education rested on Fénelon's idea that children begin to learn even before they can speak.  Their education fundamentally depends upon the environment and the behavior of people around them.  Young children should not receive strenuous instruction, or become over stimulated.  They should receive plain and precise answers to their questions, and encouragement to be inquisitive.  As far as possible, instruction should be indirect.  Teaching Latin was useless.  The fewer formal lessons the better.

I have seen various children learning to read at their play.  All that had to be done was to tell them diverting stories, taken from a book in their presence, and lead them to master the letters without knowing it.  After that they are eager to go to the source of this pleasure for

134

themselves.[45]

This was perhaps an oversimplification but represented an early statement of modern childhood learning theory.

In his general application of ideas to early childhood education, Fénelon insists on the great value of story-telling as a foundation for learning. In practice, Fénelon used this method extensively with the Duke of Burgundy. During his tenure as the prince's tutor he composed book after book as children's literature. The Fables were morality tales on personal conduct. Historical biographies in the Dialogues of the Dead created an interest in general history. Even a children's version of More's Utopia was written by Fénelon in his Telemachus (1699) as a fable on politics and government. Boyd and King believe that Fénelon's theory of educative play "has never been more completely put into practical form than in these books." This French tutor anticipated a publicly accepted children's literature by almost 150 years.[46]

The influence of royal tutors was felt throughout European society. They helped not only to popularize the use of tutors, but also led the way to the development of modern education principles by a foremost theorist of the period, John Locke.

## 5.  JOHN LOCKE--THE MODEL TUTOR

By the late seventeenth century in England and France a private tutor was a common member of the household among the landed aristocracy, gentry and rising mercantile families. A typical tutor was often a young man fresh from the university. He received an annual salary of around twenty pounds, a private room and dined with the family. He also provided intellectual conversation for the father while acting as the children's tutor. Lawson and Silver tell us that "some tutors of experience wrote about the 'breeding up' of gentlemen, advocating private education at home. . . rather than public

135

education. . . ."[47]   Aries agrees that "in the seventeenth century the advantages of a college education were disputed and many people held that education at home under a tutor was preferable."[48]

One such person was Obadiah Walker, a prominent Oxford don.   After serving as a private tutor he wrote Of Education, Especially of Young Gentlemen (1673).   The influence of "courtesy education" continued in his recommendation of traditional studies, but also virtue, urbanity and good breeding.[49]   But it was left to John Locke's Some Thoughts Concerning Education (1693) to draw on his predecessors and present a dynamic philosophy of tutoring and its attributes that still endures to our time.

Peter Gay rightly has named John Locke "the father of the Enlightenment."[50]   Locke's Essay Concerning Human Understanding (1689) laid the psychological ground-work for modern educational theory.[51]   As a humanist, Locke also favored private domestic education because of the "miserable condition of the public schools of his time . . . ."[52] In his general distrust of the existing schools he followed other social realists who advocated the tutorial system as the best agency for the education of the young.   To a modern audience, Locke's most interesting statement about tutoring was that he was writing not just for the children of the upper class. He believed that many of these educational principles applied to all children.[53]   A brief review of Locke's life reveals why Locke held private tutoring in such high esteem.

John Locke was born in 1632 at a little village in Somerset, England.   His father was an attorney and clerk to the county justice of the peace.   Locke was probably taught only at home by tutors.   At age fifteen he went to the public school, Westminster, and entered the second form.   The headmaster of Westminster was such an excessive disciplinarian that the boys called him "Richard Birch-hard."[54]   This experience undoubtedly influenced Locke's later attitudes toward the public school.   By 1652 Locke attended Christ Church, Oxford.   He was admitted to the M.A. by 1658.   Locke served as a university tutor ministering to the needs of ten pupils, ages 13-18. He kept an account book of this time that gives us a vivid picture of the tutor. From 1658 to 1664 Locke was a distinguished lecturer in Greek and ultimately received high administrative office under the Dean of Christ Church.

In 1665 an event occurred that dramatically altered Locke's work, and began his long career as a professional tutor. From November of that year to February 1666, Locke traveled to the continent as the secretary of Sir Walter Vane on a diplomatic mission to the Elector of Brandenburg at Cleves. It was not unusual for Oxford dons to assist in a government embassy, as the Crown had deep ties with Oxford. Upon returning to the university, Locke met Anthony Ashley Cooper, Lord Ashley, beginning a long friendship. He invited Locke to live at his London home as medical advisor and tutor to his fifteen-year-old son, Anthony, a feeble, small-boned boy. We will never know Locke's true reasons for accepting this new role, but at age thirty-five, he left behind his life as an Oxford don.[55] From 1666 until his death in 1704, John Locke was known and active in public affairs. He began a long career as a tutor that was distinguished by his writing on that topic and a considerable variety of other subjects.

Moving to London, Locke looked after Anthony's educational well-being. Locke was also entrusted by Lord Ashley in finding his son a wife since "being already so good a judge of men, [Lord Ashley] . . . doubted not of his equal judgement of women."[56] Three years later Anthony married Lady Dorothy Manners, from the Midlands, who Locke had found "qualified" in every respect. Locke never revealed what those "qualities" were and how he tested them. However, their tutoring relationship did not end. Years later Locke, then a political exile in France, sent to England classical grammars and French educational literature to guide the son of his student, now father to the third earl. When Lord Ashley died his grandson, Locke's "foster son," continued Locke's tutoring services for his own children. His son later wrote to Locke thanking him for having "dealt with me so like a friend in every strictest relation."[57] This typified the relation-

137

ship of tutor to student that remained prevalent in this era and continued into the nineteenth century. Rousseau took up the same theme in Emile (1762).[58]

In 1675, Locke, after graduating with a Bachelor of Medicine from Oxford, fled to Holland and France for political reasons. Later that year Locke was asked by Shaftesbury and his friend, Sir John Banks, to tutor Banks' son, Caleb, for four or five months. Instead, Locke taught Caleb for over a year. In Paris the boy saw Versailles and the Louvre; attended plays and operas; and visited the salons. The teaching situation resembled Oxford, except for the mobile tutorials. They returned to England in 1679. During this time period Locke wrote as advice to a friend on bringing up his son, Some Thoughts Concerning Education.[59]

Locke had been Oxford don, pediatrician, tutor, and travelling tutor on the "Grand Tour." Later in life he lived chiefly at the home of his friend, Francis Cudworth Masham at Oates, in Essex. There Locke tutored the grandson of his host. He died at Oates, 27 October, 1704.[60]

There can be no doubt that Locke's own educational experiences as a student and tutor influenced his writing on education. His "general method of education" stressed right habits formed early in life. The discipline of children was guided by the twin principles of building self-esteem and identifying personal dishonor with misdeeds. These were tempered by good parental example, rather than colorless and hardly-remembered rules. No excessive corporal punishment was allowed. Let children play and be what they are--children. Educational programs needed to be adapted to the child, not the other way round. Most of all, in planning to teach a child, a tutor took into account his natural and acquired talents, weaknesses and dislikes. Locke prescribed a middle-class gentry son's education to include: Roman and English history, geography, chronology, laws and statutes, parliamentary law and practices, and scripture.

Three significant educational principles emerge as a philosophical bridge between Essay Concerning

Human Understanding (1689) and Some Thoughts Concerning Education (1693). Locke was convinced that only through early childhood education can we establish "firm habits" of the mind and body. Also, the "association of ideas" must become a primary focus in any educational plan. Ideas combine to produce new thoughts resulting from each child's own educational strengths, interests and inclinations. Locke's insight was that forced book learning at school produced "pain," so that "ideas of books" in general becomes an aversion, since children join these ideas together. Finally, Locke advocated learning a foreign language including grammar, rules and spoken fluency. This continued the humanist's tradition of foreign language study.

An earlier work, The Conduct of Understanding (1679) best illuminated Locke's ideals as a tutor.[61] Locke unified his principles of education and philosophy into their application for tutoring a child. Overlearning is essential. "It is practice alone that brings the powers of the mind . . . to their perfection."[62] Love of books must be given carefully to every child.

> The sure and only way to get true knowledge is to form in our minds clear settled notions of things, with names annexed to those determined ideas. . . . It is in the perception of these [habits], and respect that ideas have one to another, that real knowledge consists.[63]

Locke did not see education as just loading the brain with trivial facts. Instead, he saw it as a process, a formation of character, a building of habits of both mind and body. The tutor's aim was to develop the child's potentiality. This would fit a child for his life's work. Tutorial education prepared the child's mental, moral and physical capabilities. The classic Greek tutors also had sought the same goal. This concept was renewed by Locke's tutorial education and became a deliberate pursuit of a living ideal human character, "his tutor should remember, that his business is not so much to teach him all that is knowable, as to raise in him a love and esteem of knowledge."[64]

In instructing his friends on how to select an instructor, Locke listed a tutor's most esteemed qualities as "sobriety, temperance, tenderness, diligence and discretion. . . . The great difficulty will be where to find a proper person."[65] Since younger persons do not qualify as able tutors, and older, more experienced tutors turn down the position,

> You must therefore look out early and inquire everywhere, for the world has people of all sorts . . . spare no care nor cost to get such a one [tutor] . . . if you get a good one, you will never repent the charge but will always have the satisfaction to think it is the best money ever spent.[66]

A sober scholarly tutor needed to be well-bred, understanding society, its manners and ways. "The tutor should know the world well, the ways, the humors, the follies, the cheats, the faults of the age he is fallen into and particularly of the country he lives in."[67] A tutor needs to help his pupil discern what is in a man's heart, not just the smile on his face.

> "to make . . . a true judgement of men . . . . He will help him pass . . . by safe and insensible degrees . . . from a boy to a man; which is the most hazardous step in all the whole course of life . . . [show] him the world as it really is. . . . He should by degrees be informed of the vices in fashion and warned of the . . . designs of those who will . . . corrupt him.[68]

The ultimate great work of a tutor is to teach good habits, principles of virtue, and wisdom, to give the child a "view of mankind." The tutor will have him learn to love what is "praiseworthy." During these years of instruction the tutor will give the child "vigor, activity, and industry." This practical education is essential, "for too often education fits the person for the university and not the world." Locke believed that unless a tutor is accomplished in all these things he will not be a good teacher. "He will never be able to set another right in the knowledge of the world..who is a novice in them himself."[69]

Locke considered knowledge of good an insufficient motive for children, unless a child also has been systematically guided and trained for many years. Here lies the importance of education by a good tutor. Locke's Education tells us how the tutor and family should work with all the features of human nature, guiding and training, harnessing the passions and emotions, and using them to form the child into a moral being. Locke saw the process of education from man to moral man. The tutor's final goal was to bring into existence through education a responsible self-conscious person.

Locke also recognized the need to allow for natural differences from child to child. But a free responsible person must also be rule-following, where rules measure both rationality and virtue. By giving children reasons for what we ask them to do, we address them as persons, not objects. The tutor's main goal was to guide the child to the age of reason and to personhood. The education process was completed only when the student as an adult became well-suited to living with others and accepted society's mores. (But when asked to bend his moral sense too far, he would fight back to correct a social evil.)

John Locke acted as the final synthesizer for the educational tradition of the Renaissance/ Reformation humanists. Rousseau and other Enlightenment philosophes expanded upon his concept of a child-centered education, but it was John Locke who first popularized this modern educational ideal. As the model tutor his thinking influenced an age and has endured to our own time.[70]

## Endnotes

1.  Andrew White Tuer, <u>History of the Horn-Book</u>, 2
    vols. (London: Leadenhall Press, 1896);
    Elizabeth Godfrey, <u>Home Life Under the Stuarts</u>
    (London: St. Paul, 1925), 46-49, 66-75, 11, 15,
    31, 32; James L. Axtell, <u>The Educational</u>
    <u>Writings of John Locke</u> (Cambridge: Cambridge
    University Press, 1968), 19; Ibid., 35.

2.  Pollock, <u>Forgotten</u>, 241-244; Nicholas Byfield,
    <u>Principles Or The Patterns Of Wholesome Words</u>,
    2nd ed. (London: S. Man, 1622); Mathurin
    Cordier, <u>Corderius Dialogues</u>, trans. John
    Bonsley The Elder (London: Anne Griffin, 1636),
    Johann Amos Comenius, <u>The Gates of Languages</u>
    <u>Unlocked</u> (London: Durgarte, 1650; Johann Amos
    Comenius, <u>The Orbis Pictus of John Amos Comenius</u>
    (Syracuse, New York: C.W. Bardeen, 1887);
    Gladys Scott Thomson, <u>Life In A Noble Household</u>
    <u>1641-1700</u> (London: Jonathan Cape, 1937), 72-
    111.

3.  Henry Peacham, <u>The Complete Gentlemen</u> (Ithaca:
    Cornell University Press, 1962), XI-XX.

4.  Ibid.

5.  Ibid.

6.  Ibid.

7.  Ibid.

8.  Henry Peacham, <u>The Complete Gentlemen</u> (Ithaca:
    Cornell University Press, 1962), XI-XX;
    Willystine Goodsell, <u>A History of Marriage and</u>
    <u>the Family</u> (New York: Macmillan, 1934), 348;
    Godfrey, <u>Home Life</u>, 40-41.

9.  Gertrude Noyes, <u>Bibliography of Courtesy and</u>
    <u>Conduct Books in Seventeenth Century England</u>
    (New Haven, Conn.: The Tuttle, Morehouse and

Taylor Company, 1937).

10. Noyes classified 477 books: One was from the fifteenth century, twenty-five were from the sixteenth century, one hundred were translations into English from Latin, Greek, Italian, Spanish, Portuguese and French works; Noyes, _Courtesy Books_, 5-6.

11. Ibid., 1, 3-4, 7-9, 27, 108-109.

12. Morris Marples, _Princes in the Making_ (London: Faber and Faber, 1965), 76.

13. David Williamson, _Debretts Kings and Queens of Britain_ (Topsfield, Massachusetts: Salem House Publishers, 1986), 134-152; Plumb, _Royal_, 94-144; Marples, _Princes_, 66-93.

14. Louis Untermeyer, _Lives of the Poets_ (New York: Simon and Schuster, 1959), 170-171, 222, 228-229; Paul Harvey, _The Oxford Companion To English Literature_ (Oxford: The Clarendon Press, 1955), 630-631; Richard Lassels, _The Voyage of Italy_, (Paris: V. du Moutier, 1670); Thomson, _Household_, 96-110; Godfrey, _Home Life_, 66-75; Paul Beale, ed. _Dictionary of Slang and Unconventional English_, 8th ed., s.v. bear-leader; Christopher Hibbert, _The Grand Tour_ (New York: G.P. Putnam and Sons, 1969), 13.

15. Godfrey, _Home Life_, 221; Kamm, _Hope Deferred_, 52-72; Howe, _Governesses_, 36-37.

16. Hannah Woolley, _The Gentlewomen's Companion_ (London: A. Maxwell, 1675); Howe, _Galaxy_, 36-39.

17. Howe, _Galaxy_, 36-39.

18. Ibid.

19. Bathshua Makin, _An Essay To Review the Ancient Education of Gentlewomen In Religion, Manners, Arts and Tongues_ (London: J.D. and Thomas Parkhurst, 1673); Reynolds, _Learned Lady_, 277-278; Uglow, _Women's Biography_, 301.

20.  Godfrey, <u>Home Life</u>, 101.

21.  Howe, <u>Galaxy</u>, 36-39; Godfrey, <u>Home Life</u>, 100-107, 220-221.

22.  Guillaume Budé, <u>De L' Institution du Prince</u> (Troyee:    Imprimé à l'Amuour Abtaye Dudict Seigneur,   Par   Maistre   Nicole   Paris,   1547); Woodward, <u>Studies In Education</u>, 130-135.

23.  Jacopo Sadoleto <u>De Liberis Recte Instituendis</u>, trans. Campagnac and Forbes (London:    Oxford University Press, 1916); Woodward, <u>Studies In Education</u>, 167-179.

24.  Francis Bacon, <u>The Works of Francis Bacon</u>, ed. Spedding, Ellis, Heath, 14 vols. (Oxford:    1857-74); Francis Bacon, "Novum Organum" in <u>Man and the Universe:    The Philosophers of Science</u>, ed Commins and Linscott (New York:    Random House, 1947),   71-154; René  Descartes,  "Discourse  on Method" in <u>Man and the Universe:    The Philosophers of Science</u>, ed. Commins and Linscott, (New York:     Random  House,   1947),   155-216;   Elmer Harrison   Wilds,   <u>The   Foundation   of   Modern Education</u> (New   York:     Rinehart   and   Company, 1936), 329-332.

25.  Michel De Montaigne, <u>Essays</u>, 3 vols. (New York: E.P. Dutton, 1935), vol. I, 165-354, vol. II, 48-385, vol. III, 24-368.

26.  Ibid.

27.  Ibid.

28.  Michel  De  Montaigne,  <u>Diary  of  a  Journey  to Italy</u>,  trans.  Trechtmann  (New  York:     E.P. Dutton, 1929), 166-169; Wilds, <u>Modern Education</u>, 210-211.

29.  Aries, <u>Childhood</u>, 194.

30.  Ibid.

31.  Aries,   <u>Childhood</u>,   196-197;   Hilaire   Belloc, <u>Richelieu</u> (London:  Lippincott, 1929), 151-152.

32. H.C. Barnard, <u>The French Tradition In Education</u> (Cambridge: Cambridge University Press, 1922), 115-118.

33. Francois de La Mothe le Vayer, <u>De l'instruction de Monseigneur le Dauphin, a monseigneur...-cardinal duc de Richelieu</u> (Paris: Chez Sebastien Cramorsy, 1640); Hardouin De Perefixe de Abbé a Sablonceau, <u>Institutio Principus</u> (Paris: 1647).

34. Francois de La Mothe le Vayer, <u>Oeuvres Nowvelle Edition</u>, 15 vols. (Paris: J. Grugnard, 1664).

35. Barnard, <u>French Education</u>, 120-122.

36. Jacques Bénigne Bossuet, <u>Oeuvres Oratoires,</u> ed. Lebarq (Paris: 1896); Jacques Bénigne Bossuet, <u>Discours sur l' Histoire Universelle à Monseigneur le Dauphin</u> (Paris: Librairie Larousse, n.d.).

37. Mrs. Horace Mann, trans. "Princes In France-Their Education and Teachers," from <u>Compayré Historie Critique de l' Education</u>, in <u>The American Journal of Education</u>, ed. Henry Barnard, 30 (1880) 465-479; Nancy Mitford, <u>The Sun King</u> (London: Hamish Hamilton, 1966), 69-81.

38. Francois Fénelon, <u>The Education of Girls</u>, trans. Lupton (Boston: Ginn and Company, 1891), iii-iv.

39. Francois Fénelon, <u>Twenty-Seven Moral Tales and Fables, French and English</u> (London: J. Wilcox, 1729).

40. Mann, <u>Princes In France</u>, 484.

41. Lucy Norton, <u>First Lady of Versailles</u> (New York: J.B. Lippincott Company, 1978), 90-91; Mann, <u>Princes In France</u>, 489-490.

42. Louis XV, in his youth, received only a superficial education. Mann, <u>Princes In France</u>, 480-490; John E. Wise, <u>The History of Education</u> (New

York:    Sheed and Ward, 1964), 236-237; William Boyd and Edmund J. King, <u>The History of Western Education</u> (Toronto:    Barnes and Noble, 1980), 264-268; Norton, <u>Versailles</u>, 71-99.

43.  Siegneur de Brantôme, <u>Illustrious Dames at the Court of the Valois Kings</u>, trans. Wormley (New York:    1898), 7; C.J. Blaisdell, "Marguerite de Navarre and Her Circle" in <u>Female Scholars</u>, ed. J.R. Brink (Montreal:    Eden Press, 1980), 36-51.

44.  Mary Stuart, <u>Latin Themes of Mary Stuart, Queen of Scots</u>, ed. Montaiglon (London:    Warton Club, No. 3: 1855); Cannon, <u>Education</u>, 124-146.

45.  Fénelon, <u>The Education of Girls</u>, 101.

46.  Francois Fénelon, <u>The Education of Girls</u>, trans. Lupton (Boston:    Ginn and Company, 1891), iii-iv,   1-7,   13-118;   Francois   Fénelon,   <u>The Adventures of Telemachus, the Son of Ulysses</u> (Philadelphia:    G. Decombaz, 1797); Francois Fénelon, <u>Dialogues of the Dead</u> (Glasgow:    R. & A. Foulis, 1754); Barnard, <u>French Education</u>, 50; Boyd and King, <u>Western Education</u>, 264-265.

47.  John Lawson, Harold Silver, <u>A Social History of Education In England</u> (London:    Methuen and Co., Ltd., 1973), 174.

48.  Aries, <u>Childhood, 369</u>.

49.  Obadiah Walker, <u>Of Education Especially of Young Gentlemen</u> (London:    H. Gellibrandfor and R. Wellington, 1699).

50.  John Locke, <u>Some Thoughts Concerning Education</u>, ed. Peter Gay (New York:    Columbia University, 1964), 1.

51.  John    Locke,    <u>Essay    Concerning    Human Understanding</u>,  2  vols.  (New  York:    Dover Publications, 1959).

52.  W. N. Hailman, <u>History of Pedagogy</u> (Cincinnati: Van Antuerp, 1874), 66-67.

53. James L. Axtell, <u>The Educational Writings of John Locke</u> (Cambridge: University Press, 1968), 52.

54. Ibid., 20, 22.

55. Ibid., 28-45.

56. Ibid., 44-46.

57. Ibid.

58. Jean-Jacques Rousseau, <u>Emile</u>, trans. Boyd (New York: Teachers College, 1962).

59. Charles W. Elliot, <u>English Philosophers</u>, <u>The Writings of John Locke</u>, vol. 37 (New York: Collier, 1910), 3, 4.

60. Elmer Harrison Wilds, <u>The Foundations of Modern Education</u> (New York: Rinehart and Co., 1936), 329-330, 332, 365; John E. Wise, <u>The History of Education</u> (New York: Sheed and Ward, 1964), 236-237; R.S. Woolhouse, <u>Locke</u> (Minneapolis: University of Minnesota Press, 1983), 1-2.

61. John Locke, <u>The Conduct of Understanding</u> (Cambridge: Cambridge University Press), 1968. He also later wrote <u>Some Thoughts Concerning Reading and Study For A Gentleman</u> (London: M. Des Maiseaux, 1720).

62. Ibid., Part IV.

63. Ibid., Part XV.

64. Locke, <u>Education</u>, 161.

65. Samuel L. Blumenfeld, <u>How To Tutor</u> (New Rochelle: Arlington House, 1973), 15-16.

66. Ibid.

67. Elliot, <u>Philosophers</u>, 78-84.

68. Ibid., 79-80.

69. Ibid.

70. Axtell, _Locke_, 53-58; John W. Yolton, _Locke_ (Oxford:  Basil Blackwell, 1985), 71-72.

CHAPTER 5

TUTORS OF THE ENLIGHTENMENT
(1700-1800)


1. ENGLAND


At the beginning of the eighteenth century in Western Europe, there were growing clusters of intelligent, educated professionals and businessmen. They continued to expand their areas of knowledge and in general supported the humanist education ideal. This group read newspapers, books, magazines, pamphlets and essays. Most knew more than a little about the writings of the philosophes. They were confident about further social progress. In short, these men and women wanted change and were ready to use any legitimate means to free society from past ignorance. They perceived tutoring as one such means to educate their families and prepare a generation for a more enlightened age.

Because of these activities, the eighteenth century was possibly the most interesting period in English educational development. It was not only a period that produced brilliant philosophic works as in the seventeenth century, but it also witnessed the actual formulation of modern education principles. England, at the start of the century, was a small island with a sparse population estimated at five to nine million persons. Even after schools had been widely established, education at home continued to increase among both the middle and upper classes. Affluent families used a residential tutor to instruct their sons in the classics. The education of young children and girls was supervised by a governess. They were assisted in specific subjects by a visiting tutor. Fathers of more modest means frequently hired traveling tutors, who were often well-known school proprietors, supplementing their income as tutors.[1]

Families used tutors to prepare their sons for school. Others employed them as a substitute for all schooling right up to entrance at the university. Some even had their sons educated entirely at home, thus dispensing with both the school and university. The cultural resources of many aristocratic homes, with their libraries and collections of art and curiosities, probably exceeded the resources of most schools and colleges of the period.[2]

N. Hans, in a review of educational trends in eighteenth century England, provides statistical evidence of the frequent use of tutors for post-primary education. Hans conducted a highly detailed study by selecting thirty-five hundred men born between 1685-1785 from the _Dictionary of National Biography_. However, not all men were automatically included who had been born during that time period. Hans excluded those whom by his definition had only vocational training, and criminals, freaks of all kinds, or men whose antecedents are unknown.[3]

This study reveals that in preparation for the university "the role of home and private tutors was more important than any group of schools."[4] We see that nine hundred sixty seven out of thirty-five hundred men were educated at home in preparation for the universities. This means that 27.62 percent of the Englishmen in his study did not attend any secondary schools, nor probably any primary institution. The nine hundred sixty seven scholars educated at home by their tutors exceeded those enrolled in the nine "great English public schools" (780); the next twenty leading English grammar schools (209); the remaining one hundred fifty English grammar schools (385); the dissenting English academies (212); or the private academies and schools (314).[5] In the eighteenth century domestic education became a dominating teaching practice, not only among the titled aristocracy, but also among the landed gentry, and reached into the professional classes as well.[6]

These conclusions are further substantiated by Hans showing that among the peerage one child in four was educated at home; among the gentry one in three;

for the clergy one in four; and for all other professions one in five. In all of Great Britain, of the three thousand children of various social origins studied, eight hundred fifty five or 28.5 percent were educated at home.[7] The aristocracy and gentry had the financial means to hire a good classical scholar to tutor their sons at home. The city merchants followed this social trend and often retained private tutors at their homes. Among the clergy their inability to maintain their sons at expensive private schools required them to tutor their own sons for the university. To some extent all these boys were educated at home because many parents did not trust the schools.[8]

Hans also completed comparisons of the educational careers and social origins of 680 scientists of the period. The number of scientists tutored at home held steady with each passing generation and increased from the seventeenth to the eighteenth century.[9]

Taking into account the observation by Lawson and Silver that some of the information found in the Hans study is "unreliable in detail," Hans still demonstrates that home tutoring remained a significant social force for that time period. He also substantiates the surprising widespread use of tutors by many different social groups throughout British society.[10]

An additional biographical review of prominent period writers disclosed the frequent use of domestic education by their families. James Boswell, William Blake, Samuel Coleridge, Oliver Goldsmith, and Sir Walter Scott, came from upper or middle class families that used home education as an alternative for school attendance.[11] This was also true at times among the lower classes. A Sussex shepherd John Dudeney, who was born at Rottingdean in 1782, was tutored by his parents to read, write and learn arithmetic. This early training gave him a taste for reading. He continued in his profession until he became a head shepherd at Rottingdean. John continued his studies with a local vicar and his aunt. He even studied Hebrew scriptures in the original. By 1804 he gave up shepherding and opened a school at Lewes.[12]

Why did private tutors become a socially acceptable alternative to the eighteenth century "public school?" The writings of Locke, Rousseau, Joseph Priestly, Maria Edgeworth, William Jones, Hester Chapone, David Williams, Mary Wollstonecraft and others, were read widely by families who had the financial means to educate their children. Almost all these philosophes advocated domestic education. Especially popular were letters of tutors to their former pupils on various aspects of education. Among the best known were Letters of A Tutor to His Pupils (1775) by William Jones and Hester Chapone's, Letters On The Improvement of the Mind Addressed To a Young Lady (1774). Locke's Some Thoughts Concerning Education (1693) influenced David Williams in his Treatise on Education (1774) and his Lectures on Education (1789) both of which defended home education against school training.[13]

This great disenchantment with a "public" education was also based on the inadequacy of the schools themselves. Henry Fielding, an Etonian, remarked that, "Public schools are the nurseries of all vice and immortality."[14] The rote Latin curriculum was too narrow and long outmoded. This frequently was accompanied by a brutal and disorderly environment of beatings, bad food and unqualified, often drunken masters. This included the so-called "fagging system" with the elder boys morally corrupting and brutally beating the younger children. In many private schools great cruelty was inflicted on helpless children. Some specialized in using a horrible weapon for discipline called a "ferule." This was a flat piece of wood widened at the end into a shape like a pear with a round hole in the middle. A stroke from this would raise a painful blister on the hand. There were exceptions to this general "rule-of-the-rod" at some of the "great" English public schools. However, the fact that even at Eton children were sometimes kicked, flogged or starved provided parents a strong motivation to tutor their children in safety at home.[15]

When John Horne Tooke was about fourteen or fifteen years old, at Eton, in

construing a passage in a Latin author, the
Master asked him why some ordinary
construction, the rule of which was very
familiar, obtained in the passage. The
pupil replied he did not know, on which the
Master, provoked by his ignorance or
perverseness, caused him to be flogged, a
punishment which he received with perfect
sang froid and without a murmur.[16]

Charles Lamb, the famous eighteenth, early
nineteenth century writer, wrote a reminiscence of
his private school education at "Christ's Hospital,"
London (1782-1789), which provided vivid details on
the dreadful existence of many public school
students. The student's diet consisted of "scanty
mutton crage," boiled beef, "rotten-roasted," or
"milk porritch blue and tasteless," and "pease soup
coarse and choking." The headmaster woke the
youngest children in the middle of the night to
"receive the discipline of a leathern thong" for
minor offenses committed by others. For major
offenses boys were put in fetters. A second trans-
gression placed him in a "little square Bedlam"
dungeon cell. Here he remained in solitary confine-
ment day and night on a diet of bread and water. For
a third offense a student was stripped of his "blue
clothes" (school uniform) in front of all the boys in
the assembly hall, and then scourged.[17]

Remarkably, these schools flourished in the
eighteenth century. It was costly for country
squires and many others to tutor their children at
home. Other unfeeling parents disposed of unwanted
children by sending them to the notorious schools in
Yorkshire and other remote parts of England. Candos,
in his study of the English Public School, found that
not until the second half of the eighteenth century
did it become "a prevailing fashion" for members of
the nobility and gentry to send their sons to one of
the great public schools. Throughout the eighteenth
century, brutality persisted in the public and
private schools. It took another one hundred years
before the school reform movement curbed these
notorious practices at many educational institutions.[18]

Even George III's admiration of Eton did not prevent him from making extensive use of private tutors for his huge family of seven boys and six girls. Twelve were born within a space of sixteen years. For a time all were being educated simultaneously. The royal tutors at Kew organized the boys in three groups, each with a set of tutors. The girls were more spread out in age so a larger number of tutors was needed for them. These arrangements were almost like a school, except the number of tutors always outnumbered those taught.

William and George, his two sons who succeeded to the throne, were educated in the classics and became proficient in French and German. George also acquired a taste for modern English literature including Lord Byron and Jane Austen.

Hannah More, the most highly respected woman intellect of her day, prepared a treatise on the education of a future queen. Following the example of Vives and Fénelon, she wrote a two-volume work, Hints Toward Forming the Character of a Young Princess (1805), dedicated to the young Princess Charlotte. It set a precedent as the first work on royal education written by a woman for the guidance of a woman. It was curious that Hannah was never hired to tutor Princess Charlotte.

The methods emphasized in the book were practical, dealing first with curriculum: modern languages, English, history, but science was excluded as superfluous for royalty and classical languages as unnecessary for a woman. Hints' second part discussed the ideal ruler's character and the "art of reigning." It appears that all these efforts had little impact on Princess Charlotte. There may not have been a serious attempt even to apply Hannah More's principles. This underscores a continued deterioration in the importance that eighteenth century society placed on the education of women, even if they were royals.[19]

It remains difficult to make a final judgement on how widespread tutoring became as a schooling alternative. Members of the educated elite obviously had good personal experiences attending the public school and made widespread use of them. As a protective measure against child abuse, tutoring offered parents few guarantees. Some tutors were also severe with their students and beat them. Henry Fielding in <u>Tom Jones</u> described how his "notorious young gentleman" suffered at the hand of his tutor, Thwackum. Even royal children were beaten by their tutors. Over the past two hundred years (1500-1700) had not many of the tutor-philosophers repeatedly counseled these tutors not to beat their charges?

Undoubtedly, tutoring was socially popular in the eighteenth century among the educated elite of England and Europe. The sons of the clergy and other professional men, as a rule, were tutored by their own fathers. City merchants invited tutors to their homes only for daily instruction. Near university towns or prominent public schools, teachers acted in a tutorial capacity to supplement their meager income by private arrangement with parents. These different circumstances required a different type of tutor. Resident tutors were expected to be well-rounded scholars. A visiting tutor could be specialized only in one subject and shared his pupil with other tutors. The teachers were combined into groups such as classical languages, modern languages, mathematics and supporting subjects; calligraphy with arithmetic and accounts, and philosophy. Teachers of mathematics and writing masters emerged as the most clearly defined groups. They published text books and other treatises on education at home. The visiting tutors usually were concentrated in larger towns, especially London.

These same middle and upper class families continued the practice of sending their sons on the "Grand Tour." The public acceptance of educational travel was due in part to the popularity of John Locke's learning theory that knowledge comes entirely through the external senses. The mind later carefully contemplates this material acquired by the memory as a result of sensory experiences. Travel became an obligation in the quest to become an educated person. Extensive observation was a critical duty for learning. The "Grand Tour" as an educational convention had started in the last century after the restoration of the monarchy in 1660 and flourished until the advent of mass rail travel around 1825. The trip could last up to a year, or was sometimes compressed to a few weeks. Its common route included: London, Dover, Calais, Switzerland, Florence, Venice, Rome, Germany and Paris.

The boy was accompanied by a tutor or "bear-leader" to protect him from corrupting foreign influences and continue his education. The tutor instructed his charge on the local history, geography, trade, climate, customs, politics, law, art and the military. An ideal tutor also taught the boy to become conversant in French, Italian and German. However, in actual practice the realities of the "Grand Tour" fell far beneath this ideal.

Many of England's leading eighteenth century intellectuals denounced this sort of peripatetic liberal education as a useless, empty exercise. Adam Smith resigned his professorship of Moral Philosophy at the University of Glasgow to accompany the young Duke of Buccleugh. Although his own pupil profited by it, most did not. Adam Smith emphasized this in his The Wealth of Nations:

> By travelling so very young, by spending in the most frivolous dissipation the most precious years of his life, at a distance from the inspection and control of his parents and relatives, every useful habit, which the earlier parts of his education might have had some tendency to form in him, instead of being riveted and confirmed, is almost necessarily either weakened or effaced.[20]

Joining in the chorus of denunciation were, other men who had been "bear-leaders" including Thomas Hobbes, Joseph Addison and John Moore. Most of the blame they placed with the boy's tutor. Instead of intellectually mature and respectable men, many tutors were incompetent place-seekers who proved quite incapable of controlling their charges. Because of their laxity the "Grand Tour" seldom encouraged original inquiry or fresh perceptions. It taught national generalizations and supported common prejudices: French courtesy; Spanish hardiness;

Italian amorous; German clownish. However, for all of its limitations this great exodus of Englishmen abroad was in part responsible for the renewed interest in the arts that swept over eighteenth century England.[21]

Upper and middle class English families had ample opportunities to educate their children at home in both modern and classical subjects. This employment of one residential tutor or several visiting teachers was rather expensive and only people of means resorted to it. Families of humble origin used the charity schools or educated themselves (autodidacts). The number of self-taught prominent men and women was comparatively large in eighteenth century England.

Private tutors enabled many children to receive a more scientific and modern education than offered at most public schools or the universities. Even when this widespread use of tutors was combined with school attendance it never became a substitute for universal public education. The lack of educational opportunities for most children caused an appalling waste of human talent in the eighteenth century.[22]


## 2. ROUSSEAU'S EMILE


As in England, the middle and upper classes of eighteenth century France made extensive use of tutors and governesses. Montaigne, Comenius, Locke and Fénelon undoubtedly influenced Jean-Jacques Rousseau (1712-1778), the century's leading philosophe. He supported tutoring as the best means to improve early childhood education. In his Emile he used the tutor to accommodate education to the nature of the child and not the child to a predetermined system of education.[23]

Rousseau was born at Geneva. His mother died of fever a week after his birth. Rousseau had little formal schooling and was largely self-educated. However, this did not prevent him from becoming a tutor. In 1740 he was hired to educate the two sons of M. Bonnot de Mably, grand provost of Lyons.  After a short time he quit the post, claiming he did not have a patient enough temperament to become an effective tutor.

More than twenty years later Rousseau was asked to advise Mme. d' Épinay on the education of her son. Emile (1762) was written as part of their discussions.  All of Europe was stimulated by this story of Jean-Jacque, the tutor and Emile his charge.  No mere hireling, once attached to the child, the tutor remained as a teacher, confidant, play-fellow until the child reached complete maturity at age twenty-five.

Rousseau prescribed methods for the tutor that allowed the child to learn his lessons as nature presented them.  The tutor stimulated the child's innate curiosity to learn by revealing the wisdom and variety of nature.  In the child's first stage of development the tutor allowed flexibility in learning, but resists the child becoming selfish. His own natural curiosity must constantly motivate the student's learning.  Mistakes are not prevented, for that too is constructive.  An elaborate attempt was made not to stimulate the imagination which discourages intellectual development.  Only at age twelve, in the second stage of childhood, did the tutor begin formal instruction.  By this time the child will demand help to learn reading, math and science.  Herein lies the key to successful tutoring. Educational problems usually arise when children lack the motivation to learn.  Many teachers rush into subjects inappropriate to the child's age and understanding.  How can a tutor teach geography before a child knows his own city?  Some will teach history before a child understands adult motivations. Tutors try to reason with children.  Thus, children learn to argue and will think that skepticism is the same as intelligence.

The tutor's main responsibility was the development of the child's senses.  Rousseau called this tutelage "negative education."  As a child matures his natural and healthy self-esteem ("amour de soi") too often gives way to vanity or conceit ("amour-propre").  This combined with the growth of passions, particularly fear of death is fed by the imagination distorting judgment that leads to a merely human or illusionary view of the world. "Negative education" became the tutor's object lessons invented to prevent the emergence in the child's personality of uncontrollable passions and conceit.

Rousseau believed that a child must always do what he wants to do. This became the source of modern progressive education principles. But what has been lost is the rest of Rousseau's basic educational concept. While a child must always do what he wants to do, he should only want to do what the tutor wants him to do! The tutor presented object lessons in a concrete form as a teaching method to determine the will of the child without using force or causing resentment. Thus the child learned to live according to natural necessity before even understanding it.

Rousseau reasoned that questions will arise naturally. When a child becomes motivated, the tutor cannot keep him from learning. By age fifteen childhood was left behind and Jean-Jacques presented literature and history to Emile. At age twenty-two they took the "grand tour" to see the world and learn politics and economics. Upon their return, Emile at age twenty-five, had reached the final stage of development and was ready to take a productive place in society.[24]

Emile took Europe by storm and began a widespread reconsideration of the nature of childhood. Rousseau represented a reaction to Locke's earlier rationalistic theory of how children learn. Rousseau held that learning was natural. Locke saw it as a learned experience. Both agreed that the tutoring method must be based on the observations of the child's individual mental and physical development. This was influenced by information gathered through the senses in accordance with the nature of the child, his talents, prowess and peculiarities. They both denounced the classical education model of learning by rote, formulae and concept. But Locke based his learning theory on the development of reason. Rousseau looked for enlightenment through feeling and sentiment. Locke assumed the existence of the supernatural to develop reason. Rousseau, always the naturalist, aimed at cultivating man's individuality, his humanity.

Rousseau saw his tutor as offering a child a more natural education through example. This life-long companion was conceived as an ideal teacher who shaped an individual's education around the child's freedom as a person and natural growth.

Emile had a great immediate effect on eighteenth century educational thought, and subsequent educational theory and method. Rousseau's ideal tutor established three significant modern principles of teaching: individualization, growth and pupil activity. From Rousseau's "neo-humanistic" thinking came the later ideas of Pestalozzi, Herbart and Froebel in the next century. He established the modern idea that the only way to educate human beings was to stimulate the activity of their own individual powers. This naturalistic movement in education starting with the Renaissance had been curtailed during the Reformation, only to be renewed now by the "neo-humanism" of Rousseau.[25]

Locke and Rousseau used a tutoring method that combined heredity and environmental factors. They pointed the way toward a modern theory of education. Through their writing the concept of one-to-one instruction became socially popular across Europe, and influenced other continental philosophers to address this theme.

### 3. THE DEVELOPMENT OF CONTINENTAL TUTORING

During the seventeenth century in continental Europe the upper classes withdrew their children from the old grammar schools and began instructing their sons at home with tutors. Theological students were often employed since they were numerous and cheap. By the eighteenth century the term "candidatus" designated a private tutor. Fathers also tutored their children with the mother sometimes helping in a child's basic education. This was not an isolated

160

social phenomenon but practiced across central Europe. Much of the educational literature for both the eighteenth and nineteenth centuries was based largely on the concept that parents tutored their children for at least part, if not all of their education.[26]

Multiple tutors for one child seem to have been the norm rather than the exception. A contemporary of Goethe, Eberhard von Rochow, was taught by not fewer than eleven private teachers between age four and his thirteenth birthday. In fact, there were so many tutors, instructors, mentors and candidates giving private lessons in the eighteenth century, that bookstores considered them an important part of their clientele.[27]

A mixture of private teachers and schooling at alternative time periods became a typical practice during the eighteenth century. An example was the education of a German boy born in 1788 whose father was a merchant. At age nine he traveled with his father on a business trip to France. The child was tutored for a time by a family friend in Le Havre. Returning home, the boy attended a private school for the next four years. He then traveled with his parents to England and was left with a tutor to learn the language. In 1805 he started his apprenticeship to become a merchant, but soon abandoned the task. After his father's death, he entered the gymnasium in Gotha and then in Weimar. A private tutor instructed him in Latin and Greek. He lived with his teacher. As a young man he studied at the university in Goettingen, then Berlin, and became the well-known scholar, Arthur Schopenhauer.[28]

It was by no means unusual to interrupt school work, change back to private lessons or resume studies at a public school at a later date. Public instruction before the university was at best supplemental to the various forms of private education then available. German society supported the existence of these dual alternatives of private and public education. It symbolized the public mistrust of institutionalized education. The quality of public education in Germany was as low as elsewhere in Europe. Parents also feared that education lost its substance when delegated to an impersonal institution within a functionalistic school system, where the lectures often formed the sole basis of instruction.[29]

The German concept of education in the eighteenth century was thought of as learning from, and relating to, one man. This remained the case even within a school. A student's relationship to his master was of far greater consequence than to an institution. Many students lived in the house of the master and quite often also worked with his family. Work and instruction were integrated as a unit. Fertig believes that this idea is found in Pestalozzi's later concept of "Wohnstubenerziehung" (living room education). In the nineteenth century this same concept expressed as "domestic education" or "fireside education" in England, France and America had great popularity in educational literature written for parents.[30]

August Hermann Niemeyer's <u>Principles of Teaching For Parents, Tutors and Teachers</u> (1796) was the leading German work on the pedagogy of tutoring. Written for parents and tutors, Niemeyer saw the teacher as a father-tutor. He suggested the best preparation for becoming a private tutor, and its beneficial status in German society. <u>Principles of Teaching</u> also gave general guidelines on educational philosophy, the content of lessons and advice to tutors on the diverse problems found when teaching a child at home.[31]

Another more influential voice on tutoring and schooling in the late eighteenth and early nineteenth centuries was Johann Friedrich Herbart (1776-1841). Born in Oldenburg, he was taught by a private tutor before he entered a <u>Lateinschule</u> for his secondary education. After Herbart graduated from the University of Jena, he tutored the three sons of Herr von Steiger, Ludwig, Karl and Rudolf in Bern, Switzerland for several years. Here he came under the influence of Johann Heinrich Pestalozzi (1746-1827), the Swiss reform educator. By 1805 he was appointed professor of philosophy at the University of Göttingen (1809) and later Königsberg (1833).

Fertig believes that Herbart has been misunderstood by many who claim he considered public
education as the criterion of all education. The
beginnings of his educational philosophy are revealed
in five surviving letters to his father reporting on
his tutorial work as a young teacher in Bern.
Herbart believed that instruction must arouse the
pupil's attention by using "a many-sided interest to
intertwine the pupil's interest with the teacher's
own, by mutual study of the same subject."[32]

Herbart viewed education as more of a personal
private experience rather than a public function.

> The teacher, as tutor to two or three
> pupils, creates his own school. To him
> who hears the true artist's call . . .
> if he would find what is best suited to his
> pupils. . . . The home, with all its
> relationships and customs, must become
> infinitely valuable to him. . . . This
> begins the education of the true teacher.[33]

Later, Herbart's _Outlines of Educational
Doctrine_ (1806) explored the relationship between
public and private education. Public schools tested
only the outward side of conduct and knowledge. They
never penetrated inner life. Herbart saw the public
school's role as a concern with the sum total of
knowledge, but not the way in which the individual
related that knowledge to himself. The schooling
only supplemented the home in moral education, which
remained essentially a home task. Since so much of
education's success was supported by the family's
moral education,

> "as much as possible, education must be
> returned to the family. In many cases
> private tutors will be found to be
> indispensable . . . the most advanced
> instruction is the easiest of all, because
> [it is] imparted with the least departure
> from the way in which it was received."[34]

In Herbart's estimation a tutor related more
closely and accurately to his students. They
perceived whether understanding had happened, or if a

163

recycling of the material was needed to reach final student cognition. Herbart insisted that tutors can be used for both "the lowest classes in [their] gymnasium as well as the brightest."[35]

Herbart always stressed that education is an ongoing interaction between the teacher and pupil so the ratio of teacher to students must be small. About 1811 he established his own seminary to prepare teachers, and quite logically used a one-to-one instructional ratio. This was in sharp contrast to the new reform pedagogy that advocated preparation of young men to work as teachers in a "public school" classroom, and not to work as a private tutor.

Herbart opposed massing children together at an early age. Fertig in The Tutors tells us that in 1810 Herbart spoke before the Deutsche Gesellschaft "About Education As A Joint Venture With The State."

> Each individual needs his own education. That is why a school cannot work like a factory, but must consider each child . . . because of the unfavorable ratio schools are only a makeshift solution that separate instruction from education. In many ways the "State" serves its own self-interest in public education and cannot be entrusted with our youth. Instead we must seek the best man in education (translator's note: Herbart refers to a Erziehungskuenstler, "a genius in education.")

> A teacher receives his real schooling through working as a private tutor for one or two boys of the same age. . . . Schools do not expand, but narrow the mission of education. They make real communication with each individual impossible . . . . The curriculum prescribes a few subjects for the teacher's lectures. It is impossible for the instructor to teach, individualize his instruction, give children close personal guidance, and keep order in a big class.[36]

Herbart speculated on an ideal teaching position that enabled a tutor to use all his knowledge without curriculum restrictions and school regulations. He saw this ideal teacher as a mediator in the community between family and state. The teacher was the point of reference concerning education. Just as you called a doctor to the house, a teacher was consulted for advice in educational matters. He worked in the community as a "free floater" paid by the families employing his services. This teacher was able to recommend the best educational possibilities and even schools for certain pupils. Several families could join together to hire a teacher, but leave him freedom of instruction. Herbart thought it was even better for a teacher to unite families that shared the same educational concerns and value system. This tutor cannot teach all subjects, leaving that task to the schools, but can use his time for student dialogues and supervision of studies. The tutor also decided a student's course of study in school. This meant that the public school cannot insist on a prescribed program for every student.[37]

Herbart hoped for an interaction between families and teachers that provided the combined benefits of private and public education. His educational philosophy was directed at the educated minority. From this privileged base, Herbart thought, education will spread in the cities and country into the lives of common people.

The professional pressure to support the prevailing idea of public education in early nineteenth century Germany was too great even for Herbart to resist. In 1831 he finally gave in to the "new regulations."[38]

Herbart's urgent appeal for small study groups, Fertig tells us, "sounded like a farewell song for a dying era."[39] Over the eighteenth and nineteenth centuries the propagation of the German state school assured that the school teacher superseded the private tutor, and the common student the "disciple." Herbart was portrayed as a public school pedagogue, rather than the best example of Germany's contribution toward a unified tutoring philosophy. His philosophy of education was a clear linkage in the development of a theory derived from earlier tutorial concepts. Herbart was representative of eighteenth century educational theorists who struggled to reconcile individual instruction with the rise of general education in European society.

## 4. TUTORS AND THEIR PUPILS

What was the influence of these educational theorists on some of the most influential children in Europe? Madame de Roucoulles, a Normandy French Protestant, was Frederick the Great's (1712-1786) tutor from birth until age seven. He was fond of her and called her "cher maman" (dear mamma). She taught him honor, clearness, truth of word and to have a dignified bearing. Frederick learned French; to speak and more importantly, to think in French. It became his second mother tongue. He also learned to read. Carlyle in his <u>History of Frederick II</u> tells us his tutor lamented that "he did not, now or afterwards, ever learn to spell. He spells indeed dreadfully ill. . . ."[40]

Jacques Duhan had the strongest formative influence of Frederick's later childhood. His father had been the secretary of Turenne, Louis XIV's Protestant general. The family immigrated to Brandenburg in 1687. Duhan educated his own son. As a soldier in the Prussian army, he was noticed by King Frederick William for extraordinary courage during a siege. The King had no idea that Duhan was also a brilliant scholar. As an anti-intellectual Frederick William would never have considered using such a tutor for his son.

After age seven Frederick had lessons in mathematics, political economy, theology, German and contemporary history from early in the morning to five in the afternoon. His father rejected a humanistic education and prohibited Latin, history before the sixteenth century, French and all the classical authors. Military science dominated the curriculum. But Duhan was unable to resist the pleadings of the young prince to teach him Latin and classical history. Though beaten by his father when these lessons were uncovered, Frederick acquired a passion for French literature, an excellent style in French prose, and a thorough grounding in history and geography. As a result he never fully mastered the German language.[41]

Duhan was a born tutor and became a surrogate father for Frederick. He remained a life-long friend of the king. Frederick, upon reaching adulthood and the throne, bore witness to his humanistic education. He rescinded, at least for a time, many of the more repressive laws of his father. His life-long friendship with Voltaire, and his court with its savants, poets, and even ballet dancers, made it appear at times that he would live up to the expectations of his tutor and the philosophes. Instead, Frederick the Great as king of Prussia regarded his enlightenment education as recreation or consolation for his true purpose in life. Duffy in Frederick the Great relates that his aide Colonel Louis Beauval observed, "His true inclinations drive him on to serious action and to war."[42]

Joannes Chrysostomus Wolfgangus Theophilus Mozart (1756-1791) received all of his education from his father, Leopold. Maria Anna, his older sister, and "Wolf" learned music with their ABC's. Their father was a rigorous tutor putting the children through tedious instruction. He gave them a thorough education in addition to notably successful music lessons. Maria Anna was at eleven a virtuoso at the Clavichord. Wolfgang, eager to imitate his sister, at age three picked out chords. At four he played several pieces from memory. By his fifth birthday "Wolf" invented composition, while his father wrote them down as the child played. This was a startling example of a "living room education." Mozart wrote a prodigious number of brilliant compositions before his early death at age thirty-five. This musical genius was compromised by his own immaturity and selfishness. His father was an effective tutor, but had forgotten parental lessons on self-restraint.[43]

Johann Wolfgang von Goethe (1749-1832), Germany's great author, was born in Frankfurt the eldest of six children. Fertig estimates that about six hundred students had private tutors at this time in Frankfurt. His attorney father, Johann Kaspar Goethe was his first tutor. The rest of his primary and pre-university education was given by tutors hired by his father. From them he acquired a reading knowledge of Latin, Greek, English, some Hebrew, and the ability to speak Italian and French.[44] Even though Goethe criticized the "pedantry and heaviness . . ." of his tutors, he did acknowledge their successes.

> The forms and inflections of language I caught with ease; and I also quickly unravelled what lay in the conception of a thing. In rhetoric, composition, and such matters, no one excelled me; although I was often put back for faults of grammar.[45]

His father's library housed an excellent collection of books that Goethe read with great delight among them Fénelon's <u>Telemachus</u>. In 1765, at age sixteen, Goethe left Frankfurt without any other formal education to study law at the University of Leipzig. He later achieved universal acclaim as Germany's greatest late eighteenth-early nineteenth century author.[46]

## 5. THE "BLUE-STOCKINGS" AND OTHER WOMEN TUTOR-SCHOLARS

If the school education available for boys was often indifferent, that provided for girls George sees as "almost always bad."[47] There were no public schools or academies for women, only private boarding-schools and home education. There were few educational institutions where even the rudiments of good teaching could be found.[48]

Boarding-school paid little attention to a young girl's health. Bedrooms were small with two or three pupils often sleeping in one bed. Schools were often terribly brutal, the rule of the rod applying to girls as well as boys. The food provided was insufficient for a healthy young child. Conse-

168

quently, many girls died from consumption called "a putrid fever."[49]

For these reasons, it was not unusual for the girls of a family to be taught at home by a governess, an aunt, or other spinster relations who were living with the family. It was a common practice for fathers to tutor their sons and daughters together. Many historians are in agreement that most of the educated women of the eighteenth century, and their numbers were not small, were educated at home by tutors.[50]

A common generalization regarding the education of eighteenth century women is that all were either educationally deprived, or had the advantages of an aristocratic education. A long list of learned, clever and interesting women undermines the first proposition. Brink also notes that a study of this group's origins: Elizabeth Elstob, Mary Astell, Elizabeth Carter, Mrs. Montague, Mary Wollstonecraft, Mrs. Vesy, Maria Edgeworth, among many others, indicates that they came from what we would today call a middle-class background.[51]

Hans' study of eighteenth century education also supports Brink's argument. He selected from the Dictionary of National Biography (DNB) 120 distinguished English women. When a comparison is made of the percentage of men and women from the upper classes included in the DNB far fewer women, only 18.3 percent, were from the upper class versus 30.8 percent of the men. A closer analysis shows that most of the outstanding women of the eighteenth century belonged to the middle or lower classes. The sixty-three cases of home education for women utilized a governess, tutor, father, elder brother, uncle or male relative who was a clergyman, scientist or teacher. Several girls were educated by their mother. Domestic education accounted for almost twice as many girls as compared to school attendance by women.[52]

Samuel Johnson's mistress, Hester Lynch Thrales (1741-1821), recorded in her Autobiography a domestic education given by a wide variety of adult instructors. As a young child her mother and uncle taught

169

her to read, write and speak French. Other relatives tutored Hester in Latin, Italian and Spanish. At age thirteen her tutor, Dr. Collier, expanded this curriculum to include logic and rhetoric. Hester's literary skills advanced to such a level that by age fifteen she began publishing poetry under an assumed name in the "St. James Chronicle." Her later Anecdotes of the Late Samuel Johnson (1786) were well received by the English public.[53]

On the continent Tobias Smollett wrote in his famous Travels Through France and Italy (1765), that most women who received any education were taught by their governess at home. Those not educated domestically were sent for a few years to a convent.[54]

As the century progressed, there seems little doubt that women's education improved. To keep a governess at home was considered genteel. Even some tradesmen's families employed them. Most governesses were treated with consideration and respect. On the whole, the eighteenth century girl was not taught the classics like her Tudor forbearers. Instead, she learned French, singing, dancing, poetry, spelling, and elegant calligraphy.[55]

It was in 1775 that the word "schoolroom" first appeared, though many a resident governess had transformed a one-time nursery into a "schoolroom" well over two hundred years before. Howe, in her study of governesses, gives us one of the few surviving descriptions (1795) of an eighteenth century schoolroom.

When Lady S___'s toilet was finished, Mary went to supper, and from there to her nursery, but how surprised was she to find it quite altered. Her play-room which before was almost empty, was now furnished with a bookcase, writing table, drawing-desk, gloves, and a harpsichord. In the room where she was accustomed to sleep was a little bed, placed by the side of a large white dimity one. She presently guessed what all this meant, and turning to the maid who accompanied her, she hastily cried, "For God's sake put me to bed that I

170

may not see her till Morning". All her good maid, Ann, replied was: "Oh, if you mean your governess, ma'am, you must make haste, for 'tis now half past seven, and she is to come at eight".[56]

A separate room was not provided for the governess-tutor before Victorian times. During the eighteenth century governesses invariably slept with their pupils. This governess more resembles the medieval "mistress" known to Chaucer than a classroom teacher. She often times took complete charge of the child's health, welfare and schoolroom education. The governess sometimes took complete charge in a country house because affluent parents were often away in London, or doing the grand tour of Europe.

Much to the credit of the eighteenth century governess was how rarely she was disliked by servants or her pupils. Besides being affectionately treated, many were honored in death. In quiet little English country churchyards can still be found records of faithful service marked on a crumbling headstone.

Here lies the body of
Anne Dear Widow who
dyed Wednesday the 27
of April Anno Domini 1720

The most famous mistress
in the west of England
for well educating and
instructing young ladies
and gentlewomen.

(Salisbury Cathedral, north transept)[57]

Miss Selina Trimmer (1765-1829) was an apt representative of the perfect family governess in this century. Educated by her mother, Mrs. Trimmer an early children's writer, Selina tutored the younger children in the family and gave her mother leisure for writing. At age twenty-one she was hired by the Duchess of Devonshire (1786) as a governess for her two small daughters, Georgiana and Harriet. Her task was not easy. The Duchess had a wild passion for entertaining. People came and went unchecked at Devonshire House, one of Landen's most stylish mansions, and no kind of routine was kept. This was hardly an atmosphere to successfully raise children. Selina soon triumphed over Lady Harriet using her authoritative voice that typified an energetic self-willed personality. But she also acquired her employer's respect and confidence, for when the Duchess went abroad in 1789, Selina was left in charge of the household.

In her eighteenth century classroom, Selina's teaching methods included the use of the magic-lantern in the same manner as educational television. She used the machine to enliven her children's lessons, making them more instructive and entertaining. She taught them grammar, geography and reading. In their leisure hours the Cavendish children played chess, read, or acted in family charades. This was hardly the rigorous tutoring endured by an earlier generation of Tudor princesses!

Later (1790) the Marquis of Hartington was born. A spoiled, very obstinate little boy, he would argue with his governess for hours on end. He too gave in eventually to a will stronger than his own. Years later, Hart paid a charming tribute to his old governess. He described her as "mild and good," possessing "mortal patience" accompanied by a charm that enabled her to endure his most obnoxious behavior. Thus an entire generation of English children was raised by a governess, more than a tutor, almost a stepmother.[58]

These learned women who acted as governess-tutors in this century departed from societal norms for their sex. Women were only to be taught what was necessary to become the mistresses of families, nothing more. Their departure from this reactionary male attitude on female education, earned them the distinction of becoming the first recognized women's activists--the "blue-stockings."[59] This contemptuous term included a large group of eighteenth century women tutors that made a most significant "blue-stocking" contribution to education.

As previously mentioned, Hannah More was a writer on the education of George III's daughter,

Princess Charlotte. She was the most notorious "bluestocking" of her day. Mrs. Mary Montague praised Hannah's denunciation of the typical education for young women that left little time for reading, serious or otherwise. If a girl received a good education, Mrs. Montague cautioned that she not parade her knowledge. Hole in English Home Life repeated Montague's advice on her granddaughter's education,

> to conceal whatever learning she attains, with as much solicitude as she would hide crookedness or lameness; the parade of it can only serve to draw on her the envy, and consequently the most inveterate hatred of all the he and she fools, . . . of all her acquaintance.[60]

Most girls were turned over to a bevy of dancing, music, drawing, French and Italian teachers. A young lady might ultimately excel in repeating a few passages in a foreign language, play like a professor, or dance like a nymph. Yet she remained very badly educated.

Hannah More was even more disturbed by the fact that these empty accomplishments were being copied by the prosperous merchant and professional classes trying to ape their betters, and give their daughters a "fashionable education." If this failed to make a girl a desirable marriage candidate, she then could become a teacher. Hannah saw this trend producing both superficial wives, and more damningly, incompetent and illiterate governesses. She foresaw the grave dilemma that overtook England's governess class in the next century. Instead, Hannah supported a revised curriculum of English grammar, knowledge of the best authors, natural history, history and poetry.[61]

However, most English girls still received a shallow education. Reynolds relates how Mary Granville (1700-1788) was tutored at home from age eight to seventeen "according to the established programme (sic) for girls destined for marriage and social position." Music, reading, writing, French and whist composed her whole education.[62]

173

Other young women like Catherine Talbot received a better education. Catherine lived with Mr. Secker, Bishop of Oxford and later Archbishop of Canterbury, who was her life-long tutor. She became proficient in French and Italian, learned a little Latin, and had other tutors in geography and astronomy.[63] Talbot's mode of tutoring was not unusual for the time. As Hans points out, many clergymen's daughters were tutored by their fathers.[64]

Elizabeth Carter's (1717-1806) father was a minister and tutored his daughter to become a classical scholar. She learned Latin, Greek and Hebrew. As a child, a Huguenot refugee minister taught her French. She later learned Italian, Spanish, German, Portuguese and Arabic. After her father's second marriage, Elizabeth tutored her half-brother Henry who was twenty-one years her junior. They became inseparable. Beginning at age seventeen, she contributed to the leading journals of the day. This career was so successful that Elizabeth was suggested for a tutorial post in the Princess of Wales' household, yet the appointment was never made. Later in life Elizabeth Carter became a friend of Elizabeth Montague and a member of her group of intellectual women, the "blue-stockings."[65]

Other clergymen were not progressive supports of women's education. Elizabeth Elstob (1683-1756) was educated by her mother who died when she was eight. She was placed in the care of her uncle, Reverend Charles Elstob, Prebendary of Canterbury Cathedral. He strongly disapproved of Elizabeth's "blue-stocking" tendencies. When Elizabeth reached the age of ten she asked him if she could be tutored in French, and he held up his hands in horror. One language, her own, was all a woman should know, he told the girl sharply. The minister's wife, however, did not agree, so she hired a French tutor for her niece. Elizabeth eventually learned Latin, Greek and Saxon. By age twenty-six she became a published author and a Saxon scholar. Her mastery of precise editorial skills were remarkable for the age. In 1718 she opened a small school in Evesham, Worcester-shire. By 1738 Elizabeth became governess to the children of the Duchess of Portland and remained there until her death.[66]

Publishing and education were the two professions followed by many of the "blue-stockings." These were among the few professional doors not barred by their lack of a university degree. This occupational trend for women continued well into the nineteenth century swelling the ranks of the English governess.

That era's most powerful statement favoring the improvement of women's education was made by Mary Wollstonecraft (1759-1797). In the same year (1787) that she took a post as governess to Lord Kingsborough's family, she published Thoughts On The Education of Daughters. Wollstonecraft's purpose was "to lay down some rule to regulate our actions . . . [to] properly educate a child . . . ."[67] She agreed with Locke that the best way to cultivate a child's mind is to let children enter into conversation with adults on subjects which will improve them. When a child asks a question, "always have a reasonable answer given it."[68] If instead their heads become "filled with improbable tales . . .," this will only breed prejudices and fear.[69]

According to Wollstonecraft education's most important goal was to teach children the power of abstract reasoning.

> Above all, try to teach them to combine their ideas. It is more use than can be conceived, for a child to learn to compare things that are familiar in some respects, and different in others. I wish them to be taught to think.[70]

She criticized the schools of the day for using rote learning that taught nothing. "If the understanding is not exercised, the memory will be employed to little purpose."[71] Mary added her voice to those of other eighteenth century educators who urged parents not use pretexts to neglect the educating of their children at home, and instead shove it off on the schools of the day. The best possible teacher for a girl, said Wollstonecraft, was her own mother, or perhaps a private governess. The boarding school was the solution only when the mother lacked the necessary time and ability or the money to hire a good governess.[72]

What was the curriculum for a girl's domestic education? Reading "should be cultivated very early in life. . . . Judicious books enlarge the mind and improve the heart. . . ."[73] But some discretion needed to be exercised in the selection of reading materials. She was sick of hearing of "the sublimity of Milton, the elegance and harmony of Pope, and the original untaught genius of Shakespeare, "many sentences are admired that have no meaning in them . . . ." Instead, for children she recommended books that are not abstract or grave. "There are in our languages many in which instruction and amusement are blended. . . . " Adventure books use "beautiful allegories and affecting tales. . . ." Wollstonecraft warned that in teaching morality, "books of theology are not calculated for young persons; religion is best taught by example."

Mary Wollstonecraft expanded Locke's ideas into a philosophy of education that also included women.

> I recommend that mind's being put into a proper train, and then left to itself. Fixed rules cannot be given, it must depend on the nature and strength of under-standing; and those who observe it can best tell what kind of cultivation will improve it. The mind is not, cannot be created by the teacher, though it may be cultivated, and its real powers found out.[74]

Wollstonecraft's career as a governess was very short. The success of her serious writing and novels led her to a literary career. She settled in London, where she was employed by a publisher as a reader and translator. She also became a member of an intellec-tual group which included William Blacke, Thomas Paine, and Joseph Priestly, In 1788 appeared her best-known work, Vindication Of The Rights Of Women. In Vindication Wollstonecraft challenged Rousseau's notions of female inferiority. Instead, she again championed the right of women to equality in educa-tion. Nash interprets the book in part "as a governess's testimony about governessing." She believed that only through intellectual companionship could an ideal of marriage be attained, and that single women had an equal right for employment as governess or tutor with single men. Wollstonecraft complained that when a woman had a superior education to teach children as a governess, "they are not treated like the tutors of sons . . . but as women educated like gentlewomen [Homemakers]."[75]

Wollstonecraft's powerful statements favoring equality for women were unconventional for her day. She also expanded the concepts of individualization in education, and supported Fénelon's earlier notion of a literature created entirely for children. It can be persuasively argued that her strong convictions regarding employment for single women helped to set the stage for public acceptance of a role for women in nineteenth century education, first as governesses, later as school teachers.

Mary Wollstonecraft's support of home instruction undoubtedly encouraged this mode of education in England. A substantial body of educational literature came into existence designed to instruct parents on both practical and philosophical aspects of education at home. They collectively assumed the name of "domestic education" or "fireside education." These books were read widely in the eighteenth and particularly nineteenth century Europe and America. Unlike early books on tutoring, these works were designed for parent-teachers, not university-trained tutors.[76] Maria Edgeworth (1768-1849) was a noteworthy early contributor to this movement. She introduced a new distinctive "children's literature," and improved educational prospects for women.

Maria was born in Ireland. Her father, Richard (1744-1817), had been educated at Trinity College, Dublin and at Oxford. Her mother, Ann Maria Elders, died when Maria was age six. Richard's second wife died in 1780. In the meantime, Maria attended school at Mrs. Latuffiere's Derby (1775) to learn penmanship, French, Italian and embroidery. In 1781 she was sent to school at Mrs. Devis' on Upper Wimpole Street in London. Maria remained there only a year. At age fourteen she arrived at the family's Irish estate (1782) to be educated by her father. By this time, her father had married a third time. There were twelve children now at home that were to be educated by Edgeworth with Maria's help.[77]

For the next two years Maria was tutored rigorously by her father. She later offered her thanks to the "father who educated me, under providence, I owe all of good or happiness I have enjoyed in life."[78] Richard read aloud to his family from Shakespeare, Milton, and Homer. He encouraged them to read on subjects they could understand, including biography, travel, literature and science. This duplicated the thinking of the "lunar group," Bolton, Walt and Kier, concerned with science, but also sharing a forward-looking progressive education attitude. They criticized the uselessness of public education that remained too remote from the business of life and morally worthless. In their educational writing Richard and Maria Edgeworth amplified these views attacking the rote learning methods found in the contemporary grammar and public schools. They denounced the narrow classical curriculum, and the failure of schools to account for individual differences.[79]

Maria later claimed that her father was the first to practice the experimental method in education. Because of her father's close association with the "lunar society," Richard used the Edgeworth family as a laboratory for educational experiments. He also remained in touch with leading reform movements on the continent. Edgeworth and his second wife, Honora, collected data for a study of children based on their actual experiences. Their goal was to develop a system to teach reading that stressed reasoning capacity and accounted for individual differences. They conducted experiments with their own children with Honora noting Edgeworth's questions, the answers of the children, and his explanations.[80]

In Practical Education (1798) Richard and Maria combined these personal observations with prevailing education theories. Nothing like Practical Education had appeared in England since Locke's Thoughts on Education (1693). It was an immediate sensation attracting a wide audience. This controversial book was widely praised by some intellectuals and strongly denounced by the education establishment. Practical Education went into numerous editions, the last in 1822. Maria wrote over half of the material, but most of the specialized curriculum chapters came from her father.

As an educational treatise Practical Education combined the best of Locke and Rousseau with scientific inquiry. It remains a key to progressive eighteenth-century educational thought. Some twentieth-century scholars view it as the most significant contemporary work on pedagogy between Locke's Thoughts in 1693 and Herbert Spencer's Essay On Education in 1861. Edgeworth accepted Locke's associationism as the explanation of how a child's mind can be formed through experientially controlled education. Of equal, if not greater importance, was Rousseau's influence on Edgeworth regarding the importance of childhood. This is a principle that revolutionized continental education. Edgeworth retained or modified many of Rousseau's theories. He stressed the importance of parents to order a child's environment, hence his clear preference for early private domestic rather than public education. He agreed that effective education must be child-centered. Rousseau's stress on infancy, boyhood and adolescence as different stages in growth and development encouraged the Edgeworths to begin writing fiction addressed to different age groups.

The Edgeworths believed that learning and happiness were to go hand in hand in a child's education. Happiness in mind was both a condition and goal of a good education. This theory was based on Locke's psychology. Like him, Edgeworth appreciated the educational nature of play, (Froebel later called this "insight"). Edgeworth also believed in practical education. He sought to mold character, to instill moral principles, to foster good attention span in children. Edgeworth's Practical Education continued the "courtesy education" tradition. The Edgeworths' writings also anticipated those works of Johann Pestalozzi (1746-1827) and Friedrich Froebel (1782-1852), setting the stage for a positive reception of these later theorists.[81]

<u>Practical Education</u> was the first basic handbook written solely for parents on how to teach, and how children learn. It was to be followed by hundreds of similar works supporting "domestic education." <u>Practical Education</u> is crowded with simple illustrations from family experience. The book's twenty-five essays cover a wide field of learning. A child's "Mental Faculties" were discussed in: "On Attention," "Memory and Invention," "Taste and Imagination" and "Wit and Judgment." For the Edgeworths a childhood "Curriculum" consisted of toys, tasks, books, grammar and classical literature, geography and chronology, arithmetic, geometry, mechanics and chemistry. "The Controlled Environment" that educated a child was composed of public and private education, servants, and their acquaintances. "Discipline" was covered in essays "On Obedience" and "On Rewards and Punishments." "Moral Habits" were governed by temper, truth, sympathy and sensibility; vanity, pride and ambition; and prudence and economy.

The basic message of the book is that the discipline of education is far more important than the amassing of factual knowledge. The Edgeworths' main goal was to teach parents to adapt the curriculum and teaching methods to the child's needs. Morality and love of learning can only be transferred by association. In the final analysis each child must acquire a sense of responsibility for his own mental culture.[82]

An earlier work, <u>The Parent's Assistant</u> (1796), established Maria Edgeworth as the leading writer for children in late eighteenth, early nineteenth century England. Her father in 1779, began writing a story about two children, Harry and Lucy. Edgeworth's story told about the beginning of a consciousness of science and morality in the mind of a young child. This story's content and approach formed the basis for Maria's classic children's stories in <u>The Parent's Assistant</u> and later in <u>Early Lessons</u> (1801).

Until this time very few books had been written especially for the young. Their entertainment was limited to literature designed for their elders. Well into the nineteenth century parents and educators clung to the concept that children were miniature adults. Adult values were presented in so-called children's books. These writers for children, however, remained preoccupied with moral and religious themes, and with educational theories.

Maria disagreed. She conceived the idea that fiction was entertainment combined with instruction. In preparing her stories, she sought to entertain her family audience of younger sisters and brothers, and demonstrated her father's educational principles. She has been judged by many as the best writer for children of her day.[83]

Moral Tales (1801) and Popular Tales (1804) featured short stories and novelettes for adolescents. "The Good Aunt," "The Good French Governess," featuring a model teacher, provided variations on pupil-teacher relationships, and Maria's theory and practice of learning. Through all her writings she drew a portrait of the ideal period governess. She told parents to appoint one superior person to be placed in sole charge of the schoolroom. Maria stressed that this governess must have a steadiness of purpose, freedom from prejudice, and great integrity. A governess was to receive 300 pounds per year so as to have adequate funds for her retirement. She would then be able to give of her best, freed from financial worry. In actual practice few governesses ever received this stupendous salary.[84]

Maria, well into the nineteenth century, continued her support of education at home by parents or a governess. Her father's influence was always present, for Maria maintained that all her educational theories came solely from him. She never credited herself as a significant contributor to educational theory. In 1847 Maria wrote,

how can I return to speak of myself and my works? In truth I have nothing to say of them but what my dear father has said for me in his prefaces to each of them as they came out. These sufficiently explain the moral design, they require no national explanations, and I have nothing personal to add.[85]

Her Essays On Professional Education (1809) offered practical advice on preparation for many professions. As late as 1825 she wrote materials designed for education at home with Harry and Lucy Concluded; Being The Last Part of Early Lessons. This book offered science lessons for older children. Her later works taught parents how education can neutralize individual differences enabling children to enter many professions.[86]

There is little doubt that Maria Edgeworth symbolized the growing influence of domestic education in eighteenth century England. Her writing's popularity underscored the widening employment of governesses for children that arose from a growing demand for tutors. The rise of this literature advocating "domestic" or "fireside education" had a significant effect on the education of women during the next century.

The eighteenth century efforts of private tutors enabled many children to receive a more advanced education than available in many public schools in England. The affluent upper class and many middle class English families made ample use of these tutoring resources to educate their children at home.

The writings of Locke and Rousseau's Emile encouraged this social trend. Their combination of heredity and environmental factors helped popularize the concept of one-to-one instruction across Europe. In Germany, Herbart continued to develop this philosophical trend and attempted to reconcile the role of the private tutor with the advent of the state controlled public school.

These philosophical works also set the stage for increased education of women at home. As an important by-product the efforts of Wollstonecraft, Edgeworth and the many "blue-stockings" assured women an expanded role in the educational profession as a governess. Without the formative influences of the eighteenth century English-tutor-scholars, the ultimate achievement of universal public education for women would have taken far longer.

# Endnotes

1.  David Wardle, <u>The Rise of the Schooled Society</u> (London: Routledge and Kegan Paul, 1974), 5-6; Rosamond Bayne-Powell, <u>English Country Life In The Eighteenth Century</u> (London: John Murray, 1935), XI; "Tutor's Diary, A School Report Book, 1799," <u>Stowe Papers</u>, Huntington Library.

2.  Lawson, <u>Social History</u>, 202, 203.

3.  Primary education was often provided by a governess for boys, but usually only male tutors gave boys instruction at the post-primary level. N. Hans, <u>New Trends In Education In The Eighteenth Century</u> (London: Routledge and Kegan Paul, Ltd., 1951), ed. Leslie Stephen, 16, 17, 26, 27; <u>Dictionary of National Biography</u>, 63 volumes (London: Smith, Elder and Company, 1885).

4.  Hans, <u>Trends in Education</u>, 23.

5.  Hans, <u>Trends in Education</u>, 18.

6.  Ibid., 17-19, 23.

7.  Ibid, 25-29.

8.  Ibid.

9.  Ibid., 32-36.

10. Lawson, <u>Social History</u>, 203; George C. Brauer Jr., <u>The Education of A Gentleman Theories of Gentlemanly Education in England 1660-1775</u> (New York: Bookman Assoc., 1959), 195-230; Hole, <u>English Home Life</u>, 120.

11. James Boswell, <u>James Boswell The Earlier Years 1740-1769</u> (London: McGraw Hill, 1985), 3-4; Untermeyer, <u>Lives</u>, 286-287, 344-345, 275-276; Sir Walter Scott, <u>Memoirs Of The Life Of Sir</u>

_Walter Scott, Bart_ (Edinburgh: Robert Cadell, 1839), 28-30.

12.  G.E. and K.R. Fussell, _The English Countryman 1500-1900_ (London: Andrew Melrose, 1955), 133.

13.  Hans, _Trends In Education_, 181; William Jones, _Letters Of A Tutor To His Pupils_ (London: Printed for G. Robinson, 1780); Hester Chapone, _Letters On The Improvement Of The Mind Addressed To A Young Lady_ (London: Printed by H. Hughes for J. Walter, 1773); David Williams, _Treatise On Education_ (London: Printed to T. Payne, etc., 1774); David Williams, _Lectures On Education_ (London: J. Bell, 1789); Locke, _Education_.

14.  Henry Fielding, _Adventures of Joseph Andrews_, Book 3 (Oxford: Oxford University Press, 1967), 201, 320.

15.  Lawson, _Social History_, 202; John Candos, _Boys Together: English Public Schools_ (Princeton: Yale University Press, 1984), 30-31; Bayne-Powell, _Country Life_, 185, 198-201; Rosamond Bayne-Powell, _The English Child In The Eighteenth Century_ (London: John Murray, 1939), 13-15; Rosamond Bayne-Powell, _Eighteenth-Century London Life_ (New York: E.P. Dulton, 1938), 265-272.

16.  James Sutherland, ed., _The Oxford Book Of Literary Anecdotes_ (Oxford: Clarendon Press, 1975), 107-108.

17.  Charles Lamb, "Christ's Hospital Five and Thirty Years Ago" in _The Essays of Elia_ (New York: Dodge Publications, n.d.), 21-38. While at Christ's Hospital Lamb formed an enduring friendship with the future poet, Samuel Taylor Coleridge. Paul Harvey, ed. _The Oxford Companion To English Literature_ (Oxford: At the Clarendon Press, 1955), 441.

18.  Bayne-Powell, _Country Life_, 182; Bayne-Powell, _English Child_, 15-16; Brauer, _Education in England_, 195-230; Candos, _English Public_

Schools, 22.

19. Williamson, Debrett's Kings, 163-183; Plumb, Royal Heritage, 163-183, 179; Marples, Princes, 97-149; Women Biography s.v., More, Hannah; Hannah More, Hints Towards Forming the Character of a Young Princess (London: Printed for T. Cadell and W. Davies, 1805).

20. Adam Smith, The Wealth of Nations (New York: Modern Library, 1937), 728.

21. Hibbert, The Grand Tour, 16-20, 222-229; Paul Fussell, ed., The Norton Book of Travel (London: W.W. Norton, 1987), 129-132.

22. Lawson, Social History, 202-203; Bayne-Powell, English Child, 9-13; M. Dorothy George, London Life in the Eighteenth Century (London: Kegan Paul, 1925), 251-252; Henry Fielding, The History of Tom Jones, A. Founding (London: MacDonald, 1953), 84; Richard Gough, The History of Myddle (Sussex, England: Galiban Books, 1982), V-VI; Hibbert, The Grand Tour, 222-229; Hole, English Home Life, 121-122; Lawson, Social History, 214; Hans, Trends In Education, 184-193.

23. Barnard, French Education, 250-254; Jean-Jacques Rousseau, Emile, trans. Boyd (New York: Basic Books, 1979).

24. Rousseau, Emile, 7-15, 55-66, 97-145; Edward J. Power, Evolution Of Educational Doctrine (New York: Appleton-Century-Crafts, 1969), 282-283; C. John Sommerville, The Rise and Fall Of Childhood (London: Sage Publications, 1982), 127-135.

25. Hailman, Pedagogy, 77-78; Mulhern, Education, 452; W.A.C. Stewart and W.P. McCann, The Educational Innovators (London: MacMillan, 1967), 23-34; John William Adamson, English Education 1789-1902, (Cambridge; Cambridge University Press, 1930), 6; Friedrich Paulsen, German Education, trans. Lorenz (New York: Scribner's 1908), 153-165; Barnard, French

Education, 253-258; Immanuel Kant, born in Prussia (1724), was a village tutor near his home town of Konigsberg. He was so greatly impressed with Emile that he read it in one day; Durant, Story of Philosophy, 198-201.

26. Friedrich Paulsen, German Education, trans. Lorenz (New York: Scribner's, 1908), 113; Ludwig Fertig, The Tutors, (Stuttgart: J.B. Metzlersche, 1979), 3, 8.

27. Fertig, The Tutors, 4.

28. Fertig, The Tutors, 4-5.

29. Ibid., 6.

30. Ibid., 7, 8.

31. August Hermann Niemeyer, Principles For Education and Teaching (Halle: Beyden Verfasser/ Waisenhaus-Buchhandlung, 1796); Fertig, The Tutors, 80.

32. Johann Friedrich Herbart, The Science of Education (Boston: Heath and Company, 1893), 6-10; Fertig, The Tutors, 82.

33. Herbart, Education, 6-10.

34. Johann Friedrich Herbart, Outlines of Educational Doctrine (New York: Macmillan, 1911), 318-320.

35. Ibid.

36. Fertig, The Tutors, 85-86.

37. Ibid., 86-87.

38. Ibid., 85.

39. Ibid., 87.

40. Thomas Carlyle, History Of Frederick II Of Prussia, vol. 1 (Boston: Estes and Company, n.d.), 313, 315-316.

41. Nancy Mitford, "The Boyhood Of Frederick The Great," _Horizon_, 12 (Winter, 1970), 107-108; Christopher Duffy, _The Military Life Of Frederick The Great_ (New York: Atheneum, 1986), 5; Robert B. Asprey, _Frederick The Great The Magnificent Enigma_ (New York: Tickman and Fields, 1986), 17-23.

42. Duffy, _Frederick the Great_, 21.

43. Otto John, _Life of Mozart_, vol. 2 (London: Novello, Ewer and Company, 1891), 437. Amadeus was not actually part of his legal Christian name.

44. Fertig, _The Tutors_, 4; Johann Wolfgang von Goethe, _Works_, vol. 1 (New York, 1902), 209-230.

45. Johann Wolfgang von Goethe, _The Autobiography of Johann Wolfgang von Goethe_, trans. Oxenford, vol. 1 (Chicago: University of Chicago Press, 1974), 28.

46. Ibid., 22-31.

47. George, _London Life_, 273.

48. Hans, _Trends In Education_, 194; George, _London Life_, 273.

49. Howe, _Governesses_, 52; Bayne-Powell, _Country Life_, 183.

50. Bayne-Powell, _Country Life_, 183; Howe, _Governesses_, 52-66; Hans, _Trends In Education_, 194-208.

51. George, _London Life_, 275; J.R. Brink, ed., _Female Scholars_ (Montreal: Eden Press, 1980), 4; Elizabeth Harden, _Maria Edgeworth_ (Boston: Tweyne Publishers, 1984); Alice C. Gausses, _A Woman Of Wit And Wisdom_ (London: Smith, Elder and Co., 1906), 3-5.

52. Hans, _Educational Trends_, 194-196.

53. Hester Lynch Piozzi Thrale, _Autobiography, Letters and Literary Remains of Mrs. Piozzi Thrale_, vol. 1 (London: Longman, Green, Longman, and Robert, 1861), 6, 7, 242, 249, 250-260; Hester Lynch Piozzi Thrale, _Anecdotes of the Late Samuel Johnson_ (London: Longman, Green, Longman and Roberts, 1862); Harvey, _Oxford English Literature_, 783.

54. Tobias Smollett, _Travels Through France and Italy (1765)_ (London: John Lehmann, 1949), 62.

55. George, _London Life_, 276; Howe, _Galaxy_, 52-53.

56. Howe, _Galaxy_, 54; _Oxford English Dictionary_, vol. 9, c.v., Schoolroom.

57. Howe, _Galaxy_, 57-58; _Oxford English Dictionary_, vol. 4, c.v. Governess.

58. Ibid., 59-66.

59. As an attributive phrase it originated in connection with gatherings held in London about 1750 at the home of Mrs. Mary Montague (1689-1762). (As a child Mary had studied with her brother's tutors learning Latin, Greek, French and Italian.) At Mrs. Montague's instead of playing cards, the chief recreation at women's evening parties, more intellectual conversation was held on literary subjects. Eminent men of letters often took part. Many attended without "full dress." One of these was Mr. Benjamin Stillingfleet. He habitually wore grey or blue worsted, instead of black silk stockings. In reference to this Admiral Boscawen (1806) derively dubbed the coterie "the blue stocking society" (as not constituting a dressed assembly). From this time on learned women who supported educational reform were depreciated by the term "blue stockingers," "blue stocking ladies," later abbreviated to "blues;" _Oxford English Dictionary_, vol. 1, c.v. Bluestocking.

60. Hole, _English Home Life_, 124-125.

61. Hannah More, <u>Strictures On The Modern System of Female Education</u> (London: Printed for T. Cadell, junior and W. Davies, in the Strand, 1799); Kamm, <u>Hope Deferred</u>, 102-119.

62. Reynolds, <u>Learned Lady</u>, 251.

63. Ibid., 246.

64. Hans, <u>Educational Trends</u>, 194-196.

65. Alice C. Gausses, <u>A Woman Of Wit And Wisdom</u> (London: Smith Elder, 1906), 3-5, 19-24, 112-113; <u>Dictionary Of Women's Biography</u>, s.v. "Carter, Elizabeth"; Reynolds, <u>Learned Lady</u>, 255.

66. Mary Elizabeth Green, "Elizabeth Elstob: The Saxon Nymph" in Female Scholars, ed. Brink (Montreal: Eden Press, 1980), 137-158; Howe, <u>Governesses</u>, 39-48; <u>Dictionary Of Women's Biography</u>, s.v. "Elstob, Elizabeth."

67. Mary Wollstonecraft, <u>Thoughts On The Education of Daughters</u> (Clifton: Augustus M. Kelly Publishers, 1972), 11.

68. Ibid., 12-16.

69. Ibid., 18.

70. Ibid., 22.

71. Ibid., 24.

72. Ibid., 25; Kamm, <u>Hope Deferred</u>, 129-130, 134.

73. Wollstonecraft, <u>Education of Daughters</u>, 48-49.

74. Ibid., 51-54.

75. Mary Wollstonecraft, <u>Vindication Of The Rights Of Women</u> (London: J. Johnson, 1792); <u>Dictionary Of Women's Biography</u>, s.v. "Wollstonecraft (Goodwin), Mary;" Nash, <u>Governesses</u>, 30, 32.

76. An example of such a work was Sarah Fielding's (1710-1768) <u>The Governess, For the Instruction of Young Ladies in Their Education (1749)</u>, ed. Grey (London: Oxford University Press, 1968).

77. Elizabeth Harden, <u>Maria Edgeworth</u> (Boston: Tweyne Publishers, 1984), 7-9; James Newcomer, <u>Maria Edgeworth</u> (Lewisburg: Bucknell University Press, 1973), 15, 17.

78. Harden, <u>Maria Edgeworth</u>, 10.

79. Ibid., 11, 5, 6.

80. Ibid., 6, 25.

81. Richard Lovell Edgeworth and Maria Edgeworth, <u>Practical Education</u>, 2 vols. (London: J. Johnson, 1798); Locke, <u>Thoughts on Education</u>; Herbert Spencer, <u>Essay on Education and Kindred Subjects</u> (London: J.M. Dent, 1914); John William Adamson, <u>English Education</u> (Cambridge: Cambridge University Press, 1930), 105-106; Newcomer, <u>Maria Edgeworth</u>, 31-38.

82. Elizabeth Inglis-Jones, <u>The Great Maria</u> (Westport, Conn.: Greenwood Press, 1959), 51; Harden, <u>Maria Edgeworth</u>, 24-27; Edgeworth, <u>Practical Education</u>.

83. Maria Edgeworth, <u>The Parent's Assistant or Stories For Children</u>, 4 vols. (London: Printed for J. Johnson by G. Woodfall, 1800); Maria Edgeworth, <u>Early Lessons</u>, 5 vols. (London: Printed by J. Johnson, 1801-1803); Newcomer, <u>Maria Edgeworth</u>, 28-29; Harden, <u>Maria Edgeworth</u>, 6, 120.

84. Maria Edgeworth, <u>Moral Tales</u>, 3 vols. (London: Printed for J. Johnson, 1802); Maria Edgeworth, <u>Popular Tales</u> (London: Printed for J. Johnson by C. Mercier, 1804); Harden, <u>Maria Edgeworth</u>, 33-34; Howe, <u>Governesses</u>, 58-59.

85. Maria Edgeworth, <u>Maria Edgeworth: Chosen Letters</u>, ed. Barry (New York: Houghton Mifflin, n.d.), 447-449.

86. Maria Edgeworth, <u>Essays On Professional Education</u>, 2 vols. (London: Printed for J. Johnson, 1811); Maria Edgeworth, <u>Harry and Lucy Concluded Being The Last Part of Early Lessons</u>, 3 vols. (Boston: Munroe and Francis, 1825); Newcomer, <u>Maria Edgeworth</u>, 18-19, 42; Harden, <u>Maria Edgeworth</u>, 75-76.

CHAPTER 6

THE AGE OF DOMESTIC EDUCATION
(1800-1900)


An increased demand for better education as Europe entered the nineteenth century did not necessarily imply an increased demand for better schooling. Widespread resistance by the upper classes continued for any kind of universal popular education. The middle and upper classes found it possible to provide at least an elementary education at home for both boys and girls. This domestic education was provided by a broad array of tutors, governesses or even parents, if they had the time and knowledge. The quality of home education varied enormously.[1]

Domestic education and school attendance were often combined during a child's education. Children might be instructed at home during childhood, with many boys sent to a formal school at adolescence, and then some attending a university to complete their education. However, for most girls instruction at home lasted far longer, even up to age fifteen or sixteen. This trend dominated the education of women until the end of the nineteenth century. The driving force behind this lack of educational opportunity was the continued discrimination against women in higher education.

It was quite common for parents to give their son a combination of public and private education that mixed lessons from a tutor with school attendance. A boy's tutor might eventually accompany him to school or the university. Young gentlemen of means, after their university graduation, continued their education with the "Grand Tour" on the

Continent accompanied by their tutors. As we will see, until the end of the nineteenth century domestic education in some form remained an important social phenomenon among the middle and upper classes of England and Europe.[2]

The publication of Education In Great Britain (1854) by Horace Mann, a London Barrister, gives a reliable picture of the general state of English elementary education by mid-century.[3] In the 1851 census questions of an educational nature were asked including inquiries regarding "scholars at home." Horace Mann's analysis of this information was made a subject of an official special report that showed the surprisingly strong influence of domestic education in Victorian England.[4]

Wardle's review of Mann's report estimates that as many children were privately educated at home as attended all of the public, proprietorial and grammar schools combined.[5] About fifty thousand children attended these schools, and approximately fifty thousand "scholars at home" were instructed by a tutor or governess. This latter number did not include the many children taught by a parent or relative at home, nor did it count the numerous children below age three receiving instruction from a nanny or governess. Though no specific number was available, a significant number of these additional "scholars at home" undoubtedly existed in these two groups. As can be seen in Table 1 on page 199 more girls ages three to fifteen (27,323) than boys (17,302), were educated at home. However, about 11 per cent of both Oxford and Cambridge then all male undergraduates were entirely educated at home before their attendance at the university.[6]

This social phenomenon of the Victorian Age was supported by the widespread use of tutors and governesses throughout English society. Most middle and upper class parents recognized an important responsibility for the education of their children. Many became their child's tutor. Pollock in her examination of the nineteenth century noted that 26 per cent of those diarists who remarked on education, related that their children either had a tutor or attended school. The higher the class the greater the

194

## Table 1

|  | Schools | Total No. of Students | Male | Female |
|---|---|---|---|---|
| "Private Schools" (Collegiate/Grammar) | 566 | 35,612 | 32,221 | 3,391 |

|  | Ages | Total No. of Students | Male | Female |
|---|---|---|---|---|
| "Scholars At Home" | 3-15 | 44,625 | 17,302 | 27,323 |

Source: Mann, Education in Great Britain, 21, 42.

delegation of the educational responsibility to others. The wealthy used in succession nannies, governesses, tutors and then the university. Governesses were far cheaper than tutors and were employed by many families of quite moderate income to prepare boys for school attendance or instruction by a tutor. But most governesses had complete responsibility for the education of daughters, since there was still considerable doubt about the advisability of sending girls to school. Visiting tutors and governesses were even cheaper to employ. For the domestic education of girls a governess was often in charge, with tutors sometimes employed for special subjects. Contemporary fiction and newspaper chronicles showed the widespread influence and use of the governess as the century progressed.

Even families of very modest circumstances commonly used domestic education. Wardle has found that in 1851 many children of Manchester shopkeepers, small businessmen and managers were privately taught at home. It was not until after 1880, when the public schools and grammar schools were sufficiently reformed, that they began to seriously rival domestic education or the private schools in public esteem.[7]

A contributing factor to the nineteenth century's increased attention to education was the rapid rise in Europe's population. It was 140,000,000 in 1750, reached 190,000,000 by 1800, and rose to approximately 265,000,000 in 1850. Much of this increase had nothing to do with improved medical science. Instead, there was a precipitous fall in the mortality rate among children. Adults did not live longer, but fewer infants died. Sommerville believes this most likely was due to dietary improvements. Children began receiving better food through advances in the transportation of foodstuffs. As a result infants were less susceptible to childhood illness.

The introduction by Edward Jenner of the smallpox vaccination (1798) had an additional positive impact on the infant mortality rate. From 1730 to 1750, 75 percent of the people of greater London died by the age of five. By 1770-1790 this number had subsided to 51 percent. After the introduction of smallpox vaccination, the child mortality figure became 32 percent by 1810-1830.[8]

Wrigley and Schofield's study of the population of England shows a dramatic rise in the population as infant mortality eased: 1706--5.1 million; 1786--7.2 million, 1801--8.6 million, 1831--13.2 million, and by 1851--16.7 million.[9] This rapid increase in the population of children, particularly at the lower end of the socio-economic scale, quickly surpassed English society's limited education resources. A cheap and efficient way was sought to expand the charity schools. Andrew Bell and Joseph Lancaster adapted a tutorial model by using student monitors in their "monitorial schools."

1. THE MONITORIAL SCHOOL MOVEMENT

The use of students to tutor other students individually or in small groups in the classroom was hardly a new idea. Quintilian in Instituto Oratoria

196

supported the concept that children can learn from children. "It is therefore best to associate a pupil with those companions whom he is first to imitate and then to outdo. Thus he will gradually develop hopes of achieving excellence."[10]

Enlightenment educators across Europe used child tutors as "monitors." In the 1530s, a German teacher, Valentin Trotzendorf, used his more advanced pupils to instruct others in his Silesian school at Goldberg. The Jesuit College of Lisbon organized a system of "decurions." A group of ten students was led by a student monitor. By 1591 the decurion system became a formal part of the Jesuit code of liberal education.[11]

By the seventeenth century the monitorial method was adapted for use with very young children. Jean Baptiste de la Salle founded the Christian Brothers to educate the young child. In Conduite des Ecoles (1680) he outlined the monitorial system he used in a school at Rheims.[12] Even earlier the influential Moravian philosopher, John Amos Comenius, supported the process of student tutors in Didactica Magna (1632).

> The saying, "He who teaches other, teaches himself," is very true, not only because constant repetition impresses a fact indelibly on the mind, but because the process of teaching in itself gives a deeper insight into the subject taught . . . . The gifted Joachim Fortius used to say that . . . if a student wished to make progress, he should arrange to give lessons daily in the subjects which he was studying, even if he had to hire his pupils.[13]

The use of monitors in England reached back to the Elizabethan grammar school of John Brinsley (c.1570-1630). He discussed the use of older students to instruct younger children in his book The Grammar Schoole (1612). Brinsley described his use of "two or foure [sic] Seniors in each fourme [sic] for overseeing, directing, examining, and fitting the rest of the children in every way."[14]

The domestic education movement of the eighteenth and nineteenth centuries encouraged parents to supplement their own instruction by allowing older children to tutor their younger siblings. The child's success and familiarity with this peer tutoring method must have been contributing factors to the widespread success of the later monitorial school movement throughout Europe.

The nineteenth century popularity of the monitorial school had its origins in the work of Andrew Bell and Joseph Lancaster. As an English schoolteacher, Andrew Bell (1753-1832), traveled to Virginia where he worked as a tutor, before returning to England and his ordination in the Church of England. In 1789 after enlisting as an army chaplain, Bell was appointed superintendent of a school in Madras, India for orphaned sons of British soldiers and Indian mothers. The boys proved stubborn, perverse and obstinate. Out of desperation Bell designed a system of one-to-one tutoring with an older boy teaching an entire class using the aid of younger boy assistants (monitors). In <u>Bell's Mutual Tuition and Moral Discipline</u> (1797) he summarized his belief,

> that the teacher profits far more by teaching than the scholar does by learning, is a maxim of antiquity, which all experience confirms - "Docemur docendo"-- "He who teaches learns."[15]

To facilitate learning Bell emphasized the fact that learning was a social act best carried out under social conditions.[16]

Almost simultaneously the schoolmaster Joseph Lancaster (1778-1838) opened a small grammar school in England (January 1, 1798). He was such an excellent teacher that his success nearly overwhelmed him. By June of 1801 he was teaching 350 boys in an enlarged school. Lancaster found himself with too many pupils and little money to hire assistants. The idea of student monitors came to him. Lancaster thought he had made one of the most "useful discoveries" in the history of civilization.[17]

Lancaster soon published Improvements In Education As It Respects The Industrious Classes Of The Community (1803) that gave a detailed description of how to operate a monitorial school using student tutors.

Both Bell and Lancaster later became very contentious over the origin of "their" idea. This was centered on the fact that Bell was an Anglican and Lancaster a dissenting Quaker. In 1811 the Church of England established the National Society for Promoting the Education of the Poor, based on Bell's work. It opposed Lancaster's British and Foreign School Society over their belief that children educated in a Lancasterian school would turn away from the Anglican church. Which man "invented" the monitorial tutorial concept is largely moot, since student tutors clearly existed long before the early nineteenth century. The general popularity of tutoring conceivably could have led Bell and Lancaster to develop their own monitorial systems at opposite ends of the globe. Since Lancaster was the first to outline his program with Improvements In Education, he became the far better known modern advocate of the monitorial method.[18]

The concept of the monitorial school movement came into existence in spite of continued widespread opposition to publicly-funded education for the poor. To cope with the burgeoning population of nineteenth century England, the charity schools sought a cheap and efficient educational system that could enroll large numbers of children. Both the National Society For Promoting The Education of the Poor in the Principles of the Established Church, and the British and Foreign School Society (Dissenters) supported Lancaster with the adoption of the monitorial system for their schools.[19]

Lancaster's system of monitors had 1,000 students taught by one adult teacher. It featured an elaborate set of rules, routines and methods for tutoring. Students sat in neat symmetrical rows in a huge classroom. Teaching was done mechanically and with precision. The teacher drilled older children; the older children taught groups of younger children;

199

they in turn taught still younger. This ripple effect greatly enhanced the effort of the master (teacher). Lancaster developed manuals of prescribed teaching procedures for the tutors which clearly outlined and systematized every aspect of the instructional process.

Lancaster's system featured economy of expense and efficiency of instruction. It disciplined by routine, motivated through competition.

> I have ever found, the surest way to cure a mischievous boy was to make him a monitor. I never knew anything succeed much better, if as well.[20]

Unlike a graded system, students were promoted to a new group whenever they had demonstrated their competence. Students of ten to twelve worked around a monitor. When one failed, the next child was given a chance to answer and move to a higher position. Moral discipline was at the heart of this curriculum that inculcated values of obedience, subordination, promptness and regularity. Individualized instruction made the system function. Instead of traditional schoolroom recitations and birch-enforced authority, Lancaster's student tutors aimed at internalized discipline through proper motivation.[21]

The popularity of Lancaster's student monitor system grew so rapidly that it became the basis for elementary education throughout early nineteenth century Great Britain, most of the countries of Europe except Turkey, the British colonies and in the urban areas of the United States. The very success of these schools ended in their own demise, since the public felt they could afford better schools staffed by teachers not student tutors. However, this method of tutoring served as a crucial transition that popularized the idea of an organized school system in both Europe and America.[22] While the monitorial schools enjoyed great success educating children at the bottom of the social ladder, many more middle class and upper class children began using domestic education provided by tutors and growing ranks of governesses.

## 2. THE SAGA OF THE TUTOR-GOVERNESS

For large numbers of English children, education became a domestic industry staffed in the first place by the nanny in the nursery, governess in the schoolroom and supplemented by visiting tutors, or later attendance (especially for boys) at a college preparatory school.[23]

The roles of these various child caretakers-educators became more imprecise as the nineteenth century advanced and their popularity grew. The nursery doubled now as the schoolroom. The governess or nanny was expected to teach a child to read or write at an early age. She became for the young child a "surrogate mother," nurse and teacher.[24]

When the child left the nursery and entered the schoolroom (age 7-8), girls and boys usually studied together. As the century advanced it became a common practice for most boys to start attending school outside the home by age nine or ten. However, the majority of girls remained at home to be further educated by their governess and selected tutors.

During the nineteenth century the English governess also dominated many continental school-rooms. There were few corners of the globe that did not experience this English educational-cultural phenomenon, as the English governess was called upon to tutor children in many foreign and at times exotic lands.[25]

The first fifty years of the nineteenth century saw a great crisis in the education of middle-class girls. Most girls remained ill-educated. Even though prosperous businessmen, clergy, professionals and others employed a bevy of educational servants. In the early Regency period (1815-1835) only upper-middle class and upper-class families could afford a governess. Their average salary was thirty to fifty pounds per year.

Women were seldom educated for this profession.

If a father died leaving an unmarried, ill-provided daughter, there were few other careers open to her other than a governess. Most of these young women received their first education at home. Many became apprenticed teachers. Conscientious young women also studied by themselves, particularly foreign languages, since this attracted high wages from future employers.

Hannah More and Maria Edgeworth complained that too many superficial wives and incompetent or illiterate governesses were brought up on educational short cuts. Girls now studied literature in "selections." Lessons were conducted in the form of question and answer. Superficial subjects crept into the curriculum. For some undetermined reason a special place was given in early Victorian schoolrooms to the "use of the globes" both celestial and terrestrial. However, neither geography nor fundamental astronomy were considered suitable subjects for study by young women. Only after 1850 did general educational reforms improve the preparation of the English governess.[26]

Ellen Weeton's (1776-1815?) _Journal Of A Governess 1807-1811_ was written by a highly intelligent person whose account illustrates the circumstances that forced women to become governesses and their typical daily lives.[27] Ellen was born on Christmas Day, 1776. At age five she lost her father, a privateersman and slave ship captain, in an engagement with an American ship during the Revolutionary War. Her mother soon afterwards opened a small day-school of fourteen scholars. Ellen was her assistant, teaching and helping the younger children. She was a quick learner, always reading and scribbling down verses that came easily to her. She taught nine hours each day and also acted as housekeeper. After her mother's death she continued to run the little school alone. By 1809 Ellen determined to give up the unequal struggle to teach her scholars single-handed. There was little money to hire an assistant. She answered the following advertisement in a Liverpool newspaper.

WANTED, in the neighbourhood of Kendal, a
GOVERNESS, to superintend the Education of

a Young Lady. None need apply but such as can give good references as to ability and character.--Apply to J. Gore.[28]

By January, 1810 she was engaged as a governess by Edward Peddar to undertake the joint education of his younger wife (age seventeen) and a daughter by a former marriage. They lived at Dove's Nest built on the shores of Lake Windermere. Peddar was a local banker. Mrs. Peddar had until lately been employed as a dairymaid at Mr. Peddar's other home. Margaret was an only child by his first marriage. This ten-year-old was subject to fits. As often as five times per day, Ellen was expected to hold Margaret down during these seizures. Although well provided for, Ellen was not happy with her pupil.

> The vexations that occur sometimes during the hours of instruction with a child of such strange temper would almost induce me to give up my present situation.[29]

In early 1810 Margaret set her clothes alight while standing too close to the fire. Ellen Weeton beat the flames out quickly, but the child died early the next morning. Ellen remained for two more years teaching the young dairy-maid wife.[30]

In July, 1812 Ellen became the governess to the children of Joseph Armitage, a Huddersfield manufacturer. The young parents gave Ellen complete authority over their five children who proved to be unruly, noisy, insolent, quarrelsome and ill-tempered. Ellen had a bad time managing her charges from seven o'clock in the morning to eight o'clock at night. Besides dressing, washing and feeding, she taught them in the schoolroom from nine till twelve and from two until five in the afternoon.

A growing middle-class disdain of the governess isolated Ellen socially. Though Mr. & Mrs. Armitage were pleasant to her, she was almost shut out of their society, not being treated as an equal by the heads of the house or by their friends. In nineteenth century England a governess rarely associated with other servants who adopted their master's

203

disdain of women tutors.

Beside the possession of personal fortitude, Ellen Weeton was concerned with the complete indifference of the parents for their children's education. When she asked for some new books Mr. Armitage refused. He saw no reason to spend more money equipping his governess.

Eventually Ellen succeeded in ordering a few new books from London. His attitude was not surprising since the Armitages did not take newspapers, seldom read books and were in plain words non-intellectual.

Ellen Weeton supplies few details on her curriculum as the Armitage's governess. She did stress the importance of French in the training of any prospective home educator. If she had learned French, Ellen might have earned a hundred pounds a year with a family of distinction, but her mother had dismissed the language as a very useless acquisition. Mrs. Weeton had feared that Ellen might become an intellectual woman, even a "blue-stocking" and thus become an unemployable spinster.

Unfortunately for Ellen the five Armitage children all developed whooping cough. Ellen now lacked a moment's peace and gave her employer notice. Soon afterward she married, ending her career as an active teacher. Ellen's role as an educator however, did not end.

In her precious "Letter Books" Ellen had preserved a careful diary of her life as a governess. By 1825 she had composed and carefully transcribed seven volumes. Unlike the later works of another governess, Charlotte Brontë, Ellen Weeton's ultimate frustration was that her works remained unpublished in her own lifetime. Only in the next century did the public learn of the Regency governess's empty life.[31]

By the time Queen Victoria assumed her throne (1837), the rising middle class had created a demand for even more governesses to educate their children. English parents sought the ideal governess who embodied all the "schoolroom virtues." She must be plain and quiet in style of dress, and with a fixed sad look of despair on her face. This guaranteed a humble and meek spirit that did not threaten children. These well-bred young women came mainly from three groups. The clergyman's daughter had usually taught her brothers and sisters or the illiterate poor in her father's Sunday school. The governess from an aristocratic, blue blood family was almost as highly prized. Ever-increasing numbers of suddenly impoverished young, aristocratic women were forced to enter the governess profession. An officer's daughter was also a welcomed recruit for a family governess. Thackeray in <u>Vanity Fair</u> presented an accurate portrait of these young women.

Dear Madam,

Presenting my respectful compliments to Lady Fuddleston, I have the honor to introduce to her ladyship my two friends, Miss Tuffin and Miss Hamky.

Either of these young ladies is perfectly qualified to instruct in Greek, Latin, and the rudiments of Hebrew; in mathematics and history; in Spanish, French, Italian, and geography; in music, vocal and instrumental; in dancing, without the aid of a master (tutor); and in the natural sciences. In the use of globes both are proficient. In addition to these, Miss Tuffin, who is daughter of the late Reverend Thomas Tuffin (Fellow of Corpus College, Cambridge), can instruct in the Syrian language, and the elements of Constitutional law. But as she is only eighteen years of age, and of exceedingly pleasing personal appearance, perhaps this young lady may be objectionable in Sir Huddleston Fuddleston's family.[32]

Whether they belonged by birth to the church, nobility or army, the governess' genteel accomplishments and virtuous backgrounds were exploited in Victorian times.[33]

By the 1840s over one hundred governesses

advertised daily in The London Times for a position. The highest salary was one hundred pounds a year, though the average was between thirty to forty pounds.[34] Thousands of these women were seen daily hurrying about London from seven in the morning to seven or eight at night to their next appointment. The "daily governess" became another word for a servant. In fair weather or foul she appeared as the clock struck, her professional life hemmed in by all sorts of petty snobberies and rude chauvinism. The convention of her day forbade any display of feeling between a governess and her pupils. Often she was victimized by her own male relatives as a useful source for helping to cancel debts.

The life of the live-in governess was hardly better. Their daily existence was one of general loneliness. Her employers, often of an equal or even less cultural background, inflicted social discrimination upon her. Unlike the tutor of past centuries, she did not socialize with the family, most often taking her meals alone or with the children. The tutor-governess was no longer the secretary-advisor to the master of the house. As a woman-tutor she could not fill either of the other older traditional tutor roles as chaplain or family physician, since these professions were still barred to her. The tutor-governess was intellectually belittled by her employer, even if she possessed a superior education or came from a higher social rank.

The house servants copied the attitude of their employer. They were often insolent to the governess and left her alone. Her isolation was increased by the unwillingness of many families to even allow the governess visitors.

The relationship with her pupils was a severe strain because of this rigidly enforced daily intimacy. The governess slaved away constantly running after her young charges. The children made teasing their governess a daily occupation.

"Julia, it is time for lessons. . . ."
Julia sat like a figure of wood or stone.
Miss Janet Summerhayes rose from her chair,
pale, with her eyes shining. . . . The

moment of conflict had come. . . . She
rose, and turning the key in the door as
she passed, walked up to the table at which
Miss Julia sat with her book. . . . With a
sudden swift movement she took the book
from under the reader's bent face. . . .
"Miss Summerhayes!  Give me back my book.
How dare you take my book . . . do you hear
me!" cried the girl. . . . "Sit down," said
Janet . . . and we can have it out. . . .
We are equal. . . . Now sit down and let us
talk it out."

"Equal!" said Julia, with a shriek,
"me and you, Miss Summerhayes!  You are
only the governess--that's no better than a
servant.  You may suppose they think
differently downstairs. . . . But they
think just the same.  And mama will stand
up for me . . . You, a bit of a governess
hired, just like the housemaid: and that's
exactly what mamma will say."[35]

All these conditions were exacerbated by the
indefiniteness of her professional position.  She was
a child's tutor, but also expected to be generally
useful often undertaking housekeeping duties.  Her
greatest fear was the constant threat of dismissal.
Older governesses were cast off with no retirement
provision made by a life-long employer.  Some did
needlework or accepted charity, but many women were
left totally destitute.  Most governesses dreamed of
escaping this dreary life by setting up a school or
marrying a local curate, or aristocrat.  Yet this
path too had many difficulties.

Who's this little schoolgirl that is
ogling and making love to him?  Hang it,
the family's low enough already, without
HER.  A governess is all very well, but I'd
rather have a lady for my sister-in-law.
I'm a liberal man; but I've proper pride,
and know my own station:  let her know
hers.[36]

Most  Victorian  middle-class  parents  were
indifferent  regarding  what  was  learned  by  their

child. They operated on the dual assumptions that their son's education should prepare him to enter a profession either through higher education or apprenticeship. This usually necessitated school attendance after early domestic education. Education for women was limited to preparation for motherhood. A "gentlewoman" did not require a very solid education, since she did not work for a living. Educated "blue-stockings" notoriously frightened away matrimonial suitors. "Strong-minded" was one of the most elusive terms that was applied to an educated Victorian woman, though men never claimed a preference for feeble-minded women. Indifferent, frivolous education for women by a tutor or governess was mandated for most girls.

> "And my dearest Mamselle Rönnquist," added the President persuasively and impressively, laying his hand on my arm, "remember particulary, for heaven's sake, no miracles of my girls--no miracles! I will not have them brilliant or vain ladies, nor learned, proud, and pedantic women; but simple, reasonable creatures, good wives and mothers--that is what I will have them to be! Accomplishments they may have, but only for their own amusement and that of others; to hear virtuosos I would much rather go to the concert and pay my dollar. As to reading, above all things let them read no more than is just necessary for them to be able freely and easily to converse on the subjects most current in society. All reading beyond that, and all connoisseurship [sic], are disadvantageous to a woman, and snatch her from the sphere in which alone she can gain esteem, or benefit society.[37]

Some governesses confined their tutoring to small children, while others promised to meet all educational needs without other master tutors. The majority professed to teach the contents of a solid English education including English, French, German, Italian, music and mathematics. Many schoolrooms were only a barely furnished study with a large table, chairs and a map of Europe.

Lesson content was limited and bordered on monotony. Foreign languages were taught with indifference. Instruction continued in the use of globes. Squeaking slates and the blackboard had replaced the hornbook.[38]

In addition to Miss Weeton's portrayal of the governess in her _Journal_, no one has portrayed so perfectly in poetry the education by a governess of a Victorian girl as Elizabeth Barrett Browning. An invalid, she was educated at home. Her long narrative poem, _Aurora Leigh_ (1856), might have portrayed a childhood governess.

I learnt the collects and the catechism,
The creeds, from Athanasius back to Nice,
The Articles . . . The Tracts against the times
(By no means Buonaventure's "Prick of Love"),
And various popular synopses of
Inhuman doctrines never taught by John,
Because she liked instructed piety.
I learnt my complement of classic French
(Kept pure of Balzac and neologism),
And German also, since she liked a range
Of liberal education,--tongues, not books.
I learnt a little algebra, a little
Of the mathematics,--brushed with extreme flounce
The circle of sciences, because
She misliked women who are frivolous.
I learnt the royal genealogies
Of Oviedo, the internal laws
Of the Burmese empire . . . ,
I learnt much music,--such as would have been
As quite impossible in Johnson's day
As still it might be wished - and I drew costumes
From French engravings, nereids neatly draped
With smirks of simmering godship, - I washed in
From nature, landscapes (rather say, washed out),
I danced the polka and Cellarius,
Spun glass, stuffed and modelled flowers in wax,
Because she liked accomplishments in girls. . .
I learnt cross-stitch, because she did not like
To see me wear the night with empty hands,

A-doing nothing.  So, my shepherdess
Was something after all (the pastural saints
Be praised for't) leaning love-lorn with pink
eyes
To match her shoes, when I mistook the silks.[39]

By 1850 the governess was acknowledged by
English society as the safest, healthiest,
pleasantist, the most effective and cheapest form of
education. The employment of governesses continued to
increase. The official census of 1851 listed governesses apart from schoolmistresses and assistants.
Over twenty-one thousand women were listed as
governesses with thousands more left unidentified.[40]
Their domestic education activities, and that of male
tutors teaching mainly boys, served over fifty
thousand children taught at home.[41]  Witnesses of
broad experience before the Schools Inquiry Commission reported that the fashion of educating girls at
home had now spread from the higher classes to lower
middle class, farmers and tradesmen.[42]  By the 1861
census over twenty-four thousand governesses were
teaching in private families.[43]

The governess was a testimony to the increased
economic power of the later Victorian middle-class.[44]
The fact that correspondingly large numbers of single
middle-class women were "in need of a situation" as a
governess was a by-product of several social conditions.  An unstable business climate ruined many
families.  Large numbers of single men emigrated to
the colonies.  A differential mortality rate also
favored women over men.  The effect of all these
social trends was further compounded by the fact that
the middle class Victorian male tended to marry later
in life.[45]

Governessing was the one occupation open to a
significant and always increasing number and propor-
tion of middle-class women.  Bessie Parkes (1829-
1925), a descendant of scientist Joseph Priestly and
an early feminist essayist, believed the role of
governess for "decayed gentlewomen" was "the one
means of breadwinning to which access alone seems
open and to which alone untrained capacity is equal,
or pride admits appeal."  Since every woman was by

nature a teacher, the middle-class lady in straitened circumstances was qualified as a teacher, and still enjoyed the shelter of life at home deemed to be her proper social station.[46]

No matter how "respectable" or "natural" her occupation, the life of a governess was not a happy one. A significant over-supply of governesses caused the average salary to drop between 1825 and 1860 from between thirty to fifty pounds to between twelve to fifteen pounds per year. Some of the more highly educated governesses still received up to 100 pounds. Even though their pay was notoriously low, the live-in governess could always expect to be housed and fed, but expenses such as laundry, travel and medical care were deducted from their pay. Many employers exploited this over-supply, and the intellectual and material poverty of these young women. Governesses were expected to teach and often undertake house-keeping duties. The continual support of the family governess when she reached old age was not often continued by a middle-class family. Reports of governesses in workhouses or asylums were not uncommon.[47]

Anna Brownwell Jameson (1794-1860), a governess herself, helped popularize a reform movement by writing about the plight of these women. In her Memoirs (1846), A Commonplace Book Of Thoughts, and Memories (1854) and The Communion of Labour (1859) she stated that employers should give the governess facilities for change of employment, variety and rest. Schoolrooms must be made large and airy for the comfort of the governess and her students by day. At night the governess deserved a comfortable bedroom away from the children for rest and relaxation.[48]

Other women also took up the cause for the beleaguered governess. In an endless stream of essays, pamphlets and novels they tried to better her social standing. Charlotte Younge (1823-1901) in her novels, The Governess, The Daisy Chain (1856), The Trial (1898), among others, offered vivid portraits of plain governesses, lonely governesses, governesses good, bad or indifferent. Womankind (1876) set out Younge's educational theory that a competent governess, with the support of visiting tutors, gave a girl a better education than at any school. Another reformer, Harriet Martineau (1802-76), was particularly concerned about the ultimate fate of the elderly governess.[49]

The significant popularity of the governess in nineteenth century literature can be traced to the many sheltered genteel ladies that identified with this theme from personal experience. For several centuries female education had been "the cottage industry of middle-class women." Even if they had not been governesses, many educated women had been taught by them, or shared the experience of Maria Edgeworth as the domestic educator of their families.[50]

Because of the continued inadequacy of many schools even the lower middle class were using governesses by 1865, a state of affairs reflected in fiction.[51] The family tutor became too important a social figure to be neglected by contemporary Victorian letters. Such themes were popular enough to become profitable for publishers during the rest of the century and into the next.[52]

Nash in her study of governesses found that they abound in the literature of Victorian England. They were the subjects or authors of educational works, children's books, letters, poems, newspaper articles, political manifestos, religious tracts, moral tales and early feminist literature. (See Appendices B and C.) In period fiction the governess was a common character, even a heroine at the center of a typical plot. They served as the defining element of a fictional sub-genre. Their frequent appearance was encouraged by their presence at the center of Victorian society. Contemporary interests in education, class and the status of women intertwine in governess characters.[53]

William Thackeray (1811-1863), in Vanity Fair (1845), presented an excellent example of the forlorn middle-class girl abandoned by her parents and thus forced to make her own way in the world. Rebecca Sharp as a family governess had many adventures that characterized Victorian morality and literature. In an earlier work, Barry Lyndon (1843), though a

212

governess was absent, Thackeray made the family tutor and chaplain Reverend Samuel Runt a prominent character in the novel.[54]

Even the quintessential Victorian novelist, Anthony Trollope (1815-1882) used the governess/tutor role in five of his novels. His characters led the "grand tour" (Rev. Mr. Cruse) in Bertrams (1859); acted as a family governess (Lady Cantrip) in The Duke's Children (1880), and (Lucy Morris) in The Eustace Diamonds (1873); was a family tutor (Alasco) in Gentle Euphemia (1866); and led the Oxford tutors (Tom Staple) in Barchester Towers (1857).[55]

A triumvirate of governesses, the Brontë sisters, Charlotte (1816-1855), Emily (1818-1848) and Anne (1820-1849), made the greatest and most enduring contribution to our modern conception of the English governess. Their Irish father, Patrick Brunty (changed to Brontë after his arrival in England), was an Essex clergyman. He educated his daughters at home and later at an institution for clergymen's daughters. The Brontë sisters studied history, geography, grammar, writing, arithmetic and globes in preparation for their careers as governesses. All were employed as domestic educators with a succession of families across England.

They were prolific writers and began publishing under the assumed name of Bell in the late 1840's. Charlotte Brontë's Jane Eyre (1847) was followed by Shirley (1849) and Villette (1853). Agnes Grey (1847) by Anne Brontë was followed by Tenant Of Wildfell Hall (1848). Emily Brontë's Wuthering Heights (1847) was one of the greatest novels ever written.[56]

When the manuscript of Jane Eyre was received by its future publisher, they were struck by the intensity of the character of that tale. Even Thackeray had high praise for the book.[57] The authorship of Jane Eyre at first was a closely-guarded family secret. As the Brontë sisters published, they each pledged their word not to reveal the authorship. Each satirized her employers in these remarkable novels. They felt it was a duty to reproduce every detail of their lives as a governess, (using fictitious characters, incidents and situations), as a warning to others of talents misused and positions abused. All three sisters despised being a governess. Their novels offered at times a brilliant allegorical portrait of the governess in her bitter, empty life.[58]

The history of education placed the governess at the center of English feminism, documenting the low standards of education for women. Through the popularity of the Victorian novel, a gradual public recognition of their grievances brought increased attention to the education of girls.[59]

Florence Nightingale (1819-1910), a great nineteenth century reformer, was tutored by both a governess and her father, William Edward Nightingale. Her education included Greek, Latin, German, French, Italian, history and philosophy. She developed a tender understanding of the Victorian governess when she reorganized the Institution For the Care of Sick Gentlewomen (1853). Most of the patients were governesses. Many were reluctant to ever leave this shelter since it was the cheapest lodging they could find with the added luxury of medical attention. From this experience Florence Nightingale came to recognize the miserable position of these women in England. Until the end of her life, governesses wrote to her because they viewed her as a friend and champion of their profession.[60]

Other reformers were equally moved by the plight of governesses. Nash believes that the formation of the Governess Benevolent Association (GBA) (1841) was linked directly to popular literature. Charles Dickens on 20 April 1844 was the speaker at a subscriber's dinner of the G.B.A. held at the London Tavern.

> To take the case of those ladies (governesses) in comparison with menial servants: they were paid less than the cook, . . . the butler, . . . the lady's maid; and they were even lower than those paid to liveried footmen. The power of governesses was acknowledged by the middle-aged lady . . . she felt the power of the

214

governess' knowledge in the education of her daughters; gentlemen also felt the power of the governess' knowledge; but nobody thought of the poor fagged knowledge herself, her eyes red with poring over advertisements in search of a new situation; and after having faithfully accomplished her task in one family, being thrown upon the world and going forth again among strangers to educate others. . . .

From first to last [I have] a confidence that the society [will] do its duty; and [I hope] by its means to see blotted out a national reproach, and that the profession of education would be placed on that honourable [sic] footing which in any civilized and Christian land, it ought to hold.[61]

Founded in London, the Governesses' Benevolent Institution sought to offer private relief discreetly to governesses in temporary distress. By 1846 a home was opened at 66 Harley Street, London, that accommodated twenty-five unemployed governesses and offered a free registry service. Four annuities of fifteen pounds annually initiated the first governess retirement fund. Ninety candidates applied immediately. By 1857 the GBA had 120 applicants for financial aid and admission to their retirement home. All of these women were over fifty years old, ninety-nine unmarried. Thirty-seven had very small incomes, while eighty-three were completely destitute. The profession of tutor-governess for women had fallen to a deplorable subsistence level by mid-century. Only the intervention of this private charity saved many from dire poverty or prostitution.[62]

The "Lectures For Ladies" were of great long-term educational significance. They were first sponsored in 1847 by the GBA with the idea of educating the governess before allowing her to educate others. Rev. Frederick Denison Maurice (1805-1872), Professor of English Literature at King's College, London, Charles Kingsley and Dean Trench, later Archbishop of Dublin, delivered the series of evening lectures. The lectures became so popular that a daytime course was added for women available to attend.[63]

One of the Queen's ladies-in-waiting, a Miss Murray, had collected funds for the establishment of a women's college. She gave the money to the GBA for the purchase of a house next door to their London retirement home. Miss Murray persuaded Queen Victoria to lend her name to the infant college. On May 1, 1848 Queen's College for Women opened as the first educational institution founded for the preparation of governesses. It maintained close ties with the Anglican King's College whose professors continued to voluntarily teach and examine students. Queen's was similar to male colleges, though in its early days older women chaperoned the girls ("Lady Visitors"). A four-year college program was introduced that featured a lecture examination system. Courses included English, theology, history, geography, Latin, mathematics, French, German, Italian, natural philosophy, music, the fine arts and pedagogy. Women earned both four-year degrees or single-course certification. This marked the first specific preparatory program for tutors in Western Europe. By 1850 over two hundred women had received a governess credential from the college.[64]

The college was opened to all women and became an immediate success. Among those educated at Queen's were women who did not intend to teach. This included two women poets, Jean Ingelow (1820-97) and Adelaide Anne Procter (1825-64); Sophia Jex-Blake (1840-1912) a woman pioneer in the medical profession; and the writer, Julia Wedgewood (1833-1913). Two great pioneers of women's education, Frances Mary Buss (1827-1894) and Dorothea Beale (1831-1906), were also students at Queen's.[65]

Within six months of the opening of Queen's College, a second institution, Bedford College, began teaching governesses. Mrs. Elizabeth Reid, a wealthy philanthropic widow, wanted a non-denominational college for women. She felt that the great success of Queen's proved that there was room for another school. In October 1849, Bedford College was launched from a house in Bedford Square, London.

Eventually Queen's College separated from the

GBA (1862). However, special provisions continued for governesses including tuition reduction, free evening lectures, sixteen scholarships and granting them special teaching certificates. Graduates of Queen's and Bedford Colleges later helped establish Girton and Newnham Colleges at Cambridge University. The GBA continued to flourish. By 1862 it established Kentish Town Home as an expanded governess retirement institution. The society had by then amassed 180,000 pounds in government securities to fund one hundred annual annuities for aged governesses of twenty-five pounds and aided fourteen thousand governesses to find positions through the GBA registry office. With these institutional and educational reforms, governessing had become recognized as a profession in some ways consistent with the heritage of tutors past, instead of a social misfortune.[66]


3.  THE INFLUENCE OF DOMESTIC EDUCATION PHILOSOPHY


For every child instructed at home by a tutor, governess or nanny, many more received their entire education, or a significant portion, through parental instruction. For most children there was no other alternative, since private schools or tutors remained beyond family means. Charity schools retained their odious reputation. It was not until 1914 that England created a national tax supported system of public education requiring mandatory attendance. It was hardly surprising that contemporary educators worked to fill this gaping crevasse by creating a movement for domestic education and parental tutors.[67]

The rise in the population of children (as noted earlier) certainly increased the size of families. Many diaries tell us of families with ten children or more. Unfortunately a comparative increase in low cost education failed to match the dramatic increase in the number of children requiring schooling. It was only natural that the rise of "domestic education" began at this time as a socially acceptable, and more importantly, practical educational vehicle.

Parents bought books on home education in ever-increasing numbers throughout the nineteenth century and persisting into the next. Only tax-supported public education in England and throughout Europe put an end to this social phenomenon.

As previously discussed, Maria Edgeworth had been an early advocate of parental domestic education in the late eighteenth-early nineteenth century. Others, such as Harriet Martineau, now expanded on these concepts. Her Household Education (1864) became one of the most influential books written on "domestic-fireside education."[68] It was representative of the early childhood philosophy of Pestolozzi and Froebel and anticipated Piegetian concepts. Martineau's audience was parents, not teachers. She related in practical terms the lessons learned from a life-time as a governess. "Household Education," Martineau wrote, "is a subject so important in its bearings on individual happiness." Children and parents alike must share in making the family's "education plan" a truly "family plan." All are equally members, "of the domestic school of mutual instruction."[69] Household education with parents as the tutors existed as an alternative to the tutor, governess or school attendance. Only by the end of the nineteenth century had "domestic education" assumed a supporting role as a supplement for the common school movement.

The aim of household education was, "the improvement of pupils . . . to bring out and strengthen and exercise all the powers given to every human being . . . and balance them."[70] The child's first education was through play. Close observation by parents yielded an insight into individual talents. At about age seven most children will begin learning to read, write and do arithmetic. Martineau told parents who considered sending their children at a later date to school, (especially boys), that a child is not ready to attend formal school until his parents have readied his mind to accept thinking activities.[71]

The first step in this learning process Martineau named the "concrete stage." The teaching of reading, grammar and numbers form the core activities. Whether this instruction is done by a tutor for boys, a girl's governess, or the child's parents, their "punctuality" an "undeviating regularity" was of utmost importance "to secure quiet and regularity for the children's lessons . . . it is for the mother to resist each day's temptation . . . for her to find any corner of the house where they may be undisturbed." The final results of this learning process depends simply on the diligence of the parents in establishing these learning habits.[72]

The "exercise of reasoning" is the next learning stage. Parents must gather teaching materials that enhance the child's "imaginative faculty." Martineau suggested the use of "heroic tales of virtue" to awaken a sense of justice, a knowledge of right conduct and good and evil.

"Perfecting individual growth" by equal family companionship remained as the "ultimate stage of Household Education. . . . " Though the family members are no longer all under the same roof, the intellectual discipline of their lives will never end. The deepest life impressions are "those imparted to the sensitive and tenacious mind of childhood."[73]

Johann Heinrich Pestalozzi's (1746-1827) Leonard and Gertrude represents the culmination of Pestalozzi's influence supporting the concepts of "domestic education." Here Pestalozzi presented the story of Leonard the mason, Gertrude his wife, and their seven children. Gertrude taught her children reading, writing, arithmetic, and many "moral lessons." She allowed the children of a neighbor to come in and join her children's tutoring lessons.[74]

A disciple of Pestalozzi, Friedrich Froebel (1782-1852) prepared Songs for Mother and for Nursery to assist mothers in the early education of their children at home.[75] Froebel in 1837 established at Blankenburg, German, the first educational institution exclusively for young children, the kindergarten. In this public setting Froebel sought to develop the child's individual strengths that he termed "gifts" and "occupations." The kindergarten at first surpressed by a conservative Prussian government, eventually became an international standard for many early childhood programs in Europe and America.[76]

In Italy Maria Montessori (1870-1952), the first woman doctor in that country, established her "Casa dei Bambini" (The Children's House) for young children of the tenements in Rome. She too accepted the principle of individually paced instruction and the right of a child to develop their own fullest potential. This Montessori school introduced children to learning materials that were intrinsically interesting and self-correcting, thereby helping the child correctly to perceive reality. Her schools spread throughout Europe, America and the world.[77]

The parent-tutor role as moral and academic domestic educator inspired hundreds of supporting "how-to" books written in Europe and America throughout the nineteenth and into the early twentieth century.[78] The movement was also known as "fireside-education," a term originated by S.G. Goodrich. Support for home education continued unabated so that by 1905 the "First International Congress On Home Education" was convened at Liége, though the emphasis by that time had shifted to pre-school education.[79]

As the Victorian era progressed, fireside educators continued to envision parents as the child's teacher, but the common school as "the great auxiliary of the fireside."[80] Goodrich in his seminal work, Fireside Education (1841), believed parents were the "natural seminary" and the teacher in school was only "their assistant" in teaching their children. If children enrolled in a school, Goodrich felt it was a great error to leave the minds of children wholly to "school instructors." Parents should review their lessons, aid in mastering problems, and "teach them to think and reflect upon their studies. . . . "[81]

Other contemporary educational philosophers agreed with these fireside educators. Herbert Spencer (1820-1903) in Education: Intellectual, Moral, Physical (1861), a penetrating analysis of the pedagogy's function, which exerted a profound

220

influence on the development of later education, supported the concepts of domestic education.[82] Spencer was educated entirely at home by his father and an uncle, both private school teachers. In Spencer's view the intelligent mother tutored at home by familiarizing her child step-by-step in her lessons

> with the names of the simpler attributes, hardness, softness, colour [sic], taste, size . . . he delights in the discovery of his powers. . . . As his faculties unfold she adds quality after quality to his list . . . the course she is pursuing is the one best calculated to establish a habit of exhaustive observation; which is the professed aim of these lessons.[83]

An important moral culture must pervade a child's life. This fostered the individual independent activity of the pupil, and was of greater importance than the ordinary school.[84]

Edwin Abbott was the headmaster of the City of London School. In 1883 he wrote <u>Hints On Home Teaching</u> for the use of governesses, private tutors and parents. <u>Home Teaching</u> discussed the fostering of "Moral Training" (habits). Abbott also offered tutoring methods for reading, spelling, arithmetic, English composition and grammar, French and Latin, geography, history and geometry.[85]

Immanuel Kant (1724-1804) also recognized the value of education at home. During his days as a student at the Collegium Fredericianum and the University of Königsberg he earned his living as a tutor. He felt that the teacher merely instructs, while a tutor is a director, educating for life. "The purpose of public education is the completion of domestic education." However, Kant saw public education as more desirable with its egalitarian attributes. But a close contemporary of Kant, Herbart, was also influenced by his thinking on domestic education.[86]

There were vocal English philosophers that also preferred a national public education system. John

Stuart Mill (1806-1873) wrote the classic statement for state educational responsibility in his Principle of Political Economy (1848).

> because the case is not one in which the interests and judgement of the consumer are a sufficient security for the goodness of the commodity.[87]

In part, Mill's distrust of parental judgment may have been based on his negative personal experience with domestic education detailed in his Autobiography of John Stuart Mill (1873).[88]

John was tutored by his father beginning at age three. His father, James Mill, was a minister in the Scottish Church. For several years he had served as a private tutor in various Scottish families. James Mill, and later Jeremey Bentham, attempted to give John Stuart Mill an education based on the utilitarian philosophy. First John learned Greek, then Latin in his eighth year. The curriculum material read like a Renaissance review of the classics: Herodotus, Xenophon, Socrates, Diogenes, Isocrates, Plato to name a few. His father's tutoring, "demanded of me not only the utmost that I could do, but much that I could by no possibility have done."[89] In the evenings John was given lessons in arithmetic. These formal classes were only part of the daily instruction schedule. During their walks while living in the rustic neighborhood of Newington Green, John and his father discussed what he had read the day before. The books were chiefly histories: Robertson's histories, Hume, Gibbon, Langhorne's translation of Plutarch, among many others.

In the same year he began Latin, Mill read the Iliad, and Pope. Between age eight and twelve he finished reading all of the principal Greek and Latin authors and mastered elementary algebra and geometry. Mill read very little of Shakespeare, since his clergyman father frequently attacked his idolatry, nor other English poets except Milton.

From age twelve Mill entered into more advanced education that commenced with Logic. He appreciated this part of his tutoring; "I know nothing, in my education, to which I think myself more indebted for whatever capacity of thinking I have attained."[90]

A book that contributed "largely to my education" was his father's History of India (1818). Mill read the manuscript aloud, while his father corrected the proofs. Shortly thereafter the directors of the East India Company appointed James Mill an Assistant of the Examiner of India Correspondence. It was not a surprise that his son perceived the History of India as "one of the most instructive histories ever written."[91]

This new employment did not stop the James Mill's lessons for his son. In 1819 they completed a "course of political economy," instruction in science "by a sort of lecture" and a study of Adam Smith. This concluded (at about age fourteen) Mill's education under his father's direction. He had by then thoroughly studied Greek and Latin literature, philosophy, world history, mathematics, logic, philosophy, chemistry, botany, psychology and law.[92]

Mill's later evaluation of his own education contained some kind words for his father's efforts. James guarded his son from self-conceit. Understanding was uppermost, rather than memorizing mere facts and the opinions of others. Yet he faulted his father for the,

> wretched waste of so many precious years
> . . . in what are considered the higher
> branches of education . . . in acquiring
> the modicum of Latin and Greek. . . .[93]

Another deficiency in his education was the lack of "any great amount of intercourse with other boys." He needed companions for play. As a result Mill felt he never developed any degree of manual dexterity.[94]

The education James gave John was, "much more fitted for training me to know than to do." While his father saved John from the inferior and often brutal schools of nineteenth century England, "he made no effort to provide me with any sufficient substitute for its practicalizing influences." Mill seemed unduly critical of his own education.

In 1822 he formed the plan of a little society that acknowledged, "Utility as their standards in ethics and politics." This group was to become the Utilitarian Society.[95] The fact that Mill's classical tutorial education produced the utilitarian movement in some ways gives credit to his father's teaching that, "Anything which could be found out by thinking I never was told, until I had exhausted by efforts to find it out for myself."[96]

The utilitarian training that Mill received from his father placed limitations on his capacity for absorbing some of the principal intellectual currents of the nineteenth century. However, Mill had a deep effect upon contemporary British thinking. He worked actively for the improvement of living conditions for working people, supported public education and advocated woman suffrage.

Mill's education was representative of other nineteenth century intellectual figures educated partially or entirely at home. Robert Lewis Stevenson (1850-1894) was plagued by chronic bronchial and gastric ailments. At age eight he almost died, forcing him to spend much of his childhood at home. Various family members acted as his tutors.[97] An ailing child, Thomas Hardy (1840-1928), was taught at home by his mother until age eight and again tutored at age sixteen.[98] A Rugby school headmaster, Thomas Arnold, received his early education from his mother. Miss Delafield, an aunt, directed his childhood tutoring until his later admission to a school in Wiltshire.[99]

Perhaps the most famous late-Victorian figure that experienced both a nanny and governess in his early education was Winston Churchill. Mrs. Everest was engaged as Winston's nanny in 1874. They remained very close until her death in 1895. Before he was seven, Lady Randolph Churchill engaged a governess to tutor him. He didn't like her: "He kicked, he screamed, he hid." One day the parlor maid was summoned to the room where the tutoring was done. It was not the governess who rang, but Winston, "Take Miss Hutchinson away. She is very cross." Soon after Winston was sent off to school where neither his studies or behavior improved. This combination of nanny and governess was not unusual for those educated at home. Tutoring still either preceeded or supplemented many children's schooling.[100]

Many significant women intellectuals and feminists of the nineteenth century also received a domestic education. Frances Power Cobbe (1822-1904), Irish reformer and feminist, was educated at home. The English feminist and educational reformer Sarah Emily Davies (1830-1921) was tutored at home. Catherine Booth (1829-1890), co-founder of the Salvation Army, because of ill-health received a domestic education. Josephine Butler (1828-1900), an English feminist was tutored chiefly by her mother. The daughter of a prosperous doctor from East Lothian, Jane Welsh Carlyle (1801-1866) was given a private yet rigorous classical education from the age of five. Jane married Thomas Carlyle in 1826.

The Welsh author Charlotte Elizabeth Guest (1812-1895) read widely and learned modern, classical, Hebrew and Persian languages with her brother's tutors. Felicia Hemans (1793-1835), British poet, was educated privately at home by her mother. Eglantyne Jebb, (1876-1928), child welfare worker, was educated at home before attending Oxford. The English doctor, Sophia Jex-Blake (1840-1912), progressed from her private tutoring at home to holding a tutorship in mathematics at Queen's College, London.

The Irish nationalist politician, Constance Markiewicz (née Gore-Booth) (1868-1927), was born in London. The sister of the trade unionist Eva Gore-Booth, she was educated by various governesses at the family home in County Sligo. Three English poets, Charlotte Mary Mew (1869-1928), Alice Maynell (1847-1922), and Christina Rossetti (1830-1894) were born in London and educated at home.

The Pankhurst family of suffragettes came from Manchester. Emmeline Pankhurst (1858-1928), often simply known as Mrs. Pankhurst, had three daughters Christabel (1880-1958), Sylvia (Estelle) (1882-1960) and Adela (1885-1961). All three daughters received their entire elementary education at home before attending secondary school, and were active in the early activities of the Women's Social and Political Union (WSPU). Other reformers educated at home included Maria Susan Rye (1829-1903), English feminist and Gertrude Tuckwell (1861-1951), an activist in the trade unionist movement.[101] This cross-section of British nineteenth century society was representative of the breadth and depth of the domestic education movement.

Queen Victoria (1819-1901) had supported Queen's College, perhaps in remembrance of her own governess Louise Lehzen.

> At Claremont . . . I sat and took my lessons in my Governess' bedroom. I was not fond of learning as a little child-- and baffled every attempt to teach me letters up to five years old--when I consented to learn them by their being written down before me. . . . [Miss Lehzen] was most kind, she was very firm and I had proper respect for her.[102]

Lehzen devoted her life to Victoria from the princess' fifth to eighteenth year. In addition to her basic education, in 1837 the Very Reverend George Daveys, Dean of Chester, was appointed her tutor to teach Latin and direct her general reading. Victoria liked her tutor so that years afterwards, in gratitude for his services, she made him a bishop. In addition to her study of Latin, she grew up speaking German and studied French. Victoria was a ready, if not brilliant pupil.[103]

During the period of 1870 to 1895 the British government began committing itself to the provision of a national system of elementary schools supported by public funds, and backed by compulsory attendance laws. However, not until 1914 did all children in England between the ages of twelve and sixteen continue their school attendance. As schools multiplied and improved in quality, it became increasingly popular to send both boys and girls to school to complete their education. The First World War (1914-1918) accelerated a national trend. The governess did not completely disappear, but became a teacher for only the young child.[104]

## 4. TUTORS AND GOVERNESSES ABROAD

During the late eighteenth and throughout the nineteenth centuries the influence of domestic education by the tutor-governess was felt in many regions overseas. On the Continent despite the growth of schools, private education proved almost as popular as in England. Numerous French and German works on domestic education were published or translated from English.[105]

In England between 1849 and 1862 several organizations were established that promoted the immigration of governesses around the world. The National Benevolent Emigration Society, the Society for the Employment of Women and the Female Middle-Class Emigration Society helped single women travel to the utmost corners of the globe to earn their livelihood. During the nineteenth century the reputation of the English governess stood very high. The educational value of acquiring a respectable well-trained English governess was recognized by many foreign families. A so-called "English Governess system" of genteel lady governesses exercised enormous power and disseminated the traditional English way of life through European society and much of the world. The quintessential English governess abroad combined the role of tutor with a pioneer spirit and the missionary's zeal. She became an interesting addition to the Victorian sense of a "civilizing mission" during this imperialist era. This was in apparent contradiction to the fact that while the English governess retained her high standing abroad, her position was rather low in England.[106]

Some of the best representatives from the tens of thousands of the English tutor-governesses abroad included Miss Emily Payne, who journeyed to what is now Laos to be the governess to the local Shan chief, Hsipavi Sawbwa (1862). There she died, her grave

227

marked by a simple cross on which are carved these words: "Emily Payne Lady Governess." Claire Clairmont was a typical English continental governess. She engaged herself as a governess to a Russian family in Moscow (1824). She later lived in Pisa and finally Florence, giving her English lessons at one Italian house or another.[107]

Another young Englishwoman, Maria Graham, became Brazil's first and last Imperial Governess (1823-1824). Even France's Tuileries saw a young English woman, Anna Bicknell as a governess to the two daughters of the Conte de Tascher de la Pagerie, Grand Master of the Empress Eugénie's Household (1852). Anna was,

> not a mere teacher, but also was employed in "governing" their education, superintending their studies, directing their reading, and accompanying them wherever they went . . . . The two girls being of different ages, the professors, classes, lectures, etc., were also totally different;. . . . During these lectures, etc., I had to take notes incessantly, and to prepare the work for them.

Anna Bicknell's Life In The Tuileries Under the Second Empire (1894) is a vivid account of the important role of a state governess at the French court.[108]

With the fall of France's Second Empire (1870), Vienna became the favorite European capital of English governesses. A great demand ensued for them to teach well-bred Austrian girls. To mark Queen Victoria's Jubilee (1877), the English residents of Vienna founded a home for governesses, the Queen Victoria Home for British Governesses.[109]

In 1862 the Viceroy of Egypt's London agent engaged the services of Emmeline Lott as governess to the infant son of the Grand Pasha. She wrote of her experiences in The English Governess in Egypt and Turkey (1865).[110]

Miss Eager's Six Years at the Russian Court,

(1906) told of her work as the governess to Grand Duchesses Olga, Tatania and Marie. From 1899 to 1905 she taught her pupils basic subjects supplemented by special tutors. The birth of the Tsarevitch in 1904 precipitated Miss Eager's departure, since an all-Russian educational staff was demanded for the future heir. She was not the only women acting in a teaching capacity in Imperial Russia. In St. Petersburg there was the English Governesses' Club Room operated in connection with a local English church.[111]

One of the best documented episodes of the overseas English tutor-governess was Anna Leonowens (1834-1915) at the court of Siam. A daughter of Thomas Crawford, a British officer killed in India, Anna married Thomas Leonowens also an officer in the Indian Army. After the death of her young husband, she supported herself by opening (1859) a small school in Singapore for officers' children. It attracted the attention of Mr. Tau Kim Ching, the Siamese Counsul, at Singapore. He had been instructed by King Mana Mongkut of Siam to find an English teacher for his children. In February, 1862 the King wrote Anna formally inviting her to come to the Royal Palace at Bangkok, "to do your best endeavour upon us and our children." She was to teach them the English language, science and literature. Anna accepted the invitation and one month later left Singapore for Bangkok with her son, Louis.[112]

Somdetch P'hra Paramendr Maha Mongkut (1804-1867) was the progressive king of Siam. He acquired some knowledge of Latin and science from the Jesuits, but after the arrival of Protestant missionaries selected the Reverend Mr. Caswell, an American minister, as his permanent tutor. Caswell taught him Latin, English, government, commerce and religion.[113]

During Anna's five years in Bangkok (1862-1867) she taught between twenty and twenty-five princes and princesses besides several gentlewomen and wives of the harem. Their favorite studies were geography and astronomy.[114]

Her most important pupil was Prince Chulalongkorn, the ten-year-old heir apparent. Anna found him "modest, affectionate, eager to learn and easy to influence." Anna taught the Prince privately from seven to ten in the evening. This instruction had a profound influence on Prince Chulalongkorn. When this prince succeeded to the throne, he abolished slavery and instituted many social reforms.[115]

Upon Anna's departure (1867) she travelled to the United States and published The English Governess at the Siamese Court (1870) and Siamese Harem Life (1873) on her work as a royal governess. Both books became very popular.[116] She also established (1867) in New York City a school for the training of kindergarten teachers. In 1884, having moved to Halifax, Nova Scotia, she returned to New York to meet one of her old pupils, now the ambassador of Siam to the United States.[117]

Anna maintained her contacts with her old pupil, the Crown Prince. Now King Chulalongkorn, she met him in London thirty years after her departure (1897). Her grandson Louis, a physician, travelled to Siam and became the king's close advisor. The king sent Anna a silver work box and autographed portrait, "which I prize above everything. It is quite refreshing," Anna wrote a friend, "to be remembered after so many years."[118]

After a lifetime of teaching Anna wrote her old friend wondering if she had accomplished anything of lasting importance. In January, 1911, King Chula died. In his will he left her a bequest, "it has touched me deeply that he held one so long in his loving remembrance."[119]

The phenomenal international recognition given to Anna Leonowens[120] was a fitting epitaph for all the other forgotten tutor-governesses. They had made a valuable educational contribution throughout the Victorian era. Their students were among the foremost educational and social reformers. The widespread social impact of the tutor-governess helped condition British society to favor education for women and ultimately mandatory schooling for all children. This was the last generation of widespread full-time domestic education. These teachers reflected the ideals from past humanist tutors and child-centered theorists, as well as more contemporary Victorian attitudes on education. Even with the inception of universal mandatory schooling, their rich legacy from centuries of tutoring can still be identified in the theory, and methods of twentieth-century English education.

Endnotes

1.  James Walvin, A Child's World (New York: Penguin, 1982), 111-112; Aries, Childhood, 269; David Wardle, The Rise Of The Schooled Society (London: Routledge and Kegan Paul, 1974), 68.

2.  John Burnett, ed., Destiny Obscure (New York: Penguin Books, 1982), 169-170, 231; George C. Brauer, Jr., The Education of A Gentleman (New York: Bookman Associates, 1939), 195; Wardle, Schooled Society, 68.

3.  Horace Mann, Census of Great Britain, 1851, Education In Great Britain Being The Official Report of Horace Mann (London: George Routledge and Company, 1854). How accurate was a nineteenth century census? The 1841 census was the first to be based upon householder's schedules delivered to every householder a few days before the census night. Results tended to indicate very inaccurate reporting of ages or misunderstood instructions. However, Wrigley and Schofield believe that there is some evidence that by the 1851 census the vast majority of people made an accurate return of the requested census data. E.A. Wrigley and R.S. Schofield, The Population History of England 1541-1871 (Cambridge, Massachusetts: Harvard University Press, 1981), 104.

4.  The report was submitted to George Graham, Registrar-General, who had been in charge of England's 1851 census. The material was prefaced with an introductory statement to Lord Palmerston, Secretary of State. Mann, Education

In Great Britain, A3 - A4; Frank Smith, A History Of English Elementary Education (London: University of London Press, 1931), 220.

5. This did not include the large number of students attending "charity schools."

6. Wardle, English Popular Education, 118; Wardle, Schooled Society, 68-69; Smith, Elementary Education, 221.

7. Wardle, English Popular Education, 118-119; Burnett, Destiny Obscure, 231; Pollock, Forgotten Children, 247-249. Even in higher education at Oxford and Cambridge the focus by mid-century was on the role of the university tutor as a source of moral and intellectual reforms. The tutor became the principal source of instruction. Their role gradually became a stepping stone to higher rank. The professor was eventually seen as a superior form of tutor, thus welding the two methods together. Lawson and Silver, Education, 297; E.G.W. Bill, University Reform In Nineteenth Century Oxford (Oxford: Clarendon Press, 1973), 75-77; Dacre Balsdon, Oxford Now and Then (New York: St. Martin's Press, 1970), 30-31.

8. C. John Sommerville, The Rise and Fall of Childhood (London: Sage Publications, 1982), 150-151, 156-157; Dorothy M. George, London Life In The Eighteenth Century (London: Kegan Paul, 1925), 406.

9. E.A. Wrigley and R.S. Schofield, The Population History of England 1541-1871 (Cambridge, Massachusetts: Harvard University Press, 1981), 529.

10. Quintilian, "Quintilian's Institutes of Eloquence," trans. Gutherie, in Luella Cole, History of Education: Socrates to Montessori (New York: Rhinehart and Company, 1950), 52.

11. Benjamin Wright, "Should Children Teach?" Elementary School Journal LX (April, 1960): 353.

12. Ibid., 354; Jean Baptiste de la Salle, _Conduite des Ecoles_ (Paris: J. Moronual, 1838).

13. John Amos Comenius, _The Great Didactic_, Part II, trans. Keatinge (London: A & C Black, Ltd., 1921), 47.

14. John Brinsley, _The Grammar Schoole_, ed. Campagnac (London: Constable and Company, Ltd., 1917), 272.

15. Andrew Bell, _Bell's Mutual Tuition and Moral Discipline_ (London: C.J.G. & F. Livingston, 1832), 75. A Monitorial School "text" was published in India in 1797 and 1815 as an early attempt at an English language textbook; John Miller, _The Tutor_ (Serampore, 1797; Calcutta, 1815) (Menston: The Scholar Press, 1971).

16. Vernon L. Allen, ed., _Children As Teachers_ (New York: Academic Press, 1976), 13; Val D. Rust, _Alternatives In Education_ (London: Sage Publications, 1977), 113.

17. David Salmon, ed., _The Practical Parts of Lancaster's Improvements and Bell's Experiment_ (1805) (Cambridge: University Press, 1932), VIII - IX.

18. Joseph Lancaster, _Improvements In Education As It Respects The Industrious Classes Of The Community_ (London: Darton and Harvey, 1803), 31-32; Lilya Wagner, _Peer Teaching Historical Perspective_ (London: Greenwood Press, 1982), 61-84.

19. Silver, _Popular Education_, 17-67; R.K. Webb, _Modern England_ (New York: Dodd, Mead and Company, 1971), 154.

20. Lancaster, _Improvements_, 31-32.

21. Carl F. Kaestle, ed. _Joseph Lancaster and the Monitorial School Movement_ (New York: Teachers College Press, 1973), 4, 6-8; Carl F. Kaestle, _Pillars Of The Republic_ (New York: Hill and Way, 1983), 67; Vernon L. Allen, ed. _Children As_

_Teachers_ (New York: Academic Press, 1976), 13-16.

22. Butts, _Western Education_, 407; Kaestle, _Joseph Lancaster_, 3, 4, 31-34, 37, 44-48; Allen, _Children As Teachers_, 16, 17; Gabriel Compayré, _The History Of Pedagogy_ (Boston: D.C. Heath, 1886), 514-517.

23. G.M. Young, ed. _Early Victorian England 1830-1865_, vol. 2 (London: Oxford University Press, 1934), 108-111, 491-492; Jonathan Gathorne-Hardy, _The Rise And Fall Of The British Nanny_ (London: Hodder and Stoughton, 1972), 126-128; Howe, _Governesses_, 79-128.

24. Hardy, _British Nanny_, 21, 57, 126-127.

25. Young, _Early Victorian England_, 110; Howe, _Governesses_, 12.

26. Kamm, _Hope Deferred_, 166, 170-173; Deborah Gorham, _The Victorian Girl_ (Bloomington: Indiana University Press, 1982), 20-21; Howe, _Governesses_, 81-82; Robert Mudie, _The Complete Governess_ (London: Printed for Knight and Lacey, 1826); Wanda Neff, _Victorian Working Women_ (New York: AMS Press, 1966), 164.

27. Ellen Weeton, _Miss Weeton, Journal Of A Governess 1807-1811_, ed. Hall (London: Oxford University Press, 1936), VII-XIX.

28. Ibid., 201.

29. Ibid., 210-215; Howe, _Governesses_, 83-88.

30. Ibid.

31. Ibid., 89-92; Weeton, _Journal_, XI-XII.

32. William Thackeray, _Vanity Fair_ (London: Smith, Elder, 1910), 89. This was one of the major novels of nineteenth century English literature, and presents a valuable portrayal of the governess.

33. Howe, <u>Governesses</u>, 112-113; Neff, <u>Working Women</u>, 154-156.

34. Ibid., 115.

35. M. Oliphant, <u>The Story Of A Governess</u> (New York: R.F. Fenno, 1897), 29-32.

36. Thackeray, <u>Vanity Fair</u>, 52.

37. Frederika Bremer, <u>The President's Daughter</u>, trans. Howitt, vol. 1 (London: Longman, Brown, Green and Longmans, 1843), 1-2; Lee Holcombe, <u>Victorian Ladies At Work</u> (Hamden, Connecticut: Archon Books, 1973), 4-5.

38. Ibid., 115, 125-126, 121-123; Neff, <u>Working Women</u>, 165-174.

39. Elizabeth Barrett Browning "Aurora Leigh," (1856) in <u>The Complete Poetical Works Of Elizabeth Barrett Browning</u> (New York: Houghton Mifflin, 1900), 260.

40. <u>Parliamentary Papers</u>, 1852-53, Volume LXXXVIII; Howe, <u>Governesses</u>, 115-116; M. Jeanne Peterson, "The Victorian Governess: Status Incongruence In Family And Society," <u>Victorian Studies</u> 14 (September, 1970): 8.

41. Mann, <u>Education In Great Britain</u>, 21, 42.

42. <u>Parliamentary Papers</u>, 1867-68, Part IV, Vol. XXXIII, 246, 944; <u>Parliamentary Papers</u>, 1867, Part III, Vol. XXXIII, 693.

43. G.M. Young and W.D. Handcock, <u>English Historical Documents</u> 1833-1874, Vol. XII, pt. 1 of <u>English Historical Documents</u>, ed. David C. Douglas (London: Eyre and Spottiswoode, 1956), 207-215.

44. It is difficult to find a satisfactory definition of the "middle class," but one Victorian described them aptly as "that part of the population which, on the whole, and mainly, has to earn its own living, and to earn it by headwork rather than by handwork." H.J. Roby,

National Association for the Promotion of Social Science, Transactions, XXIII (1879), 386.

45.  Peterson, The Victorian Governess, 9-10; Holcombe, Victorian Ladies, 10-11.

46.  Bessie Rayner Parkes, Essays On Woman's Work (London: Alexander Strahan, 1866), 88; Holcombe, Victorian Ladies, 5-6, 12.

47.  Ibid., 11-13; Howe, Governesses, 116.

48.  Anna Brownwell Jameson, Memoirs and Essays Illustrative of Art, Literature and Social Morals (New York: Wiley and Putnam, 1846); Anna Brownwell Jameson, A Commonplace Book of Thoughts, Memories, and Fancies, Original And Selected (London: Longman, Brown, Green and Longmans, 1854); Anna Brownwell Jameson, Sisters of Charity and the Communion Of Labour: Two Lectures on the Social Employment of Women (London: Longman, Brown, Green, Longman and Roberts, 1859)

49.  Charlotte Mary Younge, "The Governess," In Storehouse of Stories, 2 vols. (London: Macmillan, 1970), I, 89-222; Charlotte Mary Younge, The Daisy Chain, 2 vols. (New York: D. Appleton, 1856); Charlotte Mary Younge, The Trial (London: Macmillan, 1898); Charlotte Mary Younge, Womankind (London: Macmillan, 1876); Howe, Governesses, 123; Kamm, Hope Deferred, 172; Harriet Martineau, Harriet Martineau's Autobiography and Memorials of Harriet Martineau, ed. Chapman, 2 vols. (Boston: J.R. Osgood, 1877).

50.  Susan Nash, "'Wanting A Situation:' Governesses And Victorian Novels" (Ph.D. diss., Rutgers University, 1980), 335-336.

51.  Charles Dickens (1812-1870) in Nicholas Nickleby (1867) popularized the dreadful conditions persisting in the Yorkshire schools. Dickens even traveled to Yorkshire for documentation of their negligence, cruelty and pedantic incompetence. Charles Dickens, Nicholas Nickleby (New

York:   Bantam Books, 1983), XXI-XXIII, 83-85,
91-92, 191-192; Edgar Johnson, Charles Dickens
(New York:   Viking Penguin, 1952), 137-138.

52.  Wanda Neff, Victorian Working Women (New York:
     AMS Press, 1966), 153.

53.  Nash, Governesses, 4, 14.

54.  Thackeray, Vanity Fair; William Thackeray, The
     Memoirs of Barry Lyndon (London:   Smith, Elder,
     1908).

55.  Anthony Trollope, The Bertrams (London:   Chapman
     and Hall, 1859); Anthony Trollope, The Duke's
     Children (London:   Chapman and Hall, 1880);
     Anthony Trollope, The Eustace Diamonds (London:
     Chapman and Hall, 1873); Anthony Trollope,
     "Gentle Euphemia" The Fortnightly Review (May,
     1866); Anthony Trollope, Barchester Towers
     (London:   Longmans, 1857); Winifred Gerould and
     James Gerould, A Guide To Trollope (Princeton,
     New Jersey:   Princeton University Press, 1948),
     3, 41, 60, 170, 224.

56.  Charlotte Brontë, Jane Eyre (New York:   New
     American Library, 1963); Charlotte Brontë,
     Shirley, in Novels of the Sisters Brontë, ed.
     Scott, 2 vols. (Edinburgh:   John Grant, 1905);
     Charlotte Brontë, Villette, (Boston:   Houghton
     Mifflin, 1971); Ann Brontë, Agnes Grey (London:
     Oxford University Press, 1971); Ann Brontë, The
     Tenant of Wildfell Hall, vol. VI of The Life And
     Works Of The Sisters Brontë (New York:   Haworth,
     1900); Emily Brontë, Wuthering Heights (London:
     Oxford University Press, 1930); Elizabeth
     Gaskell, The Life Of Charlotte Brontë (1857) ed.
     Shelston (New York:   Viking Penguin, 1975), 97-
     111, 158, 210; Howe, Governesses, 93-110.

57.  Thackeray was later wounded by the rumor that
     Jane Eyre had been written by one of his
     daughter's own governesses in both admiration
     and revenge for his having modelled, or so
     Charlotte Brontë thought mistakenly, the
     character of Vanity Fair's Becky Sharp on her;
     Howe, Governesses, 114-115.

237

58. Neff, Working Women, 174; Gaskell, Brontë, 320, 327, 342-343; International Dictionary of Women's Biography, s.v. Brontë; Untermeyer, Lives, 514-517.

59. Nash, Governesses, 16.

60. Cecil Woodham-Smith, Florence Nightingale (London: Constable, 1950), 11; Edward Cook, The Life of Florence Nightingale (New York: MacMillan, 1942), 12-15; Deborah Gorham, The Victorian Girl and the Femine Ideal (Bloomington: Indiana University Press, 1982), 127-129; Kamm, Hope Deferred, 171; Howe, Governesses, 116.

61. J. Kaye, A History of Queen's College London 1848-1972 (London: Chatto and Windus, 1972), 11-12.

62. Nash, Governesses, 336, 338; Kamm, Hope, 172; Holcombe, Victorian Ladies, 14-15.

63. Grylls R. Glynn, Queen's College 1848-1948 (London: Routledge and Kegan Paul, 1948), 2-3, 7-8, 15, 113.

64. Nash, Governesses, 336; Holcombe, Victorian Ladies, 26-27; Kamm, Hope, 173-174; Neff, Working Women, 176-178; Stocks, Better Than Rubies, 175; Grylls R. Glynn, Queen's College 1848 - 1948 (London: Routledge and Kegan Paul, 1948), 2-3, 7-8, 15, 113.

65. M. Jeanne Peterson, "The Victorian Governess: Status Incongruency In Family and Society," Victorian Studies 14 (September, 1970): 7; Kamm, Hope, 174.

66. The Kentish Town Home was still flourishing in 1966; Neff, Working Women, 176-178; Kamm, Hope, 175; Holcombe, Victorian Ladies, 26-27.

67. Holcombe, Victorian Ladies, 33.

68. Harriet Martineau, Household Education (London: Smith, Elder and Company, 1864).

69. Ibid., 1-3.

70. Ibid., 10, 17.

71. Ibid., 194-195, 197-198.

72. Ibid., 210-211, 275-282.

73. Ibid., 228, 235, 298-300.

74. Johann Heinrich Pestalozzi, Leonard and Gertrude, trans. Channing (Boston: D.C. Heath, 1885), IX, X, 1, 53, 94-95.

75. Friedrich Froebel, The Songs and Music of Friedrich Froebel, ed. Blow (New York: D. Appleton and Company, 1911).

76. Friedrich Froebel, Die Menschenerziehung (Berlin: 1826); Friedrich Froebel, Mutter-und Koselieder (Berlin: 1844).

77. Maria Montessori, The Montessori Method, trans. George (New York: Schocken Books, 1964), 43-47, 107-118; Rita Kramer, Maria Montessori (New York: G.P. Putnam's Sons, 1976), 235-369, 374; E.M. Standing, Maria Montessori (Fresno: Academy Library Guild, 1957), 3-7, 17-34, 243-259.

78. A representative sample of the literature on "domestic education" includes: Elizabeth Appleton, Early Education (London: G. & W.B. Whittaker, 1821); Isaac Taylor, Home Education, from the second London Edition (New York: D. Appleton & Co., 1838); Edwin Abbott, Hints On Home Teaching (London: Seeley, Jackson and Halliday, 1883); Charlotte Mason, Home Education (London: Kegan Paul, Trench & Co., 1886); Oliver Joseph Lodge, Parent and Child (London & New York: Funk and Wagnalls, 1910); Edward Lytlelton, The Corner-Stone of Education; An Essay On The Home Training of Children (London & New York: G.P. Pitman's Sons, 1914).

79. Complete Report of the General Session of the First International Congress on Home Education Held At Liége, 1905 (Brussels: A. Lesigne, 1905).

239

80. S.G. Goodrich, <u>Fireside Education</u> (London: William Smith, 1841), IV.

81. Ibid., 84, 100, 109, 111.

82. Herbert Spencer, <u>Education: Intellectual, Moral, Physical</u> (New York: D. Appleton and Company, 1897).

83. Ibid., 134-135.

84. Ibid., 156.

85. Edwin A. Abbott, <u>Hints On Home Teaching</u> (London: Seeley, Jackson and Halliday, 1883), 1-12, 13-45, 49-73, 74-117, 118-150, 151-169, 170-206.

86. Immanuel Kant, <u>The Educational Theory of Immanuel Kant</u>, ed. Buchner (Philadelphia: Lippincott and Company, 1904), 127-128.

87. John Stuart Mill, <u>Principles of Political Economy</u> (London: Longmans, Green, 1923), 956; Gillian Sutherland, <u>Policy-Making In Elementary Education 1870-1895</u> (Oxford: Oxford University Press, 1973), 117.

88. John Stuart Mill, <u>Autobiography of John Stuart Mill</u> (New York: Columbia University, 1944).

89. Ibid., 1-4.

90. Ibid., 5-13.

91. Ibid., 17-18.

92. Ibid., 19-21.

93. Ibid., 21.

94. Ibid., 24-25.

95. Ibid., 26, 56.

96. Ibid., 22.

97. Steven Mintz, A Prison of Expectations (New York: New York University Press, 1983), 42.

98. Untermeyer, Lives, 533.

99. Thomas Arnold, The Life and Correspondence of Thomas Arnold, ed. Stanley (London:    T. Fellowes, Ludgate, 1858), 1-6.

100. Jonathan Gathorne-Hardy, The Rise and Fall of the British Nanny (London:    Hodder and Stoughton, 1972), 18, 19, 26; William Manchester, The Last Lion (Boston:    Little, Brown, 1983), 118-119.

101. The International Dictionary of Women's Biography, 1st ed., s.v. "Cobbe, Frances Power," "Davies (Sarah) Emily," "Booth, Catherine," "Butler, Josephine," "Carlyle, Jane Welsh," "Guest, Charlotte Elizabeth," "Hemans, Felicia," "Jebb, Eglantyne," "Sophia, Jex-Blake," "Markiewicz (née Gore-Booth) Constance," "Mew, Charlotte Mary," "Maynell, Alice," "Rossetti, Christina," "Pankhurst," "Rye, Maria (Susan)," "Tuckwell, Gertrude."

102. Queen Victoria, Queen Victoria In Her Letters and Journals, ed. Hibbert (New York:    Viking, 1985), 9-11.

103. Marples, Princes, 154-159.

104. Sutherland, Elementary Education, 2,340; West, Governesses, 213.

105. Stephanie Felicite Gendis, Lessons of A Governess To Her Pupils, 2 vols. (Dublin:    P. Wogan, P. Byne, 1793); Aime-Martin, The Education of Mothers of Families, trans. Lee (London: Whittaker and Company, 1841), iii, iv, x, xv, 4, 5-11, 69-72; J.H. Plumb, "The Great Change In Children," Horizon 13 (Winter, 1971): 11; Karl von Raumer, "Contributions to the History of Pedagogy" in American Journal of Education 7 (1859): 381.

106. Peterson, The Victorian Governess, 20-21.

107. Howe, Governesses, 127-130.

108. Ibid., 131-153; Anna L. Bicknell, Life in the Tuileries Under the Second Empire (New York: The Century Co., 1895), 13, 19.

109. Elizabeth Kyle, The Skaters Waltz; Miss May, Recollections of a Royal Governess (London: Hulchisn & Co., 1915).

110. Emmeline Lott, The English Governess in Egypt and Turkey (London: Richard Bentley, 1865).

111. M. Eager, Six Years at the Russian Court (London: Hurst and Blackett, 1906); Howe, Governesses, 182. In 1908 the Russian Imperial family did hire an Englishman, Charles Sydney Gibbes to teach English to the princesses. By 1913 they asked Gibbes to also teach the nine-year-old Tsarevich. The lessons continued until the 1917 revolution. J.C. Trewin, Tutor of the Czar (London: Macmillan, 1975), 12-33.

112. Anna Leonowens, The English Governess at the Siamese Court (London: Arthur Barker, Ltd., 1954), 1-128; Howe, Governesses, 162.

113. Leonowens, English Governess, 200-202.

114. Ibid., 203-236.

115. Ibid., 128-139.

116. Ibid., Anna Leonowens, Siamese Harem Life (Philadelphia: 1873).

117. Anna Leonowens to Annie Adams Fields, 17 May 1884, Anna Leonowens Papers, Huntington Library, San Marino, California.

118. Leonowens Papers, 3 January 1905, 5 January 1907, 15 March 1909, 5 June 1909.

119. Leonowens Papers, 7 January 1911.

120. Anna's life at the Siamese court was made into the Broadway musical play and later film, <u>The King and I</u>.

CHAPTER 7

THE AMERICAN TUTOR: THE COLONIAL EXPERIENCE
(1600-1789)


1. ORIGINS


Without doubt European tutor-theorists inspired American domestic education throughout the colonial-frontier experience. Unlike urban Europe, the American tutor had to cope with a predominantly isolated, rural, frontier environment. These teachers were professional tutor-governesses; student school monitors; rural school instructors; "circuit-riding tutors;" or family "domestic educators." Their chronicles document three centuries of melding European tutorial concepts with the teaching methods required by a distinctive American society. Tutorial education contributed to the birth of the American public school, and the rise in the early twentieth century of the Progressive "child centered" education movement.

As in Europe, the history of tutoring during the early colonial times (1600-1789) was joined closely to the development of schools in each local community. Provenzo believes that the colonial child who learned reading was as likely to be taught at home as by going to school. Domestic education was common throughout the 1600s and 1700s.[1] Josiah Cotton (1680-1756) of Massachusetts noted in his diary,

My younger days were attended with the follies and vanities incident to youth howsoever I quickly learned to read, without going to any school I remember.[2]

Cremin tells us that if a New England child grew up in a home of non-readers, neighbors often offered to tutor the child. When a mother decided to teach reading in her kitchen on a regular basis to others, in addition to her own children, she charged them a modest fee. She became a "dame school." In Virginia the same activity of tutoring was called a "petty school."[3]

Unlike comparative European society, private tutors (professional masters) for individual students were simply impractical in the colonies, except in the isolated plantation South. The primary reason was that there were not enough qualified tutors. This did not mean that tutors or governesses were entirely absent from the educational scene. Colonial newspapers were used frequently by both to advertise for students. In eighteenth century Boston, New York, Philadelphia, Savannah and other cities, newspapers provided a good medium for these prospective teachers.[4] Other tutors posted notices at the town hall, post office or local inn.

> These are to give Notice, that there is just arrived here a Certain Person and his Wife fit for any Town, to teach School, both Latin, and to Read and Write English, and his Wife for teaching Needle Work, any Person that wants such may be informed at the Post-Office in Boston (1718).[5]

These teachers often taught both children and adults, acting as schoolmasters for children by day and tutors for adults in the evening. William Elphinston advertised for students in the New York Mercury between 1765 and 1767.

### William Elphinston

> Teaches persons of both sexes, from 12 years of age and upwards, who never wrote before, to write a good legible hand, in 7 weeks one hour per day, at home or abroad.[6]

Woody believes that women were mostly educated at home throughout this time period and well into the nineteenth century. Girls' schools did not attract significant enrollment until after 1850. However, there is no accurate way to determine the exact number of children or adults taught at home by governesses or tutors. Long has concluded that colonial newspaper advertisements by tutor-governesses do provide credence that enough people paid for tutoring to keep a large number of these educators in business.[7] To obtain a more detailed understanding of these educational activities, a regional review will be made of the English colonies before the American revolution.

## 2. NEW ENGLAND

The Massachusetts Bay Puritans were heir to what Cremin calls the English, "Renaissance traditions stressing the centrality of the household as the primary agency of human association and education."[8] Imitating the earlier Royal Injunctions of the Tudors (1536, 1547, 1559) they were the first among the colonies to legislate reading instruction of children at home by their parents (1642). The idea that the family was also a "school" revealed the overbearing Puritan sense of purpose. Similar laws were adopted, somewhat later, by Connecticut (1650), New Haven (1655), New York (1665) Plymouth (1671) and Pennsylvania (1683).[9] This effort was repeated by Massachusetts in 1648. These laws ordered town officials to check that parents were teaching their children reading, religion and the laws of the colony.[10] A clear indication of domestic education's importance were specific court orders in 1670, 1674 and 1676 enforcing these statues on negligent parents. It is difficult to measure the extent of enforcement of these laws. Morris points to statistical evidence that recorded between 1640 and 1700 a 95 percent rate for New England males, compared to 54-60 percent for their Virginia counterparts. Cremin has concluded that, "there is every indication that the colonial household was even more important as an agency of education than its metropolitan counterpart (schools)."[11]

Puritan concern for education rested upon strong religious beliefs. The writings of Martin Luther, John Knox and other Reformation leaders on basic home instruction in reading and the Bible inspired the Massachusetts Puritan Cotton Mather

247

(1663-1728). He insisted upon education in order to safeguard the religious welfare of children.

> Tis the Knowledge of the Christian Religion
> that Parents are to teach their Children
> . . . without that Knowledge our Children
> are miserable to all Eternity.[12]

Instruction began as soon as children were able to understand their teacher. According to the law, (1642) at least once a week every father taught his child from a catechism. This book summarized in question and answer form the Puritan system of Christian belief. This method of tutoring required the father only to ask the questions and determine if the child answered without assistance. The child studied independently, and memorized the answers using little individual initiative. If a child developed new ideas about doctrine, they might lead to heresy. "Let the child memorize his catechism and leave originality to the devil!" But the child still had to make an effort to understand what he learned. Cotton Mather also warned parents not to let, "the children patter out by Rote the works of the Catechism, like parrots; but be Inquisitive how far their Understandings do take in the Things of God."[13] Children began studying their catechism before they were at the age of abstract reasoning. As they grew older, a good parent taught them to comprehend the significance of their answers. Increase Mather (1639-1723) recalled, "I learned to read of my mother. I learned to write of Father, who also instructed me in grammar learning, both in the Latin and the greeke Tongues [sic]."[14]

There was no doubt that domestic education was supplemented by more secular instruction in the early "Reading School" or "Dame School" of the colony. A mother tutored her own children, then took in others as young as two years old. This form of home education continued to flourish in most New England towns and villages until 1776 and even after. Here the child mastered his hornbook, speller and an easy reader like the New England Primer. He might even attend a writing school and some boys then enrolled in a grammar school.

248

Alice Earle in <u>Child Life in Colonial Days</u> chronicled how at least some "Dame Schools" used peer tutors. Reverend John Barnard of Marblehead, Massachusetts was born in 1681 and left a sketch of his school life in Boston. "[In] my sixth year . . . my mistress had made me a sort of usher appointing me to teach some children that were older than myself as well as some smaller ones." Boston was scarcely settled in 1630 before the appearance of many private teachers. These early Massachusetts' schools were very small. Many used the individual recitation method in a school setting. Little girls and young ladies from country homes in the southern colonies and Barbados boarded with Boston gentlewomen while being tutored or attending a local school.[15]

In Boston and throughout the colonies a number of children were educated by private tutors that were college students or by pastors of sectarian churches whose duties included tutoring as well as preaching. In New England ministers almost universally supplemented their meager incomes by taking young boys into their homes to tutor in residence. They also undertook the education of their own families. Reverend Timothy Edwards, father of Jonathan Edwards, tutored his son and ten daughters. Reverend Colman, President of Harvard, educated his daughter Jane at home.[16]

In colonial New England a few students ultimately attended the first American colleges. As at the English universities, these colleges incorporated a tutorial system into their overall instructional programs. After 1766 at Harvard, tutors taught a particular subject to all classes that studied it. Yale professors gave the lectures while tutors guided the individual student's absorption of books. The same Yale tutor accompanied a class up the academic ladder.

Yale recruited its tutors from its best recent graduates. The job had great prestige value, but few tutors held it more than three to four years. The typical tutor supervised fifty to seventy students and received a salary of from seventy to ninety pounds per year.

Ezra Stiles was a Yale tutor from 1749 to 1755, and kept a journal of his experiences. He meet privately with his students and reviewed their written arguments used for "disputations" twice a week. He arranged these academic exercises, appointed the students for the negative and affirmative teams and picked the topic. His tutorial methods also included drilling individual students in their assigned texts. Stiles often included his own views on the subject in the session. The activities of his European Oxbridge counterpart had a direct influence on the activities of the American New England college tutor. Since tutoring was commonly used in the schooled society of the "Puritan fathers," it was hardly surprising that the concept of individual instruction was continued at the highest level of their education institutions.[17]


## 3. THE MIDDLE AND SOUTHERN COLONIES


Societal conditions outside New England were less favorable to education. In early New Amsterdam (New York) few children received a formal education at school or home. Some children were taught by private tutors. In 1662 John Stuyvesant, Director General of the Dutch Colony, had his children taught by Aegidius Luyak. He tutored them in Latin, Greek, writing and arithmetic. He later was founder and rector of the New Amsterdam Latin School. Another teacher, Jacques Cortelyou, came to this American colony as a private tutor for the son of a Dutch family.[18] In 1664 the English seized the colony and renamed it New York. Kamen maintains that between 1695 and 1775 the majority of children in New York City learned to read and write at home. What little formal education existed in this city, Schultz also believes was largely controlled by private tutors.[19]

In neighboring Philadelphia private tutors were influential in educational development. Though William Penn regarded schooling as a public necessity, he employed a tutor for his own family. Penn had been raised as a child according to the English system of tutorial education. He preferred to "have an ingenious person in the house to teach them, then send them to school," since too many "vile impressions" were taught at the private schools of seventeenth century Philadelphia. The wide use of tutors in this colony was due in part to parents employing them to prepare sons for the Latin Schools founded in this city. These tutors were sought in England to teach boys Latin, Greek and arithmetic. According to Mulhern, the first secondary school in Pennsylvania was established (1758) on land first used by a tutor to teach local children.[20]

In the Southern colonies tutoring became the most widespread educational method for those families who could afford it. The planter class in Virginia, North Carolina and South Carolina in the early colonial period used English tutors, and later scholars from the northern colleges, for both boys and girls. Occasionally even indentured servants served as tutors. Families were scattered over such wide geographic areas that it was usually impractical to establish grammar schools. In many cases the family tutor also taught relatives and neighbors. This habitually resulted in boarding the children on a large estate. Special buildings were created on these plantations that housed the tutor and his schoolroom. Many were two stories. The tutor lived and slept on the second floor with the schoolroom below.[21] Knight tells us that during the seventeenth century this method of tutoring became known as the "Old Field School," "community school" or as the "academy." The curriculum in many cases resembled the private school or academy of that time: French, Latin, Greek and arithmetic. However, the method of instruction was one-to-one. Individualized teaching predominated rather than group activities.[22]

Berkeley Plantation, Virginia, provided an excellent profile of these educational practices. Beginning with the 1618 patent, Berkeley's history was the most thoroughly documented of all the tidewater plantations. Benjamin Harrison II bought the land in 1691. His son, Benjamin Harrison III (1673-1710), was the first child to be tutored in reading and Latin at the plantation. By 1700 his young son, Benjamin Harrison IV, was taught at a small building located on the plantation.[23] He and other neighborhood boys were instructed by a transient tutor to prepare them for the College of William and Mary. Benjamin Harrison V (1726-1791) was also educated in the same manner, becoming governor of Virginia and signer of the Declaration of Independence (1776).[24]

Some of the best insights into the work of the southern colonial tutors can be found in their letters, wills, diaries and newspaper advertisements. Many tutors' diaries of the pre-colonial and post-colonial period gave detailed descriptions of their careers as teachers. Planters used the newspaper to seek qualified men as tutors. The teachers themselves advertised their availability in the local community newspaper. From 1733 to 1774 more than four hundred advertisements relating to tutors were published alone in The South Carolina Gazette. Scores of similar notices appeared in Virginia, North Carolina, and Georgia during the later colonial and early national period.[25]

The domestic education of William C. Preston from Washington County, Virginia was typical of the period. William in his diary recollected that he was first taught to read by an Irishman named Peter Byrnes. Originally a weaver by trade, he taught successive generations of the Preston family between 1780 to 1820. When death claimed him at age 82, he was buried in the family plot. "He had always been a member of the Preston family. . . . We never failed to love and cherish him."[26]

William's next tutor was a Mr. Hercules Whaly, "a man of rare and curious accomplishments." His father had found Whaly in a remote valley of Lee County, Virginia. Whaly taught William for many years a curriculum that included: Latin, Greek, French and the literary classics. This tutor was also a talented musician who sang and played the violin. William also recorded that Whaly read and recited poetry, "with exquisite power."

> He took charge of my entire training
> (we slept in the same room) . . . we
> walked, rose and sat together . . . so that
> my process of education was continually

going on.

> Whaly and I read together most of the Latin classics and many of the English, for my father had a good library. But my parents thought (mistakenly as I have since believed) that their boy ought to be sent to a public school, and so at 14 I was sent to what was called the Washington College at Lexington (now Washington and Lee University), a college superintended by lazy and ignorant Presbyterian preachers, and filled with dirty boys of low manners and morals. In six months at this place I unlearned as much as it was possible for a boy of sprightly parts to unlearn in six months. . . .[27]

Though some ministers taught "public school" others were active in domestic education. Many ministers of the Church of England also served as tutors throughout the Southern Colonies. This parallelled their English counterparts who acted as both chaplin and teacher for families in England.[28]

John Harrower, a Scot, indentured himself to get to America (1773). Colonel William Dangerfield of Belvedira Plantation near Frederickburg, Virginia bought Harrower as a tutor for his three sons. He taught the two youngest boys to read, while the oldest son learned syllabification. In addition, Harrower taught them writing, arithmetic and annunciation. Since the Colonel had been well educated in English, he insisted that Harrower teach them proper formal English. This was not an easy task, since Harrower was not well educated, and his accent showed the distinctive Scottish "burr."

As on other plantations, the Belvedira "schoolroom" was a separate building twenty by twelve feet in size that stood near the main house. Harrower was successful in recruiting ten additional scholars. The tutors of wealthier planters' children were often engaged in teaching poorer children and adults. Harrower taught writing and arithmetic at night to Thomas Brooks, a carpenter living at the adjoining Spotswood Plantation, and on Sunday when Brooks did not go to church. Brooks earned 30 pounds a year as a carpenter as well as his room and board. He paid Harrower 40 shillings a year for this instruction. Unfortunately, for them both, after six months Brooks moved over forty miles away and his tutoring with Harrower ended.[29]

Farish tells us that the Virginia planter's goal was not professional specialization, but an education to develop a gentleman's character. In 1718 Nathanial Burnell of Carter's Grove Plantation deplored his son's inattention to this studies. His ignorance of arithmetic would hamper him in "the management of his own affairs." If he did not have a broad base of knowledge, he would be "unfit for any gentleman's conversation and therefore a scandalous person and a shame to his relations, not having one single qualification to recommend him." George Washington agreed when he later, in reference to the education of his young ward Jacky Custis (1771), admitted that "a knowledge of books is the basis upon which other knowledge is to be built." But Washington did not think that "becoming a mere scholar is a desirable education for a gentlemen."[30]

An alternative to schooling in England was the recruitment of English tutors for Virginia. They taught the planters' children at home in a building near the mansion. This was a common practice even if the family planned to send the child abroad at a later date to complete his education. The young men or women who came to tutor at southern plantations were honored members of the household. They were selected with greatest care. As the eighteenth century progressed, Virginians complained to relatives in England that it was becoming increasingly difficult to find suitable tutors. As we have seen, one frequent alternative was the employment of many Scots. This was done with some parental misgivings over the fear that they would "teach the children the Scotch dialect which they can never wear off." By the mid-eighteenth century tutors were also secured from Princeton and other American colleges.[31]

Another tutor's account, from the <u>Journal and Letters of Philip Vickers Fithian</u>, is replete with details of his life, curriculum and teaching methods.

Fithian wrote this journal during 1773-1774 while teaching the two sons, five daughters and nephew of Colonel and Mrs. Robert Carter of Nomoni Hall, Virginia.[32] Colonel Carter was a member of the Virginia Governor's Council. Two young men from Princeton also had taught the Carter children at Nomoni Hall before Fithian's arrival. Carter had hired these tutors through President Witherspoon of Princeton.[33]

Philip Vickers Fithian was a young theological graduate of Princeton College in 1773. His Northern education had prepared him to become a Presbyterian minister. In some ways this ill-suited him to enjoy, to the fullest extent, the social life of plantation Virginia. However, in addition to his extensive teaching duties, Fithian accompanied the Carters frequently to dine at their friends' homes, attend banquets and balls, converse with neighbors at the parish church, attend local races and welcome frequent guests at Nomoni Hall. He was no wall-flower.[34]

The plantation was a few miles from Belvedira, Westmoreland County and consisted of 333,000 acres of land. Rich planters as members of the southern aristocracy used tutors to instruct their sons in every branch of knowledge useful to a gentleman. Fithian's Journal is highly representative of this period's education and child-rearing practices even outside the exclusive planter class.[35]

When Fithian began his duties (November, 1773), his annual salary as a resident tutor was fixed at thirty-five pounds, use of a horse, a personal servant, borrowing books from Mr. Carter's library, and his accommodations. These were generous terms.[36]

The curriculum followed for the five girls, while liberal compared with contemporary customs in Colonial America, lacked any significant depth. Their education was limited mainly to instruction in the English language and simple arithmetic. The eldest daughter at the beginning of Fithian's instruction read the Spectator, wrote a good hand and was starting simple arithmetic. The second daughter was reading the "Spelling books and beginning to write;" the third was "reading the Spelling Books;" the fourth was "spelling in the beginning of the Spelling Books;" and the youngest daughter beginning her letters." The eldest girl, Priscilla, age fifteen, soon began studying multiplication with Fithian. All of the girls also received instruction in both vocal and instrumental music and dancing, though Fithian never identified a special tutor for these lessons. Fithian also mentioned that he instructed all the younger children, both girls and boys, in their catechism. It was the only instruction shared by both sexes.[37]

The boys of the family were given a somewhat broader tutorial education that comprised not only the study of English and arithmetic, but also Latin and Greek. The seventeen year old eldest son began reading Sallust (The Cataline Conspiracy) and Greek grammar at the inception of Fithian's teaching. Both boys were also taught Latin grammar, Virgil, the Greek Testament, English grammar, reading, writing and arithmetic.[38]

The Carter's school house was a 45 feet long and 27 feet wide brick structure with dormer windows. It was located in a square created by the school house and other buildings with the plantation's "Great House" in the center. The school building consisted of five rooms. Two bedrooms occupied the upper floor where Fithian lived with a clerk and other servants. The schoolroom occupied the lower floor with two other adjoining spaces. There was a fireplace in every room. This building seems fairly typical of others used on Southern plantations for educational purposes.[39]

Fithian's day began at about seven when he was roused by a boy who came to light the fire. By the time he was dressed the children were all gathered in the room below to hear "round one lesson." The meal bell was rung at eight o'clock and the children went out and at eight-thirty were served breakfast. School resumed at nine-thirty until the twelve o'clock bell when the children left for their free time. Lunch was served at two-thirty or three o'clock. Lessons resumed at three-thirty and continued until five o'clock. After school the tutor

256

might "continue in the schoolroom," occupy himself in private, or go over to the "Great House" and sit with Mr. and Mrs. Carter. Dinner was served between eight-thirty and nine. Fithian retired by ten or eleven each evening. This instruction routine was kept each day, Monday through Friday, though two daughters left their lessons on Tuesdays and Thursdays to practice their music. Since the eight students ranged in age from five to seventeen, many of Fithian's instructional methods were individualized for one-to-one tutorials. At other times group instruction obviously occurred, such as the younger children's catechism lessons. The children also may have tutored each other to complete mastery of a lesson.

In this way the experience of the Southern plantation tutor foreshadowed the later work of teachers in one-room, mixed-grade frontier school houses. Fithian's comments on his students also showed that the key to his success as a teacher was the recognition of individual differences.[40] His journal entries also revealed his philosophy as an educator.

Fithian gave extensive written advice to his successor John Peck on both practical teaching methods and the daily life of a tutor. Before becoming a tutor, "You had better go into the school and acquaint yourself with the method of teaching." A tutor, Fithian thought, must "have ingenuity and industry to thrive."[41] He told Peck that, "I am not urging these things to discourage you; they are hints for your direction, which, if you will attend to . . . shall make the remainder of your tasks pleasing, and the whole of it useful.[42]

Fithian warned Peck against forming hasty and ill-founded prejudices. To safeguard his reputation at all times he must "abstain totally from women . . . and acquit [himself] honorably in the character of a tutor . . . " so as to not jeopardize his example as a teacher for the Carter family. In 1773 James Marshall, a tutor at Nomoni Hall, had been asked to leave by Mr. Carter, because of his over-fondness for the opposite sex.[43]

257

The student's progress in learning and moral conduct "are wholly under your inspection." A tutor must demonstrate his wisdom but practice humility since, "you come here, it is true, with an intention to teach, but you ought likewise to have an inclination to learn." The most important attribute in a useful teacher was his diligence, for "without diligence no possible abilities or qualifications can bring children on either with speed or profit."

A tutor must "avoid visible partiality," among his students, and resist giving too many holidays for it is "a false method" to win a student's diligence. He must implement tutoring methods with deliberation, candor and precision. . . ."

> two things which are most essential for your peace and their advantage. . . . Read over carefully, the lessons in Latin and Greek, in your leisure hours, . . . for your memory is treacherous, . . . it would confound you if you should be accosted by a pert School-Boy, in the midst of a blunder . . . . You ought likewise to do this with those who are working figures . . . you will thereby convince them of the propriety of their subordination to you and obedience to your instructions. . . . The education of children requires constant unremitting attention.[44]

Tutoring each child separately while maintaining classroom discipline required ingenuity and adaptability by Fithian. Each child was guided by his temperament and capacities in the most fruitful directions. Tutors made this a commonplace practice in the eighteenth century. Based on the writings of Locke and Rousseau what was then termed the "genius" of every child was considered in planning an individual program of study.

Fithian took an obvious personal liking to the Carter children and recorded an intriguing portrait of each child. He exercised a powerful influence over these children. One of the younger boys told the tutor of his frustration over Latin grammar. Fithian told him that unless he understood Latin "he will never be able to win a young Lady of family and fashion for his wife." Latin was the most obvious mark of a gentleman in pre-revolutionary Virginia.[45]

At other times, Fithian like all other teachers, bemoaned his frustration as a tutor.

> When I am bedizen'd [sic] with these clamorous children, sometimes I silently exclaim--Once I was told, now I know I feel how irksome the Pedagogy Scheme is--Fanny--I say, Fanny, don't you hear me, Fanny and Betsy, sit down--pray, Sir, must I multiply here by 32--Yes, thick--Scull. . . .[46]

Yet we can surmise from Fithian's _Journal_ that he was somewhat reluctant to leave his pleasant life with the Carter family after a thirteen-month tenure. Southern colonial family tutors like Fithian enjoyed the highest degree of social prestige among the servants. The tutor was generally accepted in the family as a social equal. Fithian as the Carter family's educator admirably demonstrated the education precepts that the time demanded of an effective tutor.

In December, 1774 Fithian was licensed to preach by the Presbytery of Philadelphia. Less than a year later (October, 1775) he married Elizabeth Peaty. Early in 1776 Fithian enlisted as a chaplain in the Continental Army. After the battle of White Plains, New York (October 28, 1776), Fithian died in camp from dysentery and exposure. John Peck, Fithian's successor, made such a good impression as a tutor that he ultimately married one of the Carter's daughters with her father's blessing.[47]

Tutors remained popular in the South throughout the eighteenth century. _Travels of Four Years and a Half In the U.S.A._ was the chronicle of John Davis who sought employment as tutor (1798-1802) while traveling from New York to South Carolina and along the southern coast in between. Davis was born at Salisbury, England in 1776. At age eleven he first went to sea eventually visiting China, the Dutch Indies (1787) and Bombay (1790). He served on a Royal Navy frigate during the Napoleonic Wars (1793).

Though Davis never attended school he studied Greek, Latin and French, and published a total of twelve books, most on the subject of America. He allegedly was the first author to romanticize the relationship between Captain John Smith of Jamestown and Pocahontas.[48]

Upon his arrival in America Davis talked over his idea "to get into some family as a private tutor," with Mr. H. Caritat a New York bookseller. He heartily discouraged this scheme, "Alas! the labour of Sisyphus in hell is not equal to that of a private tutor in America!"[49] Caritat's description of a good American private tutor was a person who wrote with a good hand, understands all the "intricacies of calculation," and would passively submit to the title "Schoolmaster" by children, or "Cool Mossa" by the blacks. A tutor must also,

> maintain a profound silence in company to denote your inferiority; Rise at sun rise, teach till breakfast, swallow your breakfast and teach until dinner, devour your dinner and teach until tea-time, and from tea-time to bedtime sink into insignificance in the parlour.

Caritat warned Davis that tutors did not receive good wages.[50]

With these admonitions in mind Davis travelled to Charleston, South Carolina, and advertised in The Gazette for a tutorial position in a respectable family. Soon after Davis was interviewed by a local planter and his wife. The parents main interests defined the limits of their educational expectations. Could Davis "drive well?" (keep order in the schoolroom). Did he use a Southern spelling book or the odious Noah Webster Northern speller? The planter intended his wife to manage their "school," and expected total submission by a lowly hired tutor. Even with a princely salary of fifty pounds per year, Davis rejected their insulting proposal and soon after journeyed to Virginia seeking better terms of employment.[51]

Mr. Ellicott of Pecuquan Plantation, located

near the town of Colchester, Viginia sixty miles from the Potomac River, hired Davis to tutor his children for three months. The father wanted his children instructed in reading, writing and arithmetic. "As to Latin or French, he considered the study of either language an abuse of time; and very calmly desired me not to say another word about it." A little brick structure about three hundred yards from the main house contained a schoolroom with the tutor's quarters above. It looked out upon the Occuquann River.

At the end of his three month term Davis lamented that, "My condition was growing irksome . . . . I was surrounded by a throng of oafs, who read their lessons with the same tone that Punch makes when he squeaks through a comb." Unbelievably, he was now replaced by an old drunken Irishman name Burbridge. When Ellicott hired him, "he was so drunk that he could with difficulty stand on his legs." Ellicott overruled Davis' objection to hiring a sot as follows:

> Friend of all the schoolmasters I ever employed, none taught my children to write so good a hand, as a man who was constantly in a state that bordered on intoxication. They learned more of him in one month than of any other in a quarter.[52]

The journals of Fithian and Davis provide some indication of the great diversity of educational practice in colonial times. There were extreme dissimilarities among tutors in their formal preparation for teaching. Affluent southern planters did not agree on subject content, or the teaching methods used by their tutors.

Women as well as men frequently were sought as tutors, teaching not only the basics, but in some instances foreign languages, particularly French. Fithian's _Journal_ recorded that two women from England were employed as tutors near Nomoni Hall. Miss Garrot was the governess of the daughters of Colonel Tayboe. The other governess, Sally Pantan taught French, writing and English to Miss Turburville, the daughter of Richard Henry Lee.

261

During the fifty years prior to the American Revolution increasing numbers of women were employed as tutors.

Local Southern newspapers offered an extensive record of advertisements for women tutors (governesses). Conversely, women also advertized as tutors for girls. Woody believes that these private Southern teachers, of either sex, were the forerunners of the first recognized educational institutions in the South. Before 1750, "These schools supplemented in an important way the work of tutors in the household . . . but were found chiefly in the cities."[53]

It was not surprising that Walsh discovered that the majority of the "founding fathers" of the United States were educated at some point by private tutors in Latin, Greek, mathematics, science and literature. Many had been raised by distinguished Southern families. They included George Washington, Thomas Jefferson, James Madison, Charles Pickney and George Clymer. Mary Ball, the mother of George Washington, was tutored at home by a local clergyman who had been educated at Oxford. Her son was tutored first by a convict servant whom his father brought over as an indentured school teacher, then by Reverend Hobly at an "old-field school." Only later did Reverend James Marye teach George in a Fredericksburg school.

At age five Thomas Jefferson joined other children at Trickahve, Virginia in a small house in the family's plantation courtyard. There a tutor taught him in what was called "the English school."[54]

Madison was taught to read and write and the beginnings of arithmetic at home by his mother and grandmother. He boarded for a few years (1762-1767) with a Scottish schoolmaster, Donald Robertson, a well-known tutor. The course included Latin, Greek, arithmetic, geography, algebra, geometry and literature, including Locke. In 1767 a Reverend Thomas Martin, the new pastor at the Madison family parish church, was hired as the family tutor for James, his three brothers and one sister. During 1767-1768, Madison was tutored at home by Martin to prepare him for admission to the College of New Jersey

(Princeton). His college education was cut short in 1772 when he returned home to tutor, "my brothers and sisters in some of the first rudiments of literature." Madison pursued this task until the start of the American Revolution (1775).[55]


## 4. THE CORRESPONDENCE OF JOHN AND ABIGAIL ADAMS

During the transitional time in America from colony to nation the correspondence of John Adams (1735-1826) chronicled still another aspect of domestic education. John often wrote to his wife, Abigail (1774-1818), during his long absences while serving in the Continental Congress, or as an American diplomat in France. They frequently discussed Abigail's education of their four children.[56] Adams assured Abigail that she was well qualified for the role of "school mistress." He encouraged her to elevate the minds of their children by cultivating the habits of thinking and study. But their bodies also needed exercise since, "Without strength and activity and rigor of body, the brightest mental excellencies will be eclipsed and obscured."

Adams took great care in outlining the content and method for his wife's instruction of their children. He wanted them to learn a concern for "great and solid objects," a sense of moral purpose and useful skills such as writing and French. Why did John take the time to scrupulously outline this teaching program?

> I never had a regular Tudor [sic], I never studied any Thing methodically, and consequently never was compleatly [sic] accomplished in any Thing. But as I am conscious of my own Deficiency, in the Respects, I should be the less pardonable, if I neglected the Education of my children.[57]

Early youth was the best time to begin formal education, John wrote his wife, before a child forms

263

his tastes and judgments. "The Faculty of Writing is attainable, by Art, Practice, and Habit only. The sooner the practice begins the more likely it will be to succeed."

Adams also wrote his children to encourage their studies. John told Tommy (then three years old) to mind his books because, "it is only from Books and the kind Instructions of your Parents that you can expect to be useful in the World. As his sons entered their later childhood, Adams shared with Abigail his ambitions for their later education.

My sons ought to study Mathematicks [sic] and Philosophy, Geography, national History, Naval Architecture, navigation, Commerce, and Agriculture, in order to give their children a right to study Painting, Poetry, Musik [sic], Architecture, Statuary, Tapestry and Porcelaine [sic].[58]

These designs for a liberal education for his family and their progeny excluded any schooling in Europe or the "Grand Tour." "Upon no consideration whatever, would I have any of my children educated in Europe."[59] This was perhaps the reaction of his American patriotism, and disgust after prolonged exposure as a diplomat to the dissipated court life of Versailles.

Abigail Adams' positive response to her husband's educational counseling was tempered by some feelings of inadequacy. She wrote a friend Mary Warren of Plymouth that, "I am sensible I have an important trust committed to me and tho I feel myself uneaquel [sic] to it, tis still incumbent upon me to discharge it in the best manner I am capable of." Abigail's own education seems to have been a combination of home instruction and local dame schools. Her ambition for a better education and disappointment at its unavailability, led her to lament the lack of training she received in the care and early instruction of children.[60]

Faced with the education of her four children, Abigail told her friend how she had read with great interest, <u>On the Management and Education of</u>

<u>Children</u>, by the English writer Juliana Seymour (the pseudonym of John Hall). This book was one of the many such works written for parents in the eighteenth century to guide them in the "domestic education" or "fire-side" education of their off-spring. From the tone of Abigail's letter we can deduce that educating her children was not only an important intellectual task but also a role that fulfilled her as a parent. In part this daily forced intimacy with her children compensated for dreadful months of lonely separation from her husband. Over these circumstances she was not bitter. Abigail authored a poem (1773), that described her conception of a parent's duties in a child's "fire-side education."

> Parent who vast pleasure finds
> In forming her children's minds
> In midst of whom with read delight
>
> She passes many a winter's night
> Mingels in every play to find
> What Bias Nature gave the mind
> Resolving theme to take her aim
> To Guide them to the realms of fame
> And Wisely make those realms the way
> To those of everlasting day.
>
> Each Boisterous passion to control
> And early Humanize the Soul
> In side tales beside the fire
> The noblest Notions to inspire
> Her offspring conscious of her care
> Transported hang around her chair.[61]

It was obvious that not every mother in colonial America agreed with this idyllic portrayal of "domestic education." Mary Warren wrote Abigail from Plymouth and bemoaned the fact that the tutoring of her children was left wholly up to them for so many years. It appeared that parental separation notwithstanding, a great deal of colonial domestic education was left exclusively in the hands of the mother.[62]

Her friend's complaints had little effect upon Abigail's educational philosophy. Many years later she wrote her daughter, Abigail Adams Smith, instructions on how to teach her son, Johnny. Without hesitation she counseled that a child's education would occupy much of a mother's day. Education must begin early and continue in earnest. "You will always keep in mind the great importance of first principles and the necessity of instilling the precepts of morality very early into their minds.[63]

During the American colonial experience we know that a broad formal education was given in many households by a tutor or parent. Extensive use was made of the family library. In addition to the families already cited, Cremin found that domestic education was practiced in the households of famous personages such as, William Brewster of Plymouth, Gysberg van Imborch at New Amsterdam, Increase Mather at Boston and John Carter in Lancaster County, Virginia.[64] Extensive evidence exists,

> that individual reading, responsive reading, and communal reading were daily activities in many colonial households, and that reading was often taught on an each-one-teacher-one basis by parents or other elders, or by siblings or peers.[65]

Cremin has concluded that the colonial American family, "was the principal unit of social organization in the colonies and the most important agency of popular education.[66]

This combination of parents, tutors and governesses educated many children at home. America's colonial era is replete with examples of how the practice of one-to-one instruction became an integral component of existing education practices.

Endnotes

1.  H. Warren Button, Eugene F. Provenzo, Jr., History of Education and Culture In America (Englewood Cliffs: Prentice-Hall, 1983), 14-15.

2. Josiah Cotton, "Extracts from the Diary of Josiah Cotton" <u>Publications of the Colonial Society of Massachusetts</u> 24 (1927): 278.

3. Lawrence A. Cremin, <u>American Education, The Colonial Experience 1607-1783</u> (New York: Harper and Row, 1970), 128-129.

4. Wilson Smith, ed., <u>Theories of Education in Early America</u> (New York: Bobbs-Merrill Co., 1973), 61; Governesses of the period advertised for a position in: <u>Pennsylvania Gazette, American Weekly Mercury</u>, <u>New York Gazette</u>, <u>New York Mercury</u>, <u>Weekly Post Boy</u>; Thomas Woody, <u>A History of Women's Education In the United States</u>, vol. 1 (New York: Science Press, 1929), 192; Tutors of the period advertised for a position in: <u>Boston Gazette and County Journal, Gazette of the State of Georgia</u>, <u>New York Mercury</u>. Huey B. Long, "Adult Basic Education In Colonial America" <u>Adult Literacy and Basic Education</u> 7, no. 2 (1983): 55.

5. Robert Francis Seybrott, ed., <u>The Private Schools of Colonial Boston</u> (Westport, Conn: Greenwood Press, 1935), 14-15.

6. <u>New York Mercury</u>, 1 April 1765.

7. Woody, <u>Women's Education</u>, vol. 1, 51-52; Long, <u>Colonial American</u>, 66-67.

8. Cremin, <u>Colonial Experience</u>, 124.

9. Nathaniel B. Shurtleff, ed., <u>Records of the Governor and Company of the Massachusetts Bay in New England</u>, vol. 2 (Boston: William White, 1853-1854), 6-7; Hammond J. Trumbull, ed., <u>The Public Records of the Colony of Connecticut</u>, vol. 2 (Hartford: publisher varies, 1850-1890), 520-521; Charles J. Hoadley, ed., <u>Records of the Colony or Jurisdiction of New Haven, from May, 1653 to the Union</u> (Hartford: Case, Lockwood and Company, 1858), 582-584; _____, "Laws Established by the Authority of His Majesties Letters, Patents, Granted to His Royal Highness James Duke of York and Albany," <u>Collections of</u>

the New-York Historical Society, vol. 1 (No
publisher, 1809), 307, 334-335; _____,
The General Laws and Liberties of New-Plymouth
Colony (Cambridge, Mass.: no publisher, 1672),
26-27; Staughton George, Thomas Mc Camant,
Benjamin Nead, eds., Charter to William Penn,
and Laws of the Province of Pennsylvania, Passed
Between the Years 1682 and 1700 (Harrisburg:
Lane S. Hart, 1879), 142.

10. Massachusetts Records, 1642, 39-40 in Children
and Youth In America A Documentary History 1600-
1865, ed. Bremmer, vol. 1, (Cambridge, Mass.:
Harvard University Press, 1970); Laws of
Massachusetts, 1648, in Documentary History,
vol. 1, 40-41.

11. Watertown Records I, Watertown, Massachusetts,
1894, in Documentary History, vol. 1, 41;
Richard B. Morris, ed., Encyclopedia of American
History (New York: Harper and Row, 1970), 587;
Cremin, Colonial Experience, 124.

12. Cotton Mather, Cares about the Nurseries
(Boston: Printed by T. Green for Benjamin Eliot,
1702), 12-13, 34.

13. Ibid., 20.

14. Edmund S. Morgan, The Puritan Family (New York:
Harper and Row, 1966), 97-99; M.S. Hall, ed.
"The Autobiography of Increase Mather"
Proceedings of the American Antiquarian Society,
n.s., 71 (1961): 278.

15. Morgan, Family, 100-101; James . Axtell, The
School Upon a Hill: Education and Society In
Colonial New England (New Haven: Yale Univer-
sity Press, 1974), 174-176; Robert Francis
Seybolt, The Private Schools of Colonial Boston
(Westport, Conn.: Greenwood Press, 1935), 3-10;
Alice Morse Earle, Child Life In Colonial Days
(New York: Macmillan, 1904), 97-99.

16. Cremin, Colonial Experience, 500, 544; Earle,
Child Life, 83, 91, 92.

17. Ezra Stiles, <u>The Journal of Ezra Stiles</u>, <u>The Gentle Puritan</u>, Morgan, ed. (New Haven: Yale University Press, 1962), 79-80, 382-385.

18. William Heard Kilpatrick, <u>The Dutch Schools of New Netherlands and Colonial New York</u> (New York: Arm Press, 1969), 105; Newton Edwards and Herman Richey, <u>The School In The American Social Order</u> (Boston: Houghton Mifflin, 1963), 156.

19. Michael Kamen, <u>Colonial New York</u> (New York: Scribners, 1975), 249; Stanley K. Schultz, <u>The Culture Factory</u> (New York: Oxford University Press, 1973), 5.

20. Schultz, <u>Culture</u>, 5; Thomas Woody, <u>Quaker Education In The Colony and State of New Jersey</u> (Philadelphia: University of Pennsylvania, 1923), 8-10; Thomas Woody, <u>Early Quaker Education In Pennsylvania</u> (New York: Columbia Press, 1920), 29-30; James Mulhern, <u>A History of Secondary Education in Pennsylvania</u> (New York: Arvo Press, 1969), 47, 85-86, 103.

21. A structure of this type is still standing and can be visited at the Shirley Plantation on the James River near Richmond, Virginia. The famous Confederate, General Robert E. Lee, was educated at the Shirley Plantation. George Mason also built at Gunston Hall, Virginia near Mount Vernon, a special structure for the tutor's lessons, though only of one story. This plantation also has been preserved and is open for public view.

22. _____, <u>A Documentary History of Education In The South Before 1860</u>, vol. 1 ed. Knight (Chapel Hill, North Carolina: University of North Carolina, 1949), 571-573; William Arthur Maddox, <u>The Free School Idea In Virginia Before the Civil War</u> (New York: Columbia University, 1918), 6; Edgar N. Knight, <u>Public School Education In North Carolina</u> (New York: Negro University Press, 1969), 12; Woody, <u>Women's Education</u>, vol. 1, 244, 268, 273; Paul Monroe, <u>Founding of the American Public School System</u> (New York: Macmillan Co., 1940), 61-62.

23. Berkeley Plantation located on the James River near Richmond Virginia, has been restored and is open to public view.

24. Clifford Dowdey, <u>The Great Plantation</u> (Charles City: Berkeley Plantation, 1957), 29, 106, 125-126, 142-143, 197, 236-237.

25. Woody, <u>Women's Education</u>, vol. 1, 276; <u>Documentary History</u>, 573.

26. <u>Documentary History</u>, 649-651.

27. Ibid.

28. Ibid., 572-573.

29. Provenzo, <u>Education and Culture</u>, 35; Robert E. Brown and B. Katherine Brown, <u>Virginia 1705-1786: Democracy and Aristocracy</u> (East Lansing, Michigan: Michigan State University Press, 1964), 273.

30. Phillip Vickers Fithian, <u>Journal and Letters of Phillip Vickers Fithian 1773-1774: A Plantation Tutor of the Old Dominion</u>, ed., Farish (Williamsburg, Virginia: Colonial Williamsburg, Inc., 1957), XVI-XVII, 237; Provenzo, <u>Education and Culture</u>, 35-36.

31. Fithian, <u>Journal</u>, XXVI-XXXI.

32. The Carter children included: Benjamin, 17; Robert, 14; Priscilla, 13; Anne, 11; Frances, 9; Betty, 8; Harriet, 5; and John, 1. Louis Morton, <u>Robert Carter of Nomini Hall</u> (Williamsburg, Virginia, Colonial Williamsburg, 1941), 220-222.

33. Edmund Sears Morgan, <u>Virginians at Home: Family Life in the Eighteenth Century</u> (Charlottesville: Colonial Williamsburg, 1952), 13, 14.

34. Morgan, <u>Virginians At Home</u>, XXXII, 13; Provenzo, <u>Education and Culture</u>, 35-36.

35. Morgan, <u>Virginians At Home</u>, X, XXXI; Provenzo, <u>Education and Culture</u>, 35-36.

36. Fithian, <u>Journal</u>, 6-7. Mr. Carter's library Fithian described as an "over-grown library of law books," Latin and Greek classics, books on divinity and famous writers, Locke, Addison, Young, Pope, Swift and Dryden. Fithian, <u>Journal</u>, 26.

37. Ibid., 26, 62, 76; Woody, <u>Women's Education</u>, 277-278.

38. Fithian, <u>Journal</u>, 26, 127-128; Woody, <u>Women's Education</u>, 278.

39. Fithian, <u>Journal</u>, 80-81.

40. Ibid., 31-32; Woody, <u>Women's Education</u>, 278-279.

41. Fithian, <u>Journal</u>, 143.

42. Ibid., 208-222.

43. Morton, <u>Robert Carter</u>, 221.

44. Ibid.

45. Morgan, <u>Virginians At Home</u>, 16; Woody, <u>Women's Education</u>, 278; Fithian, <u>Journal</u>, 78.

46. Fithian, <u>Journal</u>, 133.

47. Morgan, <u>Virginians At Home</u>, 54-55; Fithian, <u>Journal</u>, XXXII; Morton, <u>Robert Carter</u>, 221.

48. John Davis, <u>Travels of Four Years and a Half in the U.S.A.</u> (New York: Holt, 1909), iii-x.

49. Ibid., 1-18.

50. Ibid., 18-19.

51. Ibid., 52-57.

52. Ibid., 252-255, 336-337.

53. Fithian, Journal, 142, 146, 225; Advertisement, South Carolina Gazette, April 28, 1757; Advertisement, Virginia Gazette, March 8, 1770; Advertisement, Maryland Gazette, June 14, 1764; Advertisement, Maryland Gazette, December 24, 1772; Woody, Women's Education, 280-281.

54. James J. Walsh, Education of the Founding Fathers of the Republic (New York: Fordham University Press, 1935), 33-63; Douglas Southall Freeman, George Washington, vol. 1 (New York: Scribner's, 1948), 64; Earle, Child Life, 65-66, 95; Jefferson did not like being tutored. One day he played hooky and hid behind an outhouse. He recited the Lord's Prayer that school end. Jefferson remembered how disillusioned he was by the impotence of his own prayers, and as a warning not to expect too much out of heaven, told his story to his grandchildren; Fawn M. Brodie, Thomas Jefferson An Intimate History (New York: Norton and Company, 1974), 49.

55. Irving Brant, James Madison (New York: Bobbs-Merrill, 1941), 56-67, 122-123.

56. John Adams, Adams Family Correspondence, ed. Butterfield, 2 vols. (Cambridge, Mass.: Harvard University Press, The Belknap Press, 1963). Their four children included: Abigail (b. 14 July 1765), John Quincy (b. 11 July 1767), Charles (b. 29 May 1770) and Thomas Boylston Adams (b. 15 September 1772).

57. John Adams to Abigail Adams, 26 September 1775, AFC, 1:286; 29 October 1775, AFC, 1:317-318; 28 August 1774, AFC, 1:145; 7 July 1776, AFC, 2:39.

58. John Adams to Thomas Boylston Adams, 20 October 1775, AFC, 1:305; John Adams to Abigail Adams, 12 May 1780, AFC, 3:342.

59. John Adams to Abigail Adams, 18 February 1783, Letters of John Adams Addressed to his Wife, ed. C.F. Adams, 2 vols. (Boston: Freeman and Bolles, 1841), 2:89-90.

60. Abigail Adams to Mary Warren, 16 July 1773, <u>AFC</u>, 1:85; Abigail Adams to Isaac Smith, Jr., 16 March 1763, <u>AFC</u>, 1:4.

61. Abigail Adams to Mary Warren, 16 July 1773, <u>AFC</u>, 1:85.

62. Mary Warren to Abigail Adams, 25 July 1773, <u>AFC</u>, 1: 86-87.

63. Abigail Adams to Abigail Adams Smith, <u>Letter of Mrs. Adams</u>, 2 vols. (Boston:   Charles C. Little and James Brown, 1841), 2:24; Abigail Adams to Abigail Adams Smith, <u>Letters of Mrs. Adams</u>, 2:218-219.

64. Cremin, <u>Colonial Experience</u>, 134.

65. Ibid., 128.

66. Ibid., 135.

CHAPTER 8


THE AMERICAN TUTOR:   THE FRONTIER EXPERIENCE
(1789-1900)


1.   THE EARLY NATIONAL PERIOD


The practice of domestic education continued
through the post-Revolutionary and early national
period.   Tutoring of children occurred at frontier
trading posts.[1]   In the more settled East a great
demand also continued for private instruction.   In
the early 1800s these same tutors were pioneers in
establishing commercial, military and normal schools
and courses.[2]

Almira Hart Lincoln (1793-1876) of Berlin,
Connecticut was the youngest member of her family of
seventeen children from two marriages.   The oldest
children always tutored the youngest, turning the
home into a school.   Almira was eleven before
attending her first formal school.   Her father Samuel
Hart, who was largely self-educated, taught her much
more than the fundamentals of reading, writing and
math.   Hart taught Almira the philosophies of Locke
and Berkeley.   They read plays from Shakespeare,
Rollin's Ancient History, Plutarch's Lives, Gibbon's
Rome, and the poetry of Milton.   Almira also read
contemporary works on teaching methods such as Hannah
More's Strictures on Female Education.   As an adult
Almira Hart Lincoln became a teacher and authored
science textbooks.[3]

In early nineteenth century America, some homes
offered better educational opportunities than the
local school.   This was true in the case of Edward
Everett Hale (1822-1909), the famous nineteenth
century orator.   The son of a Boston newspaper
editor, he recalled that, "My father was one of the
best teachers I know."   He introduced Hale "early and

275

painlessly to Latin." At age nine Hale began attending Boston Latin School. The school had a lending library, "but the family had more and better books at home." He had not attended school any earlier since,

> there was no public school of any lower grade, to which my father would had sent me, any more than he would have me sent to jail.

Even though Edward was from an upper class family who could afford a private tutor, his father participated in Hale's education. This exemplified the popularity of home instruction in the minds of many parents.[4]

A more typical learning experience of that time was that of Lucy Larcom's (1824-1893) education in Charlestown, Massachusetts near Boston. She started attending "school" at age two, "as other children about us did," kept by a neighbor everybody called "Aunt Hannah." This "Dame School" was conducted in Aunt Hannah's kitchen or her sitting room, "as best suited her convenience." Lucy learned her "letters" standing at Aunt Hannah's knee while she pointed them out to her in a spelling book with a pin." Aunt Hannah taught her to read a few passages from the Bible.

> whenever I read them now, [it does] not fail to bring before me a vision of Aunt Hannah's somewhat sternly smiling lips, with her spectacles just above them, far down on her nose, encouraging me to pronounce the hard words. I think she tried to choose for me the least difficult verses.[5]

A steady demand for increased schooling during the early days of the Republic, coincided with the introduction of the British Lancasterian system of education. As previously noted, Joseph Lancaster, the English educator, demonstrated the feasibility of using student "monitors" [tutors] to teach large numbers of their peers, while supervised by a few adult teachers.[6] Kaestle has called the Lancasterian system, "the most widespread and successful educational reform in the Western world during the first thirty years of the nineteenth century."[7] It was a basic tutorial method applied to classroom instruction. According to Kaestle its success was based upon increased motivation and competition that replaced cruel corporal punishment. "A child could proceed at his or her own rate in each subject."[8] Monitorial education relied on many concepts developed by earlier tutor-philosophers.

Children felt comfortable as "monitors." Many had already acted as peer tutors at home for their brothers and sisters. The "monitorial school movement" became an outgrowth of the "domestic education movement" as a form of mass education in basic skills using peer tutors of small groups, rather than teacher-conducted classrooms.

Because a large number of students were needed to make a Lancasterian school "cost effective," the system was confined largely to cities.[9] Kaestle further notes that, "the speed and breadth of its adoption in American cities was remarkable."[10] The Free School Society of New York City established its first monitorial school based on the Lancasterian system in 1805. Other cities followed: Philadelphia, through the Association of Friends for the Instruction of the Poor, 1808; Albany, New York, 1810; by 1817 the North Carolina legislature had recommended the system statewide. Monitorial schools were formed throughout New York State, Connecticut, Pennsylvania, Maryland, Virginia, Ohio and Kentucky. Joseph Lancaster rode the crest of his success. In 1818 he came to America and lectured across the country.[11]

One of the most unexpected legacies of these tutor-driven schools was that many provided the basis for later urban public school systems. Morris acknowledges the monitorial schools as one of the "origins of the free public school."[12] The New York City Board of Education (est. 1842) absorbed monitorial schools of the Free School Society in 1853. A similar process occurred in Philadelphia, Baltimore and Schenectady.[13] The related concept of actual student tutors rather than "monitors" of small groups would also prove useful on the American frontier. A reliance on children teaching children in one room schoolhouses as a supplement to direct teacher instruction, persisted into the twentieth century.[14]

The success of monitorial education and the beginning of an urban public school movement did not deter the continued use of domestic education by many families. Between 1830-1860 hundreds of books were published by clergymen, doctors, social reformers and educators for parents as their guide in "domestic" or "fireside" education. As previously discussed, this parallelled a similar movement in England and on the European continent. Many of the most popular titles on this subject were reprinted from European editions, or adapted for an American audience.[15]

The diary of Rachel Van Dyke (1810-1812) supported this view, offering a coherent picture of middle-class society's day-to-day life. Rachel (b. 1793) was the daughter of Frederick Van Dyke (b. 1751), a New Brunswick, New Jersey gentleman. Their household included several brothers and sisters and her cousin Betsy Magoffin, who was tutored almost daily by Rachel. Rachel's diary includes a frank account of her experiences as Betsy's tutor. Her cousin had come to live in their home after her father's death and virtual abandonment by her mother. "Poor girl," Rachel wrote, "she has been taken about from one place to another from her infancy and no attention has been paid to her education-I will begin tomorrow and try what I can do." Rachel shared her bedroom with Betsy and acted as an important role model for her younger cousin.[16]

Even before Betsy's arrival Rachel had formed an opinion of her cousin's educational accomplishments from a letter written to her sister. "The meaning of her (Betsy) sentences are good enough--but by the manner in which she expresses her meaning--I judge that she has not been much accustomed to letter writing." Betsy had attended school previously but,

> "she knows nothing about grammar or geography--I can see she has learnt [sic] her lefsons [lessons] as I did mine . . . Like a parrot without understanding what I recited. She is a smart girl and tho' rather lazy [like myself] yet by proper

278

instruction she might be made a sensible learned woman. I wish I was capable of teaching her as she ought to be taught.

Rachel constantly lamented her own poor education, that had combined instruction at home with limited school attendance. However, she had already studied chemistry, history and Latin. Much of Rachel's time was spent alone in her room studying Virgil. This proved very frustrating. She called Latin a "provoking language" and threatened to give up its study more than once.

Each morning Rachel attended to her own self-studies and then gave Betsy her lessons in grammar, spelling and history. "This I will try to persuade her to do every morning." It was not an easy task. her sister Lydia laughed at Rachel's attempt at teaching Betsy. But this did not deter her, "let her laugh I don't care--I will go on and help her but still I will instruct Betsy as long as she will attend to her studies.

The seventeen-year-old Rachel occasionally lamented that her task required too much time, trouble and patience. Though she found Betsy an intelligent girl, Rachel understood her own limitations and hoped a better educational program could be found at a later date for her cousin.

Betsy began to respond to Rachel's daily attentions. After several months of tutoring Rachel recorded that, "She is more industrious, more obliging, studies her lessons better and is as good natured as a girl need be." Rachel's tutoring method included teaching Betsy to "parse" (explanation of the grammatical usage of a word), a task that proved very difficult. Through daily perseverance they seemed to achieve some success.[17] Rachel also used Betsy's facility to hear and then relate stories. This helped her teach Betsy the use of better grammar and improved her vocabulary.

During Rachel's own studies she read a book by Maria Edgeworth, an advocate of "domestic education." Since Edgeworth at that time was a very popular author, Rachel may have read her books in search of tutoring methods to use with her cousin. Kuhn found, in her study of domestic education in the early history of the United States, that Maria Edgeworth's writing had a direct influence on the tutoring of many children like Betsy.[18]

Rachel's tutoring of her cousin was not a social anomoly. The fact that a young woman, without outside direction or support, shouldered the education of a distant relative appears absurd only from a modern perspective. The extended family of early ninteenth century America remained a highly self-reliant social unit including within its sphere domestic education both practical and moral. Only over the next century did "schooling" assume such a specialized place in society that most parents came to believe the home could not compete with the schoolhouse.

The "family school" education movement of the nineteenth century was characterized by parent teachers rebelling against "tasked lessons" in a schoolroom. Instead they saw the function of the educator to "draw out," not to "fill up." The origin of the term "Domestic Education" can be ascribed to a book of that title by the American Herman Humphrey in 1840. The parallel term, "Fireside Education," was given to a 1841 work by the Englishman, S.G. Goodrich. The latter book had far greater impact. It gave the family school movement both a concrete educational philosophy, and instructional methods. As we have already noted, hundreds of additional philosophical works on domestic education were written throughout the remainder of this century and into the beginning of the next. "Domestic education" was to remain a powerful educational force until supplanted by tax-based schooling.[19]

The mother's role as primary tutor was of supreme importance. Though the literature of the period spoke of both parents acting as teachers, most books were written for women. Fathers had increasingly little time to instruct their children because of work commitments. Kuhn sees the proponents of that era's "liberal mental culture" viewing learning as a continuous process. The mother was the logical educator since she was the person most closely and constantly associated with the child.

Many of these educational reformers were against educating children beyond their years. This led to the adoption of the Pestalozzian system of object teaching, rather than the "overeducating" of young children (such as teaching four-year-olds Latin, Greek and philosophy as had been common in the fifteenth through seventeenth centuries). Instead of formal teaching one mother of a seven-year-old son, "contrived to give an air of recreation to his hours of study." The "family school" rejecting the classical approach to learning embraced new principles by studying individual differences. The simple everyday observation of children provided a common meeting ground between the researcher and the practical environmentalist in the raising of children. The legacy of Rousseau, Locke, and Edgeworth were blended with pleasurable learning as the final goal.

Parental "domestic education" guides offered a unique blend of formal instruction: reading, spelling, the definition of words, penmanship, arithmetic, the expression of thought; with character formation, physical, intellectual, social, moral and religious. Education was more naturally presented at home since these philosophers contended that intellectual cultivation did not thrive in the crowded schoolroom where children's bodies are cramped and their mind stimulated only artificially. One hour well spent in the "family school" might do more good than a day spent in any schoolroom.[20]

Lydia Sigourney in her book Letters to Mothers (1838) told them that this period of home tutoring should be extended into childhood as far as possible.

> Why expose it [a child] to the influence of evil example? . . . Why yield it to the excitement of promiscuous association, when it has a parent's house, where its innocence may be shielded, and its intellect aided to expand? Does not a mother's tutoring for two to three hours a day give a child more time than a teacher at school?[21]

Goodrich in _Fireside Education_ (1841) also saw the parent as "the teacher . . . developing and perfecting the various physical, moral and intellectual faculties of their children." The home was a "Fireside Seminary" "the chief engine by which character is formed. . . . " The Common School was only an auxiliary to the fireside, not a replacement since the family had the first and primary educational role.[22]

_Home Education_ (1838) told parents that if properly conducted it was in most cases preferable to regular schooling. Issac Taylor believed this "especially so for girls." He recommended combining children from different families as a method of improving instruction.[23]

One of the few works published for fathers was John Hall's _On the Education of Children While Under the Care of Parents or Guardians_ (1835). He too argued in favor of a home education. If a parent was forced by circumstances to send a child to school, Hall counseled him to select one where the mind is "most effectually cultivated and where the moral, manner, general habits and health should be best promoted." He complained that too often the parent's inquiry is limited to "where does schooling come the cheapest? . . . The value received makes no part of the estimate. A school is a school." Hall did not view cheapness as a successful determinant of a quality education.[24]

To what extent did families follow the advice of these domestic educators? Troen, in his study of the public schools of St. Louis, Missouri between 1840 and 1870, found that both middle class and upper class children were often educated at home. Many of these children had European tutors. At the completion of their primary education, they were sent to Eastern colleges or European universities.[25] The U.S. Census of 1840 showed that only one scholar in five (266 out of 1,200) attended the St. Louis public schools. The majority were either tutored at home or attended private schools.[26] This census data, considered in isolation, does not offer conclusive evidence that contemporary domestic tutoring was a dominant force in the development of American education. However, the continuous popularity of domestic education for the remainder of this century was chronicled in numerous publications, diaries and the personal biographies of many prominent Americans.

Elizabeth Palmer Peabody (1804-1894), founder of the first English language kindergarten, was influenced by the philosophy of domestic education practiced by her parents. Both mother and father undertook her education at home and later in her mother's school. Elizabeth's father taught her Latin, Greek, French, Italian and German. Later she published translations in most of these languages and went on to study Polish, Icelandic and Sanskrit.[27]

Mrs. Peabody "was the ardent practitioner and theorist of the family." She enjoyed teaching and devised a curriculum with her husband that molded her children into well-educated adults. The basis of her educational scheme was "predominately moral--to fill my mind with images of kind, heroic and thoroughly high-principled people." Elizabeth's mother published two books on the "moral posture" of a good teacher. She trained her daughter to regard a good teacher as "the highest and proper activity of every American woman who loved her country--moral education became to my mind the essence of all education." The Peabody's philosophy showed the deep influence of the "fireside education" movement, that put moral education at center stage and academic training second.[28]

Elizabeth's curriculum was rigorous and broad. Her parents in addition to foreign language instruction, taught her from Murray's English Grammar, Blair's Rhetoric, Harme's Elements of Criticism. She read Herbert Spenser, Oliver Goldsmith's histories of England, Greece and Rome, the Iliad, the Odyssey, Fasso's Jerusalem, the writings of Maria Edgeworth on domestic education, and many works in the sciences including those of Charles Darwin.[29]

Before the age of sixteen Elizabeth was teaching in her mother's school. Afterward she became the governess of a Maine family. By 1825 Elizabeth became a member of the "transcendental movement" in

283

education, becoming the friend or acquaintance of many great nineteenth century New England figures including Ralph Waldo Emerson, Horace Mann and others. In 1834 she began teaching Latin, mathematics and geography at the Temple School in Boston. Bronson Alcott (1799-1888), a friend of Emerson, opened this innovative school with about thirty pupils. At that time Alcott was a leading educator in the domestic education movement rooted in Pestalozzi's methods. During his childhood, he had attended public school, but was also tutored at home by two neighboring clergymen. His support of the domestic education was highlighted in the 1829 article, "Maternal Instruction" in the American Journal of Education. As Alcott's co-worker, Elizabeth Peabody was deeply influenced by his philosophy in her later educational activities. In 1860 Elizabeth and her sister opened the first American kindergarten based on the concepts of Friedrick Froebel. Until her death in 1894, the educational philosophy of the domestic education movement appeared in her books, articles and lectures. Her theories and teaching methods became a permanent part of modern educational practice.[30]

Elizabeth was the eldest of three sisters. Sophia, the youngest, married Nathaniel Hawthorne. Her other sister Mary, after a long secret courtship, married Horace Mann. Mary supported her husband's quest for public education, but used her own domestic education to tutor the their children, Horace, Jr., George and Benjamin. They were nurtured by Mary's innovative methods of tutoring, sometimes with dire results. In the hope of helping Benjamin become bilingual, she and her husband tried speaking only in French to their youngest son. The boy's speech became such a muddle that she abandoned the attempt.[31]

Mary also demonstrated her scholarly concern for improved early childhood education in the translation of "Princes In France--Their Education and Teachers" (1880). This article discussed the strengths and weaknesses of the seventeenth century tutorial education of the princes of France. (Discussed in Chapter 5). Elizabeth Mann's commitment to the common school movement did not prevent her personal practice and study of domestic education.[32]

The popularity of "domestic education" was not confined to New England during America's early national period. Throughout the South, as during the colonial period, parents provided tutors for many children during their basic childhood education, except now parents also acted as teachers. Most planters lived in isolated rural areas where children would have to leave home to attend any school above the primary level. Formal education very often began at home with the mother as the domestic educator. In North Carolina, Hannah Gaston established a precise home class schedule. Each day her six year old son recited "six or seven lessons."[33] Other families employed private tutors or governesses, even building the typical plantation schoolrooms and dwellings for their teachers.[34] Many of these instructors proved highly transitory, or poor teachers. Sudden resignations were all too common.[35] A plantation parent Anne W. Johnson described this predicament (1848) and probably an equally common solution, "I am now teaching the young children, our Teacher left us about three weeks since. I think she will not return."[36]

Many parents believed their children needed more advanced schooling by the age of fourteen. However, Franklin has pointed out that many parents of girls did not view a far-away school as clearly superior to a plantation education. Young women gathered together in seminaries might become "corrupted by other students."[37]

With some variations this pattern of "domestic education" was repeated throughout the antebellum South. Morison related the educational program for the family of John Hampden Randolph, a Louisiana planter. He employed (1841) a Northern college graduate as a tutor and also itinerant music and dancing masters. The boys later attended the University of Virginia. His daughters did not remain at home. Instead they were enrolled at a fashionable Baltimore finishing school.[38] Many used these schools as a last resort because as one planter argued, "I have many objections to boarding schools generally but it is almost impossible to educate our

Daughters entirely at home."[39]   Qualified teachers
were difficult to find in many areas of the rural
South.

The tutor's own perspective helps complete our
understanding of home education in the South. Amelia
Akehurst Lines (1827-1886) arrived in America from
England in 1829.   During 1857-1858 her letters
described the difficult life of a Georgia plantation
tutor-governess.   She led both a lonely and preca-
rious professional existence.

February 7, 1858

To Mr. Lines,

Very rarely does any thing occur to
relieve the monotony of my life at present;
and yet times does not hang heavily, or
pass wearily away as I imagined it would:
every day cares and duties have given it
wings.   Through the day I am constantly
with my pupils, either in the school room,
in the nursery, at the piano or on the play
ground.   Never feel free from care until
they are locked in the arms of slumber;
then I "draw a long breath" and sit down to
read or write.

Receive this as a token of regard,
From Jennie

February 16, 1858

My Dear Sister,

Mrs. Shelman has a lady [interested]
as governess.   She is in Philadelphia and
has been South three years and liked so
well that she is anxious to return.   She
has written two letters to Mrs. Shelman,
and I should judge it very desirous to
secure this situation.   Mrs. Shelman is
very much pleased,--says she shall send for
her.   I am of course feeling very anxious.

In many respects this is not a desirable place but it is decidedly comfortable and easy; and sure. I had made up my mind to remain until I secured a pleasanter home or saved enough to take me home.

Your sister,
Jennie[40]

Like many other nineteenth century tutor-governesses, Jennie dreamed of escape from her profession. After exchanging with "Mr. Lines" (a Connecticut printer) so many woeful letters, she succeeded in marrying him in August, 1859.[41]

A completely different view of a tutor's life is contained in the diary of Jane Gibbs. She chronicled her life as a tutor in Nelson County, Virginia at the Green Pond School. On March 27, 1857 Colonel Fitzpatrick, a local planter, hired Jane to teach the local children writing, French (and possibly Latin) for a salary of fifty dollars a year and her room and board. This was typical of the arrangements local rural communities made with itinerant school masters. From that date until November, 1859, Jane recorded her daily activities with her "scholars." Fifteen children began attending daily school at Green Pond. In the summer months (July, 1857) this number had fallen to one or two students. In the autumn Jane taught about six pupils individually, each on a different day of the week. Children occasionally stayed with their teacher overnight. While teaching Jane continued her own self-study of Latin and professional reading.

The fact that she remained for at least three years was very unusual. Most similar school masters were itinerant. One possible reason was that the families around Green Pond School liked Jane's teaching. They invited her frequently to their homes for parties and religious gatherings.

A religious woman, Jane Gibbs, introduced her diary with a concise personal philosophy that gave an insight to her effectiveness as a teacher.

Marks!

Good disciple--good order is [sic] the life
of a school.   Make your pupils respect
[you] and they will have you--teach them
politeness and charity for one another.[42]


## 2.   THE LATER FRONTIER PERIOD
### (1860-1900)


Between 1850 to 1870 the population of the
United States increased by almost sixty-eight per
cent.   In contrast public school attendance almost
doubled to over 6,250,000 students.[43]   Many of these
children were taught in frontier one-room schoolhouses, where a indefinite dividing line existed
between group instruction and peer tutoring.   As late
as 1916, one-room schools still numbered over
200,000.[44]

The last forty years of the century witnessed
the rapid settlement of America's Western frontier.
Most of these new rural communities failed to provide
early public education.   Jeffrey concluded that they
did not see it, "as an important enough social
goal."[45]   In their early stages, married women often
set up simple home schools to teach or tutor local
children.   Individual pioneer mothers often tutored
their own children at home.   Cremin tells us that
family members tutored each other.   Children learned
to read at a somewhat older age than in colonial
times.[46]   A special class of "wandering schoolmasters" became itinerant travelers throughout the
rural East and Western United States.   They held
classes in many cabins of mud-daubed logs or sod-
houses were students of all ages gathered.   The
number was determined as much by local settlement, as
by crop season, and weather conditions.   These
teachers charged what they could get and boarded
around the community.[47]   Some of these pioneer
teachers were the daughters of the first generation
of literate American women.   They had increased their
life choices by preparing to become teachers.   One
teacher Flora Davis Winslow reasoned, "I teach school

because I wish to be independent and not beholden to my friends for my livelihood."[48] Teaching was one of the few professions open to the nineteenth century American women who needed an independent means of support.

Like her sister, the English governess, the independent minded frontier "school marm" often taught under less than desirable working conditions. Such was the case of Callie Wright (1830-1870) a "circuit-riding-tutor" on the south-eastern Texas frontier. Caledonia (Callie) Wright was the daughter of Dr. and Mrs. W.J. Wright. The family had come to Texas from Mississippi about 1850 and bought a farm on the Colorado River near Columbus. Callie was part of a large family and undoubtedly had much practice at domestic education before she ever became a frontier teacher. As an adult she became a school-teacher. However, because of the remote nature of the Texas frontier, she did not find a position even as an itinerant schoolmaster in a one-room school-house. Instead, between 1863 to 1867 Callie became a "circuit-riding tutor" for children on remote ranches isolated from alternative forms of rural education.[49]

Callie's letters to her family revealed the arduous nature of education that was typical of the American frontier. Some students studied at home under the guidance of their parents. Her own sister Jodie was a domestic scholar, partially for economic reasons.

> Jodie you wrote to me that you had commenced studying at home. I am glad to hear of it most especially from you for I know it is time and you will try to learn for you know that you have to pay your own schooling and you ought to try and learn all you can at home.

The long distances children travelled to school had a direct relationship on school attendance and scholarship.

> Silas is going to town to school, I don't expect he will do much good at it this winter, for it will be to cold to ride

so far . . . Silas has started to school, John Hilley, John Finchback and him started to Bartsop day before yesterday. They will get there today if nothing happens to them, they went in a little two horse wagon. . . .[50]

In some instances, frontier children who travelled a great distance to school did not live at home, but boarded in town. Callie told her sister that, "Silas is going to school in Columbus, he eats at Jack Naves and rooms with the teacher." Callie mentioned these room-and-board arrangements throughout her letters.

Other children were either too young for such arrangements, too poor to pay school tuition and boarding fees or in ill health. Many children were needed to work the family farm and could not easily attend a regular school. Callie taught these children, riding from home to home sometimes spending a few days at each location before riding on. She recorded her activities as a "circuit-riding tutor" during 1865 and 1866.

I commenced teaching Dan and Laura today, which I expect will be very tedious for neither one is scholarly enough to be interesting. I get eight dollars per month, but don't consider it a compensation for the sacrifice I make but I do it for accommodations for there wasn't a school convenient and neither one is well enough to board.

Another child boarded at a nearby ranch and was seen by Callie each week for instruction.[51] She visited other nearby ranches, weather permitting, but always returned "home" to teach Dan and Laura Alley. These arrangements continued until the end of 1865. With the start of a new year Callie began looking for "ten or twelve scholars," and had already been promised three students. After the end of the Civil War economic conditions became very depressed throughout the South. Callie told her sister, "There are more people in the South that don't know what to do than ever seen before." She would be grateful to

290

find a handful of children to teach since, "that would be better than doing nothing."[52]

Callie's days as a "circuit-riding tutor" ended in 1867, with her marriage to C.D. Clapp. Only three years later she died and was buried on the family farm near Columbus, Texas.

Any accurate representation of frontier education must take into account the unusual environment of the American West. Without doubt various methods of tutorial education were used in the far West. Hundreds of thousands of one-room schoolhouses used peer tutors. Parental tutors conducted "domestic education" programs. Professional tutors were scattered across these enormous spaces. The twentieth century concentration of children in urban areas ended most of these tutorial applications. For most of the nineteenth century tutoring remained the frontier's practical response to childhood education in a hostile, remote environment.

While Callie Wright rode the circuit as a tutor of the Civil War era on the Texas frontier, her northern counterpart also tutored children in the South as well as in the North. Margaret Griffis Clark (1838-1913) was the daughter of prosperous Philadelphian businessman. She began her career as a tutor-governess (1857-1866) after her father's business failed in the Panic of 1857.[53]

Margaret was hired as a live-in governess, by a succession of families and once as a visiting governess. Her daily curriculum was similar for all her students: English, French and music. With each family Margaret sought a personal relationship to in someway combat the lonliness created by family separation.

Margaret's first experience as a tutor-governess was at Meriwether Plantation near Tiptoville, Tennessee. There she taught for over one year the five children of William B. Isler. Margaret was such a success that Mr. Isler offered to double her salary to stay another year. "He thought the children improved under my care more than with any other teacher they have ever had." Margaret became so familiar with her pupils that they, "seem to think that I belong to them and must not go away."[54]

The next seven years witnessed her work with children near Centreville, Virginia (1859-1860), Washington D.C. (1861), and two Philadelphia families (1864-1866).[55] During this time away from home she continued her self-education by reading the poetry of Shelley, works by Maria Edgeworth, James Fenimore Cooper and studying both French and German.[56] The financial necessity of assuming the occupation of governess led Margaret to complain often and bitterly regarding this forced separation, "from the one I love best on earth [her mother]."[57] She never considered her occupation as a governess unusual, even though she worked for so many different families over such a large geographic area. Margaret's experience as a tutor-educator undoubtably was being repeated by thousands of other women throughout the United States. Later in 1871-1872 Margaret travelled to Japan to teach in a Japanese high school in Tokyo. She concluded her teaching career (1876-1898) as a teacher at a girls school in Philadelphia.[58]

Margaret Clark Griffis was not the only tutor to travel abroad to assume unusual educational duties. Margaret Miller Clark (b. 1845), a teacher from Plattsburgh, New York, imitated her British governess counterparts, by joining her brother Sylvanus M. Davidson at Yokohama, Japan. There she began tutoring Japanese children. Her diary covers her arduous trip and long residence in Japan. Margaret wrote a "commonplace book" about her experience in Japan between 1872-1916 that subsequently has been lost.[59]

Her brother, Sylvanus, (an agent for the Pacific Mail Steamship Company) arranged her trip from New York via Panama and San Francisco. Margaret arrived in Yokohama on December 31, 1871. The town then consisted of about 40,000 inhabitants, divided between about 38,000 Japanese and 2,000 Europeans and Americans. This Western enclave possessed both an Episcopal and an American Union Church. Sylvanus assisted her in immediately purchasing a house with a Chinese cook and two female Japanese servants. Margaret and her companion, Angie, set up a schoolroom in their home, but did not commence instruction until the spring. Two Japanese "scholars" arrived early in the morning (May 23) for their first lesson. Several days later one of the children brought her a basket of flowers.

> They knew their lessons very well, seems hard for them to remember the different words but they will in time I trust. . . they seem much pleased with me which is very gratifying. I was afraid at first, I could not get along as I do not understand any Japanese.

Unfortunately, Margaret never explained how she overcame this language barrier. In addition to her private tutoring she began teaching a Sunday school class. Margaret continued this activity for at least several years.[60]

By the middle of June, Margaret recorded that her scholars were making good progress, "they knew them (their lessons) very well. I feel that I am getting along very nicely with them." The local Japanese must have shared the same opinion. Three more pupils arrived for tutoring on June 17. By the next fall her "school" enrollment had risen to eight, including a father and his young son. Because of this steady increase in her "scholars" Margaret felt she could not accept any additional Japanese students.

The Japanese were by no means perfect students. Her original students, "felt quite jealous and do not like the idea of my taking them (new students)." On many days, "my scholars did not come . . . which I do not like very much I rather they could come regularly."[61]

Margaret Clark was not the only educator at work in Yokohama. Her companion Angie taught at least three children in another part of their home. Also in Yokahama a Mr. and Mrs. Pierson's school enrolled about sixteen to twenty girls. These students were taught as a group and not on an individual basis. This underlined the segregated practices of the Japanese, who sent only boys to be tutored by

293

Margaret and Angie. In the countryside a few miles from Yokahama existed an even larger school for girls.[62]

Margaret Clark was in many ways representative of the tutor-governess who travelled abroad at the height of the Age of Imperialism. As Anna Leonowens had brought British culture to the court of Siam, Margaret Clark tutored her students along a path "toward civilization." As an educator, her failure to learn Japanese seems curious only by modern standards.

The separation of education for boys and girls was reinforced in a comparison of instructional methods and content areas. Girls received group instruction in the "domestic arts." Boys were tutored in English on an individual or small group basis. Margaret openly condoned these practices, since in many ways they reflected the mainstream attitudes of American society regarding the nature and importance of male versus female education.

As the century came to an end, American women witnessed a significant improvement in general attitudes toward their professional education and wider employment opportunities throughout society. The industrial revolution increased the number of occupations open to women. Women readily accomplished the transition from governess or domestic tutor, to classroom teacher. As schools improved and teaching was feminized the nurturing of the young was more and more transferred to agencies outside the home. The general change of status of women in American society, and the growth of public tax-supported education in particular, made the mother's role as a "domestic educator" dwindle in importance by the end of the century.[63]

## 3. TWILIGHT OF THE TUTOR

The employment of tutors, governesses or parents as domestic educators did not come to an abrupt end at the close of the frontier era (1890). The number

294

of scholars at home declined as more States passed compulsory school attendance laws. Tutoring waned only slowly as a popular socio-educational custom. As in England one such indicator was the continued portrayal of the domestic tutor or governess in many Victorian novels.[64] Henry James (1843-1916), a great American novelist of that era, in The Turn of the Screw (1898), featured Mrs. Grose, the governess, as the central figure in this popular mystery story.[65]

Many of this century's principle advocates for public education: scientists, reformers, politicians, writers, feminists and others were themselves educated at home or had been employed at tutors. Sandburg recorded how Abraham Lincoln (1809-1865) as a child received a rudimentary education at home. As a young man he was tutored by Mentor Graham (b. 1814), a schoolmaster, to become a surveyor (1833). Sandburg relates how Graham's daughter woke up many nights at midnight to see Lincoln and her father figuring and explaining by the fire using a copy of Robert Gibson's The Theory and Practice of Surveying (1814). Several years later Lincoln rode into Springfield, Illinois to read the law and was taught by Henry E. Dunner and J.T. Stuart. By 1837, he became a practicing attorney with Stuart.[66] Years later, when Lincoln was President, his youngest son, Willie, was tutored at the White House. Alexander Williamson, a genteel Scotsman, taught Willie from 1861 until the child's premature death in 1862. Mary Todd Lincoln (1818-1882) who had hired Williamson thought him to be a kind, intelligent and reliable teacher.[67]

Louisa May Alcott (1832-88) received her first education at home in Boston from her famous father Amos Bronson Alcott. Each morning he read aloud to his daughters for an hour. She later recalled these sessions as the "pleasantest" recollections of her youth. As part of her educational training she was required to work intently on a daily journal in her room, as were the other members of her family. Louisa was later tutored by both Ralph Waldo Emerson and Henry David Thoreau. In 1868 she published Little Women (1868), an autobiographical novel of her childhood, followed by its sequel Little Men (1871). Its portrait of deep family loyalty and intimacy soon made these books enduring children's classics.[68]

A great diversity of distinguished nineteenth-century men and women from all across the United States experienced tutoring at home for all or part of their education. Among them were Elizabeth Seton (1774-1821), John Carroll (1735-1815), James Fenimore Cooper (1789-1851), Henry Adams (1838-1918), Harriet Stanton Blatch (1856-1940), Susan Elizabeth Blow (1843-1916), Susan B. Anthony (1820-1906), Thomas Edison (1874-1931), Grace Hoadley Dodge (1856-1914), Sarah Grimke (1792-1873), Amy Lawrence Lowell (1874-1925), Clara Barton (1821-1912), Maria Mitchell (1818-1889) and Margaret Fuller (1810-1850) to mention only a few.[69]

This selected biographical review indicates the pervasiveness of "domestic education" throughout the nineteenth century. Tutoring in America was not a socio-educational phenomenon limited to a few select children. Undoubtedly large numbers of children from every geographic region and virtually every social background, had a home tutoring experience for all or part of their education. For many women this constituted all of their formal learning. To a modern reader it is surprising the number of prominent nineteenth-century business, political and intellectual leaders whose pre-university educational preparation was based on the work of their tutors. One-to-one instruction at home remained a popular form of education until the advent of compulsory tax-supported public schooling.

The tutorial career of Clyde Augustus Duniway (1866-1944) of Albany Oregon, offers an unusual perspective of a tutor at work in the late nineteenth century. After his graduation from Cornell University (B.A., 1912) its President recommended Duniway as a tutor for Childs Frick (1883-1965), the son of Henry Clay Frick, founder of U.S. Steel. From 1892 to 1896 Childs received his entire education from Duniway in both Pittsburg and at Harvard University. Duniway's papers provided a detailed account of his tutoring methods, Childs' response to this education; and comments from his father Henry Clay Frick and others on the results of this adventurous program.[70]

Duniway came to Pittsburgh on 24 June 1892 and accepted the job of tutoring the nine-year-old Childs for a salary of $2,000 per year. He began in August after Childs had finished at the School of Applied Ethics in Pittsburgh.[71]

During a trip to Europe 4 March 1893 to 19 May 1893, Duniway first described in his diary the content and methods of Childs tutoring. Each morning and afternoon they worked together on reading, writing and arithmetic. Duniway required Childs to study at least two hours each day. Duniway accompanied the entire Frick family on this trip. Mr. Frick and Duniway became good friends often exploring museums and historic sites together, while the rest of the family was elsewhere. This was only the first of several European trips on which Duniway traveled with the family. A deeper friendship seemed to develop between the steel baron and his son's tutor, more than at anytime with Childs.[72]

Frick was obviously pleased with his son's tutor, for he rehired Duniway for the 1893 school year. However, Duniway and Childs had moved to Cambridge, Massachusetts, while Duniway attended Harvard University to complete a Masters and Doctorate Degrees in History.

During this fall term Duniway enlarged his curriculum to include science. He purchased entomological materials, a compass and drawing instruments. Did Childs already have a personal fascination for science, or did Duniway evoke this interest through his tutoring? We only know that in later life Childs Frick developed an interest in paleontology, natural history and the conservation of natural resources. He became a trustee of the American Museum of Natural History in 1921, a post he occupied until his death.[73]

Childs continued with Duniway during the 1895-1896 school year. Drawing lessons, dancing lessons and geography were added to the boy's curriculum.[74] At the outset of his third year at Harvard (1895-1896), Duniway had made little academic progress with his pupil. Frick was unhappy with his report on

Childs, "Suppose we will have to bear with him patiently, with the hope that he will some time wake up." The father counseled Duniway to introduce Childs to older and brighter friends who might have a good influence on the boy.[75]

During his fourth year of private tutoring, Childs convinced his father to send him for the following year to the Shady Side Academy in Pittsburgh. Exactly how he brought this about was never clarified by Duniway. Perhaps Frick was discouraged over his lack of scholastic progress. His father was certainly not happy about Childs decision.

Duniway's tutoring sowed enough good seed that Childs later pursued a successful academic career. He graduated from Princeton in 1905 with a B.S. degree in paleontology and received his doctorate in 1941. In 1912 he led a scientific expedition to Ethiopia. Childs authored numerous articles in scientific journals and a book, Horned Ruminants of North America.[76]

How much of this later academic success began during the years (1892-1896) of the Duniway-Frick tutorials? The close daily interaction between the nine to thirteen year old Childs with the scholarly Duniway must have been at the very least, a partial determinant. Duniway's life showed him to be a highly creative scholar and successful educational leader. Duniway, after receiving a Ph.D. in history from Harvard University (1897), was appointed Assistant Professor at Harvard (1897-1899). He later became a Professor at Stanford University (1899-1908) and among a lifetime of appointments in higher education served as the President of the University of Montana (1908-1912), University of Wyoming (1912-1917) and Colorado College (1917-1924). His personality and obvious interest in teaching made him an exemplar tutor and a positive force in the future life of Childs Frick.

American tutors borrowed a great deal from their European counterparts. Comparatively, they were far more successful in spreading domestic education throughout their society, and across the vast reaches of a rugged frontier environment. They adopted the Lancastrian peer-tutorial system (the monitorial school) for urban centers, that formed a core for many Eastern public school systems. On the frontier they made the one-room public schoolhouse function by using the peer tutors found in the ordinary domestic education of large rural families. By the end of the nineteenth century widespread domestic education was displaced, at least partially, because of the success of these adaptations.

The writing of these tutors in America showed the influence of the humanist-enlightenment philosophers' child-centered educational theory. The successful expansion of the American tax-supported public school absorbed these tutorial concepts, and adapted them for schooling through the progressive education movement of the twentieth century.

## Endnotes

1. Lloyd P. Jorgenson, The Founding of Public Education In Wisconsin, (Madison, Wisconsin: State Historical Society of Wisconsin, 1956), 5.

2. James Mulhern, A History of Secondary Education In Pennsylvania, (New York: Arvo Press, 1969), 282-287. Just out of Yale University in 1793, Eli Whitney (1765-1825) journeyed South to earn his living as a tutor at a plantation near Savannah, Georgia. While there he invented a cotton gin, making cotton for the first time an important cash crop that bolstered the institution of slavery and helped guarantee the future Civil War (1861-1865). Shirley Abbott, The National Museum of American History (New York: Abrams, 1981) 131.

3. Lois Barber Arnold, Four Lives In Science, Women's Education In Nineteenth Century (New York: Schocken Books, 1984), 38-39.

4. Hale was the "other person" who spoke at Gettysburg on the same program with Abraham Lincoln. Carl F. Kaestle, <u>Pillars of the Republic</u> (New York: Hill and Way, 1983), 52-53.

5. Lucy Larcom, <u>A New England Girlhood</u> (Boston: Northeastern University Press, 1986), 38-48.

6. See Chapter 7.

7. Carl F. Kaestle, <u>Pillars of the Republic</u> (New York: Hill and Wang, 1983), 41.

8. Ibid.

9. Ibid., 18, 41-43.

10. Ibid., 42-43.

11. Lancaster had moved from city to city constantly complaining, planning great things and never doing them. In 1838 he was living in New York working on yet another unfinished book. While crossing a city street he was trampled and killed by a run-away horse. Ibid., 41-43.

12. Morris, <u>Encyclopedia of American History</u>, 588.

13. John Franklin Reigart, <u>The Lancasterian System of Instruction in the Schools of New York City</u> (New York: Arno Press, 1969), 1-6; William Oland Bourne, <u>History of the Public School Society of the City of New York</u> (New York: Willow Woods, 1870), 28-47; Kaestle, <u>Republic</u>, 56-57.

14. "<u>Little Schools On The Prairie Still Teach A Big Lesson</u>," <u>Smithsonian</u>, 16 (October 1985): 118-128; Lilya Wagner, <u>Peer Teaching Historical Perspective</u> (London: Greenwood Press, 1982), 134-202.

15. Kuhn's annotated bibliography lists hundreds of books on "domestic education" or "fireside education." Anne L. Kuhn, <u>The Mother's Role In Childhood Education: New England Concepts 1830-1860</u> (New Haven, Conn: Yale University Press, 1947), V.

16. Rachel Van Dyke, _Diary_, 6 October 1810 - 16 May 1811, Rutgers University Library, New Brunswick, New Jersey; _Diary_, 27 November 1810; _Diary_, 12 December 1810.

17. _Diary_, 16 October 1810; 28 February 1811; 27 October 1810; 21 January 1811; 4 December 1810; 3 November 1810; 22 January 1811; 29 January 1811; 31 January 1811; 9 February 1811; 14 February 1811.

18. _Diary_, 28 November 1810; 25 February 1811; Kuhn, _Childhood Education_, 12, 37, 41, 159.

19. Herman Humphrey, _Domestic Education_ (Amherst, Mass.: J.S.C. Adams, 1840); S.G. Goodrich, _Fireside Education_ (London: William Smith, 1841); Kuhn, _Childhood Education_, 108.

20. Kuhn, _Childhood Education_, 72, 79, 101, 106, 107, 108, 119, 175, 178-203. Other representative works on "domestic education" included: John Abbott, _The Mother At Home_ (Boston: Crocker and Brewster, 1833), Theodore Dwight, _The Father's Book_ (Springfield, Mass.: G.&C.Merrian, 1834), Warren Burton, _Helps To Education In the Homes of Our Country_ (Boston: Anesly and Nichols, 1863), Annie Allen, _Home, School and Vacation_ (Boston: Houghton, Mifflin, 1907), Ellen Celia Lombard, _Home Education_ (Washington D.C.: Government Printing Office, 1919), Ellen C. Lombard was the Secretary of the Home Education Division, U.S. Bureau of Education.

21. Lydia Sigourney, _Letters of Mothers_ (Hartford, Conn.: Hudson and Skinner, 1838), 107.

22. Goodrich, _Fireside Education_, IV-V, 15-20.

23. Isaac Taylor, _Home Education_ (New York: D. Appleton and Company, 1838), 10-11.

24. John Hall, _On the Education of Children While Under the Care of Parents or Guardians_ (New York: John P. Haven, 1835), 11, 33-34, 153-154.

25. Selwyn Troen, <u>The Public and the Schools Shaping the St. Louis System 1838-1920</u> (Columbia, Missouri: University of Missouri Press, 1975), 10-11.

26. <u>The Sixth Census</u>, 1840, 6 (Washington: U.S. Census Office, 1840), 203-211.

27. Hersha Sue Fisher, "The Education of Elizabeth Peabody" (ED.D. diss., Harvard University, 1980), 23, 29, 42-43; Megan Marshall, "The Sisters Who Showed the Way," <u>American Heritage</u> 38 (September-October 1987): 58-66.

28. Ibid., 30, 31, 35.

29. Ibid., 36, 37, 43.

30. Ibid., i, ii, iii, 23; Kuhn, <u>Childhood Education</u>, 59-61; Robert E. Spiller, ed., <u>Literacy History of the United States</u> (New York: the Macmillan Company, 1959), 229.

31. Marshall, <u>The Sisters</u>, 60, 62.

32. Mann, <u>Princes in France</u>, 465-490.

33. Alexander Gaston to William Gaston, 9 July 1813, <u>Gaston Papers</u>, Southern Historical Collection, Library of the University of North Carolina.

34. John D. Hawkins to ABC, 31 August 1828, <u>Hawkins Family Papers</u>, Southern Historical Collection, Library of the University of North Carolina.

35. William P. Little to William Polk, 11 November 1822, <u>Polk and Yeatmann Family Papers</u>, Southern Historical Collection, Library of the University of North Carolina.

36. Ann W. Johnson to Charles E. Johnson, Jr., May, n.d. (ca. 1848), <u>Johnson Papers</u>, Duke University Library.

37. John Hope Franklin, <u>A Southern Odyssey: Travelers in the Antebellum North</u> (Baton Rouge: Louisiana State University Press, 1976), 73.

38. Samuel Eliot Morison, <u>The Oxford History of the American People</u> (New York: Oxford University Press, 1965), 502.

39. Joseph Pearson to William Gaston, 3 July 1823, <u>Gaston Papers</u>, Southern Historical Collection, Library of the University of North Carolina.

40. Amelia Akehurst Lines, <u>To Raise Myself a Little: The Diaries and Letters of Jennie, a Georgia Teacher 1851-1886</u>, ed. Dyer (Athens, Georgia: University of Georgia Press, 1982), XIII, 74, 77-78, 78-79.

41. Ibid., 9.

42. Jane Gibbs, <u>Diary</u>, 27 March 1857 to 30 November 1859, Virginia State Library.

43. <u>The Statistical History of the United States</u> (Stanford, Conn.: Fairfield Publishers, 1965), 8, 207; Spiller, <u>Literary History</u>, 517.

44. <u>Statistical History</u>, 208.

45. Julie Roy Jeffrey, <u>Frontier Women, The Trans-Mississippi West, 1840-1880</u>, (New York: Hill and Wang, 1979), 87.

46. Ibid., 70, 88, 90; Lawrence A. Cremin, <u>American Education: The National Experience 1783-1876</u>, (New York: Harper and Row, 1980), 374-377.

47. Spiller, <u>Literary History</u>, 653-654.

48. Polly Wetts Kaufman, <u>Women Teachers On the Frontier</u> (New Haven, Conn.: Yale University Press, 1984), XXI-XXII.

49. Josepha Wright, <u>Papers</u>, 1863-1867, The University of Texas Library, Austin. Callie wrote these letters on her frontier teaching experiences to her youngest sister Josepha (Jodie) Wright.

50.  Callie Wright to Jodie Wright, 11 November 1864, _Josepha Wright Papers_; Callie Wright to Jodie Wright, 30 March 1863, _Josepha Wright Papers_; Callie Wright to Jodie Wright, 11 November 1864, _Josepha Wright Papers_; Callie Wright to Jodie Wright, 26 January 1865, _Josepha Wright Papers_.

51.  Callie Wright to Jodie Wright, 16 June 1865, _Josepha Wright Papers_.

52.  Callie Wright to Jodie Wright, 8 October 1865, _Josepha Wright Papers_; Callie Wright to Jodie Wright, 9 January 1866, _Josepha Wright Papers_.

53.  Margaret Clark Griffis, _Diary_ 1 January 1858; 27 September 1866, Rutgers University Library.

54.  Griffis, _Diary_ 2 January 1858; 2 June 1858; 29 June 1858; 22 September 1858.

55.  Griffis, _Diary_ 18 November 1859; 10 February 1860; 1 February 1861, 20 November 1964; 17 November 1865.

56.  Griffis, _Diary_ 2 January 1858 to 4 June 1858; 5 November 1859; 17 February 1861; 13 March 1861.

57.  Griffis, _Diary_ 11 February 1860.

58.  Griffis, _Diary_.

59.  Margaret Miller Clark, _Diary_, 14 October 1871 to 10 October 1872, Rutgers University Library, New Brunswick, New Jersey.

60.  Clark, _Diary_, 31 December 1871; 7 January 1872; 21 May 1872; 31 January 1872; 23 May 1872; 27 May 1872; 26 May 1872; 31 August 1872.

61.  Clark, _Diary_, 11 June 1872; 17 June 1872; 5-6 September 1872; 2 October 1872; 17 June 1872; 2 September 1872; 10 September 1872; 18 September 1872; 19 September 1872.

62.  Clark, _Diary_, 10 October 1872; 19 September 1872; 24 October 1872.

63. Kuhn, Childhood Education, 185.

64. See Chapter 7.

65. Henry James, The Turn of the Screw, ed. Kimbrough (New York: W.W. Norton, 1969), 2, 7, 8, 89.

66. Carl Sandburg, Abraham Lincoln: The Prairie Years, vol. 1 (New York: Harcourt, Brace, 1926), 169, 203-204, 217.

67. Justin G. Turner, Linda Levitt Turner, Mary Todd Lincoln (New York: Alfred A. Knopf, 1972), 247-248.

68. Steven Mintz, A Prison of Expectations (New York: New York University Press, 1983), 23-35; Johnson Allen, Dictionary of American Biography, s.v. "Alcott, Louisa May."

69. Joseph I. Dirvin, Mrs. Seton (New York: Farrar, Straus and Cudahy, 1962), 64, 277; Annabelle Melville, John Carroll (New York: Charles Scribner's Sons, 1955), 25-37; Dictionary of American Biography, s.v. "Cooper, James Fenimore;" Henry Adams, The Education of Henry Adams (London: Covotable and Co. Ltd., 1928), 31, 35-36; Women's Biography, s.v., "Blatch, Harriet Stanton;" Harriet Stanton Blatch, Challenging Years (New York: G.P. Putnam, 1940; Women's Biography, s.v. "Blow, Susan (Elizabeth);" Dictionary of American Biography, s.v., "Anthony, Susan B.;" Abbott, American History, 289-290; Women's Biography, s.v. "Dodge, Grace (Hoadley);" Ibid., s.v., "Grimke;" Ibid., s.v., "Lowell, Amy Lawrence;" Dictionary of American Biography, s.v., "Barton, Clara;" Ibid., s.v., "Mitchell, Maria;" Ibid., s.v., "Ossoli, Margaret Fuller."

70. Clyde Augustus Duniway, Papers, David C. Duniway, Personal Collection, University of Oregon Library, Salem. Mrs. Frick's maiden name was "Childs." It is possible that the name of their son "Childs Frick" in some way symbolized the partnership of their marriage.

71. Henry Clay Frick to C.A. Duniway, 9 June 1892, <u>Duniway Papers</u>; H. C. Frick to C.A. Duniway, 18 July 1892, <u>Duniway Papers</u>. Frick made the offer to Duniway shortly after a failed assassination incident. This was never mentioned in their correspondence. Did Frick decide to have Childs tutored privately for fear of a similar attempt against his son's life?

72. C.A. Duniway, <u>Diary</u>, 8 March 1893, 19 May 1893.

73. C.A. Duniway, <u>Account Book</u>, October 1893, 115, 117, <u>Duniway Papers</u>.

74. C.A. Duniway, <u>Account Book</u>, October 1894, 145, 153, <u>Duniway Papers</u>; C.A. Duniway, <u>Account Book</u>, January 1895, 159, 161, <u>Duniway Papers</u>.

75. H.C. Frick to C.A. Duniway, 29 October 1895, <u>Duniway Papers</u>.

76. Obituary, <u>New York Times</u>, 10 May 1965; Jaques Cattell, ed., <u>American Men of Science</u>, seventh edition (Lancaster, Pa.: The Science Press, 1944), 605.

# CHAPTER 9

## TUTORS IN THE AGE OF COMPULSORY SCHOOLING
## (THE TWENTIETH CENTURY)


### 1. A BRIDGE TO MODERNITY


Education in twentieth century America has been defined almost exclusively as a school experience. Tutorial philosophy and methods were forgotten or quietly absorbed by tax-supported public schools. The progressive education movement embraced the concepts of individual differences and child-centered education as first proposed by the philosopher-tutors Erasmus, Elyot, Vives, Thomas More, Locke, Fénelon, Rousseau, Edgeworth, Hannah More, Herbart, Humphrey, Goodrich and others. Their ideas were adopted by the progressive education movement and adapted to the American public school. John Dewey saw education as a shift in the center of teaching back to the student, "to facilitate and enrich the growth of the individual child." Dewey defined education as, "a continuous process of reconstruction of experience . . . which is always the actual life-experience of some individual."[1]

Much of what the progressive educators considered as the "teacher's role in her classroom," corresponded to, "the ideal tutor in his schoolroom." Cremin complains that the modern-day teacher's task became overwhelming,

> From the beginning, progressiveness cast the teacher in an almost impossible role: he was to be an artist of consummate skill, properly knowledgeable in his field, meticulously trained in the science of pedagogy, and thoroughly imbued with a burning goal for social improvement.[2]

Emile became every child!  Group instruction now replaced the one-to-one teaching relationship. However, only the instructional method changed since the ideas of the humanist-enlightenment tutors were largely adopted by American progressive educational theorists.

The triumph in the first two decades of the twentieth century of the American common school guided in part by these progressives, did not bring the immediate demise of "domestic education." Instead, home educators now told parents how to establish "the home nursery school" as an early childhood program in preparation for school. They also encouraged the formation of parent-teacher associations to help bring the needs of the home and school together. Three "International Congresses On Home Education" held between 1905 to 1910 focused on these themes. The Secretary of the Home Education Division of the U.S. Bureau of Education was among the 250 attending delegates from Europe, Japan, North America and South America that gathered in Brussels for these Congresses. The Bureau of Education published a report on the 1910 meeting and even later in 1919 issued Home Education.[3]

During the same period "domestic education" also included the "visiting teacher movement." These teachers had come into existence to supplement the work of the classroom teacher, especially in cases of retarded or failing pupils. In the 1910 Report of the Commissioner of Education the "visiting teacher movement" was characterized as prevalent throughout the entire country. These teachers offered one-to-one instruction for remedial education and special education. They also helped delinquent youths, and served as a vehicle to cope with the needs of foreign parents as they integrated their children into the American public school. The National Education Association (NEA) devoted an entire section of its 1910 Annual Convention in New York City to programs for "the Visiting Teacher." By 1929 these teachers had evolved into the "adjustment teacher," an early form of school social worker concerned with preventing delinquency.[4]

308

## 2. THE MODERN ONE-ROOM SCHOOL

Comprehensive compulsory school attendance was accomplished only after a considerable struggle throughout the United States. Massachusetts in 1852 enacted the first truly comprehensive school attendance statute. It was not until 1918 that Mississippi became the last state to embrace mandatory public education.[5] But these statutes failed to specify the method of classroom instruction. For well into this century many school children found that tutorial instruction remained an essential classroom teaching activity.

Table II on page 316 indicates that a majority of American public schools before 1930 were one-room schoolhouses. Though by the 1920s the majority of Americans lived in cities, tens of thousands of these small educational units persisted in remote rural areas for most of this century. Since the children in these one-room schoolhouses were all at such different educational levels and ages, teachers found they could not do the entire instructional job alone. The teachers designated older students as tutors to help younger children or their own peers.[6]

Continuing into the twentieth century was this daily adaptation of the earlier monitorial in most country schools. Many teachers have documented the fact that rural schools functioned effectively because of the use of peer tutoring following group recitation periods. The younger children were receptive in part because they had already learned many selections by listening to older students present their lessons. The consensus among these educators and parents was that this method helped both the younger child's education and simultaneously strengthened the learning and self-image of the older peer tutor. Rural teachers testified as to how and why this tutoring system worked.

> I don't believe any rural school-
> teacher ever taught without help from

TABLE II

One-Room Schools In the U.S.[7]

| Year | One-Room Schools | Total Schools | % of Total |
|------|------------------|---------------|------------|
| 1916 | 200,100 | NA | NA |
| 1920 | 190,700 | NA | NA |
| 1930 | 149,282 | 247,769 | 54% |
| 1940 | 113,600 | 238,169 | 48% |
| 1950 | 61,247 | 166,473 | 37% |
| 1956 | 34,964 | 146,732 | 24% |
| 1960 | 23,695 | NA | NA |
| 1970 | 1,800 | NA | NA |
| 1985 | 800 | NA | NA |

older students. That's the truth of it! I don't believe you could handle that many grades without a cooperative effort from everybody.

The kids in the sixth grade would teach the first grade how to read. . . . The boys would teach arithmetic. . . . It would be accurate to say the children did lots of teaching.

If they got their own work and were making good enough grades, the older children always helped the small ones. I used them that way all the time when I taught.

They [the peer tutors] would try to imitate the teacher. I had children I couldn't, like, teach long division. [sic] So I said, "Well . . . I'm going to let some of these children try it." And they did a pretty good job of it . . . all of them would want to do that, some of them that couldn't even do it. They'd want to help this child when they couldn't even help themselves.[8]

The use of student tutors was not confined only to rural schools. In 1924, 1933 and 1940 H.M. Horst published the results of studies on peer-tutoring conducted in urban midwestern high schools. Both pre-test and post-test scores and questionnaires were used to measure the benefits of peer-tutoring programs. He estimated the majority of tutors and tutees benefited scholastically from the program. Student participants also acquired a more positive attitude regarding learning and school attendance.[9]

As late as 1961, an international survey conducted by UNESCO of sixty-nine countries found that fifty-eight (84%) made extensive use of one-room school houses. Sixteen nations including Austria, Canada and the United States made extensive use of peer-tutors ("monitors") in these schools.[10]

Sitton and Rowold found in their historical

review of Texas county schools that contemporary one-room schools were successful because of their tutorial atmosphere. Teachers felt an increased responsibility for children's learning. Their in-depth knowledge of their students facilitated individualized instruction. The use of peer-tutors allowed the teacher to attain a detailed under-standing of each student's personality and degree of subject mastery. "At time the system resembled the British 'tutorial' approach. As in the tutorial system, recitation periods in the country school were not primarily for learning but for displays of learning already mastered."[11] The effective use of peer tutoring created a "familiar classroom atmo-sphere," and acted as "an instructional secret weapon" that helped many teachers get through the day.[12] The use of peer tutors was not confined to only country schools. As the century progressed they were "rediscovered" in many urban American class-rooms.

## 3.  TUTORS IN MODERN ENGLAND

Contemporary English tutoring has developed as an integral part of the higher education system. In the twentieth century this remained particularly true at Oxford and Cambridge Universities. Today Oxford refers to a "teacher-pupil-contact hours" as "tutorials." It had been known previously as "private hours." Balsdon tells us that, "A good don [tutor] is the servant of his pupils and not their master." Each student prepares an essay with extreme care each week for his tutor's review. The tutor and student in their hour together review this essay. He challenges him to produce evidence, and refutes him by citing other evidence. "A good tutorial should be a sparring match, keeping the two of you in training. It should not be a substitute for a lecture.[13]

A notable contemporary example of this tutorial relationship was Ruth Lawrence, a thirteen year old, who graduated from St. Hugh's College, Oxford in August, 1985, taking an honors degree in math. She was the youngest person ever to graduate from Oxford.

Her tutor, Mary Lunn, commented that, "Ruth is exhausting. It takes all my time to keep up with her." Ruth and her sister Rebecca were tutored at home by both parents for all their primary and secondary education. Even though Ruth had already planned her Ph.D. by age sixteen, her tutor reminded her, "You are not a genius until you have left a personal mark on your subject."[14]

Contemporary England has institutionalized tutoring in an alternative school form, "the tutorial college." d'Overbroeck's Tutorial College at Oxford remained one among many other such educational institutions that allowed students to complete their high school studies and prepare for the university entrance examination.

> The College aims to give a good alternative education to that normally received in the school sixth form and to prepare students for Higher Education. Students are taught for O-levels, A-levels and the Oxford and Cambridge Entrance Exam. . . . The option of one-to-one tuition allows a student to study almost any subject in any combination and enables some to cover a syllabus in less time than would have been possible at school. Individual tuition may also help those with special learning difficulties.[15]

Approximately 230 students ranging in age between sixteen and twenty attended d'Overbroeck's in the 1980s. Students from all parts of Great Britain live in Oxford while attending d'Overbroeck's for one to two years.[16]

The use of private tutors at home or "private tuition" remained popular in England. In April, 1985 The London Times estimated that tens of thousands of teacher supplemented their annual income through private tutoring. However, this multi-million pound educational activity remained highly secretive for both tutor and child. "Full-time teachers don't want their own school to know for fear it might harm their school image and promotion prospects, as well as for tax reasons." Parents also want the tutoring to

313

remain confidential fearing, "that their children's school teacher will interpret it as a lack off confidence in their abilities." (Many American parents expressed the same concern.)[17]

Tutors have continued to function in many educational roles throughout modern Great Britain. Though their use as live-in domestic educators has ended almost completely, large numbers of tutors still provide formal and informal educational services in primary, secondary and higher education.


## 4. THE RENEWAL OF TUTORING IN AMERICA

The early 1960s witnessed a general revival of peer tutoring, initially in the Detroit public schools, and with the "Mobilization For Youth" program in New York City. Population mobility changed the nature of student learning in many classrooms. The quality of education was questioned due to the decreasing performance of many children. Peer tutoring helped meet public demand for new methods, new instructional materials and new resources. Student tutors were soon supplemented with both adult volunteers and paid tutors. Numerous contemporary studies pointed to their general success in improving student attitudes and academic skills.[18]

By 1973 the National School Volunteer Program estimated that 2,000,000 volunteers were tutoring 3,000,000 children in 3,000 programs.[19] Tutors (student and adult) were not only helping in regular classroom work, but were also used as a supplement for the education of the handicapped. Tutoring helped the schools "mainstream" these children both as "as academic learning experience and as a socializing experience."[20] It was also recognized that tutoring for gifted children was "a useful form of individualized study in harder subjects." This was one of the best methods to challenge, pace and motivate bright young learners. "Special tutors for the highly precocious child may be, however, preferable to radical acceleration."[21]

314

The U.S. Department of Education, "Parents As Teachers" became part of the National Basic Skills Improvement Program (1975 Title II Education Act). This return to the concepts of "domestic education" sought to help parents develop skills that improve a child's oral communication skills. Parents were given written instruction to help their children at home from pre-school age to senior year in high school. This program begun in the mid-1970s was still active in 1988.[22]

This resurgence of tutors in the schools induced its re-evaluation by educators as an education process. Contemporary peer-tutoring was recognized as a variation of the nineteenth century "Monitorial School." Douglas Ellson in "Tutoring" presented perhaps the most thoughtful contemporary analysis, equating the procedure to individualized instruction, based on a diagnosis and possibly related to the group learning process. He criticized contemporary tutoring programs for dwelling too much on content and too little on methods.[23]

The most elaborate response to this criticism was Grant Von Harrison's "structured tutoring." Using his method manuals students were taught specific tutoring behavior and the expected correct student response. Harrison conducted many studies using this model and empirically demonstrated the benefits of peer tutoring.[24]

Benjamin S. Bloom's research also supported the effective use of tutoring for modern education programs. He found that eighty per cent of students who did poorly in conventional instruction profited from tutoring. Tutoring was effective because of the "constant feedback and correction between the tutor and tutee." These activities helped develop the "higher mental processes of problem solving, application of principles, analytical skills and creativity." This was far superior to the factual learning emphasized in typical classroom instruction.[25]

During the 1960s and 1970s the educational benefits of public school peer tutoring programs were seen in thousands of classrooms across the United

States.   Both published and unpublished reports empirically verified many academic benefits. Unfortunately, these factors were promptly ignored as schools rushed to use teacher driven programmed instruction (PI) materials.  If volunteers were used in these programs, adults were recruited rather than peer tutors.   Very few schools continued to use pupils as tutors.   They cited numerous mechanical programs of matching student time-tables and the public resentment that a child attended school not to act as a tutor, but to be taught by a teacher.  Some peer tutoring programs persisted in both urban and rural schools.   A diversity of published peer-tutoring methods materials became available in the 1980s that facilitated these remaining peer tutorial programs.[26]

### 5.   THE REVIVAL OF THE "VISITING TUTOR"

In the 1960s, as public awareness of the tutoring process increased, many parents sought private tutorial help for their children.   Yates found parents often perceived the school as not responsive to either the specific academic needs or motivational needs of their children.  The majority of parents did not seek the cooperation of the school either in the selection or effective utilization of a private tutor.   However, this lack of professional guidance did not prevent growing numbers of parents from seeking after-school educational programs.[27]

It has been estimated that tens of thousands of tutors annually taught at least one million school age children in the United States (1986).  Many of these tutors were classroom teachers working after-school with local children.   Teachers, college students even high school students were employed as tutors by national corporations including The Reading Game (Encyclopedia Britannia Learning Corporation), Huntington Learning Centers and Sylvan Learning Centers.   Sylvan's outlets were so uniform in their use of programmed instruction materials that Newsweek magazine dubbed them the "McDonalds of Teaching."[28]

The lack of tutorial program supervision by public or private regulatory agencies resulted in some tutors making unfair claims regarding academic improvement that unduly raised student and parent expectations. If not attained by the student during the tutoring program, this process added to increased achievement frustrations. In recognition of a significant change in public attitudes toward the use of private tutorial instruction, the North Central Association of Colleges and Schools (NCA) in 1982 accredited Imperial Tutoring and Educational Services as a special function school for after-school home tutoring. This was the first instance of professional recognition for any tutorial program in the United States. Between 1968 and 1987 Imperial had tutored over 5,000 children and adults at home on a one-to-one basis using its own written "Individualized Instructional Program" (IIP) curriculum.[29]

In 1980-1982 a study conducted by the Los Angeles public schools (1980) measured the achievement results of children tutored by teachers at home compared with students attending school on a daily basis. For two years 430 students from grades four to eight participated in the program. Achievement results for children attending school at home, "were encouraging, if not startling." Home tutored students also showed impressive results in the areas of maturation and social growth.[30]

There is little doubt that after-school tutorial education is a permanent phenomenon in the American education environment. In order to be taken seriously by other professional educators and the public, tutors must substantiate that they provide valid teaching services. This can be done in two ways. They must verify their results through professional recognized, published research. Also, both private and public regulatory agencies must establish proper criteria for recognition of valid tutorial programs. If these activities take place the public will be better served through enhanced community education, and protected from the incompetent, nefarious, or strictly "corporate raider." Other parents sought tutoring at home for more than remedial help. Families revived the "domestic education" idea of the nineteenth century and estab-

317

lished their own home schools.


## 6. MODERN "DOMESTIC EDUCATION:" THE HOME SCHOOL MOVEMENT

Attending school at home is certainly not a new concept in America. In the 1980s tens of thousands, perhaps hundreds of thousands of children met state compulsory education requirements at home rather than attending school.

The world of "domestic education" remains vigorous and diverse. Families kept their children at home as a matter of choice, often a "value-laden choice." Some parents objected to political or cultural values taught at school. Other did not like instructional methods. Many parents wanted to spend more time with their child. Precocious children were recognized by their parents as needing highly individualized programs. Even some handicapped children responded well to individualized home tutoring. Many fundamentalist religious groups also objected to the secular nature of the public schools. For these reasons parents all across America were once again tutoring their children at home.[31]

Lines, in a study of modern home schooling, has found that the actual number of children in home instruction seems to have increased from about 15,000 during the 1970s to 120,000-200,00 by 1987.[32] As Table III on page 325 shows, a wide variety of home instruction groups supported this parental tutoring. These organizations provided instructional guides, tests and books. The largest group, Christian Liberty Academy, also graded tests and employed teachers to evaluate papers. Christian Liberty Academy published its own monthly newspaper, The Christian Educator (March, 1985). The publication offered parents "news articles" exposing the so-called inferiority of public education, and encouraging them to fight for the right to a "domestic education."[33]

As the 1980s advanced, an increasing number of

318

TABLE III

Number of K-8 Children in
Home Instruction (1985-86)[34]

| Provider | N |
|---|---|
| Abbott Loop Christian Center, Anchorage, AK | 67 |
| Accelerated Christian Education, Lewisville, TX | 3,600 |
| Alpha Omega Publications, Tempe, AZ | 2,700 |
| American Christian Academy, Colleyville, TX | 700 |
| American Heritage Christian Academy, Sacramento, CA | 150 |
| Baldwin Park Christian School, Baldwin Park, CA | 75 |
| Calvert School, Baltimore, MD | 4,168 |
| Christian Liberty Academy, Arlington Hts., IL | 21,000 |
| Clonlara School, Ann Arbor, MI | 1.560 |
| Discovery Christian School, Concord, CA | 240 |
| Evangelistic & Faith Enterprises of America, Inc., Oliver Springs, TN | 300 |
| Family Centered Learning Alternatives, Arlington, WA | 150 |
| Hewitt-Moore Child Development Center, Washougal, WA | 4,000 |
| Home Study International, Takoma Park, MD | 1,509 |
| International Institute, Park Ridge, IL | 1,000 |
| Learning at Home, Honaunau, HI | 800 |
| Our Lady of Victory, Mission Hills, CA | 600 |
| National Academy of Christian Education, Columbus, Ohio | 1,050 |
| Pensacola Christian School, Pensacola, FL | 1,870 |
| Pilgrim Schools, Porterville and three other sites in California | 200 |
| Pilgrim Christian School, Maywood, CA | 80 |
| Santa Fe Community School, Santa Fe, NM | 200 |
| School of Home Learning, Escondido, CA | 80 |
| Seton School Home Study, Front Royal, VA | 500 |
| Summit Christian Academy, Dallas, TX | 1,800 |
| Sycamore Tree, Costa Mesa, CA | 175 |
| State Department of Education, Juneau, AK | 800 |
| 15 organizations with fewer than 50 children in 1985-86 | 123 |
| Subtotal | 49,497 |
| Estimate of number whose parents prepare own curriculum | 50,000-150,000 |
| | 100,000-200,000 |

state and local education agencies permitted home schooling. Lines found that twenty-nine states allowed instruction at home by a parent or tutor. Twelve other states mandated school attendance or "equivalent instruction." However, nine states still require "school attendance with no exceptions."[35]

Contemporary "home schools" appeared as American society's current adaptation of the previous "domestic education" movement. The small overall percentage of children educated at home does not pose a serious threat to the vitality of the public school.

Tutoring in America though largely informal continues to exist in our schooled society. The current interest in individualized learning in the schools, and its broader application in adult education and training programs, has encouraged even American business to consider the tutor as an alternative for corporate literacy programs. The future use of tutors across society will likely increase as educators continue to focus on individual differences and the means to increase productivity in all modes of learning.[36]

Endnotes

1. Lawrence A. Cremin, The Transformation of the School (New York: Vintage Books, 1964), 118, 119, 122, 217-218; John Dewey, Experience and Education (New York: Collier Books, 1963), 87, 89.

2. Cremin, Transformation, 168.

3. _____, The Complete Proceeding of the First International Congress On Home Education (Brussels: Lesigne, 1905), 5-60; Content Report On the 3rd International Congress On Home Education Held At Brussels, August 21-25, 1910 in U.S. Bureau of Education, Reports On International Congresses 1 (1910): 579-601; Ellen C. Lombard, Home Education (Washington

D.C.: Government Printing Office, 1919), 3-13;
A.A. Berle, <u>The School In the Home</u> (New York:
Moffat, Yard and Co., 1912), 1-21.

4.    Frederic Schoff, "Education In the Home," <u>Report</u>
<u>of the Commissioner of Education</u> (Washington
D.C.: GPO, 1910), 289-302; Mabel Brown Ellis,
<u>The Visiting Teacher In Rochester</u> (New York:
Joint Committee On Methods of Preventing
Delinquency, 1925), 39-55; Jane F. Culbert, <u>The</u>
<u>Visiting Teacher At Work</u> (New York: The Common-
wealth Fund's Division of Publication, 1929), 3-
45.

5.    August W. Steinhiller, <u>State Law On Compulsory</u>
<u>Attendance</u> (Washington D.C.:   U.S. Government
Printing Office, U.S. Department of HEW, 1966),
3.

6.    Between 1930-32, 54.33% of all schools in the
U.S. were one-room schools.  These schools were
common across the entire country as the
following state percentages indicate: New York-
63%, Illinois - 70%, Michigan - 69%, North
Dakota - 94%. Kate Wofford, <u>Modern Education In</u>
<u>the Small Rural School</u> (New York: The Macmillan
Co., 1938), 329; Sophie Bloom, <u>Peer and Cross-</u>
<u>Age Tutoring in the Schools</u> (Washington D.C.:
Department of Health Education, and Welfare,
December, 1976), 3; G. Ray Musgrave, <u>Indivi-</u>
<u>dualized Instruction</u> (Boston: Allyn and Bacon,
1975), 68-89.

7.    _____, <u>Historical Statistics of the</u>
<u>United States</u>, Part 1 (Washington, D.C.: Bureau
of the Census, 1975), 368; _____, <u>The</u>
<u>Statistical History of the United States from</u>
<u>Colonial Times to the Present</u> (Stanford, Conn.:
Fairfield Publishers, Inc., 1965), 208; Nelson
B. Henry, ed., <u>The Fifty-First Yearbook of the</u>
<u>National Society for the Study of Education</u>,
Part 2, <u>Education In Rural Communities</u> (Chicago:
University of Chicago Press, 1952), 92-95; Mark
M. Kindley, "Little Schools on the Prairie Still
Teach a Big Lesson" <u>Smithsonian</u>, 16 (October
1985): 119.

8. Thad Sitton and Milan C. Rowold, <u>Ringing the Children In, Texas Country Schools</u> (College Station: Texas A&M University Press, 1987), 85-86; Wayne E. Fuller, <u>The Old County School</u> (Chicago: University of Chicago Press, 1982), 14, 195.

9. H.M. Horst, "Student Participation in High School Responsibilities," <u>The School Reunion</u>, 23 (May 1924): 346; H.M. Horst, "An Experiment With Student Tutors," <u>National Educational Association Journal</u>, 22 (November 1933): 206; H.M. Horst, "Student Tutors Reduce High School Failure," <u>American School Board Journal</u>, 101 (July 1940): 51-52.

10. _____, "The One-Teacher School," <u>Proceedings of the 24th International Conference on Public Education (UNESCO)</u> (Geneva: International Bureau of Education, 1961), 13-14, 27, 28.

11. Sitton, <u>Texas Country Schools</u>, 207.

12. Ibid., 208.

13. Dacre Balsdon, <u>Oxford Now and Then</u> (New York: St. Martin's Press, 1970), 153-156.

14. Ezra Bowen, "Oxford's Amazing Adolescent," Time, 126 (August 5, 1986): 55.

15. <u>d'Overbroeck's Tutorial College Catalog 1986-87</u>, (Oxford, England), 1-24. "O-levels" and "A-levels" are national examinations taken by all students at the completion of their secondary education.

16. Elizabeth Ann Gallagher, interview with author, Chicago, IL, 24 April 1987. Ms. Gallagher was a tutor at d'Overbroeck's Tutorial College.

17. Nick Baker, "A Bit On the Side" <u>The Times Educational Supplement</u>, 16 April 1985, 22-23.

18. Peggy Lippitt and John E. Lohman, "Cross-Age Relationships An Education Resource," Children, 12 May-June 1965): 113-117; Robert Cloward, "Studies In Tutoring," The Journal of Experimental Education, 36 (Fall 1967): 14-25; Judy Rogers, "The Effects of Tutoring By 6th Graders On the Reading Performance of 1st Graders," (Ph.D. diss., University of San Francisco, 1979), 16.

19. Samuel L. Blumenfelf, How To Tutor (New Rochelle: Arlington House, 1973) 9-10.

20. Virginia May Cole-Mahan, "Tutoring As A Support Service For Mainstreaming Handicapped Children In Rural and Urban Schools," (Ph.D. diss., University of Cincinnati, 1980), 1, 2, 5, 96.

21. A. Harry Passov, "The Gifted and the Talented: Their Education and Development," in The Seventy-Eighth Yearbook of the National Society for the Study of Education (Chicago: University of Chicago Press, 1979), 120-121.

22. _____, Parents: The Missing Link in Education Reform, Hearing (Washington, D.C.: Government Printing Office, 1988); _____, Parents As Teachers: Helping Your Children To Become Better Communicators (Springfield: Illinois State Board of Education, 1980).

23. S. Thiagarajan, "Madras System Revisited: A New Structure For Peer Tutoring," Educational Technology, (December 1973): 10-13; Douglas G. Ellson, "Tutoring" in The Psychology of Teaching Methods (Chicago: University of Chicago Press, 1976), 130-141.

24. David G. Reay, Grant Von Harrison, Conrad Gottredson, "The Effect On Pupil Reading Achievement of Teacher Compliance With Prescribed Methodology" Research In Education, 32 (November 1984): 17-23; Grant Von Harrison, Ronald E. Guymon, Structural Tutoring (Englewood Cliffs: Educational Technology Publication, 1980), 15-76.

25. Benjamin S. Bloom, "The Search for Methods of Group Instruction As Effective As One-to-One Tutoring," <u>Educational Leadership</u> 41 (May 1984): 12, 14, 16; Benjamin S. Bloom, <u>All Our Children Learning</u> (New York: McGraw-Hill, 1981), 160, 162, 166.

26. D.T. Tosti, "The Peer Proctor In Individualized Programs," <u>Educational Technology</u>, 8 (August 1973): 29-30; Harrison, <u>Prescribed Methodology</u>, 17; Cole-Mahan, <u>Tutoring</u>, 12-13.

27. Donald Crombie Yates, "Home and School Relations: The Private Tutor and the School," (Ed.D., Columbia University Teachers College, 1980), 1-170.

28. "McDonalds of Teaching," <u>Newsweek</u>, 7 January 1985, 61; Susan Becker, "What You Should Know About Tutoring Centers," <u>Instructor</u>, 95 (February 1986): 88.

29. Edward E. Gordon, "Home Tutoring Programs Gain Respectability" <u>Phi Delta Kappan</u>, 64 (February 1983): 398.

30. Roy A. Weaver, Anton Negri, Barbara Wallace, "Home Tutorials vs. The Public Schools in Los Angeles," <u>Phi Delta Kappan</u> (December 1980): 254.

31. Patricia Lines, "Home Instruction: Law, Legislation and Practice," Law and Education Center, <u>Education Commission of the States, Working Paper</u>, December, 1984, LEC-84-7; Patricia Lines, "An Overview of Home Instruction," <u>Phi Delta Kappan</u>, 68 (March 1987): 510; Jim Gallagher, "Home Schools Protest 'Evils of Humanism'," <u>Chicago Tribune</u>, 4 December 1983, sec. 1; "Intensive Program Frees Autistic Children, Scientists Say," <u>Chicago Tribune</u>, 24 May 1987, sec. 3.

32. Lines, <u>Home Instruction</u>, 510.

33. Some of the articles included: "Time Wasted In Many U.S. Schools," "Schools Take Mom To Court," "Fear Cuts Teacher Ranks," "Survey Assails

Teacher Training," "More Teens Turning To Cocaine," "10% of Teachers Flunk Skills Test," "When The Teacher Can't Speak English," "New Jersey Orders School Drug Tests," The Christian Educator 1 (March-November 1985).

34. Lines, Home Instruction, 512.

35. Lines, Home Instruction, 514; "Nonpublic School," Planning and Policy Committee, Illinois State Board of Education Memorandum, 30 November 1984, 3-29.

36. Edward E. Gordon, "Assessing Training Alternatives In Today's Corporations," Training Today, (December 1986): 8; Larry Green, Wendy Leopold, "Workers Get New Look At Three R's," Los Angeles Times, 13 February 1987, Section 1; N.J. Eurich, Corporate Classrooms (Princeton: The Carnegie Foundation for the Advancement of Teaching, 1985), IX, XIII, 12-13, 52-54, 61-63.

# CHAPTER 10

## RETROSPECTIVE: THE TUTORS' LESSONS

Tutoring has made a significant contribution in the history of education regarding the evolution of schooling. Today, we view the schools as being synonymous with education. This was not always true. There is much evidence that a sizable amount of education took place in the home using one-to-one instruction by a variety of tutors, including parents. Some of the most important philosophers of the West developed educational theories based upon their practical experience as tutors, rather than as school teachers. Their tutorial philosophy developed into many of our modern educational principles.

What were these ideals? The development of the individual's thinking processes became a fundamental educational goal. The recognition of individual differences guided the instruction of each student. Education became a culturally broadening experience, that at the same time recognized the child's own talents and prepared him for a specific lifetime vocation. Students learned far better through rewards than punishments. A teacher best motivated a child to study through kindness, exciting natural curiosity, recognizing personal interests and unique abilities. Women should receive the same educational opportunities as men for their own intellectual development. The best teacher established for his student a moral and ethical standard, reinforced by his own example. A child's education helped him acquire a sense of individual responsibility for the betterment of society through his own personal contribution.

Like other forms of education, tutoring had a checkered past that followed the norms and expectations of society and individuals. An excellent example occurred between 1500 and 1900 with the alternating periods of advance and decline in the history of women's tutorial education. Philip Jackson, in The Practice of Teaching, described these varying patterns of instruction by contrasting "mimetic education" with "transformational education." He defined a mimetic teacher instructing children to imitate their instructors at school. Tutors that came from this mold included: the Sophists, rhetoricians, medieval scholars, the classicist tutors of the Renaissance, tutors of the "salon" and "academy" for women in 18th and 19th century Europe, the "monitorial school movement," contemporary computerized tutorials, and the "back to basics" tutoring programs of the 1980s.

By contrast "transformational education," according to Jackson, was an effort by the teacher to guide a child toward independent thinking based on the classic "human ideal" originated by Socrates, Plato and Aristotle.[1] The tutors that enlarged this theme included Thomas Elyot, Roger Ascham, Thomas More, Juan de Vives, John Cheke, Bethusa Makin, Francois Fénelon, John Locke, Jean Jacques Rousseau, Maria Edgeworth, Hannah More, Mary Wollstonecraft, John Herbart and many other more obscure philosophers.

In addition to chronicling the history of women's education, tutoring was fundamental in the development of our conception of childhood. A considerable collection of books, teaching methods and materials laid the foundation of early childhood education that for the first time was differentiated from adult education.

Much of the history of tutoring was recorded by anonymous individuals whose obscure work evaded public recognition. Our past ignorance of their work left modern educators with an incomplete picture. We continued to portray tutoring as an exclusive elitist form of education available only for a few wealthy children, who were taught by university scholars. Until now historical scholarship ignored the instruction of many other children from professional or mercantile families. We now know they were educated at home by an array of tutors, governesses and parents, who brought different levels of sophistication to their task.

A unified history of tutoring clearly exists. The "classic ideal" of the tutor-pupil relationship began in the Greco-Roman era. It was subordinated by the Church of the Middle Ages, only to be resecularized during the Renaissance revival. The Reformation scholar reinforced parental responsibility to provide a basic education at home. The tutor theorists of the fifteenth century began to shape a definitive educational literature that played a major role in the history of childhood and the education of women. The following two hundred years formalized a philosophy of tutoring that broadened its appeal from the royal court to the homes of the newly emerging professional classes and laid the foundation of many modern education principles.

By the early nineteenth century tutoring had spread from the fireside to the quasi-tutoring of the popular monitorial charity school. At the same time "domestic education" increased women's educational opportunities, first as tutor-governess, and later in the establishment of the first institutions of higher education for women.

Schooling has dominated the twentieth century, but tutoring still holds an important role. Peer-tutors, after-school remedial programs, home-bound instruction and the "home-schooling movement" are tutoring's modern expressions.

Future advances in education may be based on "mastery learning," computerized instruction or skill/content directed education, but they remain conceptual expressions of individualized learning. Centuries of tutors demonstrated that a child's education was a personal process, supported by the family, and guided through the assistance of moral, literate, open-minded women and men. At their best tutors remained the best equipped to account for individual differences and adjust a child's educational experience.

329

In the late nineteenth and early twentieth centuries educational theorists incorporated concepts from the tutor-philosophers into the far broader context of the common school movement. As part of this transition, educational historians tended to ignore tutoring as a distinctive form of instruction. One underlying reason for this exclusion was that they predictably sided with the argument that "schooling" was superior to "tutoring."

The history of tutoring contains two lines of educational development. In its earlier origins and use tutoring was recognized intrinsically as an educational process. Only much later in the nineteenth and particularly in the twentieth centuries did tutoring become a part of "schooling." Schools absorbed and used certain aspects of tutoring.

Modern historians obscured this issue by describing one-to-one instruction using other expressions rather than "tutoring." As we have seen over the centuries, many terms came into daily use that described the work of the tutor. This is no longer easily discerned by a modern audience, since contemporary history seldom characterized or classified these instructional activities in a tutorial context. Cremin provides a good example in his comments on colonial American education, "that reading was often taught on an each-one-teacher-one basis by parents. . . ."[2] Through this exclusionary process tutoring has been almost eliminated from our modern notion of educational development in the history of the West.

A far greater educational concern was the erroneous adaptation of tutorial concepts to the classroom. Modern educators overlooked the fact that the original context of the tutor-philosopher was one-to-one instruction at home, not group instruction in a classroom. This remains a fundamental reason why many classroom teachers experience daily frustrations as they attempt to carry out many educational principles originally formulated in a tutorial environment.[3]

The history of tutoring is largely the study of individuals, not institutions. Our focus has been on how men and women joined with parents to teach the young values, ideas and skills for the improvement of society. In sharp contrast contemporary education remains focused on the study of its own bureaucracy. For many education has become the pursuit of personal material success, rather than an awakening of the individual's responsibility for societal improvements. Ever fewer parents share a sense of personal responsibility with the teacher in educating their children. The institutionalization and bureaucratization of modern American education has stifled the initiative for change in our schools, and dropped from education's working agenda the basic tenets of the tutor-philosophers.

What has been lost is the evolution of the one-to-one instructional process during its many years of successful use both in the home and in school. "Schooling" and "tutoring" did not develop as a socio-educational phenomenon isolated one from the other. Instead, at many times they mutually supported each other in providing for the broader educational needs of society. As we have already seen, compelling evidence exists that classroom tutors, (students, parents or professionals), and a mixture of home tutoring with school attendance, enhanced many children's educational foundations in one-to-one relationships. In other instances one-to-one and group instruction blended through peer-tutors or student monitors becoming quasi-tutorial-schooling.

Today the challenge of better schooling requires a much broader study of tutorial philosophy and methods. This activity will not promote "anti-schooling" or "elitist" attitudes, but offers a viable design to increase "educational productivity" in the classroom.[4] This reassessment acknowledges the tutor as a vital part of our Western educational heritage. The tutor and teacher are not in competition with one another. Instead they seek an answer to the question of how a new alliance of "tutoring" and "teaching" will best serve society's learning requirements.

# Endnotes

1.  Philip Jackson, <u>The Practice of Teaching</u> (Chicago: University of Chicago Press, 1985), 115-145.

2.  Cremin, <u>Colonial Experience</u>, 135. "Domestic education" of the eighteenth and nineteenth centuries portrayed the many forms of one-to-one tutoring found in the home. Today this term is related to the "home economics" programs taught at secondary educational institutions.

3.  A fundamental criticism of "progressive education" has been its lack of specific teaching methods. This can be partially attributed to its misapplication of individualized tutorial concepts to classroom teaching.

4.  Douglas G. Ellson, <u>Improving the Productivity of Teaching: 125 Exhibits</u> (Bloomington, Indiana: Phi Delta Kappa, 1986).

APPENDIX A

# APPENDIX A

Tutors have described their methods and philosophy over the centuries of recorded history through a variety of publications. The following material provides a chronological and developmental continuum of the "tutorial ideal."

| DATE | AUTHOR | WORK | COUNTRY | TYPE OF INSTRUCTION |
|------|--------|------|---------|---------------------|
| 400 B.C. | Aristotle, | Ethics, | Greece | Socratic Method |
| 400 B.C. | Plato, | The Dialogue of Plato, | Greece | Socratic Method |
| 100 B.C. | Cicero, | De Oratore, | Rome | Rhetorical Education |
| 150 A.D. | Marcus Quintilian, | De Institutione Oratoria, | Rome | Rhetorical Education |
| 1100? | _____, | Boke of, Curtasye, | England | Courtesy Education |
| 1412 | Thomas Hoceleve, | The Regiment of Princes, | England | Princely Tutorial Education |
| 1431 | Leo Battista Alberti, | Trattato della Cura della Faniglia, | Italy | Renaissance Education |
| 1450 | Matteo Palmieri, | Della Vita Civile, | Italy | Renaissance Education |
| 1450 | Aeneas Sylvinus, | De Liberorum Educatione, | Germany | Princely Tutorial Education |

| DATE | AUTHOR | WORK | COUNTRY | TYPE OF INSTRUCTION |
|---|---|---|---|---|
| 1501 | John Skelton, | Speculum Principis (A Prince's Mirror), | England | Princely Tutorial Education |
| 1505 | Pietro Bembo, | Gli Asolani, | Italy | Courtly Education |
| 1511 | Desiderius Erasmus, | De Ratione Studii, | Netherlands | Rhetorical Education |
| 1513 | Machiavelli, | The Prince, | Italy | Princely Education |
| 1516 | Desiderius Erasmus, | The Education of a Christian Prince, | Netherlands | Princely Tutorial Education |
| 1516 | Guillaume Budé, | The Instruction of a Prince (De l'Institution du Prince), | France | Princely Education |
| 1521 | Alexander Barclay, | Here Begynneth the Introductory to Write and Pronounce French, | England | Foreign Language Tutoring |
| 1523 | Juan de Vives, | On the Education of Christian Women, | Spain/ England | Humanistic Tutoring of Women |
| 1523 | Juan de Vives, | Plan of Studies, | Spain/ England | Princely Tutorial Education |
| 1524 | Richard Hyrde, | "On the Education of Women," | England | Humanistic Tutoring of Women |
| 1526 | Desiderius Erasmus, | De matrimonio Christiano, | Netherlands | Tutorial Education of Women |

336

| DATE | AUTHOR | WORK | COUNTRY | TYPE OF INSTRUCTION |
|------|--------|------|---------|---------------------|
| 1528 | Baldassare Castiglione, | The Courtier, | Italy | Courtesy Education |
| 1529 | Martin Luther | "Duties of Parents in Training Children," | Germany | Domestic Education |
| 1529 | Desiderius Erasmus, | De Pueris Instituendis, | Nether- lands | Tutorial Education |
| 1529 | Henricus Cornelius Agrippa, | De Nobilitate et Praecellentia Feminei Sexus, | Germany | Education of Women |
| 1530 | John Palsgrave, | L' Esclaircisse- ment de la Langue Francoyse, | England | Foreign Language Tutoring |
| 1530 | Jacopa Sadoleto, | De Liberis Recte Instituendis (The Freedom To Choose Instruction), | France | Humanistic Tutoring, Courtesy Education |
| 1531 | Thomas Elyot, | The Boke Named the Governor, | England | Courtesy Education |
| 1535? | Thomas Elyot, | The Defense of Good Women, | England | Tutoring of Women |
| 1535 | Plutarch, | Discourse Touching the, Training of Children, | Italy | Courtesy Education |
| 1549 | Ludovico Domenichi, | La Nobiltá della Donne, | Venice | Education of Women |
| 1552 | Roger Ascham, | The School Master, | England | Princely, Courtesy Education |
| 1552 | William Bercher, | The Nobylytye of Women, | England | Education of Women |

337

| DATE | AUTHOR | WORK | COUNTRY | TYPE OF INSTRUCTION |
|------|--------|------|---------|---------------------|
| 1555 | _____, | Institution of a Gentleman | England | Courtesy Education |
| 1568 | _____, | The Instruction of a Gentleman, | London | Courtesy Education |
| 1572 | _____, | Queen Elizabeth's Academy, | England | Courtesy Education |
| 1574 | Jerome Turler, | De Perigrinatione, | England | The Grand Tour |
| 1596 | Edmund Coate, | The English Schoolmaster, | England | Tutorial Education |
| 1607 | James Cleland, | Institution of a Young Nobleman, | England | Courtesy Education |
| 1620 | Henry Peacham, | The Complete Gentleman, | England | Courtesy Education |
| 1630 | Richard Brathwait, | The English Gentleman, | England | Courtesy Education |
| 1632 | John Amos Comenius, | The Great Didactic, | Germany | Tutorial Education |
| 1640 | Francois de La Mothe Le Vayer, | De l'instruction de Monseigneur le Dauphin, | France | Princely Education |
| 1647 | Hardouin De Perefixe, | Institutio Principis, | France | Princely Education |
| 1655? | Francois de La Mothe Le Vayer, | Morale du Prince, | France | Princely Education |
| 1656? | Francois de La Mothe Le Vayer, | Logique du Prince, | France | Princely Education |

| DATE | AUTHOR | WORK | COUNTRY | TYPE OF INSTRUCTION |
|------|--------|------|---------|---------------------|
| 1661 | Pierre Nicole, | Essais de Morale, | France | Princely Education |
| 1668 | Gilbert Burnet, | Thoughts on Education, | England | Domestic Tutoring |
| 1673 | Obadiah Walker, | Of Education, Especially of Young Gentlemen, | England | Courtesy Education |
| 1673 | Bathsua Makin, | "An Essay to Revive the Ancient Education of a Gentlewoman," | England | Education of Women |
| 1675 | Hannah Woolley, | The Gentlewoman's Companion, | England | Education of a Governess |
| 1678 | Jean Gailhard, | The Complete Gentleman, | England | Domestic Education |
| 1679 | Jacques Bénigne Bossuet, | Discours sur l' Histoire Universell a Monseigneur le Dauphin, | France | Princely Education |
| 1687 | Francois Fénelon, | The Education of Girls, | France | Education of Women |
| 1690? | Francois Fénelon, | Recueil des Fables Composées pour l'education, | France | Princely Education |
| 1693 | John Locke, | Some Thoughts Concerning Education | England | Tutorial Education |
| 1696 | Charles Augrste d'Allonville, | Mémoire sur l' Education des Ducs de Bourgogne, Anjou, et Berry, | France | Princely Education |

| DATE | AUTHOR | WORK | COUNTRY | TYPE OF INSTRUCTION |
|------|--------|------|---------|---------------------|
| 1722 | Jacques Bénigne Bossuet, | De la Connaissants de Dieu et de Soi-même, | France | Princely Education |
| 1762 | Jean Jacque Rousseau, | Emile, | France | Natural Social Education |
| 1774 | Hester Chapone, | Letters on the Improvement of the Mind Addressed to a Young Lady, | England | Home Education |
| 1774 | David Williams, | Treatise On Education, | England | Home Education |
| 1775 | William Jones, | Letters of a Tutor to His Pupils, | England | Home Education |
| 1780? | Jakob Long, | Der Hofmeister (The Tutor), | Germany | Domestic Education/ Tutoring |
| 1782 | Percival Stockdale, | Liberal Education, | England | Domestic Education |
| 1787 | Gottfried Leibnitz, | The Education of a Prince (Project de l'Education d'un Prince, | Germany | Princely Education |
| 1787 | Mary Wollstonecraft, | Thoughts On the Education of Daughters, | England | Domestic Education |
| 1789 | David Williams, | Lectures on Education, | England | Home Education |
| 1796 | Maria Edgeworth, | The Parent's Assistant, | England | Domestic Education |

| DATE | AUTHOR | WORK | COUNTRY | TYPE OF INSTRUCTION |
|------|--------|------|---------|---------------------|
| 1796 | August Herman Niemeyer, | Principles of Teaching for Parents, Tutors and Teachers, | Germany | Domestic Education |
| 1797 | John Miller, | The Tutor, | India/ England | Monitorial Education (Peer Tutoring) |
| 1798 | Maria Edgeworth, Richard Lovell Edgeworth, | Practical Education, | England | Domestic Education |
| 1799 | Hannah More, | Strictures On the Modern System of Female Education, | England | Domestic Education for Women |
| 1801 | Maria Edgeworth, | Early Lessons, | England | Domestic Education |
| 1801 | Maria Edgeworth, | Moral Tales, | England | Domestic Education |
| 1803 | Joseph Lancaster, | Improvements In Education, | England | Monitorial Education |
| 1804 | Maria Edgeworth, | Popular Tales, | England | Domestic Education |
| 1805 | Hannah More, | Hints Toward Forming the Character of a Young Princess, | England | Princely Education |
| 1809 | Maria Edgeworth, | Essays On Professional Education, | England | Domestic Education |
| 1821 | Elizabeth Appleton, | Early Education, | England | Domestic Education |

| DATE | AUTHOR | WORK | COUNTRY | TYPE OF INSTRUCTION |
|------|--------|------|---------|---------------------|
| 1825 | Maria Edgeworth, | Harry and Lucy Concluded; Being the Last Part of Early Lessons, | England | Domestic Education |
| 1826 | Robert Mudie, | The Complete Governess, | England | Domestic Education/ Governess Education |
| 1830 | Pestalozzi, | Letters, | Italy | Domestic Education |
| 1832 | Andrew Bell, | Bell's Mutual Tuition and Moral Discipline, | England | Monitorial Education |
| 1833 | John Abbott, | The Mother At Home, | United States | Domestic Education |
| 1834 | Theodore Dwight, | The Father's Book, | United States | Domestic Education |
| 1835 | John Hall, | On The Education of Children . . . , | United States | Domestic Education |
| 1838 | Isaac Taylor, | Home Education, | United States/ England | Domestic Education |
| 1840 | Herman Humphrey, | Domestic Education, | United States | Domestic Education |
| 1841 | S.G. Goodrich, | Fireside Education, | England | Domestic Education |
| 1842 | Aimé Martin, | The Education of Mothers of Families, | France | Domestic Education |
| 1846 | Anna Brownwell Jameson, | Memoirs, | England | Training of Governesses |

342

| DATE | AUTHOR | WORK | COUNTRY | TYPE OF INSTRUCTION |
|------|--------|------|---------|---------------------|
| 1854 | Anna Brownwell Jameson, | Books of Thoughts, | England | Training of Governesses |
| 1859 | Anna Brownwell Jameson, | Social Employment of Women, | England | Training of Governesses |
| 1863 | Warren Burton, | Helps To Education In The Homes of Our Country, | United States | Domestic Education |
| 1864 | Harriet Martineau, | Household Education, | England | Domestic Education |
| 1883 | Edwin Abbott, | Hints On Home | England | Domestic Education |
| 1905 | _____, | Complete Report of the Grand Session of the International Congress On Home Education Held at Liége, 1905, | Europe | Domestic Education |
| 1907 | Annie Allen, | Home, School and Vacation, | United States | Domestic Education |
| 1910 | U.S. Bureau of Education, | Report On The 3rd International Congress On Home Education Held at Brussels August 21-15, 1910, | Europe/ United States | Domestic Education |
| 1910 | Oliver Lodge, | Parent and Child, | England/ United States | Domestic Education |

| DATE | AUTHOR | WORK | COUNTRY | TYPE OF INSTRUCTION |
|------|--------|------|---------|---------------------|
| 1914 | Edward Lyttelton, | The Corner-Stone of Education; An Essay On the Home Training of Children, | England/ United States | Domestic Education |
| 1919 | Ellen Celia Lombard, | Home Education, | United States | Domestic Education |
| 1976 | Douglas Ellson, | "Tutoring," | United States | One-to-One Instruction |
| 1980 | Grant Von Harrison, | Structured Tutoring, | United States | Peer Tutoring |
| 1984 | Benjamin Bloom, | "The Search For Methods of Group Instruction As Effective As One-To-One Tutoring," | United States | Mastery Learning |

APPENDIX B

APPENDIX B:  GOVERNESSES AND EDUCATION BOOKS

The following books discuss female education before 1870. They detail the duties and rewards of governesses as a sub-category of tutoring, or employ the metaphor of the book as governess. (Source: Nash, Governesses, 433-436.)

Advice to Governesses. London: John Hatchard & Sons, 1827.

Amica, pseud. The Calling and Responsibilities of a Governess. London: Longman, Brown, Green & Longmans, 1852.

Darwin, Erasmus. A Plan for the Conduct of Female Education. 1797.

Edgeworth, Maria. Letters for Literary Ladies. 1795.

Edgeworth, Maria and Richard Lovell Edgeworth. Practical Education. 1801.

The Elements of Tuition and Modes of Punishment: In Letters From Mlle. Dobouleau, a Celebrated Parisian Tutoress, Addressed to Miss Smart Bum, Governess of a Young Ladies Academy at -----. London: George Canmon, 1794. (Cat. Lib. Prohib.)

Emerson, Joseph. Female Education. 1822.

An Experienced Teacher [Robert Mudie]. The Complete Governess: A Course of Mental Instruction for Ladies. London: Knight & Lacey, 1826.

[Fénelon, Francoise de Salignac de la Mothe-]. The Accomplished Governess; or, Short Instruction for the Education of the Fair Sex. London: Printed for the editors, 1752.

Fruse, J.W. <u>Latin Governess</u>. London: Simpkin, 1843.

Genlis, Mme. de.

A Governess. <u>Hints to Governesses, by One of Themselves</u>. London: [Printed] Chichester, 1856.

<u>The Governess: First Lesson Book for Children</u>. London: Cox, 1856.

[Johns, C.A.]. <u>The Governess: A First Lesson Book for Children Who Have to Read, By a Schoolmaster of Twenty Years Standing</u>. London, [1855].

<u>Governess Life: Its Trials, Duties, and Encouragements</u>. See Maurice, Mary A.

<u>The Kind Governess; or, How to Make Some Happy</u>. Edinburgh: Simpkin, 1869.

A Lady. [Farrar, Eliza Ware (Rotch)]. <u>The Young Lady's Friend. A Manual of Practical Advice and Instruction to Young Females on their Entering Upon the Duties of Life after Quitting School</u>. Boston: American Stationer's Co., 1836; 3rd ed. London, 1840.

Le Prince de Beaumont, Jeanne-Marie. See Appendix A.

<u>Legacy of Affection, Advice and Instruction from a Retired Governess to the Present Pupils of an Establishment near London for Female Education, Which She Conducted for Upwards of 40 Years</u>. London, 1827. 2nd ed. London: Poole & Edwards, 1830.

Makin, Bethusah. <u>An Essay to Revive the Ancient Education of a Gentlewoman in Religion, Manners, Arts and Tongues</u>. London: Printed by J.D. to be sold by Tho. Parkhurst, 1673.

Maurice, Frederick Dennison, Charles Kingsley, et al. <u>Lectures to Ladies</u>. 1855.

Maurice, Mary Atkinson.

A Mother. <u>Female Excellence; or, Hints to Daughters</u>
<u>Designed for their Use from the Time of Leaving</u>
<u>School to their Settlement in Life</u>. London,
1832.

A Mother. <u>Thoughts on Domestic Education; the result</u>
<u>of experience</u>. London, 1826.

<u>Mothers and Governesses</u>. London, 1847. See Maurice,
Mary A.

More, Hannah.

<u>Essays on Various Subjects, Principally Designed</u>
<u>for Young Ladies</u>. London, 1777; 2nd. ed.
London: J. Wilkie, 1778.

<u>Hints toward Forming the Character of a Young</u>
<u>Princess, . . .</u> [With special reference to
Charlotte Augusta Princess of Wales.] 2 vols.
T. Cadell & W. Davies, 1805.

<u>Observations on the Effect of Theatrical</u>
<u>Representations with Respect to Religion and</u>
<u>Morals, . . .</u> Bath: J. Hume, 1804.

<u>Strictures on the Modern System of Female Education</u>
<u>with a View of the Principles and Conduct</u>
<u>Prevalent Among Women of Rank and Fortune . . .</u>
2 vols. London: T. Cadell & W. Davies, 1799.

<u>Nursery Governess</u>. London: Seeleys, 1854.

<u>Nursery Governess Model Lessons</u>. London:
Groombridge & Sons, 1853.

Peart, Emily.

<u>The Polite Lady; or, A Course of Female Education in</u>
<u>a Series of Letters from a Mother to her</u>
<u>Daughter</u>. London: J. Newbury, 1760.

<u>The Relative Position of Mothers and Governesses</u>.
See Jameson.

Ridout, S.F.  Letters to a Young Governess on the Principles of Education.  2 pts.  London: E. Fry, 1838-40.

[S.,G.].  Houlston's Industrial Library: Pamphlet #18 - The Governess.  London: Houlston and Wright, 1849.  May be a re-issue of S.,G. [Sir George Stephen].  The Guide to Service: #14 - The Governess.  London, 1838-44.

Smith, Jane.

Smith, Lucy.  The Music Governess.  Edinburgh: W. Oliphaunt & Co.; London: Hamilton, 1868.

T., R.  The Mother, The Best Governess: A Practical System for the Education of Young Ladies.  London, 1839.

[Three Young Ladies].  Letters to a Governess on Different Useful and Entertaining Subjects.  London: Harvey & Darton, 1828.

Wells, Helena, afterwards Mrs. Whitford.

Letters on Subjects of Important to the Happiness of Young Females, addressed by a Governess to her Pupils.  London: Peacock, [1799?]; 2nd ed. London: Sabine & Son, 1807.

Thoughts on Establishing an Institution for the Support and Education of Impoverished Females.  London: Hurst, Rees, Orme, et al., 1809.

[A Lady].  The Step-Mother: A Domestic Tale, from Real Life.  2 vols.  London: Printed for T.N. Longman, 1798.

Wollstonecraft, Mary.

Woolley, Hannah.

A Word to A Young Governess: By an Old One.  London: Bennett, 1860.

APPENDIX C

# APPENDIX C: GOVERNESSES AND FICTION

These English novels (and, occasionally, "tales" or short stories) contain at least one of the following: governesses as heroines or prominent characters who work in a group of "feminine" professions, especially teaching, professions which often involved training as a governess. (Source in Part: Nash, _Governesses_, 437-444.)

1749  [Sarah Fielding], _The Governess; or, The Little Female Academy_.

1756  J. M. Le Prince de Beaumont. _Magasin des Enfants_.

1760  [C. Allen], _The Polite Lady_.

1766  [Oliver Goldsmith?], _The Renowned History of Little Goody Two-Shoes_.

c. 1766  _The Rival Pupils; or, A New Holiday Gift for a Boarding School_.

c. 1782  [Lady Fenn], _School Occurrences under the tuition of Mrs. Teachwell_.

    [Kilner, Dorothy], _Anecdotes of a Boarding School; or, An Antidote to the Vices of those Useful Seminaries_.

1783?  [Sophia Lee], _The Recess; a Tale of Other Times_.

1785  [Mme. de Genlis], _Moral and Instructive Tales for the Improvement of Young Ladies_.

1786  C. Stanhope. _The New Polite Tutoress; or, Young Ladies' Best Instructor_.

1788        Mary Wollstonecraft, <u>Original Stories from Real Life</u>.

1795        H. S., <u>Anecdotes of Mary; or, The Good Governess</u>.

1797        Maria Edgeworth, "Mademoiselle Panache," Part I.

            <u>The Governess; or,, Courtland Abbey</u>.

            Ann Radcliffe, <u>A Sicilian Romance</u>.

            Mary Wollstonecraft, <u>Maria; or, The Wrong of Woman</u>.

c. 1798     <u>Three Days' Chat . . . between Young Ladies and their Governesses</u>.

1800        <u>The Governess, or Evening Amusement at a Boarding School</u>.

c. 1800     <u>Christmas Holidays; or, Anecdotes of Mrs. Truegood's Scholars</u>.

1801        Maria Edgeworth, "The Good French Governess," <u>Moral Tales</u>, III.

            Mrs. Harriet Ventrum, <u>The Amiable Tutoress</u>.

1804        [Dorothy Kilner], <u>First Going to School; or, The Story of Tom Brown, and His Sisters</u>.

            [Sophia Lee], <u>The Life of a Lover, in a Series of Letters</u>.

1806        Eliza Kirkham Mathews, <u>Ellinor; or, The Young Governess</u>.

1809        Catherine Bayley, <u>Vacation Evenings; or, Conversations between a Governess and her Pupils</u>.

            Lamb, Charles and Mary, <u>Mrs. Leister's School; or, The Histories of Several Young Ladies Related by Themselves</u>.

c. 1811    Mrs. Rachel Hunter, <u>The Schoolmistress; a Moral Tale for Young Ladies</u>.

1811       Maria Edgeworth, <u>Vivian</u>.

           <u>The Ladies' School; or, The Approach of the Holidays</u>.

1813       Jane Austen, <u>Pride and Prejudice</u>.

           Eaton Stannard Barrett, <u>The Heroine; or, Adventures of Cherubina</u>.

           Damina [A. Kent], <u>York House; or, Conversations in a Ladies' School: Founded on Fact</u>.

1814       Jane Austen, <u>Mansfield Park</u>.

           Mary Brunton, <u>Discipline; A Novel</u>.

           Barbara Hofland, <u>Ellen, the Teacher; A Tale for Youth</u>.

           Sydney Owenson Morgan, <u>O'Donnel; A National Tale</u>.

1816       Jane Austen, <u>Emma</u>.

1818       Elizabeth Sandham. <u>The School-Fellows; A Moral Tale</u>.

           Mary Martha Sherwood. <u>The History of the Fairchild Family</u>.

1820       Mrs. Mary Martha (Butt) Sherwood, <u>The Governess; or, the Little Female Academy</u>.

1821       M. Hughes, <u>The Rebellious Schoolgirl</u>.

1822       E.A. Dove, <u>Tales for My Pupils</u>.

1823       <u>The Boarding School; or, Familiar Conversations Between a Governess and Her Pupils</u>.

The School for Sisters.

W.E.W., The Journal of a Governess.

1826 Anna Brownwell Jameson, Diary of an Ennuyee. "The Private Governess." The Literary Souvenir.

1827 Blue-Stocking Hall; A Work of Fiction Designed to Inculcate the Various Duties of Domestic Life.

Selina Bunbury, Annot and Her Pupil.

1830 Anna Maria Hall, Chronicles of a School-Room. The Schoolmistress; or, The True Story of Jenny Hickling (Relig. Tract Society).

W. H. White, The Governess' Story.

1833 Aunt Ellen and Her Pupils; or, A Week at Beech Grove.

1834 Elizabeth Napier, The Nursery Governess.

1835 Anna Maria Hall, Tales of Woman's Trials.

c. 1835 Mrs. Sherwood, Caroline Mordaunt; or The Governess.

A. Strickland, Tales of the Schoolroom.

Eliza T_____, The Village School-Girls: A Tale.

1836 [Miss Ross?], The Governess; or, Politics in Private Life.

Mrs. Mary M. Sherwood, The Schoolgirl.

1838 Joseph Le Fanu, "Passage in the Secret History of an Irish Countess."

1839 Marguerite, Countess of Blessington, The Governess.

Joseph Sheridan Le Fanu, "Chapter in the History of a Tyrone Family."

Harriet Martineau, <u>Deerbrook</u>.

1840    Anna Maria Hall, <u>Marian</u>.

Rachel MacCrindell, <u>The Schoolgirl in France</u>.

c. 1840  <u>Helen's Schooldays</u>.

1841    Mrs. Leckie, <u>The Village School; A Story for Girls</u>.

Harriet Mozely, <u>The Fairy Bower</u>.

[Harriet Mozely], <u>The Lost Brooch</u>.

1843    Bremer, Fredrika, <u>The President's Daughters, A Narrative of a Governess</u>. New York: J. Munroe & Co., 1843.

1843-44  Charles Dickens, <u>Martin Chuzzlewit</u>.

1844    Rachel MacCrindell, <u>The English Governess; A Tale of Real Life</u>.

Elizabeth Missing Sewell, <u>Amy Herbert</u>.

1845    <u>Distinction</u>.

<u>The Nursery Governess</u>.

1846    Elizabeth Grey, <u>Sybil Lennard</u>.

Ann Marsh-Caldwell, <u>Emilia Wyndham</u>.

1847    Anne Brontë, <u>Agnes Gray</u>.

<u>Annie Sherwood; or, Scenes from School</u>.

Charlotte Brontë, <u>Jane Eyre</u>.

Elizabeth Missing Sewell, <u>Laneton Parsonage</u>.

William Makepeace Thackeray, <u>The Book of Snobs</u>.

Augusta Wicks, "Education; or, The Governesses' Advocate," <u>La Belle Assemblee</u>.

1847-48     Anne Brontë, <u>The Tenant of Wildfield Hall</u>.

<u>Edna Morton and Her Cousins; or, School-Room Days</u>.

Elizabeth Gaskell, <u>Mary Barton</u>.

Geraldine Jewsbury, <u>The Half-Sisters</u>.

Joseph Sheridan Le Fanu, "Some Account of the Latter Days of the Hon. Richard Marston of Dunoran."

Rachel MacCrindell, <u>The Convent; A Narrative Founded on Fact</u>.

Anne Marsh-Caldwell, <u>Angela</u>.

M.A.Y., "The Young Governess," <u>La Belle Assemblee</u>.

1849     Charlotte Brontë, <u>Shirley</u>.

<u>The Governess</u> (Mass. Sabbath School Society).

1850     Anne Marsh-Caldwell, <u>Lettice Arnold. Chance and Choice; or, The Education of Circumstances</u>.

Dinah Mulock Craik, <u>Ohio</u>.

Elizabeth Gaskell, <u>The Moorland Cottage</u>.

Mrs. S.C. Hall, <u>Stories of the Governess</u>.

Harriet Martineau, "The Old Governess."

Francis Trollope, <u>Petticoat Government</u>.

1851     Geraldine Jewsbury, <u>Marian Withers</u>.

         Joseph Sheridan Le Fanu, <u>Ghost Stories and
              Tales of Mystery</u>.

         Anne Marsh-[Caldwell], "Lizzie Wilson; or,
              The Governess' Christmas Holiday."

         George Henry Miles, <u>The Governess; or, The
              Effects of a Good Example</u>.

1852     Dinah Mulock Craik, <u>Bread Upon the Waters</u>.

         Anna Maria Hall, <u>Stories of the Governess</u>.

         Franck Smedley, <u>Lewis Arundel</u>.

         "Wanted, A Governess," <u>The Leisure Hour</u>.

         Charlotte Yonge, <u>The Two Guardians</u>.

1852-53  Charles Dickens, <u>Bleak House</u>.

1853     Anna Atkins, <u>The Colonel</u>.

         Charlotte Brontë, <u>Villette</u>.

         Elizabeth Gaskell, <u>Ruth</u>.

         Geraldine Jewsbury, <u>The History of an
              Adopted Child</u>.

         J. Todd. <u>The Daughter at School</u>.

1853-54  Charles James Lever, <u>The Dodd Family
              Abroad</u>.

1853-55  William Thackeray, <u>The Newcomes</u>.

1854     Gabriel Alexander, <u>Adelaide; or, The Trials
              of a Governess</u>.

         Mary Clarke, <u>The Iron Cousin</u>.

         Leith Ritchie, <u>Wearyfoot Common</u>.

         Charlotte Yonge, <u>The Castle-Builders</u>.

1855        Geraldine Jewsbury, <u>Constance Herbert</u>.

              Frederick William Robinson, <u>The House of Elsmore</u>.

              Charlotte Yonge, <u>The Clever Woman in the Family</u>.

1855-57  Charles Dickens, <u>Little Dorrit</u>.

1856        Rosina Doyle Wheeler Lytton, <u>Very Successful</u>.

              Holme Lee [Harriet Parr], <u>Kathie Brande: The Fireside History of a Quiet Life</u>.

              Emma Jean Worboise. <u>Grace Hamilton's Schooldays</u>.

              Charlotte Yonge, <u>The Daisy Chain</u>.

1857        Matilda Bentham-Edwards, <u>The White House by the Sea; A Love Story</u>.

              Charlotte Brontë, <u>The Professor</u>.

              Dinah Mulock Craik, <u>John Halifax, Gentleman</u>. "Ellen Maynard; or, the Death Wail of the Hawkshaws," <u>Family Herald</u>.

              Sir Arthur Hallam Elton, <u>Below the Surface; A Story of English Country Life</u>.

              Anna Maria Hall, <u>A Woman's Story</u>.

              Fanny Aiken Kortwright, <u>Anne Sherwood</u>.

              Georgiana Craik May, <u>Riverston</u>.

              Eliza Meteyard, <u>Lillian's Golden Hours</u>.

              Anthony Trollope, <u>Barchester Towers</u>.

              Charlotte Yonge, <u>The Pillars of the House</u>.

1858        George Eliot, <u>Scenes of Clerical Life</u>,

"Janet's Repentance."

George John Whyte-Melville, _The Interpreter_.

1860    George Eliot, _The Mill on the Floss_.

Janet Maugham, _Charley Nugent_.

William Thackeray, _Lovel the Widower_.

Charlotte Yonge, _Hopes and Fears; or Scenes from the Life of a Spinster_.

1861    [Sarah Maly Fitton], _How I Became a Governess_.

Holme Lee [Harriet Parr], _Warp and Woof_.

_She Would be a Governess; a Domestic Tale_.

Mrs. Gordon-Smythies, _The Daily Governess_.

Mrs. Henry Wood, _East Lynne_.

Charlotte Yonge, _The Young Stepmother_.

1862    J.T. Barr, _The Governess_.

Mary Elizabeth Braddon, _Laddy Audley's Secret_.

Wilkie Collins, _No Name_.

Charles Stuart Saville, _Walter Langley_.

J. Saunders, _Abel Drake's Wife_.

Mrs. Henry Wood, _The Channings_.

Charlotte Yonge, _Countess Kate_.

1863    Mark Lemon, _Wait for the End_.

Margaret Stourton, _M.S.; or, a Year of Governess Life_.

| 1864 | Mabel S. Crawford, The Wilmot Family. |
| --- | --- |
| | Kenner Deene [Charlotte Smith], Anne Cave, A Tale. |
| | Jean Ingelow, "Dr. Dean's Governess," Studies for Stories. |
| | Joseph Sheridan Le Fanu, Uncle Silas. |
| | Mrs. Emma Jean Worboise, Thornycroft Hall: Its Owners and Heirs. |
| 1864-66 | Elizabeth Gaskell, Wives and Daughters. |
| 1865 | Mortimer Collins, Who is the Heir? |
| | Dinah Mulock Craik, Christian's Mistake. |
| | Eliza Lynn Linton, Grasp Your Nettle. |
| | Catherine E. Spence, Mr. Hogarth's Will. |
| | Charlotte Yonge, The Clever Woman in the Family. |
| 1866 | Louisa May Alcott, "Behind a Mask." |
| | Wilkie Collins, Armadale. |
| | George Eliot, Felix Holt. |
| 1867 | The Governess and her Pupil; and other Stories (Pres. Board of Publication). |
| | Anne French Hector, Which Shall It Be? |
| | Anne Thackeray Ritchie, The Village on the Cliff. |
| 1868 | Rev. Francis Edward Paget, Lucretia; or, The Heroine of the Nineteenth Century. |
| | Catherine E. Spence, The Author's Daughter. |
| | Tales of My Governess (Relig. Tract Society). |

Mrs. Henry Wood, <u>Anne Hereford</u>.

1869      Dinah Mulock Craik, <u>The Women's Kingdom</u>.

Henry Kingsley, <u>Stretton</u>.

Joseph Sheridan Le Fanu, <u>The Wyvern Mystery</u>.

1870      Wilkie Collins, <u>Man and Wife</u>.

1871?     [Henry Courtney Selous], <u>The Young Governess; A Tale for Girls</u>.

1871-72   George Eliot, <u>Middlemarch</u>.

1871-73   Anthony Trollope, <u>The Eustace Diamonds</u>.

1872      George MacDonald, <u>The Vicar's Daughter</u>.

Guernsey, Lucy Ellen, <u>Lady Betty's Governess</u>. New York: T. Whittaker, 1872.

1873      Louisa May Alcott, <u>Work</u>.

Georgiana C. May, <u>Miss Moore, A Tale for Girls</u>.

1873-76   <u>The Romance of Lust; or, Early Experiences</u>.

1875      Elizabeth Wetherell, <u>Daisy</u>.

E.W., <u>Ellen Manners; or, Recollections of a Governess</u> ("Sunday Lib. for Young People").

1876      Julia Horatia Ewing, <u>Six to Sixteen</u>.

Mrs. Henry Wood, <u>Edina</u>.

Charlotte Yonge, <u>Hopes and Fears</u>.

Charlotte Yonge,, <u>Womankind</u>.

1878      Ricard Jefferies, "Mademoiselle, the Governess," in <u>Hodge and his Masters</u>.

1880 <u>In Adventures of a Young Lady, Who Was First a Governess</u>.

Craik, Dinah Maria [Mulock], <u>The Half-Castle, An Old Governess' Tale</u>. New York: G. Munro, 1880.

1881 J.R.H. Hawthorn, pseud. [John Richard Houlding], <u>The Pioneer of a Family; or, Adventures of a Young Governess</u>.

1883 Mrs. Emma Raymond Pitman, <u>My Governess Life; or, Using My one Talent, . . .</u>

Ferner, William Mason, <u>Gertrude the Governess</u>. New York: N.L. Munro, 1883.

1886 Kathleen O'Meara, <u>Mabel Stanhope</u>.

1888 Rosa Nouchette Carey [Le Voleur], <u>Only the Governess</u>.

Carey, Rosa Nouchette, <u>Only the Governess</u>. New York: J. W. Lovell Co., 1888.

c. 1890 <u>My Secret Life</u>.

1891 Sir Arthur Conan Doyle, <u>The Adventures of Sherlock Holmes</u>.

Fleming, May Agnes [Early], <u>A Pretty Governess</u>. New York: J.S. Ogilvie, 1891.

1892 Charlotte Yonge, <u>That Stick</u>.

MacGregor, Annie, <u>John Waids' Governess</u>. New York: 1892.

1893 George Gissing, <u>The Odd Women</u>.

1894 Robert Hitchins, <u>The Green Carnation</u>.

1895 Kenneth Grahame, <u>The Golden Age</u>.

Thomas Hardy, <u>Jude the Obscure</u>.

Miles, George Henry, <u>The Governess</u>. Boston: T.B. Noonan, 1895.

1897 Henry James, <u>What Maisie Knew</u>.

Oliphant, M.O.W., <u>The Story of a Governess</u>. New York: R.F. Fenno & Co., 1897.

1898 Henry James, <u>The Turn of the Screw</u>.

1903 Samuel Butler, <u>The Way of All Flesh; or, Ernest Pontifex</u>.

1904 I. Zwangwill, <u>The Serio-Comic Governess</u>.

1909 Francis Marian Crawford, <u>The Undesirable Governess</u>.

1912 Mrs. Alfred Hunt and Viola Hunt, <u>The Governess</u>.

1914 Joseph Conrad, Chance.

Saki [H.H. Munro], "The Schwartz-Metterclume Method," <u>Beasts and Super-beasts</u>.

1916 Kingsley, Charles, <u>The Tutor's Story</u>, Lucas Malet, ed. New York: Dodd, Mead and Company, 1916. This was an unpublished Victorian novel revised and completed by Kingsley's daughter. It is an excellent representation of the impact that tutors, governesses and nannies had on English fiction in the nineteenth century.

1924 Virginia Woolf, <u>Mrs. Dalloway</u>.

1930 Vita Sackville-West, <u>The Edwardians</u>.

1958 Stewart, Mary, <u>Nine Coaches Waiting</u>, Greenwich, Conn.: 1958. A contemporary example of the tutor-governess in fiction.

# LIST OF TABLES

Bibliography

PRIMARY SOURCES

1. Manuscript Collections

Adams, Abigail. Letters of Mrs. Adams. 2 vols. Boston: Charles C. Little and James Brown, 1841.

Adams, John. Adams Family Correspondence. Edited by Butterfield. 2 vols. Cambridge: Harvard University, The Belknap Press, 1963.

_____. Letters of John Adams Addressed to his Wife. Edited by C.F. Adams. 2 vols. Boston: Freeman and Bolles, 1841.

Alcuin. Disputatio and De rehetoricca. In Thought and Letters in Western Europe A.D. 500 to 900, edited by Laistner. Ithaca, New York: Cornell University Press, 1957.

_____. The Letter of Alcuin. Translated by Page. New York: The Forest Press, 1909.

Arnold, Thomas. The Life and Correspondence of Thomas Arnold. Edited by Arthur Penrhnyo Stanley. London: T. Fellowes, Ludgate, 1858.

Clark, Margaret Miller. Diary, 14 October 1871 - 10 October 1872. New Brunswick, New Jersey: Rutgers University Library.

Duniway, Clyde Augustus. Papers, 9 June 1892 - 24 March 1896. Salem, Oregon: David C. Duniway Personal Collection, University of Oregon Library.

Edgeworth, Maria. Maria Edgeworth: Chosen Letters. Edited by Barry. New York: Houghton Mifflin, n.d.

Edward VI. The Chronicle and Political Papers of King Edward VI. Edited by Jordan. Cambridge, Mass.: The Belknap Press of Harvard University Press, 1968.

Fithian, Phillip Vickers. Journal and Letters of Phillip Vickers Fithian 1773-1774: A Plantation Tutor of the Old Dominion. Edited by Hunter D. Farish Williamsburg, Virginia: Colonial Williamsburg, 1957.

Foxe, Richard. The Letters of Richard Foxe. Edited by Allen. vol. 7. Oxford: Oxford University Press 1929.

Gaston, William. Letters. William Gaston Papers. Library for the University of North Carolina, Chapel Hill.

Gibbs, Jane. Diary. 12 March 1857-30 November 1859. Richmond, Virginia: Virginia State University.

Griffis, Margaret Clark. Diary, 1 January 1858-27 September 1866. New Brunswick, New Jersey: Rutgers University Library.

Hawkins, John D. Letters. Hawkins Family Papers. Library of the University of North Carolina, Chapel Hill.

Henry VIII. Miscellaneous Writings of Henry the Eight. Edited by MacNamara. London: Golden Cockerel Press, 1924.

Henry VIII. The Letters of King Henry VIII. Edited by Byrne. London: Cassell and Company, 1936.

Johnson, Charles E. Letters. Charles Earl Johnson Papers. Duke University Library, Durham, North Carolina.

Leonowens, Anna. Papers. Huntington Library, San Marino, California.

Lines, Amelia Akehurst. To Raise Myself a Little: The Diaries and Letters of Jennie, a Georgia Teacher 1851-1886. Edited by Dyer. Athens,

Georgia: University of Georgia Press, 1982.

More, Sir Thomas. _The Correspondence of Sir Thomas More_. Edited by Rogers. Princeton: Princeton University Press, 1947.

Pestalozzi, Johann Heinrich. _Letters of Pestalozzi on the Education of Infancy_. Boston Carter and Heder, 1830.

Polk, William. _Polk and Yeatman Family Papers_. Library of the University of North Carolina, Chapel Hill.

Stowe, William. _Tutor's Diary 1799_. _William Stowe Papers_. Huntington Library, San Marino, California.

Van Dyke, Rachel. _Diary_. Rutgers University Library, New Brunswick, New Jersy.

Victoria, Queen. _Queen Victoria in Her Letters and Journals_. Edited by Christopher Hibbert. New York: Viking, 1985.

Weeton, Ellen. _Miss Weeton, Journal of a Governess 1807-1811_. Edited by Hall. London: Oxford University Press, 1936.

Wright, Josepha "Jodie." _Papers_ 1845-1884. Austin Texas: University of Texas Archives.

2. Public Documents

Complete Proceeding, _First International Congress On Home Education_. Brussels, 1905.

_____. Congress of the United States, House Select Committee on Children, Youth and Families. _Parents: The Missing Link in Education Reform, Hearing_. Government Printing Office, 1988.

_____. "Content Report on the 3rd International Congress on Home Education Held at Brussels 21-25 August 1910." _Report of the Commissioner of_

Education. Washington D.C.: Government Printing
Office, 1910.

Deering, Albert R. "Homework Helper Program, Fact
Sheet." U.S. Department of Health Education, and
Welfare. Educational Resource Information
Center, Research in Education. Washington, D.C.:
Goverment Printing Office, 1968.

The General Laws and Liberties of New-Plymouth
Colony, Cambridge, Mass., no publisher, 1672.

Great Britain, Public Records Office. Calendar of
State Letters and Papers, Foreign and Domestic of
the Reign of Henry VIII. Vol. IV. London:
Longman and Company, 1875.

Hoadly, Charles J., ed., Records of the Colony or
Jurisdiction of New Haven, from May, 1653, to the
Union. Hartford: Case, Lockwood and Company,
1858.

Laws and Liberties of Massachusetts. In Children and
Young in America a Documentary History. Edited
by Robert Bernover. Cambridge, Mass.: Harvard
University Press, 1970.

"Laws Established by the Authority of His Majesties
Letters, Patents, Granted to His Royal Highness
James Duke of York and Albany," Collections of
the New York Historical Society, vol. 1, no
publisher, 809.

Lines, Patricia. "Home Instruction: Law, Legislation
and Practice." Education Commission of the
States Working Papers. December, 1984.

Lombard, Ellen Celia. Home Education. Washington
D.C.: Government Printing Office, 1919.

Mann, Horace. Census of Great Britain, 1851
Education in Great Britain Being the Official
Report of Horace Mann. London: George Routledge
and Company, 1854.

Massachusetts Records II (1853). In Children and
Youth in America a Documentary History. Edited

by Robert Bremmer. Vol. 1 1600-1865. Cambridge, Mass.: Harvard University Press, 1970.

_____. "The One-Teacher School." In <u>Proceedings of the 24th International Conference on Public Education (UNESCO)</u>. Geneva: International Bureau of Education, 1961.

_____. <u>Parents As Teachers: Helping Your Children to Become Better Communicators</u>. Illinois State Board of Education: 1980.

<u>Parliamentary Papers of Great Britain</u> 1852-53. Vol. LXXXXIII.

<u>Parliamentary Papers of Great Britain</u> 1867. Vol. XXVIII.

<u>Parliamentary Papers of Great Britain</u> 1867-68. Vol. XIII.

_____. "Planning and Policy Committee Memorandum." Illinois State Board of Education. Springfield, Illinois, 30 November 1984.

Schaff, Mrs. Frederic. "Education in the Home." <u>Report of the Commissioner of Education</u>. Washington, D.C.: Government Printing Office, 1910.

Scottish Education Department. <u>Primary Education in Scotland</u>. Edinburgh: Her Majesty's Stateway Office, 1965.

Shurtleff, Nathanial B., ed., <u>Records of the Governor and Company of the Massachusetts Bay In New England</u>, 5 vols., Boston: William White, 1853-1854.

_____. Tutorial Assistant Center. <u>Tutorial Survey</u>. Washington, D.C., 1968.

_____. U.S. Bureau of Education. Reports On International Congresses. Vol. 1. <u>Content Report On the 3rd International Congress On Home Education Held At Brussels</u>. Washington, D.C.: Government Printing Office, 1910.

373

_____. U.S. Bureau of Education. <u>Education In the Home</u>. Washington, D.C.: Government Printing Office, 1910.

_____. U.S. Bureau of Education. <u>A Manual of Education Legislation</u>, Bulletin, 1910, no. 4, Department of the Interior. Washington, D.C.: Government Printing Office, 1919.

<u>Watertown Records I</u>. Watertown, Mass., 1894. In <u>Children and Youth in America a Documentary History</u>. Edited by Robert Mermner. Cambridge, Mass.: Harvard University Press, 1970.


3. <u>Published Works</u>

Abbott, Edwin. <u>Hints On Home Teaching</u>. London: Seeley, Jackson and Halliday, 1883.

Abbott, John. <u>The Mother At Home</u>. Boston: Crocker and Brewster, 1833.

Abelard, Peter. <u>The Story of My Misfortune</u>. Translated by Bellows. Glencoe, Illinois: The Free Press, 1958.

Adams, Henry. <u>The Education of Henry Adams</u>. London: Constable and Company, 1928.

Allen, Annie. <u>Home, School and Vacation</u>. Boston: Houghton Mifflin, 1907.

Appleton, Elizabeth. <u>Early Education</u>. London: G. and W.B. Whittaker, 1821.

Aristotle. <u>Ethics</u>. Translated by D.P. Chase. Edited by Ernest Rhys. London: Walter School, n.d.

_____. <u>Politics</u>. Translated by Rackham. Boston: Harvard University Press, 1932.

Arnold, Matthew. "Reports on Elementary Schools, 1852-1882." In <u>Matthew Arnold and the Education</u>

of the New Order, edited by Smith, and
Summerfield. Cambridge: At the University Press,
1969.

Ascham, Roger. The Schoolmaster. London: Cassell,
1900.

Ascham, Roger. The Whole Works of Roger Ascham.
Edited by Rev. Dr. Giles. New York: A.M.S.
Press, 1965.

Aurelius, Marcus. The Meditations of Marcus Aurelius
Antoninus Book 1 in The Scola Philosophers.
Edited by Saxe Commins and Robert N. Linscott.
New York: Random House, 1947.

Austen, Jane. Emma (1816). New York: New American
Library, 1980.

Bacon, Frances. The Works of Frances Bacon. 14
vols. Edited by Spedding, Ellis, Heath. Oxford:
Oxford University Press, 1857-74.

_____. "Novum Organum." In Man and the Universe:
The Philosophers of Science, edited by Commins
and Linscott. New York: Random House, 1947.

Barclay, Alexander. Here Begymneth the Introductory
to Write and Pronounce French. London: Robert
Coplande, 1521.

Bell, Andrew. Bell's Mutual Tuition and Moral
Discipline. London: C.J.G. and F. Livingston,
1832.

Benoist, A. Quid de puerorum institutione senserit
Erasmus. Paris: 1876.

Berle, A.A. The School in the Home. New York:
Moffat, Yard and Company, 1912.

Bhagavad - Gita (The Song Celestial). Translated by
Arnold. Boston: Robert Brothers, 1885.

Bicknell, Anna. Life In the Tuileries Under the
Second Empire. New York: The Century Company,
1895.

Blackburn, Keith. _The Tutor_. London: Heinemann
Educational Books, 1975.

Blatch, Harriet Stanton. _Challenging Years_. New
York: G.P. Putman, 1940.

Blois, Peter of. "Literature vs. Logic." In
_University Records and Life in the Middle Ages_,
edited by Thorndike. New York: Octagon Books,
1971.

Blundevile, M. _Exercises of M. Blundevile_. London:
1593-4.

Bonhours, Dominique. _The Arts of Logick and
Rethorike_. Adapted by John Oldmixon from _La
Menierede Bien Penser_. London: Printed for J.
Clark etc., 1728.

_Book of the Dead_. Translated by Hillyer in Mark Van
Doren, _Anthology of World Poetry_. New York:
Harper, 1928.

Bossuet, Jacques Benigne. _Oeuvres Oratoires_. Edited
by Lebarq. Paris, 1896.

Boswell, James. _James Boswell The Earlier Years
1740-1769_. London: McGraw Hill, 1985.

Brathwait, Richard. _The English Gentleman_. London:
1630.

Bremer, Frederiker. _The President's Daughters_. Vol.
1. Translated by Horvitt. London: Longman,
Brown, Green and Longman, 1843.

Bremmer, Robert H., ed. _Children and Youth In
America a Documentary History_. Vol. 1 1600-1865.
Cambridge, Massachusetts: Harvard University
Press, 1970.

Brenton, Humphrey. _The Most Pleasant Song of Lady
Bessy_. London: Percy Society, R. Taylor, 1829.

Brinsley, John. _The Grammar School_. Edited by
Campagnac. London: Constable and Company, 1917.

Brontë, Ann. <u>Agnes Gray</u>. London: Oxford University Press, 1971.

_____. <u>The Tenant of Wildfell Hall</u>, vol. VI of <u>The Life and Works of the Sisters Bronte</u>. New York: Haworth, 1900.

Brontë, Charlotte. <u>Jane Eyre</u>. New York: New America Library, 1960.

_____. <u>Shirley</u> in <u>Novels of the Sisters Brontë</u>. Edited by Scott, 2 vol. Edinburgh: John Grant, 1905.

_____. <u>Villetee</u>. Boston: Houghton Mifflin, 1971.

Brontë, Emily. <u>Wuthering Heights</u>. London: Oxford University Press, 1930.

Browning, Elizabeth Barrett. "Aurora Leigh." In <u>The Complete Poetical Works of Elizabeth Barrett Browning</u>. New York: Houghton Mifflin, 1900.

Budé, Maiftre Guillaume. <u>De L'institution du Prince</u>. Farnborough, England: Gregg Press Limited, 1966.

Burnet, Gilbert. <u>Thoughts on Education</u>. Edited by John Clarke. Aberdeen: 1914.

Burnett, John, editor. <u>Destiny Obscure</u>. New York: Penguin Books, 1982.

Burton, Warren. <u>Helps To Education In the Homes of Our Country</u>. Boston: Crosley and Nichols, 1863.

Byfield, Nicholas. <u>Principles or the Patterns of Wholesome Words</u>. London: Printed by T.S. for S. Man, 1622.

Castiglione, Baldassare. <u>The Courtier</u>. London: J.M. Dent and Sons, 1928.

Cavendish, George. <u>The Life of Cardinal Wolsey</u>. London: George Routledge and Sons, 1885.

Chamberlayne, Edward. <u>An Academy For Women</u>. London:

1671.

Chapone, Hester. _Letters On the Improvement of the Mind Addressed to a Young Lady_. London: Printed by M. Hughes for J. Walter, 1773.

Chetardie, Cherialier Trotti de la. _Instructions For a Young Nobleman_. Translated by Ferrand Spence. London, 1683.

Cicero. _De Oratore_. Translated by E.W. Sutton. Cambridge, Masschusetts: Harvard University Press, 1942.

Cleland, James. _Institution of a Young Noble Man_. New York: Scholars Facsimiles and Reprints, 1948.

Clement, Francis. _The Pelie Schole_. London: Imprinted by T. Vautroilier, 1587.

Comenius, Johann Amos. _The Gates of Languages Unlocked_. London: Printed by W. Du-gard for T. Slater, 1650.

_____. _The Orbis Pictus of John Amos Comenius_. Syracuse, NY: C.W. Bardeen, 1887.

_____. _The Great Didactic_. Part II. Translated by M.W. Keatings. London: A. and C. Black, 1921.

Confucius. _The Sacred Books of China, The Texts of Confucianism_. Vol. 28. Translated by Legg in _The Sacred Books of the East_. Edited by Muller. Oxford: At the Clarendon Press, 1885.

_Complete Report of the General Session of the 1st International Congress On Home Education Held at Liege 1905_. Brussels: A. Lesigne, 1905.

Connor, Frances P. _Education of Homebound or Hospitalized Children_. New York: Bureau of Publications Teachers College, Columbia University, 1964.

Cordier, Mathurin. _Corderius Dialogues_. Translated by John Bunsley the Elder. London: Anne Griffin, 1636.

Cox, Richard.  The Necessary Doctrine and Erudition
     for Any Christian Man.  London: Thomas Berthelet,
     1543.

Davis, John.  Travels of Four Years and a Half In the
     U.S.A.  New York: Holt, 1909.

Descartes, René.  "Discourse on Method."  In Man and
     the Universe: The Philosophies of Science, edited
     by Commins and Linscott.  New York: Random House,
     1947.

Dewey, John.  Experience and Education.  New York:
     Collier Books, 1963.

Dickens, Charles.  Nicholas Nickleby.  New York:
     Bantam Book, 1983.

Dunlop, Agnes Mary Robertson  [Kyle, Elizabeth,
     pseud.]  The Skater's Waltz.  London: P. Davies,
     1944.

Dwight, Theodore.  The Father's Book.  Springfield,
     Mass.: G. and C. Merriam, 1834.

Eager, M.  Six Years at the Russian Court.  London:
     Hurst and Blackett, 1906.

Edgeworth, Maria  and  Edgeworth, Richard  Lovell.
     Practical  Education.   2  vols.   London:  J.
     Johnson, 1798.

Edgeworth, Maria.  The Parent's Assistant or Stories
     for Children.  4 vols.  London: Printed for J.
     Johnson by G. Woodfall, 1800.

_____.  Moral Tales for Young People.  3 vols.
     London: Printed for J. Johnson, 1802.

_____.  Early Lessons.  5 vols.  London:  Printed
     for J. Johnson 1801-1803.

_____.  Popular Tales.  London:  Printed  for  J.
     Johnson by C. Mercier, 1804.

_____.  Essays  on  Practical  Education.   2  vols.

London: Printed for J. Johnson, 1811.

_____. Harry and Lucy Concluded Being the Lost Part of Early Lessons. 3 vols. Boston: Munroe and Frances, 1825.

Eginhard. Early Life of Charlemagne. Translated by A. J. Grant. London: Chatto and Windus, 1926.

Ellson, Douglas G. "Tutoring." In The Psychology of Teaching Methods. Chicago: University of Chicago Press, 1976.

Elyot, Thomas. The Boke Named the Governour. Edited by Foster Watson. London, 1907.

Elyot, Thomas. "The Defense of Good Women." In Vives and the Renascence Education of Women. Edited by Foster Watson. New York: Longmans, Green and Company, 1912.

Erasmus, Desiderius. The Education of a Christian Prince. Translated by Born. New York: Columbia University Press, 1936.

_____. De Matrimonia Christiano. Lugdieni Batavorum: J. Maire, 1650.

_____. De Pueris Instituendis. Paris: Ex Officina Christiani Wechelf, 1536.

_____. De Ratione Studii. Paris: Ex Officina Simonis Colinali, 1526.

_____. Opera omnia emendatiora et auctiora. Bavaria: 1703.

_____. Precatio dominica in septem portiones distributa. Basel: J. Frobenius, 1523.

Examples For Kings or Rules For Princes To Govern By. London: 1642.

Fénelon, Francois de Salignae de la Mothe. Dialogues of the Dead. Glascow: R. and A. Foulis, 1754.

_____. Twenty-Seven Moral Tales and Fables.

London: J. Wilcox, 1729.

_____. The Adventures of Telemachus, the Son of Ulysses. Philadelphia: G. Decombax, 1797.

_____. The Education of Girls. Translated by Kate Lupton. Boston: Ginn and Company, 1891.

Fielding, Henry. The Adventures of Joseph Andrews. Book 3. Oxford: Oxford University Press, 1967.

Fielding, Sarah. The Governess, For the Instruction of Young Ladies In Their Education. Edited by Gray. London: Oxford University Press, 1968.

Froebel, Freidrich. The Songs and Music of Freidrich Froebel, ed., Blow. New York: D. Appleton and Company, 1911.

Gailhard, Jean. The Compleat Gentleman. London: 1678.

Gaskell, Elizabeth. Wives and Daughters. London: Smith, Elder and Company, n.d.

Genlis, Stephanie Felicite, Marquise de Sillery. Lessons of a Governess to Her Pupil. 2 vols. Dublin: P. Wogan, P. Byrne, 1793.

Gilbert, Sir Humphrey. Queen Elizabeth's Academy. Edited by Frederick James Furnivall. Queene Elizabethes Achademy (by Dir Humphrey Gilbert). London: Published for the Early English Text Society by N. Trubner & Co., 1869.

Goethe, Johann Wolfgang Von. Works. 7 vols. New York: 1902.

_____. The Autobiography of Johann Wolfgang von Goethe. Vol. 1. Translated by John Oxenford. Chicago: University of Chicago Press, 1974.

Goodrich, S.G. Fireside Education. London: William Smith, 1841.

Gough, Richard. The History of Myddle. Sussex, England: Caliban Books, 1982.

Hall, John. On the Education of Children While Under the Care of Parents or Guardians. New York: John P. Haven, 1835.

Hardouis, De Porefixe de Abbe a Sabbonceau. Institutio Principus. Paris: 1647.

Harrison, Grant Von and, Ronald Edward Grymon. Structural Tutoring. New Jersey: Educational Technology Publishers, 1980.

Hayward, Sir John. The Life and Reign of King Edward the Sixth. London: John Partridge, 1636.

Henry VIII. Assertio Septem Sacramentorum. Edited by O'Donovan. New York: Harper and Row, 1908.

Herbart, John Frederick. Outlines of Educational Doctrine. New York: Macmillan, 1911.

Hewitt, John. "A Tutor For the Beaus." A comedy acted at the Theatre Royal in Lincoln's Inn-Field. London: Ward and Chandler, 1737.

Hoare, Louisa Gurney. Hints for the Improvement of Early Education and Nursery Discipline. 2nd edition. London: J. Matchard and Son, 1819.

Hocalene, Thomas. Works. Edited by Furnivall. Vol. 3. EETS, 1897.

Homer. The Iliad. Translated by Rieu. New York: Viking Penguin, 1986.

_____. The Odyssey. Translated by Bryant. Boston: Estes and Company, 1898.

Humphrey, Heman. Domestic Education. Amherst, Massachusetts: J.S.C. Adams, 1840.

Hyrde, Richard. "On the Education of Women." In Vives and the Renascence Education of Women, edited by Foster Watson. New York: Longmans, Green and Company, 1912.

Isocrates. Works. 2 vols. New York: Loeb Library,

n.d.

Isocrates. <u>Panegyricus, Antidosis Against the Sophists, Panathenaicus Areopagiticus, and to Philip.</u> Translated by Norlin. London: Loeb Classical Library.

_____. <u>Institution of a Gentleman.</u> Edited by C. Whittinghand. London: 1839.

Jaeger, Werner. <u>Paideia: The Ideals of Greek Culture.</u> Translated by Highet. New York: Oxford University Press, 1945.

James, Henry. <u>The Turn of the Screw.</u> Edited by Kimbrough. New York: W.W. Norton and Company, 1969.

Jameson, Anna Brownwell. <u>Memoirs and Essays.</u> New York: Wiley and Putnam, 1846.

_____. <u>Memoirs and Essays Illustrated of Art, Literature and Social Morals.</u> New York: Wiley and Putnam, 1846.

_____. <u>A Commonplace Book of Thoughts Memories, and Francies, Original and Selected.</u> London: Longman, Brown, Green and Longmans, 1854.

_____. <u>Sisters of Charity and the Communion of Labour: Two Lectures on the Social Employment of Women.</u> London: Longman, Brown, Green, Longman and Roberts, 1859.

Jones, William. <u>Letters of a Tutor To His Pupils.</u> London: Printed for G. Robinson, 1780.

Josceline, Mrs. Elizabeth. <u>Treatise of Education of a Daughter.</u> London: 1684.

Kant, Immanuel. <u>The Educational Theory of Immanuel Kant.</u> Edited by Edward F. Buchner. Philadelphia: Lippincott & Co., 1904.

Kaye, Elaine. <u>A History of Queen's College, London 1848-1972.</u> London: Chatto and Windus, 1972.

Kempe, William. The Education of Children in Learning. London: T. Orwin for I Porter and T. Gubbin, 1588.

Knight, Edgar, editor. A Documentary History of Education In the South Before 1860. Vol. 1. Chapel Hill: University of North Carolina Press, 1949.

Knox, John. "Bible Reading, Family Instruction, Singing." Translated by David Laing. In Early Protestant Educators, edited by Frederick Ely. New York: McGraw Hill, 1931.

Lamb, Elia Charles. "Christ's Hospital Five and Thirty Years Ago." In The Essays of Elia Charles Lamb. New York: Dodge Publishing Company, n.d.

La Mothe le Vayer, Francois de. De l'instruction de Monseigneur le Dauphin a monseigneur . . . Cardinal duc de Richelieu. Paris: Chez Schastien Cramory, 1640.

_____. Oeuvres Nouvelle Edition. 15 vols. Paris: J. Grugnard, 1664.

Lancaster, Joseph. Improvements In Education. 1803. Reprint. Edited by Francesco Cordasco. Clifton: Augustus M. Kelly Publisher, 1973.

Larcom, Lucy. A New England Girlhood. Boston: Northeastern University Press, 1986.

Lassels, Richard. The Voyage of Italy . . . London: Printed for E.C, F.R. and A.C., 1686.

Long, Jakob. The Tutor, De Hofmeister or The Advantages of Private Education. Translated by William E. Yuill. Chicago: University of Chicago Press, 1972.

Leonowens, Anna. The English Governess at the Siamese Court. London: Arthur Barker, 1954.

_____. Siamese Harem Life. London: 1873.

Liebnitz, Gottfried. "The Education of a Prince."

In <u>The Tutors</u>. Stuttgart: Metzler, 1979.

Locke, John. <u>Some Thoughts Concerning Education</u>. Edited by Peter Gay. New York: Columbia University, 1964.

_____. <u>An Essay Concerning Human Understanding</u>. 2 vols. New York: Dover Publications, 1959.

_____. <u>Some Thought Concerning Reading and Study for a Gentleman</u>. London: M. Des Maiseaux, 1720.

Lodge, Oliver Joseph. <u>Parent and Child</u>. London and New York: Funk and Wagnalls, 1910.

Lombard, Ellen Celia. <u>Home Education</u>. Washington: Government Printing Office, 1919.

Lott, Emmeline. <u>The English Governess in Egypt and Turkey</u>. London: Richard Bentley, 1865.

Lull, Raymond. <u>The Book of the Order of Chivalry</u>. Edited by Byles. London: Kegan Paul, 1926.

Luther, Martin. "Duties of Parents In Training Children." Translated by Henry Barnard. In <u>Early Protestant Education</u>, edited by Frederick Ely. New York: McGraw Hill, 1931.

_____. "Letter to the Mayors and Aldermen of All the Cities of Germany In Behalf of Christian Schools." In <u>Early Protestant Educators</u>, translated by F.V.N. Painter. New York: McGraw Hill, 1931.

Lynacre, Dr. <u>Rudiments of Grammar</u>. Paris: Ex officina R. Stephani, 1533.

Lytlelton, Edward. <u>The Corner-Stone of Education: An Essay on the Home Training of Children</u>. London and New York: G.P. Pitnam's Sons, 1914.

Machiavelli, Niccoló. <u>The Prince</u>. Translated by Marriott. London: J. M. Dent and Sons, 1958.

MacLeod, Norman. <u>The Home School or Hints On Home Education</u>. Edinburgh: Paton and Ritchie, 1856.

Makin, Bathshua. An Essay to Revive the Ancient Education of a Gentlewoman in Religion, Manners, Arts and Tongues. London: Printed by J.D. to be sold by Tho. Parkhurst, 1673.

Marguerite, de'Angouléme, Queen of Navarre. The Mirror of Glass of the Sinful Soul. London: Asher and Co., 1897.

Martin, Aimé M. The Education of Mothers of Families or The Civilization of the Human Race by Women. Translated by Edwin Lee. London: Whittaker and Company, 1842.

Martineau, Harriet. Household Education. London: Smith Elder and Company, 1864.

Mason, Charlotte Maria Shaw. Home Education. London: K. Paul, Trench and Company, 1886.

Mather, Cotton. Cares About the Nurseries. Boston: Printed by T. Green for Benjamin Eliot, 1702.

Matteo, Palmieri. Libro della Vita Civile. Firenze, 1529.

May, Miss. Recollections of a Royal Governess. London: Hutchison and Company, 1915.

Melanchthon, Philip. Corpus Reformatiorium, Melanchthon Opera. Vols. 20, 25, 26. Edited by Bretschneider and Bindscih. Brunswick: C.A.: Schwetschke and Son, 1852-1858.

Mill, John Stuart. Autobiography of John Stuart Mill. New York: Columbia University, 1944.

_____. Principles of Political Economy. London: Longman Green, 1923.

Miller, John. The Tutor. Menston: The Scholar Press, 1971.

Milton, John. Tractate On Education. London: Macmillan, 1918.

Montaigne, Michel de. <u>The Diary of Montaigne's Journey to Italy in 1580 and 1581</u>. Translated by E.J. Trechmann. New York: Harcourt Brace and Company, 1929.

_____. <u>Essays</u>. 3 vols. New York: E.P. Dutton, 1935.

_____. <u>The Essays of Michel de Montaigne</u>. Translated by Ives. New York: The Heritage Press, 1939.

Montessori, Maria. <u>The Montessori Method</u>. Translated by George. New York: Schocken Books, 1964.

More, Cresacre. <u>The Life of Sir Thomas More, Knight</u>. Edited by J. L. Kennedy. Athens, Pennsylvania: 1941.

More, Hannah. <u>Strictures on the Modern System of Female Education</u>. London: Printed for T. Codell and W. Davies, in the Strand, 1799.

More, Margareta. <u>The Household of Sir Thomas More</u>. New York: Charles Scribner, 1852.

_____. <u>Hints Towards Forming the Character of a Young Princess</u>. London: Printed for T. Cadell and W. Davies, 1805.

More, Thomas. <u>Utopia</u>. London: Walter Scott, 1890.

Mudie, Robert. <u>The Complete Governess; A Course of Mental Instruction for Ladies with a Notice of the Principal Female Accomplishments</u>. London: Printed for Knight and Tacey, 1826.

Niemeyer, August Hermann. <u>Principles of Teaching For Parents, Tutors and Teachers</u>. Halle: Beydem Verfasser and in commission for Waisenhaus-Buchhandburg, 1796.

Oliphant, Margaret (Wilson). <u>The Story of a Governess</u>. New York: R.F. Fenno and Company, 1895.

Pace, Richard. "De Fructu." In The Babees Book. Vol. 32. Edited by F. J. Furnivall. London: Early English Text Society, 1868.

Palmieri, Mattheo. Libro della Vita Civile. Firenze: 1529.

Palsgrave, John. L'Esclaircissement de la Langue Francoyse. London: John Hawkins, 1530.

Parkes, Bessie Rayner. Essays On Woman's Work. London: Alexander Strahan, 1866.

Patrizi, Francesco. De Regno et Regis Institutione. Paris: 1567.

Peacham, Henry. The Complete Gentleman. Ithaca: Cornell University Press, 1962.

Péréfixe, Hardouin de Beaumont de. Institutio Principis ad Ludovicum XIV. Paris: A. Vitre, 1647.

Pestalozzi, Johann Heinrich. Leonard and Gertrude. Translated by Channing. Boston: D.C. Heath, 1885.

Pieper, Josepfs. Scholasticism. Translated by Winston. New York: McGraw Hill, 1960.

Plato. The Dialogues of Plato. Vol. 1. Translated by B. Jowett. New York: Bigeloie, Brown and Company, n.d.

Plato. The Collected Dialogues of Plato. Edited by Cairns Hamilton. Princeton, New Jersey: Princeton University Press, 1961.

Plutarch. Plutarch's Lives. Vol. IV. Translated by A.H. Clough. New York: The Nottingham Society, n.d.

Plutarch. Discourse Touching On the Training of Children. Translated by Elyot. London: Thomas Barthelet, 1535.

Prendilacqua, Francesco. Intorno alla vita di

<u>Vittorino de Feltre</u>.  Como: 1871.

Quintilian, Marcus Fabius.  <u>The Institutio Oratoria</u>.
New York: G.P. Putnam's Sons, 1921-22.

_____.  <u>Quintilian</u>.  Translated by H.E. Butler.  New
York: Putnam, 1921.

Raleigh, Sir Walter.  <u>The Prince or Maxims of State</u>.
London: 1642.

Rousseau, Jean Jacques.  <u>Emile or On Education</u>.
Translated by Bloom.  New York: Basic Books,
1979.

Russell, Bertrand.  <u>The Autobiography of Bertrand
Russell</u>.  Boston:  Little and Brown, 1967.

Russell, Bertrand.  <u>Education and the Good Life</u>.  New
York: Liveright Publishing Company, 1926.

Sabbadini, Remigio.  <u>Epistolario di Guarino Veronese</u>.
Salerno: 1885.

Sadoleto, Jacopo.  <u>Sadoleto on Education:  A
Translation of the De Pueris Recte Instituendis</u>.
Noted and translation by E.T. Campagnac and K.
Forbes.  London: Oxford University Press, 1916.

Saint-Simon, Duke of.  <u>Memoirs of Louis XIV; and the
Regency</u>.  Translated by Bayle St. John.  New
York:  St. Dunstan Society, 1901.

Salisbury, John of.  "The Education of John of
Salisbury."  In <u>University Records and Life in
the Middle Ages</u>, edited by Thorndike.  New York:
Octagon Books, 1971.

Salle, Jean Baptiste de la.  <u>Conduite des Écoles</u>.
Paris: J. Moronval, 1838.

Salmon, David, ed.  <u>The Practical Parts of
Lancaster's Improvements and Bell's Experiment</u>.
Cambridge: University Press, 1932.

_____.  <u>The Schollers Medley or A Survey of History</u>.
London: 1614.

Schurman, Anna A.  The Learned Maid or Whether a Maid
    May Be a Scholar?  Translated by C.B.   London:
    1659.

Scott, Sir Walter.  Memoirs of the Life of Sir Walter
    Scott, Bart.  Edinburgh: Robert Cadell, 1839.

Seymour, Jane.  A Century of Disputes Upon the Death
    of Mary of Navarre.  Edited by Denisot.   Paris:
    Michel Fezandal and Robert Granier, n.d.

Skelton, John.   Works.   Edited by Dyce.   London:
    1843.

Shakespeare, William.   The Life of Henry the Fifth.
    New Haven: Yale University Press, 1961.

Sheridan, Richard.  The Governess.  Performed at the
    Theatre-Royal, Crow Street, Dublin, 1777.

Sigourney, Lydia.   Letters to Mothers.   Hartford,
    Connecticut: Hudson and Skinner, 1838.

Smith, Adam.  An Inquiry Into the Nature and Causes
    of the Wealth of Nations.  New York: Modern
    Library, 1937.

Smollett, Tobias.  Travels Through France and Italy.
    London: John Lehmann, 1949.

Spencer, Herbert.  Education: Intellectural, Moral,
    Physical.  New York: D. Appleton and Company,
    1897.

Spencer, Herbert.  Essay on Education and Kindred
    Subjects. London: J.M. Dent, 1914.

Stockdale,  Percival.    Liberal  Education  an
    Examination of the Important Question, Whether
    Education at a Great School, or by Private
    Tuition is Preferable.  London, 1782.

Stuart, Mary.  Latin Themes of Mary Stuart, Queen of
    Scots.  Vol. 3.   Edited by Montaiglon.   London:
    Warton Club, 1855.

Suetonius, Gaius. The Twelve Caesars. New York: Penguin Books, 1957.

Tacitus, Cornelius. The Complete Works of Tacitus. Translated by Chruch. New York: Random House, 1942.

_____. The Reign of Nero. Translated by Ramsey. London: The Folio Society, 1962.

Taylor, Isaac. Home Education. New York: D. Appleton and Company, 1838.

Thackeray, William Makepeace. The Memoirs of Barry Lyndon. London: Smith, Elder and Company, 1908.

_____. Vanity Fair. London: Smith, Elder and Company, 1910.

Thrale, Hester Lynch Piozzi. Anecdotes of the Late Samuel Johnson. London: Longman, Green, Longman, and Robert, 1862.

_____. Autobiography, Letters and Literary Remains of Mrs. Piozzi (Thrale). Vol. 1. London: Longman, Green, Longman, and Robert, 1861.

Ticozzi, Stefano. Storia dei Letterati e degli Artisti del Departimento Della Piarie. Belluno: 1813.

Trollope, Anthony. The Bertrams. London: Chapman and Hall, 1859.

_____. The Duke's Children. London, Chapman and Hall, 1880.

_____. The Eustace Diamonds. London: Chapman and Hall, 1873.

_____. Barchester Towers. London: Longman, 1857.

Turler, Jerome. The Traveiler. London: William How for Abraham Veale, 1575.

Vives, Juan Luis. The Instruction of a Christian Woman. London: 1540.

_____. _Vives and the Renascence Education of Women_. Edited by Foster Watson. New York: Longmans, Green and Company, 1912.

Walker, Obadiah. _Of Education Especially of Young Gentlemen_. London: Printed by H. Gellibrand for R. Wellington, 1699.

Williams, C.H., editor. _English Historical Documents_. Vol. 5. London: Eyre and Spottiswood, 1967.

Williams, David. _Treatise On Education_. London: Printed for T. Payne, 1774.

_____. _Lectures On Education_. London: J. Bell, 1789.

Wollstonecraft, Mary Goodwin. _Thought on the Education of Daughters_. Clifton: Augustus N. Kelly Publisher, 1972.

_____. _Vindication of the Rights of Women_. London: J. Johnson, 1792.

Woolley, Hannah. _The Gentlewomen's Companion_. London: Printed by A. Maxwell for Edward Thomas, 1675.

Young, G.M. and Handcook, W.P. _English Historical Documents 1833-1874_. Vol. XII, part 1. In _English Historical Documents_, edited by David C. Douglas. London: Erye and Spottiswood, 1956.

_____. _The Young Maiden's Tutor_. London 1677.

Younge, Charlotte Mary. _The Daisy Chain_. 2 vols. New York: D. Appleton, 1856.

_____. "The Governess." In _Storehouse of Stories_. London: Macmillan, 1970.

_____. _The Trial_. London: Macmillan, 1898.

_____. _Womankind_. London: Macmillan, 1876.

4. <u>Catalogs - Brochures</u>

d' Overbroeck's Tutorial College Catalog 1986-87.
Oxford, England.

_____. The Home Study Journal (1983). Christian
Liberty Academy, Satellite Schools, Prospect
Heights, Illinois.

Lindstrom, Paul D. 1983. "There's no place like home
. . . to educate your child!" Christian Liberty
Academy Satellite Schools, Prospect Heights,
Illinois.

5. <u>Interview</u>

Gallagher, Elizabeth Ann. Interview with
d'Overbroeck's College Tutor. Chicago, Illinois,
24 April 1987.

SECONDARY SOURCES

## 1. <u>Books</u>

Abbott, Shirley. <u>The National Museum of American History</u>. New York: Abrams, 1981.

Adamson, John William. <u>English Education 1789-1902</u>. Cambridge: Cambridge University Press, 1930.

Aiken, Luch. <u>Memoirs of the Court of Elizabeth, Queen of England</u>. London: Alex, Murray and Son, 1869.

Allen, Vernon L. "Cross-Age Interaction in One-Teacher Schools," Madison: Wisconsin Research and Development Center for Cognitive Learning, 1974. In <u>Children As Teachers</u>, edited by Allen. New York: Academic Press, 1976.

Altman, Leslie. "Christine De Pisan: First Professional Woman of Letters." In <u>Female Scholars</u>, edited by Brink. Montreal: Eden Press, 1980.

Angeles, Peter A. <u>Dictionary of Philosophy</u>. New York: Barnes and Noble, 1981.

Aries, Phillippe. <u>Centuries of Childhood</u>. New York: Alfred A. Kmopf, 1962.

Arnold, Lois Barber. <u>Four Lives in Science, Women's Education in the Nineteenth Century</u>. New York: Shocken Books, 1984.

Asprey, Robert B. <u>Frederick The Great The Magnificent Enigma</u>. New York: Tickman and Fields, 1986.

Axtell, James L. <u>The Educational Writings of John Locke</u>. Cambridge: University Press, 1968.

395

Axtell, James L.  The School Upon A Hill:  Education and Society In Colonial New England.  New Haven: Yale University Press, 1974.

Balsdon, Dacre.  Oxford Now and Then.  New York: St. Martin's Press, 1970.

Barclay, William.  Educational Ideals in the Ancient World.  London: Collins, 1959.

Barnard, H.C.  The French Tradition in Education.  Cambridge: Cambridge University Press, 1922.

Bateson, F.W.  The Cambridge Bibliography of English Literature 1800-1900.  Vol. III.  Cambridge: At the University Press, 1969.

Bayne-Powell, Rosamond.  Eighteenth Century London Life.  New York: E.P. Dutton, 1938.

_____.  English Country Life in the Eighteenth Century.  London: John Murray, 1935.

_____.  The English Child in the Eighteenth Century.  London, John Murray, 1939.

Beale, Paul, editor.  A Dictionary of Slang and Uncoventional English.  New York: MacMillan, 1984.

Beck, Frederick.  Greek Education.  London: Methuen, 1964.

Belloc, Hilaire.  Richelieu.  London: Lippincott, 1929.

Bennett, Harold.  No More Public Schools.  New York: Random House, 1972.

Berle, A.A.  The School In the Home.  New York: Moffat, Yard and Company, 1912.

Bill, E.G.W.  University Reform in Nineteenth Century Oxford.  Oxford: Clarendon Press, 1973.

Bishop, Morris.  The Horizon Book of the Middle Ages.  New York: American Heritage, 1968.

Blackburn, Keith. The Tutor. London: Heinemann Educational, 1975.

Blaisdell, C.J. "Marguerete de Navarre and Her Circle." In Female Scholars, edited by J.R. Brink. Montreal: Eden Press, 1980.

Bloom, Benjamin S. All Our Children Learning. New York: McGraw Hill, 1981.

Bloom, Sophie. Peer and Cross-Age Tutoring in the Schools. Washington, D.C.: Department of Health, Education and Welfare, December 1976.

Blumerfeld, Samuel L. How To Tutor. New Rochelle, New York: Arlington House, 1973.

Bonner, Stanley F. Education in Ancient Rome. Berkeley: University of California Press, 1977.

Bowrne, William O. History of the Public School Society of the City of New York. New York: William Wood, 1870.

Boyd, William and King, Edmund J. The History of Western Education. Toronto: Barnes and Noble Books, 1980.

Brant, Irving. James Madison. New York: Bobbs-Merrill, 1941.

Bremer, Fredricka. The President's Daughters, A Narrative of a Governess. New York: J. Munroe and Company, 1843.

Broudy, Harry S. and Palmer, John R. Exemplars of Teaching Method. Chicago: Rand McNally and Company, 1965.

Brantome, Siegneur de. Illustrious Dames at the Court of the Valois Kings. Translated by Wormley. New York: 1898.

Brauer, George C. Jr., The Education of a Gentleman. Theories of Gentlemanly Education in England 1660-1775. New York: Bookman Association, 1959.

Brink, J.R., editor. <u>Female Scholars</u>. Montreal: Eden Press, 1980.

Brink, J.R. "Bathsua Makin: Educator and Linguist." In <u>Female Scholars</u>, edited by Brink. Montreal: Eden Press, 1980.

Brodie, Fawn M. <u>Thomas Jefferson an Intimate History</u>. New York: Norton and Company, 1974.

Bronfenbrenner, Urie. <u>Two Worlds of Childhood: U.S. and USSR</u>. New York: Russell Sage Foundation, 1970.

Brooke, Christopher. <u>From Alfred to Henry III</u>. London: Sphere Books, 1969.

Brown, Robert E. and Brown, B. Katherine. <u>Virginia 1705-1786: Democracy or Aristocracy</u>. East Lansing, Michigan: Michigan State University Press, 1964.

Burckhardt, Jacob. <u>The Civilization of the Renaissance in Italy</u>. Translated by Middlemore. London: Phaidon Press, 1940.

Bury, J.B. <u>A History of Greece</u>. London: Macmillan, 1931.

Bush, Douglas. <u>The Renaissance and English Humanism</u>. Toronto: University of Toronto Press, 1939.

Button, H. Warren and Provenzo, Eugene F., Jr. <u>History of Education and Cultures in America</u>. Englewood Cliffs: Prentice-Hall, 1983.

Butts, R. Freeman. <u>The Education of the West</u>. New York: McGraw Hill, 1973.

Candos, John. <u>Boys Together: English Public Schools 1800-1864</u>. New Haven: Yale University Press, 1984.

Carey, Rose Nouchette. <u>Only the Governess</u>. New York: J. W. Lovell Company, 1888.

Carlyle, Thomas. History of Friedrich II of Prussia. Boston: Estes and Company, n.d.

Caspari, Fritz. Humanism and the Social Order in Tudor England. New York: Teachers College Press, 1968.

Castle, E.B., Ancient Education and Today. Baltimore: Penguin Books, 1961.

Censer, Jane Turner. North Carolina Planters and Their Children. Baton Rouge: Louisiana State University Press, 1984.

Chambers, R.W. Thomas More. London: Jonathan Cape, 1935.

Clarke, M.L. Rhetoric At Rome. New York: Barnes and Noble, 1963.

Charlton, Kenneth. Education in Renaissance England. London: Routledge and Kegan Paul, 1965.

Cole, Luella. History of Education: Socrates to Montessori. New York: Rhinehart and Company, 1950.

Commanger, Henry Steele. Documents of American History. Vol. 1. New York: Appleton Century Crofts, 1963.

Compayré, Gabriel. The History of Pedagogy. Boston: D.C. Heath, 1886.

The Concise Oxford Dictionary. Oxford: Clarendon Press, 1964.

Cook, Edward. The Life of Florence Nightingale. New York: Macmillan, 1942.

Craik, Dinah Maria (Mulock). The Half-Castle, An Old Governess' Tale. New York: G. Munro, 1880.

Cremin, Lawrence A. American Education, The Colonial Experience 1607-1783. New York: Harper & Row, 1970.

399

_____. American Education: The National Experience 1783-1876. New York: Harper & Row, 1980.

_____. The Transformation of the School. New York: Vintage Books, 1964.

Culbert, Jane F. The Visiting Teacher At Work. New York: The Commonwealth Funds Division of Publication, 1929.

Dirvin, Joseph I. Mrs. Seton. New York: Farrar, Straus and Cudahy, 1962.

Disick, Renne. Individualizing Language Instruction. Chicago: Harcourt Brace, 1975.

Dowdey, Clifford. The Great Plantation. Charles City, Virginia: Berkeley Plantation, 1957.

Drake, William. The American School in Transition. New York: Rentice-Hall, 1955.

Dudley, Donald R. The Civilization of Rome. New York: New American Library, 1962.

Duffy, Christopher. The Military Life of Frederick The Great. New York: Atheneum, 1986.

Duggan, Stephen. A Student's Textbook in the History of Education. New York: Appleton Century Crofts, 1948.

Dunbar, Willis F. The Michigan Record in Higher Education. Detroit: Wayne State University Press, 1963.

Durant, Will. The Story of Philosophy. New York: Simon and Schuster, 1953.

Dyhouse, Carol. Girls Growing Up in Late Victorian and Edwardian England. London: Routledge and Kegan Paul, 1981.

Earle, Alice Morse. Child Life in Colonial Days. New York: Macmillan, 1904.

Edwards, Newton and Herman Richey. <u>The School in the American Social Order</u>. Boston: Houghton Mifflin, 1963.

Elliot, Charles W. <u>English Philosophers</u>. Vol. 37. New York: Collier, 1910.

Elliott, J.H. <u>Imperial Spain</u>. New York: New American Library, 1963.

Ellis, Mahel Brown. <u>The Visiting Teaching in Rochester</u>. New York: Joint Committee on Methods of Preventing Delinquency, 1925.

Ely, Frederick. <u>The History and Philosophy of Education Ancient and Medival</u>. New York: Prentice-Hall, 1940.

_____. "History of Education." In <u>Encyclopaedia Britannica</u>, Vol. 18. Chicago: Encyclopaedia Britannica, 1985.

Erickson, Carolly. <u>The First Elizabeth</u>. New York: Summit Books, 1983.

Eurich, N.J. <u>Corporate Classrooms</u>. Princeton: The Carnegie Foundation for the Advancement of Teaching, 1985.

Fertig, Ludwig. <u>Die Hofmeister</u> (The Tutors). Translated by Margaret Schieser. Stuttgart: Metzler, 1979.

Fielding, Henry. <u>The History of Tom Jones, A Foundling</u>. London: MacDonald, 1953.

Fleming, May Agnes (Early). <u>A Pretty Governess</u>. New York: J.S. Ogilvie, 1891.

Flexner, Abraham. <u>Universities</u>. London: Oxford University Press, 1930.

Forster, E.M. <u>A Room With a View</u>. New York: Vintage Books, 1986.

Franklin, John Hope. <u>A Southern Odyssey: Travelers in the Antebellum North</u>. Baton Rouge: Louisiana

State University Press, 1976.

Fraser, Antonia. _The Weaker Vessel_. New York: Knopf, 1984.

Freeman, Douglas Southhall. _George Washington_. Vol. 1. New York: Scribner's, 1948.

Freeman, Kenneth J. _School of Hellas_. New York: Teachers College Press, 1969.

_____. "Education in Sparta and Crete." In _Education and Western Civilization_, edited by George C. Simmon. Arlington: College Readings, 1972.

Frere, Walter Howard, and William McClure Kennedy, editors. _Visitation Articles and Injunctions of the Period of Reformation_. 3 vols. London: Longmans, Green and Company, 1910.

Fuller, Wayne E. _The Old Country School_. Chicago: University of Chicago Press, 1982.

Fussell, G.E. and K.R. _The English Countrywoman 1500-1900_. London: Andrew Melrose, 1953.

_____. _The English Countryman 1500-1900_. London: Andrew Melrose, 1955.

Fussell, Paul, editor. _The Norton Book of Travel_. London: W.W. Norton, 1987.

Gagné, Robert M. _The Conditions of Learning_. Chicago: Holt, Rinehart and Winston, 1977.

Gartner, Alan, May Conway Kohler, and Frank Riessiman. _Children Teach Children_. New York: Harper & Row, 1971.

Gaskell, Elizabeth. _The Life of Charlotte Brontë_. Edited by Shelston. New York: Viking Penguin, 1975.

Gathorne, Hardy Jonathan. _The Rise and Fall of the British Nanny_. London: Hodder and Stoughton, 1972.

Gausses, Alice C. _A Woman of Wit and Wisdom_. London: Smith Elder and Co., 1906.

George, M. Dorothy. _London Life in the Eighteenth Century_. London: Kegan, Paul, 1925.

Gerould, Winifred, and James Gerould. _A Guide to Trollope_. Princeton: Princeton University Press, 1948.

Gibbon, Edward. _The History of the Decline and Fall of the Rome Empire_. Vol. V. London: Methuen and Company, 1909.

Gibbons, Maurice. _Individualized Instruction_. New York: Teachers College Press, 1971.

Gies, Frances. _The Knight in History_. New York: Harper & Row, 1984.

Gmeiner, Hermann. _The SOS Children's Villages: Modern Homes for Destitute Children_. Innsbruck: SOS-Kinderdorf Publishers, 1976.

Godfrey, Elizabeth. _English Children in the Olden Time_. Williamstown: Corner House Publishers, 1980.

_____. _Home Life Under the Stuarts_. London: St. Paul, 1925.

Goodsell, Willystine. _A History of Marriage and the Family_. New York: Macmillan, 1934.

Gorham, Deborah. _The Victorian Girl and the Feminine Ideal_. Bloomington: Indiana University Press, 1982.

Graham, H. _The Early Irish Monastic Schools_. Dublin: Talbot Press, 1923.

Grant, Michael. _Nero_. New York: American Heritage Press, 1970.

Graves, Frank. _A History of Education_. Westport: Greenwood Press, 1970.

Grees, Mary Elizabeth. "Elizabeth Elstob: 'The Saxon Nymph'." In _Female Scholars_, edited by Brink. Montreal: Eden Press, 1980.

G. Grote. _Aristotle_. 2 vols. London: 1872.

Grun, Bernard. _The Timetables of History_. New York: Simon and Schuster, 1979

Grylls, R. Glynn. _Queen's College 1848-1948_. London: Routledge and Kegan Paul, 1948.

Guernsey, Lucy Ellen. _Lady Betty's Governess_. New York: T. Whittaker, 1872.

Gwynn, S.J. Aubrey. _Roman Education from Cicero_. New York: Teachers College Press, 1926.

Hackett, Francis. _Henry the Eighth_. London: Jonathan Cape, 1929.

Hagelman, Charles, Jr. Introduction to _A Vindication of the Rights of Women_, by Mary Wollstonecraft. New York: Norton, 1967.

Hailman, W.N. _History of Pedagogy_. Cincinnati: Van Artways, 1874.

Hamilton, Edith. _The Echo of Greece_. New York: W. W. Norton, 1957.

Hans, Nicholas. _New Trends in Education in the Eighteenth Century_. London: Routledge and Kegan Paul, 1951.

Harden, Elizabeth. _Maria Edgeworth_. Boston: Twayne Publisher, 1984.

Harvey, George. _Henry Clay Frick_. New York: Charles Scribner's Sons, 1928.

Harvey, Paul. _The Oxford Companion to English Literature_. Oxford: The Clarendon Press, 1955.

Hawes, Joseph M., and N. Ray Hiner, editors. _American Childhood_. London: Greenwood Press,

1985.

Heltzel, Virgil. A Check List of Courtesy Books in the Newberry Library. Chicago: Newberry Library, 1942.

Hibbert, Christopher. The Grand Tour. New York: G.P. Putnam, 1969.

Hill, Brian V. Education and the Endangered Individual. New York: Teachers College Press, 1973.

Historical Statistics of the United States, Part 1. Washington D.C.: Bureau of the Census, 1975.

Hogrefe, Pearl. The Life and Times of Sir Thomas Elyot, Englishman. Ames, Iowa: University of Iowa Press, 1967.

Holcombe, Lee. Victorian Ladies At Work. Hamden, Conn.: Archon Books, 1973.

Hole, Christina. English Home Life 1500-1800. London: B.T. Batsford, 1947.

Howe, Bea. A Galaxy of Governesses. London: Derek Verschoyle, 1954.

Hunt, David. Parents and Children in History. London: Basic Books, 1970.

Inglis-Jones, Elizabeth. The Great Maria. Westport, Conn.: Greenwood Press, 1959.

The International Dictionary of Women's Biography. Edited by Jennifer Uglow and Frances Hinton. New York: Continuum, 1982.

Irwin, Joyce L. "Anna Maria Van Schurman: The Star of Utrecht." In Female Scholars. Montreal: Eden Press, 1980.

Jackson, Philip W. The Practice of Teaching. New York: Teachers College Press, 1986.

Jahn, Otto. *Life of Mozart*. 3 vols. London: Novello Ewer and Company, 1891.

Janowitz, Gayle. *After-School Study Centers Volunteer Work in Reading*. Chicago: Mayor's Commission on New Residents, Commission on Human Relations, 1964.

Jarrett, Derek. *England in the Age of Hogarth*. London: Yale University Press, 1986.

Jeffrey, Julie Roy. *Frontier Women, The Trans-Mississippi West 1840-1880*. New York: Hill and Way, 1979.

Johnson, Allen, editor. *Dictionary of American Biography*. 20 vols. New York: Scribners, 1943.

Johnson, Edgar. *Charles Dickens*. New York: Viking Penguin, 1952.

Jorgeson, Lloyd P. *The Founding of Public Education in Wisconsin*. Madison, Wisc.: State Historical Society of Wisconsin, 1956.

Kaestle, Carl F., editor. *Monitorial School Movement*. New York: Teachers College Press, 1973.

_____. *Pillars of the Republic*. New York: Hill and Wang, 1983.

Kamen, Michael. *Colonial New York*. New York: Scribners, 1975.

Kamm, Josephine. *Hope Deferred, Girl's Education in English History*. London: Methuen and Company, 1965.

Kaufman, Polly Wetts. *Women Teachers on the Frontier*. New Haven: Yale University Press, 1984.

Kennedy, George. *Quintilian*. New York: Twayne Publishers, 1969.

Kilpatrick, William Heard. *The Dutch Schools of New*

Netherlands and Colonial New York. New York: Arno Press, 1969.

Kingsley, Charles. The Tutor's Story. Edited by Lucas Malet. New York: Dodd, Mead and Company, 1916.

Knight, Edgar W. Public School Education in North Carolina. New York: Negro University Press, 1969.

Kramer, Rita. Maria Montessori. New York: G.P. Putnam's Sons, 1976.

Kuhn, Anne L. The Mother's Role in Childhood Education: New England Concepts 1830-1860. New Haven: Yale University Press, 1947.

Lacey, Robert. Majesty. New York: Avon Books, 1977.

Lawson, John, and Harold Silver. A Social History of Education in England. London: Methuen and Company, 1973.

Lehmberry, Standford E. Sir Thomas Elyot. Austin: University of Texas Press, 1960.

Lodge, R.C. Plato's Theory of Education. New York: Russell and Russell, 1970.

Lombard, Ellen C. Home Education. Washington: Government Printing Office, 1919.

Lucas, Christopher J. Our Western Educational Heritage. New York: Macmillan, 1972.

Lynch, John Patrick. Aristotle's School. Los Angeles: University of California Press, 1972.

MacGregor, Annie. John Wards' Governess. New York: 1892.

Maddox, William Arthur. The Free School Idea in Virginia Before the Civil War. New York: Columbia University Press, 1918.

Manchester, William. The Last Lion. Boston: Little Brown and Company, 1983.

Manschreck, Clyde Leonard. Melanchthon. New York: Abingdon Press, 1953.

Marrou, H.I. A History of Education in Antiquity. Translated by Lamb. New York: New American Library, 1956.

Marchant, J.R.V. Cassell's Latin Dictionary. New York: Funk and Wagnalls, 1953.

Marius, Richard. Thomas More. New York: Vintage Books, 1985.

Marples, Morris. Princes in the Making. London: Faber and Faber, 1965.

Mason, W.A. History of the Art of Writing. New York: Macmillan, 1920.

Mattingly, Garrett. Catherine of Aragon. New York: Vintage Books, 1941.

Maxwell, Constantia. A History of Trinity College Dublin. Dublin: The University Press, 1946.

Medway, F.J. "Tutoring As a Teaching Method." In The International Encyclopedia of Education, Vol. 9, edited by Torsten Housen. New York: Pergamon Press, 1985.

_____. "Philip Melanchthon." In A Cyclopedia of Education. New York: Macmillan, 1913.

Melville, Annabelle. John Carroll. New York: Charles Scribner's Sons, 1955.

Miles, George Henry. The Governess. Boston: T.B. Noonan, 1895.

Mintz, Steven. A Prison of Expectations. New York: New York University Press, 1983.

Mitford, Nancy. The Sun King. London: Hamish Hamilton, 1966.

Monroe, Paul. Founding of the American Public School System. New York: Macmillan, 1940.

Morgan, Edmund S. The Gentle Puritan. New Haven: Yale University Press, 1962.

_____. Virginians at Home: Family Life in the Eighteenth Century. Charlottesville: Colonial Williamsburg, 1952.

_____. The Puritan Family. New York: Harper & Row, 1966.

Morrison, Samuel Eliot. The Oxford History of the American People. New York: Oxford University Press, 1965.

Morris, Richard B., editor. Encyclopedia of American History. New York: Harper & Row, 1970.

Morton, Louis. Robert Carter of Nomoni Hall. Williamsburg, Virginia: Colonial Williamsburg, 1941.

Mulhern, James. A History of Education. New York: Ronald Press, 1959.

_____. A History of Secondary Education in Pennsylvania. New York: Arno Press, 1969.

Musgrave, G. Ray. Individualized Instruction. Boston: Allyn and Bacon, 1975.

Myers, Edward D. Education in the Perspective of History. New York: Harper and Brothers, 1960.

Neale, J.E. Queen Elizabeth. New York: Harcourt, Brace and Company, 1934.

Neff, Wanda. Victorian Working Women. New York: AMS Press, 1966.

Nelson, B. Henry, editor. The Fifty-First Yearbook of the National Society For the Study of Education, Part 2, Education in Rural Communities. Chicago: University of Chicago

Press, 1952.

Newcomer, James.   _Maria Edgeworth_.   Lewisburg:
Bucknell University Press, 1973.

Noar, Gertrude.   _Individualized Instruction: Every
Child a Winner_.  London: Wiley and Sons, 1972.

Norton, Lucy.  _First Lady of Versailles_.  New York:
J.B. Lippincott, 1978.

Noyes, Gertrude.   _Bibliography of Courtesy and
Conduct Books in Seventeeth Century England_.  New
Haven: The Tuttle, Morehouse and Taylor Company,
1937.

Ojala, Jeanne A.   "Madame de Serigne: Chronicles of
an Age."   In _Female Scholars_, edited by Brink.
Montreal: Eden Press, 1980.

Oldenbourg, Zoe.  _Catherine the Great_.  Translated by
Anne Carter.  New York: Random House, 1965.

Orme, Nicholas.  _English Schools in the Middle Ages_.
London: Methuen, 1973.

Orme, Nicholas.  _From Childhood to Chivalry_.  London:
Methuen, 1984.

_Oxford English Dictionary_.  Vol. 11.  Oxford: Oxford
University Press, 1933.

Passov, A. Harry.   "The Gifted and the Talented:
Their  Education  and  Development."   In  _The
Seventy-Eighth Yearbook of the National Society
for the Study of Education_.  Chicago: University
of Chicago Press, 1979.

Paulsen, Friedrick.  _German Education_.  Translated by
T. Lorenz.  New York: Scribner's, 1908.

Plumb, J.H.   _The Horizon Book of the Renaissance_.
New York: Doubleday, 1961.

Pollock, Linda A.   _Forgotten Children, Parent-Child
Relations  From  1500  to  1900_.   Cambridge:
Cambridge University Press, 1983.

Popkewitz, Thomas S. "The Sociological Basis for Individual Differences: The Relation of Solitude to the Crowd." In Individual Differences and The Common Curriculum, edited by Gay P. Fenstermacher, and John Goodlak. Chicago: University of Chicago Press, 1983.

Power, Edward J. Evolution of Educational Doctrine: Major Educational Theorists of the Western World. New York: Appleton Century Crofts, 1969.

Prescott, William. Prescott's Histories. Edited by Blacker. New York: Viking Press, 1963.

Rashdall, Hastings. The Universities of Europe in the Middle Ages. Vols. I, III. Edited by F.M. Pourcke and A.B. Erden. Oxford: Clarendon Press, 1936.

Reigart, John Franklin. The Lancasterian System of Instruction in the Schools of New York City. New York: Arno Press, 1969.

Renault, Mary. Fire From Heaven. New York: Pantheon, 1969.

_____. The Nature of Alexander. New York: Pantheon, 1975.

Reynolds, Myra. The Learned Lady in England. Boston: Houghton Mifflin, 1920.

Ridley, Jasper. Henry VIII. New York: Viking Press, 1985.

Robbert, Louise Buenger. "Caterina Corner, Queen of Cyprus." In Female Scholars, edited by J.R. Brink. Montreal: Eden Press, 1980.

Rogness, Michael. Philip Melanchthon. Minneapolis: Augusburg Publishing House, 1969.

Ross, Charles. Richard III. Berkeley: University of California Press, 1981.

Rust, Val D. Alternative in Education. London: Sage

Publications, 1977.

Ryan, John.  Irish Monasticiem.  Ithaca, New York: Cornell University Press, 1972.

Sandburg, Carl.  Abraham Lincoln, The Prairie Years. Vol. 1.  New York: Harcourt, Brace, 1926.

Standing, E.M.  Maria Montessori.  Fresno: Academy Library Guild, 1957.

Sarbin, Theodore R.  "Cross-Age Tutoring and Social Identity."  In Children As Teachers, edited by Vernon L. Allen.  New York: Academic Press, 1976.

Scarisbrick, J.J.  Henry VIII.  Los Angeles: University of California Press, 1968.

Schultz, Stanley K.  The Culture Factory.  New York: Oxford University Press, 1973.

Sedgwick, Henry Dwight.  Marcus Aurelius.  New Haven: Yale University Press, 1927.

Seybolt, Robert Francis.  The Private Schools of Colonial Boston.  Westport, Connecticut: Greenwood Press, 1935.

Shahar, Shulamith.  The Fourth Estate.  London: Methuen, 1983.

Shattuck, Roger.  The Forbidden Experiment.  New York: Farrar Straus Giroux, 1980.

Silver, Harold.  The Concept of Popular Education. London: Mac Gibbon and Kee, 1965.

Sim, Myre.  Tutors and Their Students: Advice From a Psychiatrist.  London: E. & S. Livingstone, 1970.

Simon, Joan.  Education and Society in Tudor England. Cambridge: University Press, 1966.

Simon, Brian.  Studies in the History of Education 1780-1870.  London: Lawrence and Wishart, 1960.

Sitton, Thad, and Milan C. Rowold.  Ringing the

Children In, Texas Country Schools. College
Station: Texas A&M University Press, 1987.

Smith, Frank. A History of English Elementary
Education 1760-1902. London: University of
London Press, 1931.

Smith, L. Glenn. Lives in Education. Ames, Iowa:
Education Studies Press, 1984.

Smith, Wilson, editor. Theories of Education in
Early America. New York: Bobbs-Merrill, 1973.

Sommerville, C. John. The Rise and Fall of
Childhood. London: Sage Publications, 1982.

Spiller, Robert E., editor. Literary History of the
United States. New York: Macmillan, 1959.

The Statistical History of the United States from
Colonial Times to the Present. Stanford, Conn.:
Fairfield Publishers, 1965.

Stephen, Leslie. Dictionary of National Biography.
63 vols. London: Smith, Elder and Company, 1885.

Steinhiller, August W. State Law On Compulsory
Attendance. Washington, D.C.: U.S. Government
Printing Office, U.S. Department of Health,
Education and Welfare, 1966.

Stewart, Mary. Nine Coaches Waiting. Greenwich,
Conn.: Fawcett Publications, 1958.

Stewart, W.A.C., and W.P. McCann. The Educational
Innovators. London: Macmillan, 1967.

Stock, Phyllis. Better Than Rubies, A History of
Women's Education. New York: G.P. Putnam's Sons,
1978.

Stratton, Joanna L. Pioneer Women: Voices From the
Kansas Frontier. New York: Simon and Schuster,
1981.

Strickland, Agnes. The Life of Queen Elizabeth.
London: Hutchinson and Company, 1904.

Strodtbeck, Fred L. "Tutoring and Psychological Growth." In Children As Tutors, edited by Vernon L. Allen. New York: Academic Press, 1976.

Strype, John. The Life of the Learned Sir John Cheke. Oxford: Clarendon Press, 1821.

Sutherland, Gillian. Policy-Making in Elementary Education 1870-1895. Oxford: Oxford University Press, 1973.

Sutherland, James, editor. The Oxford Book of Literary Anecdotes. Oxford: Clarendon Press, 1975.

Talmage, Harriet. "What Is Individualization?" In Approaches to Individualized Education, edited by Jan Jeter. Alexandria, Virginia: Association for Supervision and Curriculum Development, 1980.

Taylor, Robert. The Computer in the School: Tutor, Tool, Tutee. New York: Teachers College Press, 1980.

Thomson, Gladys Scott. Life in a Noble Household 1641-1700. London: Jonathan Cape, 1937.

Trewin, J.C. Tutor of the Czar. London: Macmillan, 1975.

Troen, Selvyn K. The Public and the Schools. Columbia, Missouri: University of Missouri Press, 1975.

Tuchman, Barbara W. A Distant Mirror. New York: Alfred A. Knopf, 1979.

Tuer, Andrew White. History of the Horn-Book. 2 vols. London: Leadenhall Press, 1896.

Turner, Justin G., and Linda Levitt Turner. Mary Todd Lincoln. New York: Alfred A. Knopf, 1972.

Turner, William Mason. Gertrude the Governess. New York: N. L. Munro, 1883.

Ulich, Robert, editor. Three Thousand Years of Educational Wisdom. Cambridge, Mass.: Harvard University Press, 1965.

Untermeyer, Louis. Lives of the Poets. New York: Simon and Schuster, 1959.

U.S. Census Office. 6th Census, 1840. Washington: Blair and Rives, 1841.

Viola, Herman J. The National Archives of the United States. New York: Abrams, 1984.

Wade, Theodore. School At Home: How Parents Can Teach Their Own Children. Colfax, California: Gazelle Publications, 1980.

Wagner, Lilya. Peer Teaching Historical Perspective. London: Greenwood Press, 1982.

Walden, John W. H. The Universities of Ancient Greece. Freeport: Books for Libraries Press, 1970.

Walsh, James J. Education of the Founding Fathers of the Republic. New York: Fordham University Press, 1935.

Walvin, James. A Child's World. New York: Penguin, 1982.

Wardle, David. English Popular Education. Cambridge: Cambridge University Press, 1970.

_____. The Rise of the Schooled Society. London: Routledge and Kegan Paul, 1974.

Webb, R.K. Modern England. New York: Dodd, Mead and Company, 1971.

Webster's New World Dictionary. New York: New World Pub., Co., 1964.

West, Katherine. Chapter of Governesses, A Study of the Governess in English Fiction 1800-1949. London, Cohen and Est, 1949.

Wheldon, Huw, and J. H. Plumb. _Royal Heritage_. New York: Crescent Books, 1985.

Wilds, Elmer Harrison. _The Foundation of Modern Education_. New York: Rinehart and Company, 1936.

Wilkins, A.S. _Roman Education_. Cambridge: University Press, 1905.

Williamson, David. _Debrett's Kings and Queens of Britain_. Topsfield, Mass.: Salem House Publishers, 1986.

Wilson, Joan Hoff, and Sharon L. Bollinger. "Mercy Otis Warren: Playwright, Poet, and Historian of the American Revolution." In _Female Scholars_, edited by Brink. Montreal: Eden Press, 1980.

Wise, John E. _The History of Education_. New York: Sheed and Ward, 1964.

Wofford, Kate. _Modern Education in the Small Rural School_. New York: Macmillan, 1938.

Woodham-Smith, Cecil. _Florence Nightingale_. London: Constable, 1950.

Woodward, William Harrison. _Studies in Education During the Age of the Renaissance 1400-1600_. New York: Teachers College Press, 1967.

_____. _Erasmus, Desiderius: Concerning the Aims and Methods of Education_. Cambridge: Cambridge University Press, 1904.

_____. _Vittorino da Feltre and Other Humanist Educators_. New York: Teachers College Columbia University, 1963.

Woody, Thomas. _A History of Women's Education in the United States_. 2 vols. New York: Science Press, 1929.

_____. _Early Quaker Education in Pennsylvania_. New York: Columbia University, 1920.

_____. Quaker Education in the Colony and State of New Jersey. Philadephia: University of Philadephia, 1922.

Woofter, T. J. Teaching in Rural Schools. Boston: Houghton Mifflin, 1917.

Wright, Thomas. The Homes of Other Days. New York: D. Appleton and Company, 1871.

Wrigley, E.A., and R. S. Schofield. The Population History of England 1541-1871. Cambridge, Mass.: Harvard University Press, 1981.

Young, G.M., editor. Early Victorian England 1830-1865. 2 vols. London: Oxford University Press, 1934.

Ziegler, Philip. The Black Death. New York: Harper and Row, 1969.

Zimmern, Alice. The Home Life of the Ancient Greeks. Translated by H. Blummer. New York: Cooper Square Publishers, 1966.


2. Journal Articles

Barnard, Henry, editor. "Princes in France-Their Education, and Teachers." In Compayré Historie Critique de l'Education, translated by Mrs. Horace Mann. The American Journal of Education 30 (1880): 465-490.

Becker, Susan. "What You Should Know About Tutoring Centers." Instructor 95 (February 1986): 88-90.

Bloom, Benjamin S. "The Search for Methods of Group Instruction as Effective as One-to-One Tutoring." Educational Leadership, 41 (May 1984): 12-16.

Bowen, Ezra. "Oxford's Amazing Adolescent." Time 126 (5 August 1985): 55.

Cloward, Robert. "Studies in Tutoring." The Journal of Experimental Education 36 (Fall 1967): 16-25.

417

Ellson, Douglas. "Improving Productivity." Phi Delta Kappan 68 (October 1986): 111-124.

Frederiksen, Lee W., John B. Myers, and Anne W. Riley. "A Case For Cross-Training." Training 23, (February 1986): 37-43.

Goodwin, Laura, and William Goodwin. "Cognitive and Affective Effects of Various Types of Microcomputers Use By Preschoolers." American Educational Research Journal 23 (Fall 1986): 348-355.

Gordon, Edward E. "John Locke the Model Tutor." Vitae Scholasticae 5 (Spring/Fall 1986): 275-285.

_____. "Home Tutoring Programs Gain Respectability." Phi Delta Kappan 64 (February 1983): 398-399.

Hall, M.G., editor. "The Autobiography of Increase Mather." Proceedings of the American Antiquarian Society. 71 (1961): 260-289.

Harrison, Grant Von. "The Effect on Pupil Reading Achievement of Teacher Compliance with Prescribed Methodology." Research In Education, 32 (November 1984): 17-23.

Horst, H.M. "An Experiment with Student Tutors." National Educational Association Journal 22 (November 1933): 200-206.

_____. "Student Participation in High School Responsibilities." The School Review 32 (May 1924): 341-348.

_____. "Student Tutors Reduce High School Failures." American School Board Journal 101 (July 1940): 49-54.

Howitt, Doran. "Experimental Software Boosted." Info World 29 (October 1984): 29-30.

Kaestle, Carl F., and Lawrence C. Stedman. "Literacy and Reading Performance in the United States, From 1880 to the Present." Reading Research

Quarterly 21 (Winter 1987): 8-45.

Kindley, Mark M. "Little Schools On the Prairie Still Teach a Big Lesson." Smithsonian 16 (October 1985): 118-128.

Lines, Patricia M. "An Overview of Home Instruction." Phi Delta Kappan 68, (March 1987): 510-517.

Lippitt, Peggy. "Cross-Age Relationships - An Educational Resource." Children 12, (May-June 1965): 113-117.

Long, Huey B. "Adult Basic Education in Colonial America." Adult Literacy and Basic Education 7 (1983): 55-68.

Mann, Mrs. Horace, translator. "Princes in France Their Education and Teachers." From Compayre Historie Critique de l'Education, The American Journal of Education 30 (1880): 465-479.

Marshall, Megan. "The Sisters Who Showed the Way." American Heritage, 38 (September-October 1987): 58-66.

"McDonalds of Teaching." Newsweek 105 (7 January 1985): 61.

Melmed, Arthur. "The Technology of American Education: Problem and Opportunity." Technological Horizons In Education Journal 14 (September 1986): 77-81.

Mitford, Nancy. "The Boyhood of Frederick the Great." Horizon 12 (Winter 1970): 104-111.

Neidermeyer, Fred C., and P. Ellis. "Remedial Reading Instruction by Trained Pupil Tutors." Elementary School Journal 26 (1971): 68-75.

Peterson, M. Jeanne. "The Victorian Governess: Status Incongruency in Family and Society." In Victorian Studies 14 (September 1970): 7-25.

Plumb, J.H. "The Great Change in Children." Horizon
13 (Winter 1971): 4-13.

Raumer, Karl von. "Contributions to the History of
Pedagogy." Translated by Henry Barnard. The
American Journal of Education 7 (1859): 381-400.

Rayman, Ronald. "Joseph Lancaster's Monitorial
System of Instruction and American Indian
Education 1815-1838." History of Education
Quarterly 21, (Winter 1981): 395-409.

Rollin, Charles. "The Education of Youth." The
American Journal of Education 23 (1872): 2-46.

Rothrock, Dayton. "The Rise and Decline of
Individualized Instruction." Educational
Leadership 83 (April 1982): 528-530.

Schultz, Mary Alice. "An Alternate Effort for
Troubled Students." Momentum 13, (May 1982): 23-
25.

Simons, Carol. "They Get by with a Lot of Help from
Their Kyoiku Mamas." Smithsonian 17, no. 12
(March 1987): 44-53.

Thiagarajan, S. "Madras System Revisited: A new
Structure for Peer Tutoring." Educational
Technology 3 (December 1973): 10-13.

Weaver Negri, Wallace. "Home Tutorials vs. The
Public Schools in Los Angeles." Phi Delta Kappan
60 (December 1980): 250-255.

3. Dissertations

Cannon, Mary Agnes. "The Education of Women During
the Renaissance." PhD. diss., Catholic
University of America, 1916.

Cole-Mahan, Virginia May. "Tutoring as a Support
Service for Mainstreaming Handicapped Child in
Rural and Urban Schools." Ph.D. diss.,
University of Cincinnati, 1980.

Fisher, Hersha Sue. "The Education of Elizabeth Peabody." Ed.D. diss., Harvard University, 1980.

Florian, Robert Bruce. "Sir John Checke, Tudor Tutor." Ph.D. diss., West Virginia University, 1973.

Hurney, Frances Mary. "Hospital Schools in the City of Chicago." M.A. thesis, DePaul University, 1944.

Nash, Susan. "Wanting a Situation: Governesses and Victorian Novels." Ph.D. diss., Rutgers University, 1980.

Peryon, Mary Charleen Dolphin. "An Analysis of the Instructional Process in Tutoring Using Teachers and Paraprofessionals with Kindergarten Children." Ph.D. diss., Utah State University, 1980.

Richter, Sharon Jane. "A Computer-Managed Tutorial Reading System." Ed.D. diss., University of Alabama, 1981.

Rogers, Judy. "The Effects of Tutoring by 6th Graders on the Reading Performance of 1st Graders." Ed.D. diss., University of San Francisco, 1979.

Ustick, W.L. "The English Gentleman in the 17th and Early 17th Century: Studies in the Literature of Courtesy and Conduct." Ph.D. diss., Harvard University, 1932.

Willis, Craig Dean. "The Tudors and Their Tutors: A Study of Sixteenth Century Royal Education in Britain." Ph.D. diss., Ohio State University, 1969.

Yates, Donald Crombie. "Home and School Relations: The Private Tutor and the School." Ed.D. diss., Columbia University Teachers College, 1980.

# INDEX

## BIOGRAPHICAL SKETCH

Edward E. Gordon is a Lecturer in history and education at DePaul University, Chicago. He has published scholarly works in both fields. In 1968 he founded Imperial Tutoring, that later became America's first nationally accredited after-school tutoring program. Gordon received his B.A. and M.A. at DePaul, and his Ph.D. from Loyola University, Chicago.

Elaine H. Gordon is the Instruction Librarian at DePaul University, Chicago. She received her B.A. from Manhattanville College, White Plains, New York; M.A. in Political Science from Georgetown University; and her M.A.L.S. from Rosary College, River Forest, Illinois. Before teaching at DePaul, Elaine H. Gordon was on the library staff of the University of Illinois, Chicago.